CHRISTOPHER HADLEY is a
popular subjects as eight
appeared in the *Independen*
of Books, Esquire and his l
publications. Christopher i
hopes will never grow out
in the Hertfordshire countr

Praise for

Hollow Places

A *Sunday Times* Best History Book of the Year 2019

'Impossible to summarise and delightfully absorbing, Hadley's book is comfortably the most unexpected history book of the year. In effect, it is a quest for the truth behind a tombstone, apparently medieval, in a rural Hertfordshire church . . . Hadley's journey takes him through the centuries, peeling back the layers of myths and legends, like some real-life version of an M.R. James ghost story'   *Sunday Times*

'The past is animated with imagination and knowledge . . . Shonks and his story, the tomb and the now vanished yew are a starting point for a digressive and affectionate exploration of a local tradition that has survived for 800 years . . . Authoritative and well-researched'

Spectator

'Christopher Hadley's celebration of English folklore across 800 years delights in these imaginative tales which have shaped and coloured the cultural landscape of the nation . . . Enriching and at times surprising . . . Anchored by memorable tales, the narrative overturns long-held historical beliefs as it goes . . . *Hollow Places* has an innate charm . . . The book's real success lies in being alert to what makes these superstitions and rituals special – the understanding that imagination trumps truth'   *TLS*

'Hadley wears his scholarship lightly but at the heart of this antiquarian wild goose chase is an ingenious meditation on what history, in all its complexity and unevenness, really is'   *Guardian*

HOLLOW PLACES

An Unusual History of Land and Legend

CHRISTOPHER HADLEY

WILLIAM COLLINS

William Collins
An imprint of HarperCollins*Publishers*
1 London Bridge Street
London SE1 9GF

WilliamCollinsBooks.com

First published in Great Britain in 2019 by William Collins
This William Collins paperback edition published in 2020

1

A catalogue record for this book is available from the British Library

ISBN 978-0-00-831952-6

Typeset in Garamond by Palimpsest Book Production Ltd, Falkirk, Stirlingshire

Printed and bound in Great Britain by CPI Group (UK) Ltd, Croydon

To my dad Harry Raymond Hadley, and in loving memory of
my mum Joan Mary Hadley, a born storyteller

Dummling set to work, and cut down the tree; and when it fell, he found in a hollow under the roots a goose with feathers of pure gold.

—'The Golden Goose' in *German Popular Stories*,
collected by Jakob and Wilhelm Grimm,
from oral tradition, London, 1823

Contents

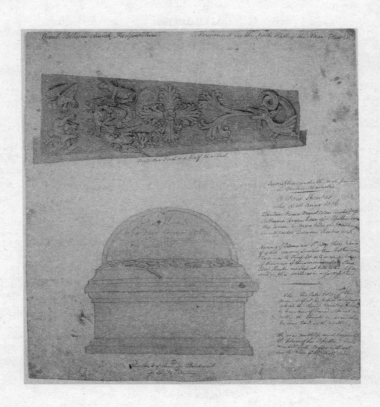

THE SHONKS EPITAPH, BRENT PELHAM.
— I should be grateful for information
regarding the epitaph on O. Piers Shonks in Brent
Pelham Church, Hertfordshire. The tomb of this
worthy lies in a recess cut into the north wall of
the church and bears the following inscription in
Latin (I quote from memory):—

> Tantum fama manet Cadmi Sanctique Georgi
>   Postuma; tempus edax ossa sepulchra vorat.
> Hoc tamen in muro tutus qui perdidit anguem
>   Invito positus Daemone Shonkus erat.

There is also a neat rhyming translation in
English which I cannot recall.

Who was Shonks? What is the point in
the reference to Cadmus and St. George (in
itself a curious conjunction of names)? What
is the significance of 'who destroyed the
snake' (the Devil?) as applied to Shonks?
What is the point of 'invito Daemone'?

I understand that a field in the village still
bears the name 'Shonks' field.'

D. C. THOMPSON.
Notes and Queries, 1932

In the High Middle Ages, on the Hertfordshire–Essex border, a remarkable tomb was carved out of grey-black marble to cover the bones of an English hero whom legend calls Piers Shonks. For centuries, tales about dragons, giants and the devil have gathered around the tomb and spread into the surrounding countryside. How and why that happened is the subject of this book: it is both a historical detective story and a meditation on memory, belief, the stories we used to tell – and why they still matter.

Part I

Tree

I begin on the edge of Great Pepsells field on a cold winter's morning in the early nineteenth century.

LITHETH AND LESTENETH AND
HERKENETH ARIGHT

S he was the oldest living thing thereabouts.

Alone, on the wide plateau between the rivers Ash and Quin, the old yew tree had stood since time out of mind and beyond the memory of man.

Did old Master Lawrence think of her great age when he tested the cold edge of his felling axe that winter's morning? He would have known that bringing her down was going to be an *'umbuggin* job, but he had no idea how things would turn out; that before the day was over he and his axe would become part of a story already ages old. Two hundred years hence, people would still be talking about the yew in Great Pepsells field, of the day she fell and of what the woodcutters found in her roots.

For some twenty years now she had stood alone: resolute but incongruous in that heavy-clay field where tracks and parishes met; her evergreen boughs prey to lightning, the knots and sinews of her trunk rivened by wind and hail. She had once marked the northernmost boundary of a wood, but the acres of ash and maple had been grubbed up in the years between Trafalgar and the death of Old Boney.

Perhaps the landowner, or his steward, had left her standing for her grandeur. Generations must have paused to admire her or sheltered beneath her thick crown. Children, dallying on their way to gather brushwood or flints or rushes, would have carved their names in her bark and picked her blood-red arils – breakfasting on the bitter flesh and spitting the poisonous seeds to the ground.

The tree stood in the village of Furneux Pelham, 500 yards from the parish boundary. Half a mile further east across the level fields rose the tower and Hertfordshire spike of St Mary the Virgin in Brent Pelham. That the church was the only building in sight is not incidental, nor was the presence of yet another parish boundary just 200 yards to the west along the widening ditch: strange things happen where three parishes meet.

There she grew in this remote spot near the Hertfordshire–Essex border, within five or six feet of where a Roman road lay beneath the soil of the field. (Did her shadow once fall on the Eagle of the Ninth?) Trees of that age – like the famous churchyard yews at Tandridge and Crowhurst in Surrey – have many textures: on one face she might be red and hairy and corded, a trunk of immense ropes twisted into terrible strength, yet on another, bleached and moth-eaten, misshapen like driftwood. From certain angles, in certain lights, vermicular, flayed, mutating.

She had grown into a storybook tree, long before she became part of a story.

They say that she had 'split open, as such trees do, with extreme old age'. A great wound. Split enough and large enough to have a stile and steps set in her trunk. The Reverend Soames, pursuing rumours of piglets or turnips (one in every ten was his), might easily follow the track across Pipsels Mead and Nether Rackets, through the great tree into Pepsells, and on through Long Croft or Lady Pightle towards Johns a Pelham Farm.

Was she as prodigious as the yew at Crowhurst with its small door set in its hollow trunk? Or more wonderful still? Like the greatest of all surviving British yews at Fortingall in Perthshire. Once fifty-six feet round there was plenty of space between her trunks through which to lead a horse and cart. Today, both trees are thought to have taken seed in the reign of the Emperor Augustus.

Was the Pepsells yew already centuries old when Peola gave his name to Peola's-ham, the homestead that became Pelham? Did the militia enter the village butts with longbows from her boughs? Did a Saxon, a Roman, a scout from the Trinovantes tribe 2,000 years ago take his bearings from her? *Generations pass while some trees stand, and old families last not three oaks.* Nor one yew.

Master Lawrence, the woodcutter, was unlikely to think of these things. He would have thought of village stories. Perhaps of poor Widow Bowcock stabbed to death in the fields thereabouts in the last century, or the handles of grubbing axes broken in the heavy ground when clearing the roots from Ten Acres Field to make way for barley; of tall tales told by old men as they coppiced the horn-beam to make charcoal on a morning such as that one; tales about the black tomb in the church wall and the man called Shonks who sleeps in it, about his winged dogs, the monster they killed and the immense double-jointed finger bones that gave Mr Morris so much trouble.

Master Lawrence heard from the pulpit on the first day of Lent that *cursed be he who removeth his neighbour's landmark.* He may have fretted that his first job that winter's morning was to bring down such a singular tree. *A landmark, which they of old time have set.* Might he pay more heed to an old wife's 'no-good-will-come-of-it'? Perhaps there was little room in such a life for superstition. I think he pulled his stockings up to meet his breeches in the light of the hearth and rush-light and thought that his business was no one else's concern, turning his mind instead to how hard the ground was that morning – yet not as hard as yew wood from which he might fashion axle pins or mill cogs. A practical man who kept his concerns to himself. After the event, I don't suppose he would have had much truck with foolish enquiries about a morning's work.

> *Gone, the merry morris din*
> *Gone, the song of Gamelyn.*

And yet years later he would talk about the ordeal of felling that tree – and the 'girt hole underneath it, underneath its roots, a girt cave like' – and in this way the simple woodcutter became as important to this story as the stonemason had 800 years earlier, no less important than the map-maker, the fundamentalist, the poet and all those who are caught in its weave.

It is the early 1830s: a time of great change. The sailor King William IV is on the throne, a young Charles Dickens has begun writing under the pen name Boz, Charles Darwin is on board HMS *Beagle*, and in a Hertfordshire village Master Thomas Lawrence and a gang of farm labourers are about to find a dragon's lair beneath the roots of a tree.

1

The Reader will rather excuse an unsuccessful Attempt to clear up the Truth where so little Light is to be had, than giving Things up for nursery Tales to save the Pains of Inquiry.

—Nathaniel Salmon, *The History of Hertfordshire,*
1728

I like to know where dragons once lurked and where the local fairies baked their loaves, where wolves were trapped and suicides buried, who cast the church bells, which side the Lord of the Manor took in the Civil War and which modern surnames were found in the first parish register (and which in the records of the assize). I am with Walter Scott, who was 'but half satisfied with the most beautiful scenery if he could not connect it with some local legend'. To map a place and to know its stories is to belong, to find companionship with the living and the dead, to time-travel on every visit to the Brewery Tap or the Black Horse. Sometimes you spot something – a burial mound, a scratch dial in the church porch – and then set out to find its story. Other times you hear a story and go in search of it in the landscape, or the archive or someone's memories, and that is how my journey to Great Pepsells field and the spot where Master Lawrence felled a yew tree began.

I first encountered the name Shonks some years ago on the Pelhams' website. Piers Shonks, a local hero, was buried in a tomb in the wall of the church in Brent Pelham. Apparently, he was a giant who had slain a dragon that once had its lair under a yew tree in a field called Great Pepsells. As one rustic supposedly said, 'Sir, it's one of the rummiest stories I ever heard, like, that 'ere story of old Piercy Shonkey, and if I hadn't see the place in the wall with my own eyes I wouldn't believe nothing about it.'

To know Shonks is to wander the margins of history: the margins of the Bayeux Tapestry where strange creatures gather, the margins of ancient woodland where hollow trees hide secrets, of eighteenth-century manuscripts where antiquaries have scribbled clues to the identity of folk heroes. It is to encounter the many other folk legends we find around the country: stories about dragons and giants and devils, avenging spirits and outlaws, which all have their echoes in the legend of Piers Shonks. It is to rediscover a world where the community was in part defined by its collective memory, by its pride in its past, and a story its members had passed down through the generations: to wrestle with their superstition, what they really believed and what that tells us about them, their priorities and their needs (and about us too for that matter, how we are different and how very much still like them).

To know Piers Shonks is to sit shivering in a church in Georgian

England sketching the dragon on his tomb, to stand atop its tower triangulating the Elizabethan countryside, and to confront the zealous Mr Dowsing and his thugs looting the brasses and smashing the masonry during the Civil War. It is to ask why Churchwarden Morris could not sleep at night, and how long bones last in a crypt, and where a medieval stonemason found his inspiration. It is to wonder what a thirteenth-century tomb is doing in the wall of a fourteenth-century church, who is really inside it, and why he was immortalised by generations of storytellers.

At first, and for many months, to know Piers Shonks was to wonder that less than 200 years ago some farm labourers supposedly uncovered a cave under a tree in a field where a centuries-old folk legend said that a dragon had lived. Did they really? Surely not. This is where people usually wrinkle their brow. 'You're writing a children's book?' they ask.

No, it's a history book, a historical detective story . . . People generally look confused at this and then venture: 'Oh, it's a novel.'

It's non-fiction, I explain.

'But no one really found a dragon's lair under a tree.'

Maybe not, I concede, but they believed they did.

'They didn't really.'

I think they did.

'Really?'

This book began with that question, and in trying to answer it I discovered things even more puzzling, things that eventually brought home to me the importance and the power of the folk legends we used to tell and why they still matter. The story of Piers Shonks is not the legend that changed the world, it did not forge the nation or launch a thousand ships. It is an obscure tale, of small importance, but it has endured: the survivor of an 800-year battle between storytellers and those who would mock or silence them. Shonks' story stands for all those thousands of forgotten tales that used to belong to every village.

This rumour of a tree that once housed a dragon caught my imagination, as the tree itself must have bewitched those farm labourers. It took root and grew, putting out feelers, tapping the furthest horizons of my mind, where the magical and mysterious lay buried, becoming a solitary and crooked shape in a field far away from a winding road, both sinister and oddly pleasing. Perhaps frightening and anatomical in silhouette, with claws like the tree at the bend by Jack's Bridge as you enter the village at dusk, but much larger and more substantial: *Girth enourmous* like the Yardley Oak in Cowper's poem, with 'moss cushion'd root / Upheav'd above the soil, and sides emboss'd / With prominent wens globose', a *shatter'd veteran, hollow-trunk'd, embowell'd,* and with *excoriate forks deform.* Cowper, the great Hertfordshire poet of nature, has appropriated all the right adjectives for the job.

I hoped, rather ridiculously, that I could somehow identify the tree on old maps. An early estate map of the Pelhams has lovely water-coloured woods and springs of trees with shadows pooling to the east, but no individual trees. The Ordnance Survey followed the same convention, so that the sun is always setting in nineteenth-century mapscapes, but whereas the earlier maps showed trees merely to indicate the presence of woodland, the second half of the nineteenth century saw the arrival of OS maps so detailed that they showed every non-woodland tree in fields or hedgerows that was more than thirty feet from another tree. Oliver Rackham, the historian of the countryside, estimated that nationwide the surveyors plotted some twenty-three million individual trees, and many are still there to be found.

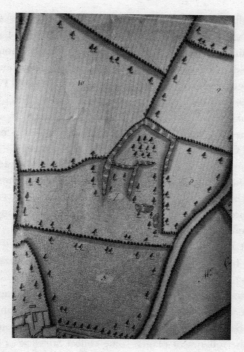

While single trees were marked on the published maps, single tree stumps might be plotted on the original boundary sketch maps because they were meres marking the beginning and end of a hedge that the farmer had uprooted half a century before. I once spent an enjoyable hour searching for the vestiges of the 'Hornbeam Stub' that marked a stretch of boundary between Furneux Pelham and Great Hormead. My search was in vain, as it was for the yew tree. Sadly, as I later learned, Master Lawrence's axe had struck the yew some forty years before the first large-scale sheets of north-east Hertfordshire. Still the *looking* was almost as rewarding as the *finding* would have been.

The tree was just the start. I was soon fascinated by the tomb in the wall, the inscription above it, and other places associated with the hero: *Shonks Garden*, his wood, and his moat. At first, I kept coming across intriguing references to Piers Shonks when I was looking for something else: in old newspapers and county histories, guidebooks and letters. He was even in the old Post Office directories: at Brent Pelham in 1862 with its reported 1,601 acres and population of 286, I read that in the church 'In the north wall of the nave there is a curious monument to the memory of one Piers O'Shonkes, the legendary slayer of dragons'.

Ever since the Elizabethan map-maker John Norden passed through Brent Pelham and found the place name and Shonks' tomb the only things worth noting down, people had been trying to get to the bottom of the legends attached to that curious monument. In the words of the eighteenth-century antiquary and tombstone enthusiast Richard Gough – pretending to disapprove – the tomb had long 'furnished matter for vulgar tradition, and puzzled former antiquaries'.

Folklorists collect things. Fully paid-up folklorists might collect legends associated with a place, such as those who compiled the Folklore Society's classic county series. Others focus on a theme such as the folklore of plants, some collect fairy-lore, playground chants or dances.

For my part, I found myself simply collecting the legend of Piers Shonks; that is instead of just happening upon accounts of the legend, at some point I started hunting for them. In the preface to his *Italian Folktales*, Italo Calvino describes perfectly what this is like, the sometimes obsessional searching, his feeling that some 'essential, mysterious element lying in the ocean depths must be salvaged to ensure the survival of the race'. At the same time, he knew that there was a risk of disappearing into the deep. 'I was gradually possessed by a kind of mania, an insatiable hunger for more and more versions and variants. Collating, categorizing, comparing became a fever.'

As I spent ever more time in the company of Shonks, I liked to seize on anything that helped me to justify it, not least the notion that along the way I would learn a thing or two about something worth knowing about. In her 1914 *The Handbook of Folk-Lore*, Charlotte Sophia Burne suggests that studying 'folk-lore' will advance the study of ethnology, history, economics, politics, sociology and psychology. There are certainly worse ways to get your bearings in an English village than to study its old stories, examine its tombs and dig up its potsherds. The father of antiquaries, Joseph Strutt, wrote that the study of such things 'brings to light many important matters which (without the study) would yet be buried in oblivion, and explains and illustrates such dark passages as would otherwise be quite unknown'.

That sounds like a suitably gothic enough reason for us to go in search of Piers Shonks. And where better to start than at the house that Shonks built?

2

And as imagination bodies forth / The forms of things unknown, the poet's pen / Turns them to shapes, and gives to airy nothing / A local habitation and a name.

—*A Midsummer Night's Dream*, Act 5, Scene 1

On a summer's afternoon in the early years of the twentieth century, a group of Edwardian gentlemen processed through a field of close scrub in Brent Pelham like men who had lost something important. The ground was unremarkable, broken and tumbled down to woodland, but was bound by wide and now stagnal ditches dug with great effort some seven or eight centuries earlier to fashion a moat. The members of the East Hertfordshire Archaeological Society were searching for signs of a half-remembered house that had once stood there, but I hope that some among them were looking for something more, hoping to catch sight of a great rumour in its infancy, to detect, in a broken blade of grass perhaps, the long-ago path Piers Shonks took on the day legend says he bested a dragon.

See you the dimpled track that runs,
All hollow through the wheat?
O that was where they hauled the guns
That smote King Philip's fleet.

Rudyard Kipling's 'Puck's Song' didn't appear in print until the following year, but the archaeological imagination it embodies was no doubt at work that summer's day in 1905 as those men tried to find something hidden beneath tussock and root that would carry them back to the distant past.

A local newspaper report of the day's excursion called it 'a moated site of some two and a half acres across upon which once stood the castle of the celebrated Piers Shonks, the slayer of the Pelham Dragon'. The castle (if not the dragon and its slayer) was a fiction. Most moats that trench the countryside are not the stuff of medieval sieges, but are homestead moats built around new farms and manor houses in the thirteenth and fourteenth centuries by men ostentatiously proclaiming their independent status and their membership of the knightly class – or their aspirations to it. They were especially popular on the boulder clay of East Anglia. Oliver Rackham has written that anyone who has dug as much as a post-hole in the clay will be in awe of the labour that went into excavating an entire moat, so people must have had a good reason to do it. They may have served a practical purpose as fishponds, or as a ready water supply for putting out fires, or for drainage or sewerage, and they must have offered some degree of deterrence to passing robbers and rapists, the notorious *trailbastons* – vagabonds with big sticks – of the period, but many historians agree that moats were first and foremost a status symbol.

William Blyth Gerish, the man who had organised the trip that afternoon, was careful to call the vanished building a house and not a castle. To the Elizabethans, the moated site had been plain old *Shonkes*. It was by then an 'ancient and decayed place'. Known as *Shonkes Barn* in the eighteenth century, it was said it would soon 'lose its name in all likelyhood with its substance, which is in a very tottering condition'. The prediction proved partly true. Thomas Hollingworth's beautiful Georgian estate map of Beeches Farm in green and yellow watercolours shows a neat four-sided moat identified in the key simply as *Nursery & Moat*, the building forgotten and seemingly the hero's name as well, but all is not lost: the adjacent fields are labelled *Shonks Farmyard* and *Shonks Hoppett*. Some forty years later, a new survey showed that the moat had been extended and gained an extra enclosure; it was now *The Hoppits & Shonks Garden*. Shonks played on people's minds and their superstitions in those parts: writing at Clifton School in Bristol in 1872, one pretentious schoolboy from near the Pelhams noted that by night *Shonks Garden* is 'studiously avoided by the simple villagers'. Other locals were less easily spooked, treasuring the moated old pasture, not only for its association with their hero, but also for its early summer carpet of narcissus, the double white jonquil.

The earliest large-scale Ordnance Survey map has it as *Shonk's Moat* (in the gothic typeface reserved for antiquities) and clearly shows a double moat arrangement forming two islands. By 1905, when the archaeological society visited, a fishpond remained, and the arms of the moat were mostly dry. The only clues that there had once been a building were the traces of foundations, which still dimpled the turf.

A photograph, perhaps taken earlier that day, shows William Gerish standing behind the Brent Pelham stocks and whipping post, looking younger than his forty-one years, his face framed by a neat dagger-shaped beard and a straw boater. A bank clerk by day, the indefatigable Mr Gerish is best characterised by pointing to his magnum opus, *Monumental Inscriptions*, for which he trawled the churches and graveyards of Hertfordshire recording some 70,000 inscriptions on strips of paper that he and his wife pasted into thirteen volumes in alphabetical order– a pursuit that was said to have destroyed his health and contributed to his premature death at the age of fifty-six.

Gerish was part of what became known as the nationwide folk-lore revival, avidly collecting local stories and publishing them in one shilling pamphlets. It was one of these that Gerish read to his fellow archaeological society members that Thursday afternoon in July 1905. It was called *A Hertfordshire St George, or the story of Piers Shonks and the Pelham Dragon*. While he had chosen for his stage the countryside where Shonks once lived, Gerish's pamphlet paid greater attention to the home of his adversary. In fact, Gerish's chief claim to originality is his treatment of the yew tree, its felling and the dragon's lair beneath it. He had first written about the incident in an article for *Folklore* three years earlier; written about a 'terrible dragon kennelled under a yew tree which stood between what were afterwards two fields called Great and Little Pepsells', adding the surprising news that the tree had been chopped down some years before and the dragon's cave found in its roots. Gerish's papers in the Hertfordshire Archives reveal the original source for this story to be a series of letters in the *Hertfordshire Mercury* from some fifteen years earlier. A correspondent identified only as D.E. set the ball rolling with a query published in late February 1888:

> *Brent Pelham: There is a man buried under the foundation on the north side of Brent Pelham Church of the name of Shonks. Can any of the readers of the Mercury give the reason why he was buried there, and also the date of the year he was buried? —D.E.*

The year 1888 was a good one for enquiring about bones. On 23 January, the remains of a skeleton were discovered in a stone coffin in the eastern crypt of Canterbury Cathedral that some would claim were the lost relics of St Thomas Becket. The story broke in *The Times* early in February, sparking a series of letters to the editor and a controversy that has lasted to the present day. I cannot help but wonder if D.E., whoever he or she was, thought to question the identity of Shonks because of the excitement over Becket's bones.

There were several replies: quoting the various county historians on the matter, describing the tomb and giving versions of the inscription over it. Between them, the authors of each letter managed to encompass most of the traditions: here was Shonks the Lord of the Manor who supposedly died in 1086, Shonks the giant who got the better of a rival, Shonks the dragon-slayer, and Shonks who cheated the devil. But the most interesting letter by far ran in the paper on 17 March, and came from a local vicar with a name like a hardwearing fabric; he was the alliterated Reverend Woolmore Wigram, and what he had to say would change the centuries-old folk legend for ever.

3

On what occasions are stories told? Is there a story-telling season? Do particular stories belong to particular occasions? For what purposes are they told? For instruction or warning, or simply for amusement?

—Charlotte Sophia Burne,
The Handbook of Folk-Lore, 1914

In a letter written towards the end of his life, Reverend Woolmore Wigram recalled that the story of the dragon's lair found under a yew tree belonged to a particular occasion in the 1860s; to one of his traditional tithe luncheons. This was the annual meeting when the parson and the farmers agreed – or more likely disagreed – on the tax due to the church. Traditionally held in Brent Pelham on the second Friday in December, there could hardly be a more apt occasion to discuss the old stories. Tithes were part and parcel of the customs of the village. Onerous, contentious and unedifying, tithes are an entertaining way to glimpse the lives of the folk, their personalities, their world and their preoccupations.

Though familiar themes crop up everywhere, ancient tithing customs were particular to each parish. Today they read like magic potions: *toad under cold stone, days and nights has forty-one*, could well be the vicar's due at Lammastide. As well as the joy of otherness and unfamiliar words to justify time spent with tithe records, they are also especially instructive for anyone chasing old stories. They challenge us to unravel them, to reveal lost ways of making sense of the world and to shed light on the long-forgotten machinations of the stock characters of village life: impecunious parsons, resentful husbandmen and bombastic squires.

Tithes were organic and multi-layered, built out of cunning millers and higglers' horses, village personalities, stolen land, ancient disputes, forgotten farming practices and lost ways of life. While farmers and most tithe payers of the past would be delighted to know of their utter obliteration, we are right to be anxious that something has been lost with their passing, and we should treasure the traces we have left. In this they are like local legends: Piers Shonks has fought many battles but none more important than the battle between memory and forgetting.

In about 1902 Wigram wrote to Gerish, 'I will send you another time the legend of O. Piers Shonks; as I heard it from the Inhabitants, at my Tithe Audits when the good folk used to pay their 1/6 or 2/ worth of tithe (quite punctually) and sit down to cold beef bread & cheese & conversation; and give me all the folk-lore.'

Was it simply that the luncheon was held at the Yew Tree Inn, a popular village meeting place since the middle of the previous century, and Wigram asked about village yews and one story led to another? Perhaps someone was talking about the tithes due on mature timber in the old days when his neighbour mentioned what was found under the oldest of all trees in those parts, back when Reverend Soames was vicar and busy writing his books instead of earning his tithes, back when churchwarden Morris was farming the tithes in Brent Pelham and making himself very unpopular? A story to impress or entertain the new vicar. 'Are dragon's eggs tithable, Reverend?' somebody quipped.

Woolmore Wigram became vicar of both Brent and Furneux

Pelham in 1864 and held the post for twelve years. In his early thirties when he arrived, Wigram was a mutton-chopped and muscular Christian, a founding member of the Alpine Club. Just two years before he arrived in the Pelhams, he had braved storms that had turned his hair white with icicles and driven frozen spicules into his face as he made the first successful ascent of the White Tooth, *La Dent Blanche*, near Zermatt. At over 14,000 feet, it was considered one of the hardest climbs in the Alps. How would he occupy himself in countryside that was pleasantly undulating but with no discernible peaks? Perhaps he might turn his hand to more scholarly pursuits, to folklore and local history.

The clergy had gradually been replacing the squire as the keepers of parish history. An early local history manual urged clergymen to collect field names and look into the parish chest to find accounts from the Overseers of the Poor so they could write the history of ordinary people. Wigram was one of the more enlightened local historians, someone who would not restrict himself to title deeds and the genealogies of those in the Big House. He also cared about the folk and their customs: what they remembered and what they valued.

Tithes are almost as alien to most of us today as dragons, but baffling customs, grumbling farmers and greedy vicars added piquancy to life in your average village. For centuries tithes were paid in kind – in other words, the tithe on piglets was paid in piglets. As endless legal cases testified, what was owed to the church was often cause for much debate: at times desperate clergy, eager to increase their incomes, had been known to claim that stones in a field were subject to tithe. Others were said to have demanded tithe on the '*germins*' or shoots growing from the roots of felled trees (although these anecdotes, told against the church, have the ring of the apocryphal, or at least exceptional, about them). In 1727, Alexander Pope in his description of a fictional parish clerk's memoirs jokes that there are 'seventy chapters containing an exact detail of the Law-suits of the Parson and his Parishioners concerning tythes, and near an hundred pages left blank, with an earnest desire that the history might be compleated by any of his successors, in whose time these suits should be ended'.

There were two main types of tithe: great and small. Great tithes were paid on the produce of the land – grain, hay, fruit, timber – and these usually went to the rector, who in the Pelhams, owing to a shady deal done in 1160, was the Treasurer of St Paul's Cathedral. After the dissolution of the monasteries in Henry VIII's reign, some third of all great tithes in the country ended up in the hands of lay rectors, who had nothing to do with the church. Once tithes could be bought and sold like any other property, the moral and religious argument for paying them became increasingly hard to make.

The small tithes were paid on those things resulting from the produce of the land – pigs, chickens, milk, cheese, eggs, fatting beasts, geese and bees. In the Pelhams, by custom, the small tithes also included potatoes, turnips, clover, herbs and aftermouth (grass from the second mowing). These were paid to the rector's representative on the ground, the vicar, who was wise to keep detailed accounts and records of parish customs. In the 1730s, the vicar of Furneux with Brent Pelham, Reverend Charles Wheatly, did just that. On 4 May 1732, Wheatly visited the aptly named Farmer Pigg to claim his tithe of seven lambs. By this date, he would normally accept a cash payment, but the two men were unable to agree on a price. Wheatly set down what happened in his account book: '[Mr Pigg] had 75 lambs, offered 3 s. a piece for my seven: But I refused it & drew them out in kind . . . I took one Ram, 5 Ewes & one Weather [sic]: & in lieu of the tithe of the remaining 5 lambs, I took a lame infirm one.'

Other parishioners paid with a fat goose on Lammas Day, in honey or wax or bushels of apples. Tithe eggs were due in Lent: two for every hen and three for every cock, 'whether they be fowls ducks or turkeys' according to custom. Some paid by work: a William Keene settled his tithe by 'making the hay of the Close'. Among the more unusual forms of payment were brass 'nozels', pricked bricks or bottles of tent – a low-alcohol Spanish wine used for the sacrament.

The tithe customs had been written down at much the same time as the first references to the exploits of Piers Shonks. In the reign of Queen Elizabeth, William Bishop, the vicar of Brent Pelham, sued Richard Dalton for seven years' worth of tithes on the underwood, that is the smaller woodland trees that were used for fuel or to make poles or fences and such like. Dalton, however, knew the customs of his village, which included such arcane and impenetrable rules as: 'If a lamb was sold with its Damme between Lady Day and St George's Day the tithe for every lamb would be 4 d.' Another dictated that not all the underwood in the Pelhams was tithable; they were usually paid on coppice wood, lopped wood and wood from springs and hedgerows, but they were not paid on any underwood that was used to repair hedges and fences. And so Dalton won the case, and all the customs that were confirmed and written down at the time would still be guiding the villagers and confusing the vicar when Master Lawrence felled the yew tree centuries later.

Tithes, like old stories, were under threat in the early nineteenth century. They were gradually monetised, stripped of their interest, homogenised and made intangible. The traditions that went with them would soon fade from memory. Over the years, clergy and tithe farmers found it increasingly tiresome to keep track of all the ringes of wood and bushels and pecks of barley. The counting, weighing, transport, storage and use of tithes in kind could be costly and burdensome. It distracted incumbents from less worldly concerns and it was in most people's interest to convert tithes to regular cash payments. This had happened in many places in a piecemeal way since the Middle Ages, and by the eighteenth century many tithe owners agreed on fixed sums known as compositions. For a while, some agreed a fixed sum, but still settled their bill in kind. Like Richard Hagger who paid his annual 3s. 6d. in honey and apples.

By the 1830s, it was observed that no tithe had been collected in kind in living memory. Wrested from tradition, they would eventually be easier to do away with. Throughout the early years of the nineteenth century, there was growing agitation nationally to reform the system. Tithes were accused of being a tax on industry and land improvement and caused particular resentment among the growing ranks of non-conformists, who did not see why they should be financing the Church of England. As agricultural methods changed, it became ever harder to decide whether something was tithable and in what way. Turnips might be tithable, but then again not, it depended on whether they were grown to feed animals or people. How about partridges? Acorns? Charcoal?

When Master Lawrence felled the yew tree, the last days of the old tithe system had come, but vestiges of it lingered on, and traditions such as tithe luncheons were still around thirty years later, when two members of his family played a prominent role at them. The brothers Thomas and James Lawrence were variously master carpenters, constables, sub-postmasters, grocers, innkeepers and, for many years, parish clerks in both Furneux and Brent Pelham. One or both of them were also good storytellers.

Before his death in 1907, the then *Canon* Wigram, casting his mind back some forty years to his tithe luncheons, wrote two letters to W. B. Gerish about Shonks that provide several clues to the identity of the man who told him about the yew tree. His informant was a Master Lawrence, who was not only related to the woodcutter, but also remembered the tree. This Lawrence worked at the post office and was also his parish clerk, which should narrow things down, but describes both Thomas in Furneux and his brother James in Brent Pelham. Perhaps both regaled Wigram with village history, but in Wigram's last known letter to Gerish, written in July 1905, which he begins by saying he has already told Gerish everything he can about Shonks, we learn that it was Thomas Lawrence who told Wigram old stories about the village, and so he emerges as the prime candidate for tale-spinner-in-chief.

What Wigram didn't learn about the yew tree at the tithe luncheon he must have found out later through conversations with Thomas, facts he finally set down on paper in February 1888 when he wrote to the *Hertfordshire Mercury*, replying to D.E.'s question about Piers Shonks' tomb. His letter concluded with the following story:

> In subsequent ages the yew tree was cut down by a labourer well known to my informant, the parish clerk. The man began his work in the morning, but left it at breakfast time, and on his return found that the old tree had fallen, collapsing into a large cavity underneath its roots. That such cavities have been found in other cases under old yew trees I have been told. Whether this one was simply enlarged by the dragon for his own convenience, or whether it was wholly dug out by that creature's claws, there is no evidence to show.

This is the earliest account of the felling of the tree. Was Wigram preserving custom or creating it? If true, it posed some fascinating questions. Was the cavity visible before the tree came down? Had it played a role in the origin of the legend, or at least in the tradition that the dragon lived under a tree in that field? Many of the written accounts said that the dragon had lived in Great Pepsells field, others said it had lived under a yew tree in the field. Had tradition always associated the dragon with that particular tree and, more to the point, had Master Lawrence known that when he set his axe to its roots?

4

The Variety of Wonders caused some Suspition of the Truth of his
Relations; but all things that seem improbable are not impossible,
and the ignorance of the Reader does oftentimes weaken the Truth
of the Author . . .

—Henry Chauncy, *The Historical Antiquities*
of Hertfordshire, 1700

Folk legends, with their origins buried deep in the past, owe much to unseen forces; they are crafted gradually like limestone pillars on the seashore, eroded imperceptibly to their present shape by sea and wind and rain. For a time at least, they might resemble something recognisable: a witch's face in profile, say, or a giant's fist. Can we say what the rock originally looked like or what other shapes it has taken over thousands of years? Occasionally, however, it changes in a moment – when a storm sweeps away a large chunk – and the cause of the new shape can be discovered by listening to the old people or turning up the water-damaged logbook of a ship.

The shifting themes and motifs in the different versions of the Shonks legend made it clear that his story had changed many times over the centuries. Oral accounts must have morphed in the telling, and then, once people started writing them down, they could not resist dreaming up a detail or two of their own; eventually the oral tradition became a garbled version of early written accounts and vice versa. Old motifs were embellished by an eager storyteller, others borrowed, new emphases were made, traditions were misconstrued, meanings were forgotten and re-remembered back to front, small details were tacked on to add colour.

Was it possible to say where the detail that the dragon lived in a yew tree in Great Pepsells field had come from? Had it been there from the beginning? How was it passed down through the generations? Who first wrote it down? It was not mentioned by the cartographer John Norden in 1598, nor by the county historian Nathaniel Salmon, who was very taken with the legend in the early eighteenth century, nor even by Edward Brayley, who wrote at length on the tomb in his *Beauties of England and Wales* in 1808. In over twenty accounts of the legend by locals, antiquaries and journalists written before Wigram set down his version, not one mentioned the tree or the fields.

It is not impossible that an oral tradition about Pepsells had been overlooked by all these early chroniclers, but it is unlikely when every other element of the legend that we will meet in this book had found its way onto the page. By the early nineteenth century there were vague references to where the dragon lived. An account published in 1827 mentioned a location for the battle between Shonks and the dragon that took place on somewhere called Shonks' Hill, which villagers still pointed out at the time. In 1865, the same year that Woolmore Wigram became vicar, Frances Wilson wrote to *The Reliquary (A Depository for Precious Relics Legendary, Biographical and Historical, Illustrative of the Habits, Customs and Pursuits of our Forefathers)*. She had grown up in neighbouring Little Chishill, the daughter of the village blacksmith, and for the first time, in print at least, she associated the dragon's lair with a tree, mentioning in passing that the beast occupied a tree in a meadow. But not one text in the first two hundred and ninety years of written accounts mentioned Great or Little Pepsells field, or a yew tree, until Wigram wrote his letter to the *Hertfordshire Mercury*. Anyone reading it in 1888, or since, would assume that the location of the dragon's lair was part of the tradition before the men chopped down the yew. Subsequent accounts take Wigram at face value and name the field as if it had been a key part of the story long before the labourers uncovered the cavity beneath the tree. The woodcutters' belief in the dragon's cave became entwined with the story in such a way that the cave appears to have always been part of the tradition, but the textual evidence was clear: it was simply Wigram's narrative conceit. The felling of the tree, especially Wigram's account of that day years later, was a storm that in an instant changed the limestone pillar. I love W. G. Hoskins' axiom that most things in the landscape are older than we think, but it is not always true, even of trees and fields and dragons' lairs, but especially not the stories we tell about them.

In his famous essay 'On the Cannibals', Montaigne wrote that he would rather have a story from a plain ignorant fellow than an educated one:

> *for your better-bred sort of men are much more curious in their observation, 'tis true, and discover a great deal more; but then they gloss upon it, and to give the greater weight to what they deliver, and allure your belief, they cannot forbear a little to alter the story; they never represent things to you simply as they are, but rather as they appeared to them, or as they would have them appear to you, and to gain the reputation of men of judgement, and the better to induce your faith, are willing to help out the business with something more than is really true, of their own invention.*

Wigram could not forbear to *gloss* and *help out the business*, but we should be glad of it, glad he played the storyteller. Wigram enriched the legend from the moment he responded to that newspaper query in 1888. Contrast that with the reaction of his contemporary John Edwin Cussans who had already called the stories about Shonks' tomb 'absurd traditions' in his *History of Hertfordshire*. In 1888, the so-called 'laughing historian' followed the correspondence in the newspaper and then waded in with his own *ex cathedra* pronouncement. After trying to pour cold water on another Hertfordshire tradition, he added a spiteful coda: 'I forebore to address you on the discussion which has recently taken place in your columns on the subject of Shonk's tomb, as I thought I had sufficiently demolished the ridiculous tradition in my account of Furneaux [sic] Pelham.' We will run into others like him, who boast of demolishing things and are proud of their own drag-on-slaying and giant-killing exploits. Give us the Wigrams any day, even if they cannot resist tinkering.

'If stories remain undisturbed they die of neglect,' writes Philip Pullman, and Italo Calvino said something similar when he justified his own tampering with Italian folk tales with a Tuscan proverb: 'The tale is not beautiful if nothing is added to it.' That is not to say anything goes. The wrong kind of change destroys more than it creates: you have to be true to the fact that people used to believe folk legends were true.

It was a clever bit of storytelling by the vicar, but we would not be happy if he had just made up the yew tree, the fields and the felling. We would feel cheated. As the folklorist Jacqueline Simpson has pointed out, we want a reason to say of our dragons and their slayings, 'there was something in it after all'.

The realisation of Wigram's conceit not only provided an unusually detailed instance of a folk legend metamorphosing – and perhaps a model for how other parts of the legend had been seeded or transformed – it completely changed the nature of my curiosity. I no longer had to wrestle with what it meant to find a cave under a tree that according to tradition grew over a dragon's lair, because that was back to front: the tradition did not begin until the day the tree was felled. But the question remaining is even more curious: why on finding a cavity under a tree in a field with no previous connection to the legend did those nineteenth-century labourers think of the dragon that Shonks slew?

This hints at much about folk legends and their status within communities as recently as the 1830s. Stories about dragons and their holes are assumed to have medieval origins, conjured by medieval minds as they conjured up other strange creatures to populate bestiaries, adorn the edges of manuscripts and support the corbel tables of churches, but nineteenth-century agricultural labourers? Was the legend so powerful and so ubiquitous in the Pelhams that when uneducated farm workers found an unexpected cavity under a yew tree they immediately turned to the legend of a dragon-slayer for an explanation?

That such wonders hid in the fields and spinneys of the English countryside so recently is a delight, as well as a reminder that folk *legends* differed from folk *tales* – that were never believed and told only for entertainment – by the evidence in the real world as well as in the story: the hilltop, the gravestone, the tree that sages can point at and say: 'You can still see it today'. It proves the legend.

I was first attracted to Shonks' story by the yew tree in a named field. Finding such survivals, tangible evidence for stories and folk legends, is psychologically very appealing. At the beginning of *Albion*, her compendium of English folk legends, the folklorist Jennifer Westwood quotes Walter de la Mare: 'Who would not treasure a fragment of Noah's Ark, a lock of Absalom's hair, Prester John's thumb-ring, Scheherazade's night lamp, a glove of Caesar's or one of King Alfred's burnt cakes?'

Such wonders have been called mnemonic bridges that help us connect with the past. It is the reason people have venerated fragments of the cross, or followed in the footsteps of Caesar and Alexander. It is the attraction of the perennial plot device in children's stories where the young hero or heroine awakes in bed thinking they dreamed it all, only to find the golden coin in their dressing-gown pocket, proving they had really been there. Coleridge once imagined a dream about Paradise where he was given flowers and awoke to find them beside him, and Hans Christian Andersen knew the power of objects that crossed the boundary between fantasy and reality when at the end of his little story 'The Princess and the Pea' he wrote: 'The pea was exhibited in the royal museum; and you can go there and see it, if it hasn't been stolen. Now that was a real story!'

Objects that locate legends in a real landscape possess some archetypal magic. Some place the story in a distant, fantastical past, while others root it in the everyday. Some tales explain oddly shaped hills and standing stones by the antics of immense dragons, giants or the devil, but a yew tree in a field has the commonplace about it, the evidence is on a more human scale. There was a real tree, chopped down by real people, in a field with a name. It was important for the legend. Such things can be the reason stories prevail. Yet here was a strange instance of that rule because the yew did not ensure the survival of the legend by providing a regular, visible reminder of that story, since on the very day it became part of that story someone removed it from the landscape. It was an artefact, both in the sense that its significance lay in the workmanship of the woodcutters and in the sense that its place in the story was a remnant of the storytelling process. In spite of this, it undoubtedly helped to perpetuate the tale and did so largely thanks to Wigram's rhetorical device.

The Shonks legend had the moat named for him and a mysterious tomb, and now it had a magical tree on the edge of Great Pepsells field as well.

5

*Field names and Folk-lore are naturally classed together; both
alike speak to us of the lives and customs of our forefathers; of
creeds and cults, long since abandoned, but still surviving, though
unrecognised, to these modern days.*

—U. B. Chisenhale-Marsh, 1906

In the late 1930s, the English Place-Name Society asked schoolchildren to save the names of England's fields before they were
lost and forgotten for ever. In the fourteenth year of her forty-
four-year reign as headmistress of Furneux Pelham School, Miss
Evelyn Prior heard the call to arms and sent her pupils out to
interview the farmers and field hands. The parish magazine for
March 1937 records that: 'With the aid of the school children
and an Ordnance map and a few other helpers, and at the request
of the County Council, Miss Prior, the headmistress of our
school has drawn up a list of the names of all the fields of the
parish.'

Did they find Great and Little Pepsells?

These names situate the yew in the real world, and evoke a bygone
landscape. As with tithe customs, field names once again bring us
into the territory of collective memories and tradition. The folklore
collector Charlotte Burne said that all such 'trifling relics' were
important for the study of social history: local sayings, rhymes, even
the bell-jingles (the words that the different peals of church bells

44

are supposed to 'say'). 'They reflect the rural life of past generations, with its anxieties, its trivialities, its intimate familiarity with Nature, and its strong local preoccupations.' They helped make us what we are.

In Reverend Wigram's day, the countryside was not numbered by bureaucrats but named by, and for, the people who worked it. Our landscapes and sense of the spaces around us were richer and more highly developed than today, or at least that is what the names would suggest. Today field names can help us recover that landscape from the blandscapes of modernity and to see our world with fresh eyes. Every parcel of cultivated land in the country had a name – more often than not one that can tell us something interesting about the land and put us in touch with the past.

It has been said that place names are linguistic fossils containing within them extinct words; they are often dense with information. They carry echoes of the dead, how they worked the land, their hopes and struggles, and the stories they told each other.

In many places, the fields themselves have disappeared. The London Borough of Ealing is not somewhere you naturally associate with the countryside, but it is the subject of the first of the English Place-Name Society's series of *Field-Name Studies* written in 1976. Here beneath the pavements and Victorian villas are forgotten pastures that remember the names of local men known to have been on an early fourteenth-century list of the local militia. Other names will tell you where those men and their descendants built a dovecote, a menagerie, or ice house, where they quarried clay, farmed rabbits, or struggled to make crops grow in a stony field.

John Field, the aptly named historian and taxonomist of English field names, arranged them into useful categories. There are names that describe the shape of a field (*Harps*), its wild plants (*Cockerels*), the productivity of the land (*Smallops*), or long-lost buildings

(*Duffers*). Its size (*Pightle* or *Thousand Acres*), how it was farmed (*Lammas Meadow*), and industrial uses (*Brick Kiln Meadow*). He came up with twenty-six types in all.

The meanings, as you have probably noticed, are not always self-explanatory, although Harps is easy: it should be a triangular-shaped field. Cockerels on the other hand is a false friend. Field names can morph in a process that gradually transforms a strange-sounding word into something familiar that seems to fit – philologists call this 'popular etymology'. So Cockerels was originally *Cocklers* – from the weed corn cockle – and nothing to do with male chickens. Similar forces tinker with our folk tales and our urban myths, and in such ways dragons are sometimes born and giants set free to stalk the land. A well-known instance of popular etymology is Gravesend; there is one in Kent and another on the border of the Pelhams, and no doubt elsewhere. A friend told me recently that the local Gravesend was named for the plague victims who were buried there in the seventeenth century; she suspected this because Gravesend in Kent was apparently so-called because the London dead were washed down the Thames and ended up there, where they were buried. It is a good story, but a quick check of the place-name dictionaries tells us that both places were so-called centuries before the plague, before the Black Death even, and probably owed their monikers to local land-owners called Graves.

Some field names have simply become mumbles of the original: how does Smallops tell us about the productivity of the land? For Smallops read *Small Hopes*. The meaning of Duffers has also been submerged in the argot of the agricultural labourer. For Duffers read *Dovecote*. Other names are made from obsolete words: a pightle is a small field, while a *croat* or *croft* is a small piece of land often attached to a house and usually enclosed. Thousand Acres is, of course, usually a very small field. If we ask why Lammas Meadow tells us something about how a field was farmed we can find an answer rich with history between *Lamb Pits* and *Lamp Acre*:

'"Meadow lands used for grazing after 1 August". The hay harvest occupied the time between 24 June and Lammas, when the fences were removed and the reapers turned their attention to the corn. The cattle were meanwhile allowed to graze on the aftermath. Loaves made from the new wheat were taken to the church at this time for a blessing and a thanksgiving – hence the name *hlāfmæsse*, "loaf festival".'

Sometimes the name is the only surface remnant of a field's claim to fame. There is no brick kiln to be seen in Brick Kiln Mead. Names can also help identify mysterious features still visible in the landscape. Aerial photographs reveal two circular mounds in a large field – ancient burial mounds perhaps? It is more likely they are remnants of a medieval coney, or rabbit, farm because it is remembered as *The Warren*. Other commonplaces of the medieval past live on only in the name: in the south-east corner of Furneux Pelham is *Woolpits*, which perhaps means 'land near a wolf pit'. Although others have argued that rumours of wolves, like those of dragons, might just as easily refer to metaphorical beasts.

Field names remind me of Entish, the language of Tolkien's giant tree shepherds, in which 'real names tell you the story of the things they belong to', but words in Entish were impossibly long agglomerations of meaning, so I suppose field names are in some ways the opposite: they contain much in a very small space, like poetry. Treebeard, the leader of the Ents declares that *hill* is 'a hasty word for a thing that has stood here ever since this part of the world was shaped', but Margaret Gelling counted some forty different words for a hill in Old English; after all, the Saxons needed to know one type of hill from the other when giving directions. The word *hill* may be lost somewhere in the name of the fields we are hunting for: Pepsells. The name is not in the field-name dictionaries, but some forty miles away, on the Bedfordshire border, there is a Pepsal End Farm with various spellings recorded, including in

1564 'Pepsel'. The meaning is 'Pyppe's Hill' from the Anglo-Saxon personal name Pyppa, suggesting a very venerable field name indeed. Did Pyppa till the earth with Payn of Paynards – perhaps the oldest surviving field name in those parts – and with Peola, who gave his name to Pelham in the early days of the Anglo-Saxon migration? It is fun to think so, but it does not help us find the field we are looking for, a field where some once thought a dragon took up residence.

The schoolchildren did a wonderful job of collecting the names for Miss Prior and posterity. Across Hertfordshire as a whole, the operation was a great success. Two luminaries of the English Place-Name Society, Allen Mawer and Sir Frank Stenton, wrote: 'We have been able in this county, possibly with more success than in any other that we have hitherto attempted, to get a lively picture of the field-names as they still survive and through the help of the school-masters and mistresses and their scholars we have again and again been able to obtain information which has been invaluable in throwing light upon the history of these names.'

The procedure was copied all over England and some of the information was used in lists in the early county volumes. The complete lists and maps were safely stored at University College London; safe until disaster struck in September 1940 when bombs fell from the sky. All the records were destroyed and the small number of names not already in print were lost along with their locations.

Fortunately, there are maps of Brent and Furneux Pelham rolled up in the Furneux church chest that are almost certainly the result of Miss Prior's exertions. They are brittle and yellow: the parish boundary in red; the roads and woodland in green; the river, the field boundaries and their names marked in dark blue ink. The crossings-out, illegible pencil notes and childlike handwriting add to their charm.

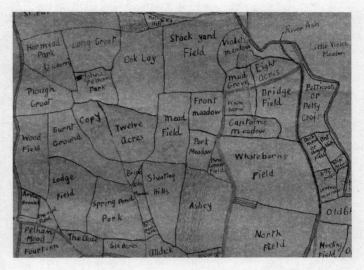

Carefully unrolling the maps for the first time, I eagerly skimmed them in search of Pepsells, but could not see the name. I worked systematically from field to field following the names from Furneux Pelham church through *Alldick* and *Little Pasture* to the field boundary between *Shooting Hills* and *Brick Kiln Meadow*. I kept the pond on my left through *Copy* and skirted the ruins in *Johns Pelham Park*, emerging in *Long Croat*. Into Brent Pelham through *St Patricks Hill*, *Chalky Field* and *Broadley Shot*, my eye passed over 300 distinct field names: poetry like *Moat Duffers*, *Malting Meadow* and *Mile Post Field*, *Ashey* and *Dumplings* and *Hitch*. There were meads and leys, crofts, croats, pightles, springs and shots. Pepsells, great or small, was nowhere. Looking at that map for the first time, I began to entertain an idea that had not even occurred to me until that moment: what if Woolmore Wigram had just made the whole thing up? Maybe there never were a Great and Little Pepsells, no credulous labourers, no venerable yew set with a stile, not even a dragon's lair.

6

It is distinctly remembered by the old inhabitants of these parishes that at the time the boundaries used to be trod a great deal of amusement was occasioned by the party always dragging with a rope one man through the ponds situated upon the heath.

—Thomas Bray, Meresman for Furneux Pelham
—John Cork, Meresman and Overseer of Albury
Ordnance Survey Boundary Remark Book, 1875

In my mind's eye I can see Major Barclay, tall and rangy, with very fine wind-blown hair, standing up to his knees in flood water one summer morning, trying to unblock the ditches on the Roman road by Chamberlains Moat and recalling the number of oyster shells found there when it was last dredged; on the tile-strewn platform at St John's Pelham Moat on a summer's evening explaining how a boy who went to his school started the First World War by insulting the Kaiser; or on Shonks' Moat, leaning against an old oak tree which he calls Shonks: 'There's him himself,' he says smiling. 'He's impressive close up, isn't he?'

Ted Barclay has been fascinated by Shonks since his childhood when his grandfather Maurice told him stories about the hero. He is the current custodian of Beeches Manor and of all the Brent Pelham moats. In fact, he has owned much of Brent Pelham since the 1860s, or rather his family has, but Ted has the totally disarming habit of talking about the distant past as if recalling his own part in it. Casting his mind back perhaps to the day in 1905 when his great-grandfather played host to W. B. Gerish and the East Hertfordshire Archaeological Society, playing the immortal Comte de St Germain: 'Hmmm. I told Shonks to stay at home that day there were dragons abroad.'

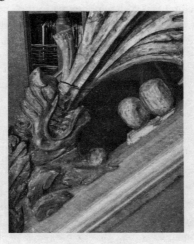

On the mezzanine stairs in his library are carvings taken from a staircase that was originally made for Brent Pelham Hall in the late seventeenth century. On the inside of the balusters, the head of Shonks' dragon snarls with sabretooth fangs; on the outside, it bares its teeth in a demonic grin, breathing flames of foliage – opposites that nicely reflect the Barclays' longstanding relationship to the story, which is both tongue-in-cheek and entirely in earnest. Ted's father, Captain Charles Barclay, adopted a stray Irish wolfhound in the 1960s, which was promptly named Shonks. The three-foot-high beast proceeded to menace the neighbourhood, chasing cars, stealing food from kitchens and pulling clothes from washing lines, earning him immortality in Frank Sheardown's book, *The Working Longdog*, in which Shonks the Dog's most notorious exploit was to remove a dish of rice pudding from inside an oven: 'How he did it, no one was able to tell, but did it he did and duly delivered the empty pot back home.' The stuff of village legend.

The library is a recent addition to Beeches. The house was built in the seventeenth century and is dominated by nine exceedingly tall octagonal chimneys, with windows set in the stacks at the gable ends. The west wing is oddly stunted in contrast to the east, because six rooms were haunted and had to be demolished.

Ted pulled a small slipcase from the shelves and unfolded an old cloth-backed 25-inch Ordnance Survey map onto the carpet. It had been coloured and annotated over the years to show the extent of the Barclays' Brent Pelham estate. Joseph Gurney Barclay, the banker and prominent Quaker, bought the manor of Brent Pelham in the middle of the nineteenth century and over time the family expanded their holdings, so the Barclays owned a fair portion of farmland in Furneux Pelham too. Surveying his domain, Ted traced a long finger across fields, across Nether Rackets, High Field and Lady Pightle.

He was looking for dragons and eventually tapped his finger on an irregularly shaped field defined by two blocks of ancient woodland: Great Hormead Park at the south-western corner and Patricks

Wood on the eastern edge. It was labelled *St Patricks Hill* on the 1930s school map, but Ted was sure: this was Great Pepsells. After all, the land had been part of the Barclay estate for over a hundred years. It is in Furneux Pelham, bounded by Brent Pelham to the east and Great Hormead to the west.

If Ted was right, Woolmore Wigram may well have been telling the truth after all. There was certainly plenty of room for a dragon's lair in the field, one of the largest in the Pelhams. Ted recalled that it had been the longest run of the steam plough, and during the Second World War the farmers filled it with old machinery to stop enemy planes landing. (Patricks Wood still concealed the rusting carcasses.)

Just so there could be no doubt, Ted produced an old notebook marked: *Fields in Brent and Furneux Pelham: Owner-Occupiers-Area 1784*. It was an eighteenth-century tithe book that had once belonged to a Robert Comyns, and inked into the columns of the first page were the fields owned by the Lord of the Manor in Furneux. There was no Great or Little Pepsells, but there were Pipsels and Pepsels in company with Nether Rackets, High Field and Lady Pightle, locating them just where Ted said they ought to be.

Great Pepsells was not the only field I discovered that day in Beeches. Next to the library in the old gunroom, hung a Victorian copy of 'The Field of Cloth of Gold'. The original print was once famous for its vastness and for the man-hours expended to make it cover twelve square feet of plaster with so many tents and Tudor courtiers. Completed in 1773, it was the largest print ever made. The painter Edward Edwards spent 160 days at Windsor Castle copying the original oil for James Basire the Elder, who then took another two years to engrave the copper plate. Four hundred copies were pressed onto bespoke sheets of paper made for the occasion by the great paper-maker James Whatman in a sheet-size still known as Antiquarian. It was a print as ambitious as the event it commemorated.

It depicts the extraordinary pageant held in June 1520 when Henry VIII and the French King Francis I tried to outdo each other for excess and machismo in the Pale of Calais. Here was an endlessly diverting blend of historical detail, make-believe and mythmaking. Here were hundreds of richly costumed courtiers and halberdiers parading through a Barnum and Bailey landscape constructed specially for the occasion. The two larger-than-life kings embrace in a Big Top as knights gallop through the lists behind them, and men drink claret from fountains.

The Society of Antiquaries valued such paintings as historical documents, and scholars tried to tease out the factual from the fabulous – no easy task when the facts were so extraordinary anyway and the fabulous might symbolise much that was real. Take the statues of the three dragon-slayers on Henry's extraordinary temporary palace. The showy Renaissance edifice was richly decorated with figures, but when Sydney Anglo published a detailed examination of the painting in the 1960s, he ruled that the dragon-slayers were figments of the painter's imagination.

Another, much larger dragon, a magnificent, bearded wyvern, is painted in the sky above Calais. Whereas it is uncertain whether the painter portrayed the dragons on the gate accurately, presumably we can say with some confidence that there was no real dragon at the event, although chroniclers did write of one screaming through the sky above the crowd as Cardinal Wolsey sang the Corpus Christi mass. Historians cannot agree what this was. Some say that there was a 'Flying Dragon' firework display, others that it was perhaps a kite in the shape of a salamander released prematurely during the service. Whatever it was, it must have been a strange omen to some sixteenth-century minds. Today, the airborne dragon stands for the spirit of the piece: the myth and history, the real and the make-believe side by side. It stands as a cipher for all the fabulous but true features of the occasion, because ambitious as the painting and its print are, they cannot hold a torch to the real event.

There were not hundreds of soldiers, gentry and nobility, but over ten thousand. Their clothes were so fine that one French eyewitness said noblemen were walking around with their estates on their back because they had mortgaged their lands to finance the cloth. The temporary palace contained five thousand square feet of the finest glass ever made. A fountain ran with claret, but if you preferred beer, the English had brought 14,000 gallons with them – presumably to wash down their other rations: 9,000 plaice, 8,000 whiting, 4,000 sole, 3,000 crayfish, 700 conger eels, 300 oxen, 2,000 chickens, 1,200 capons, 2,000 sheep and over 300 heron. As Melvyn Bragg said when his BBC Radio 4 programme *In Our Time* tackled the occasion, 'The fun is in the detail.' And that great dragon in the sky stands for the detail that the picture, for all its intricacy, can only hint at.

Encountering that print during my quest for Great Pepsells was serendipitous: with its associations, its mysteries, its vivid historical detail, its poetic licence, its riddles, its unwitting challenge to find out just how much history it contained, and, of course, its dragons.

7

It is not down in any map; true places never are.

—Herman Melville, *Moby Dick*, 1851

Ancient yews stand few and far between. Did one really straddle the boundary of Great and Little Pepsells until the early nineteenth century? A four-foot by three-foot oblong of greying parchment lies unfolded on the chart table at the Hertfordshire Archives, held flat by weighted leather snakes to reveal a jigsaw puzzle of Furneux Pelham's fields. The 1836 Act of Parliament that did away with tithes had the wonderful side effect of creating remarkable encyclopedic maps and surveys, covering some 80 per cent of English parishes. Every field within the parish bounds is there, numbered and surveyed at six chains, or 132 yards, to every inch, some enclosed shortly before the map was made, neat and geometrical, others with edges softened by time and use, squashed polygons, their boundaries meandering and dog-legged to attest to their antiquity. The odd large field bears a dotted line intersected by S-marks to tie fields together that were not then enclosed, but considered separate. Thin yellow roads run east to west and north to south partitioning the village. Along them, in two or three places, buildings cluster in plan: red for homes and grey for all the others, the church indicated by a cross, the windmill a small crude X on a stick. There are avenues of trees, blocks of woodland, ponds and the River Ash roughly bisecting the map.

It was surveyed a hundred years before Miss Prior's school map, and whereas her students had found some 300 field names, the tithe maps for Brent and Furneux Pelham list over 400. Some names had swapped fields over time: Handpost Field is on the other side of the road – perhaps the handpost moved, or more likely the children or the surveyors made a mistake. Many changed their names, becoming more poetic, like Moat Duffers, which was originally Dove House Field, or less so, like Violets Meadow, which was once the much lovelier Fylets. The field identified as Great Pepsells by Ted Barclay, but St Patricks Hill by the school map, is five separate fields on the tithe: ancient enclosures amalgamated by Victorian landowners. On the western boundary, no. 7 is simply Spring, and no. 8 the self-explanatory eleven-acre field called Ten Acres. On the eastern edge is no. 10 Wood Field, and part of no. 12, the delightful Lady Pightle. There, in the middle, is no. 9, Pepsels and directly to the north is field no. 5, known then as Pipsels Mead.

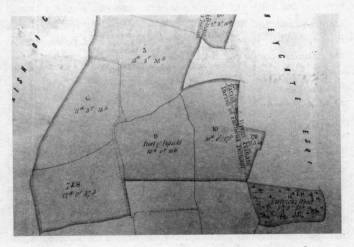

Strikingly, a track is marked on the tithe map crossing the inter-section of Pepsels, Nether Rackets, Pipsels Mead and Ten Acres fields.

This track might have passed straight through the stile in the yew tree. The track – a tunnel of dashed lines on the map – goes no further, as if it led to something no longer there. The countryside is marked with these strange paths to nowhere, or rather paths to the past.

The good Reverend Wigram had not made up the names of Great and Little Pepsells after all, so perhaps no one had invented the tree either. The boundary between them was a real place and you could visit it still. There may even be something in the rest of the tale, if once again we allow the logic of that rustic who would not have believed a word of Shonks' tale if he hadn't seen the place in the wall with his own eyes. There was certainly a field, so we might as well believe that there was a tree, but what was an ancient yew of all trees doing growing there astride a track in the middle of nowhere?

A single yew alone outside a churchyard is a great rarity – with or without a dragon's lair. Of the 311 ancient yews known in Britain, very few are not – and have never been – associated with a known church or religious site, and an ancient yew growing anywhere at all is an unfamiliar sight in the countryside around the Pelhams: there are none in Cambridgeshire, Essex or Bedfordshire, and just two surviving ancient yews known in Hertfordshire – both in churchyards. There are a further seven *veteran* yews in the county – that is trees between 500 and 1,200 years old according to the latest classification by the Ancient Yew Group – but they are all linked to a church.

The nearest non-churchyard yew is a lone veteran growing in Hatfield Forest some sixteen miles away. Although Oliver Rackham insisted that it was only 230 years old, 'and should be remembered by anyone who supposes that big yews must always be of fabulous age'. Recent analysis by an arborist suggests that the tree is much older and has a smaller circumference than you'd expect because it has spent much of its life in the shade. Perched on the edge of the decoy lake, sloughing off the bark of its many-corded bole, it conceals the mysterious cavities of ancient yew. Its existence gives us some confidence that our yew is within the geographical distribution of these curious trees.

Nearer to the Pelhams, a remarkable specimen lingers in the churchyard of St James the Great, in Thorley, near Bishop's Stortford. Ringed by precarious gravestones, the main trunk appears to be made from many closely packed smaller trunks, like the product of black fairy magic, an impenetrable palisade of thick stakes imprisoning some secret. A terrible secret: the tree has been hollowed out by arson, its innards gone, and what remains is dreadfully tormented and charcoaled. Yet still it lives and grows and puts out new leaves. Yews are extraordinary trees. In the church is a certificate, from when the Conservation Foundation ran its Yew Tree Campaign in the 1980s, attesting that the tree is 1,000 years old. *Ancient* yews are now defined as those over 800 years old, with no upper age limit, but determining the age of yews is about as controversial as botany gets. Tim Hills of the Ancient Yew Group writes that the science has moved on a lot since those certificates were awarded based on the ideas of Allen Meredith in his influential *The Sacred Yew.* Regardless of its age, the yew at Thorley is rightly something to be revered.

Robert Blair in his eighteenth-century poem 'The Grave' calls the yew a cheerless, unsocial plant that loves to spend its time in the midst of skulls and coffins. Illustrating the poem, William Blake depicted the tree's only merriment as ghosts and shades performing their mystic dance around the trunk under a wan moon, but in his watercolour the tree is at the centre, it is evergreen and blue, not dull, but bright in contrast to the pale spectres encircling it; a tree, like the burned-out Thorley yew, that defies death.

There are many theories as to why yews are found in churchyards, ranging from the prosaic (useful shelter from the storm) to the poetic (yews were symbolic of the journey to the underworld). The church guidebook to St James the Great lists other reasons: as a symbol of immortality, to stop villagers allowing their cattle to stray into the graveyard (its leaves are poisonous), or because Edward I decreed that yews be planted to protect churches from storms. Wherever they grow, it is generally assumed that their siting has some significance, if only because they must have been preserved from the needs of longbow production for some special reason (by the late sixteenth century, Europe had been almost completely denuded of yew wood). Although others have argued that they were planted in churchyards precisely because they were needed for longbow production and they would be protected from livestock. John Brand, the eighteenth-century compiler of superstitions thought this was nonsense, approving instead of Sir Thomas Browne's conjecture 'that the planting of yew trees, in Churchyards, seems to derive its origin from the ancient funeral rites, in which, from its *perpetual verdure*, it was used as an emblem of the resurrection'. Yews are not accidental trees, they mark things, they remember things: wells or springs, boundaries, lost settlements, meeting places, pagan religious sites or perhaps even the burial places of people who dropped dead along a pilgrimage route. What did the Pelham tree mark on its lonely boundary between two fields?

Was it originally planted to mark the site of an early Christian saint's cells? In about 940 the Welsh King Hywel Dda threatened a fine of sixty sheep for felling yews associated with saints. Or did people gather around the yew long ago? Surviving lone trees may have been moot trees – meeting trees – like the Ankerwycke Yew at Runnymede where King John might have signed *Magna Carta*, and Henry VIII was said to have met Anne Boleyn for the first time. From Anglo-Saxon times until the modern period many southern and Midlands counties were divided into Hundreds, which took their names from the original moots or meeting places of the Hundred Court. Such places were often marked by a significant tree or stone. The Pelhams were in the Edwinstree Hundred – literally Edwin's Tree – and early records indicate that the meeting place was somewhere in the Pelhams. Place-name historians have guessed that Meeting Field housed the tree, although that name appears for the first time in the late nineteenth century. Great Pepsells was much closer to the centre of the Hundred, bounded by three parishes and fed by ancient paths and trackways. Was Edwin's Tree a venerable old yew? One early medieval source links Edwin's Tree to woodland, and woodland may hide the reason for a lone Hertfordshire yew and that track to nowhere.

At the turn of the nineteenth century, villagers across Essex and Hertfordshire were warned not to be startled by strange lights on the horizon. The engineers of the Ordnance Survey were at large, hauling Ramsden's immense horse-drawn theodolite from village to village, along with their 100-foot steel chains, twenty-foot high white flags, and their brand-new draught-proof white lights. This was the earliest of the surveys made some eighty years before the large-scale 25-inch with its individual trees. The maps would be plotted at just 1 inch to the mile, but it was a revolution in cartography.

There are remarkable preliminary pencil drawings, made at a larger scale than the published sheets. The fields seem to stand out from the paper in relief, like anatomical specimens in cross section, finely hachured to look more like a coral reef than rural Hertfordshire. Zoom in and the map covering Great Pepsells is heavily shadowed as if seen through storm clouds, the gathering clouds of the Peninsular War perhaps, which hurried the surveyor's hand. The field boundaries, which would disappear from the published version, are clearly drawn in, and the house and settlements picked out brightly in red ink. Right in the centre of the drawing between the little red dots labelled Johns Pelham and Lily End is Hormead Park Wood, the woodland that adjoins the southwest corner of Great Pepsells. But it is much larger on the 1 inch than it is today. Instead of the tidy rectangle of later maps, the wood meanders across the fields of Furneux Pelham drawing a shape far more typical of an original ancient woodland boundary.

But were these early small-scale maps accurate? They were surveyed in two parts. First the large-scale trigonometry was completed, and then a second survey filled in the resulting triangles with fields and roads, rivers and hills: this was the interior or topographical survey. Map historians write that the very first OS sheets of Kent had been plotted at the end of the eighteenth century to the exacting standards of the pioneering military map-maker William Roy, who insisted that 'The boundaries of forests, woods, heaths, commons or morasses, are to be distinctly surveyed, and in the enclosed part of the country at the hedge, and other boundaries of fields are to be carefully laid down.' It was a slow and expensive process, so when they came to do Essex, the chief surveyors were told to make it faster and cheaper, but in the end they only sacrificed the exact shape of fields. So while the 1804 sheets might not be as detailed as the later large-scale maps, it was a proper military survey, and the towns, villages, rivers and hills were plotted accurately. As were the woods, because they could provide cover for ambushes – a French invasion was still feared when the surveyors were at work.

Assured of the map's accuracy, I laid a copy over later maps, and found that where a finger of the wood points to its northernmost edge, *it precisely matches the shape of the boundary between Great and Little Pepsells.* (I use italics in an effort to convey the excitement I felt at this discovery. It was as if I had unearthed a fragment of an ancient cuneiform clay tablet and found it joined up perfectly with another found years before to reveal the location of Noah's ark.) Was it an echo of the northernmost tree-line of Great Hormead Park Wood? Did an ancient yew tree once mark this boundary? Yews, as well as other trees, had been used as meres or boundary markers since Anglo-Saxon times. And there was that telltale path that the yew had straddled, hence the stile in its split trunk, a path terminating at a tree that is no longer there.

There is a later map, one of the last private county maps made before the OS swept all before it: Mr Bryant's 1822 map reveals that sometime between then and the start of the century, the section of Hormead Park projecting into Furneux Pelham was grubbed up, or, in the terms of the Lord of the Manor's tenancy agreement for the land, the timber was felled, cut down, stocked up, peeled, hewn, sawn, worked out, made up and carried away. Why was the Yew left untouched?

The same military zeal that saw the birth of the Ordnance Survey saw the felling of thousands of trees not for timber for ships or for the war effort as is sometimes said, but simply because corn prices went through the roof. The militaristic language used to describe the campaigns against Napoleon were used to describe the agricultural revolution against the inefficient use of land. 'Let us not be satisfied with the liberation of Egypt or the subjugation of Malta,' wrote the first President of the Board of Agriculture, in 1803. 'Let us subdue Finchley Common; let us conquer Hounslow Heath, let us compel Epping Forest to submit to the yoke of improvement.'

The transformation of the ancient clay or heavy-lands of Eastern England from medieval bullock fattening into intensive arable is now recognised as one of the key stages of the agricultural revolution. Arable land in the Pelhams increased by 130 acres in the half-century after 1784, but pasture fell by only three. It was woodland and hedgerow that gave way to the plough. Hertfordshire was one of the counties with the least waste – or uncultivated land – as so much of it had already been enclosed and cultivated in the Middle Ages; little wonder then that farmers were grubbing up trees and not just scrub when corn prices were so high. 'What immense quantities of timber have fallen before the axe and mattock to make way for corn,' wrote one observer in 1801.

If you are felling and grubbing up fifteen acres of trees, felling them by hand and digging up the roots, when you get to an ancient yew, perhaps some thirty foot or more in circumference, magnificent and stately and – more importantly – notoriously hard to chop down, you might well leave it standing, along with its stile that allowed people on the track from the north to clamber into the woodland.

It was not only a mere but also a shelter. The presence of these evergreens in churchyards and elsewhere is often said to be because of the shelter they offer. Deer have been spotted sheltering under a yew at Ashridge Park, in Hertfordshire, and there are yews on the banks of John of Gaunt's deer park at King's Somborne, probably dating from when the deer park was set out in the thirteenth century. Of course, they can shelter more than game. An ancient yew at Leeds Castle in Kent was lived in by gypsies in 1833, and the hollow Boarhunt yew in Hampshire reputedly housed a family for a whole winter.

'I know of no part of England more beautiful in its stile than Hertfordshire,' wrote Sir John Parnell in 1769. Here the ancient fields were bordered by ancient hedgerows that were practically small strips of woodland. In an 1837 article lamenting the fall of an ancient yew in a hurricane, one eulogist wrote: 'There are few objects of nature presenting more real interest to the mind, or richer points of beauty to the eye, than a noble aged tree; and at times these glories of the forest become associated, either from intrinsic character or local situation, with our best and purest feelings.' We know that folk, and not just poets, loved trees. In Matilda Betham-Edwards' novel about rural Suffolk in the 1840s, *The Lord of the Harvest*, Kara Sage the wife of the farm headman finds companionship in a magnificent elm. She 'never tired of gazing at that ancient tree'. But we are told that in her love of nature she was 'unlike her neighbours'. Still, she was not alone in literature: Thomas Hardy's eponymous *Woodlanders* Marty South and Giles Winterborne were also said to be rare in their 'level of intelligent intercourse with Nature', when they knew by a glance at a trunk if a tree's 'heart were sound, or tainted with incipient decay; and by the state of its upper twigs the stratum that had been reached by its roots'.

Even if we doubt that in such a practical age someone left the tree standing simply for its grandeur, we cannot doubt the effect such a tree might have had on the superstitious – that fear may have stopped their axes. At Old Oswestry Hillfort in Shropshire, the countryside has been stripped of trees except for a single old yew. 'It was probably spared because of a superstition about felling yews or because yews are very hard and so difficult to fell,' suggests one Shropshire natural historian. In his 1896 article 'Folk-Lore in Essex and Herts', U. B. Chisenhale-Marsh wrote that 'All about our own neighbourhood it is very customary, in clipping hedges, to leave small bushes or twigs standing at intervals, originally, no doubt, to keep away the evil spirits, or as propitiation to those that were cut away.' What better way to appease the spirits of the vanished woodland than to leave them the sanctuary of an ancient yew, to watch, and wait, and guard the secret at its roots for a few years more?

8

*Many writers at different times have engaged passionately by proxy
in the fairy world. Most of the accounts of encounters in fairyland
report incidents and adventures that occurred to someone else. This
is the terrain of anecdote, ghost sightings, and old wives' tales, of
oral tradition, hearsay, superstition, and shaggy dog stories: once
upon a time and far away among another people . . .*

—Marina Warner, *Once Upon a Time*, 2014

'Except for their gravestones and their children, they left nothing
identifiable behind them,' wrote historians George Rudé and
Eric Hobsbawm of the nineteenth-century agricultural labourer, 'for
the marvellous surface of the British landscape, the work of their
ploughs, spades and shears and the beasts they looked after bears
no signature or mark such as the masons left on cathedrals.' They
are right that the traces are few, but the fields themselves carried
names and sometimes they were the names of men who had worked
them and, if the land bore names, so I expect did the men's tools,
their initials cut plainly into hafts alongside the initials of their
fathers who swung them at other trees on other mornings. Did the
yew tree itself also bear their names? One historian has noted that
boundary trees 'were deeply scored with carved and ever enlarging
parish initials, from which the ivy was regularly stripped'. Did local
men carve their names into the trunk of the yew as plainly as they
did into the stone window jambs and leadwork of the Pelham

churches? Even if they did, the tree is long gone, the tools are lost, and the field names are slipping from memory. Where now can we find Master Lawrence the carpenter and the labourers who believed in dragons?

In October 1904 the Hertfordshire historian Robert Andrews went to Anstey, a village next to Brent Pelham, chasing the legend of a secret tunnel, a blind fiddler and the devil. 'The tenant of the little house at Cave Gate near Anstey was digging upon the premises held by him and found that the tool he was using suddenly sunk into the ground almost throwing him down,' wrote Andrews. This tenant was old Thomas Skinner and he had found the entrance to a tunnel in the chalk. Skinner was a carpenter who had 'passed his early years in the near neighbourhood' and had recently retired to Cave Gate, 'where he can, if he chooses, smoke his pipe under one of the most magnificent trees in Hertfordshire'. Perhaps it was while sitting under this tree talking to his guest about local folklore that he mentioned that in his boyhood his family had taken loppings from an ancient yew tree felled on the boundary of Great Pepsells field.

This was a tantalising reference. Not only did it place the felling of the tree in Thomas Skinner's boyhood in the 1830s – tallying with the map and other evidence – but the Skinner family were agricultural labourers who just happened to share a house in Brent Pelham with another labourer, Thomas Lawrence, the cousin of the carpenter William Lawrence whose sons would one day become Wigram's parish clerks. I would never know for sure, and it did not really matter, but I was unlikely to do better than to send these men to fell the tree one winter's day in 1834.

Like many agricultural labourers in the early nineteenth century, the Skinners awoke in a single room in a house shared with another family. There was scant light on a winter's morning and a ceiling open to the rough rafters did little to keep the place warm. If a labourer's wife were house-proud, he would take his breakfast sitting on a chair varnished with homemade beer, and there might be bread with dripping washed down with 'tea' (made from burned toast), or perhaps 'coffee' (made from burned toast). Many labourers spent half their week's wages on bread, but could not settle the baker's bill until they had killed their pig at the end of the year. These are the generalisations of the historian, but the 1830s were not a happy time for agricultural labourers, especially in the winter months when trees were traditionally felled. Winter was also the time for job creation schemes (or as the historians of the rural poor, the Hammonds, put it in their inimical and depressing way, 'Degrading and repulsive work was invented for those whom the farmer would not or could not employ'). One economic historian has estimated that 17 per cent of agricultural labourers were out of work in winter in the early 1830s. They would get poor relief, but it also meant that labourers could find themselves shared out between farmers who would find them things to do. The winter of 1834 was particularly bad, because the harvest had failed. 'I am fearful we shall experience much difficulty this Winter in finding employment for the Poor,' wrote a prominent Essex land agent, in a letter to his client, insisting they must reduce the burden of tithe payments that year.

Across the country, and especially in the south, large numbers of agricultural labourers had been turned into paupers by a system that saw the rate-payers, who were also their employers, agree to pay or subsidise their wages through the poor rate. The money they took home each week was linked to the size of their family and the price of a loaf of bread. There were many variations to this system. In some villages, labourers were auctioned weekly to the highest bidders. One Nathan Driver explained to the Select Committee on the Poor Laws how things worked in Furneux Pelham. There were some ninety agricultural labourers in a parish of 2,500 acres, which according to Mr Driver meant there were eighteen labourers too many. The solution was to put the names of all ninety labourers in a hat and share them out between the farms in Furneux Pelham – according to their size – on a daily basis. The farmers would then have to find something for them to do – chopping down a tree, for example.

Twenty-five children were born in the Pelhams in 1834, to a thatcher, a shoemaker, two yeoman farmers and twenty-one agricultural labourers. At the beginning of the 1830s, 62 per cent of men over twenty in the three Pelhams were agricultural labourers, a little higher than the Hertfordshire average and nearly three times the national one. By then considerably more families earned their living in England from trade, manufacturing or handicrafts, than worked on the land, but still agricultural labourers made up the single largest occupation group – some 745,000 of them. Most of us have more agricultural labourers in our family tree than any other ancestors. 'Agricultural labourer' does not necessarily tell the whole story. In the column marked 'Occupation' on the 1841 Census, the enumerators would have written the diminutive 'Ag Lab' *ad nauseam*, so it is disappointing that they didn't relieve the boredom by being more precise. Where were the ploughmen, the carters, the hedgers, the headmen, the woodcutters and the common taskers? It has been said that there were hierarchies among farm workers as intricate as that among the gentility.

It is impossible to consider this period without turning to the campaigning journalist and chronicler of the pains and pleasures of rural life William Cobbett. On one of his 'rural rides' around England in the 1820s he encountered a group of women labourers in 'such an assemblage of rags as I never before saw'. And of labourers near Cricklade: 'Their dwellings are little better than pig-beds and their looks indicate that their food is not nearly equal to that of a pig. Their wretched hovels are stuck upon little bits of ground on the road side . . . It seems as if they had been swept off the fields by a hurricane, and had dropped and found shelter under the banks on the road side! Yesterday morning was a sharp frost; and this had set the poor creatures to digging up their little plats of potatoes. In my whole life I never saw human wretchedness equal to this; no, not even amongst the free negroes in America.'

Accommodation for these people was notoriously bad: 'The majority of the cottages that exist in rural parishes,' wrote the Reverend James Fraser in the late 1860s, 'are deficient in almost every requisite that should constitute a home for a Christian family in a civilized community.'

Labourers in the Pelhams were probably not living on roots and sorrel, nor had they – in the words of Lord Carnarvon – been reduced to a plight more abject than that of any race in Europe. Housing may also have been better than mud and straw hovels found elsewhere. Over forty new houses were built in the first thirty years of the nineteenth century, which might suggest a benevolent land-owning class, but the population of the villages increased as well, so the ratio of families to houses barely changed. In the early 1830s, some 228 families shared 177 homes.

The Reverend Fraser disapproved of such cramped conditions, adding that, 'it is impossible to exaggerate the ill effects of such a state of things in every aspect – physical, social, economical, moral, *intellectual*'. What did such an existence do to their minds? Did it make them more or less likely to see holes and think of dragons?

Reading contemporary accounts of agricultural labourers, we are told that they are not just ill-paid and ill-fed and ill-clothed but also unimaginative, ill-educated, ignorant, illogical and brutish. 'They seem scarcely to know any other enjoyments than such as is common to them, and to the brute beasts which have no under-standing . . , So very far are they below their fellow men in mental culture,' wrote John Eddowes in his 1854 *The Agricultural Labourer as He Really Is*. This is the cruel stereotype that christened every Ag Lab 'Hodge' and gave him an awkward gait, ungainly manners, a slow wit and an indecipherable patois. Another observer described the limited horizons of such a labourer: 'Like so many of his friends, he had never been out of a ten-mile radius; he had never even climbed to the top of yonder great round hill.' And there were said to be rustics who lived within ten miles of the sea but had never seen it. They were 'intellectual cataleptics', interested only in food and shelter, according to one mid-century journalist.

In one of his characteristically oblique and brilliant studies, the historian Keith Snell set out to uncover whether this really was all that the labourer wanted by scouring letters home from emigrants. Several themes stood out. They valued their families, wanted to be free from the overseer of the poor, craved secure work and better treatment by those offering it, and they demonstrated a marked interest in their environment – in the land and the livestock.

This only tells us about those who could write, but it gets around the famous reticence of the labourer, the mysterious barrier of 'Ay, ay', 'may be', 'likely enough' that greeted any enquiry, and contemporary observers attributed to stupidity.

Labourers were not alone, their employers were not celebrated for their conversational skills: In his *Professional Excursions* around Hertfordshire published in 1843, the auctioneer Wolley Simpson gives a wonderful description of a farmer which reads like the children's game where you have to avoid saying 'yes' or 'no'.

Q. The Land you hold of the Marquis, is very good is it not Mr. Thornton?

A. It ai'nt bad Sir.

Q. The Timber I understand in this neigh-bourhood is very thriving.

A. Why I've seen worse Sir.

Q. You have an abundance of chalk too which is an advantage?

A. We don't object to it Sir.

Q. You are likewise conveniently situated for markets?

A. Why we don't complain Sir.

Q. You are plentifully supplied with fruit if I may judge from your Orchards?

A. Pretty middling for that Sir.

Q. Corn is at a fair price now for you?

A. It be'nt a bit too high Sir.

Q. The Canals must facilitate the convey-ance of produce considerably?

A. They are better than bad roads to be sure Sir.

And so on in the same vein. Simpson concludes that 'evasion had become habitual, and I believe it to be a principle in rural education'.

Did village schools teach anything else besides?

The traditional way to measure literacy is to count the number of people who could sign their name on marriage licences and other documents. Although the method has its detractors, it is still a useful ready reckoner. In 1834, two marriages in the Pelhams involved agricultural labourers. All made their mark, with the exception of one witness, sixty-five-year-old Mary Bayford. This is not surprising as not all their employers could write: in the previous year the farmer and Vestry (local council) member John Hardy made his mark in the Overseers accounts.

There had been a charity school in Furneux Pelham since 1756 thanks to a bequest by the widow of the Reverend Charles Wheatly to provide a proper master to teach eight poor boys and girls to read and write. In an 1816 report to the parliamentary Select Committee somebody observed of the Pelhams: 'The poor have not sufficient means of education; but the minister concludes they must be desirous of possessing them.' By 1833, there was a schoolmaster and mistress looking after twenty-one boys and girls, but even with the existence of a school and the growing attendance figures, there were no guarantees that children would turn up regularly. In January

1854, the Hertfordshire school inspector wrote: 'In country parishes boys are employed from three to five months in the year after the age of seven, and they are withdrawn from school altogether between ten and eleven. I believe that at present there are scarcely any children of agricultural labourers above that age in regular attendance at schools in my district.'

While the gentry endowed and managed the schools, their tenant farmers were less than enthusiastic, insisting that workers brought their children to the fields with them. Many, if not most, parents could not afford to forfeit the extra pennies the children would bring home. A survey of over 500 labouring families in East Anglia in the 1830s found that only about half the income of an average family came from the husband's day-work. Nearly 80,000 children were permanently employed as agricultural labourers in the middle of the century. At least 5,500 of these were between the ages of five and nine. At harvest time classrooms would be empty.

They could be kept off at short notice for reasons that would baffle us, writes Pamela Horn: 'Sometimes a strong wind would loose branches and twigs, and children would be kept from school to collect this additional winter firing.' In the winter months, hard-pressed parents needed their children to earn extra money picking stones, rat-catching or beating for the squire's shooting parties. These jobs not only kept them from the classroom, they provided them with little alternative stimulation. Common occupations such as bird scaring were an isolating and literally mind-numbing activity. Children would be on their own from dawn to dusk, because it was thought they wouldn't work as hard if they had someone to talk to; as one chronicler of rural life in Norfolk observed, farmers thought that 'One boy is a boy, two boys is half a boy, and three boys is no boys at all.'

If children did get past the classroom door, what did the schools teach them? The gentry might have been eager to do their duty and help provide an education to the agricultural workers, but their idea of what constituted that education was not ours. Needlework,

73

cleaning and the catechism were often the extent of it. In the 1840s, girls were taught such rigorous academic subjects as the 'art of getting up linen' – but only as a reward if they showed good conduct and industry.

At the first school inspection of Furneux Pelham, in February 1845, seventy-one children turned up for the examination. There were nearly three times as many girls as boys, and just over half were older than ten. Twenty-four were, 'Able to read a Verse in the Gospels without blundering', twenty-six girls were 'Working sums in the Simple Rules', but only two boys; not one child had advanced to 'Sums in the Compound Rules' or the even loftier 'Working Sums in Proportion and the Higher Rules'.

One school inspector a few years later lamented that children's copy books rendered a dull study duller: 'For of what use can it be to copy ten and twelve times over such crackjaw words as these: "Zumiologist", "Xenodochium" . . .? Or such pompous moral phrases as "Study universal rectitude"?'

Pamela Horn gives examples of long-winded sums from the period designed perhaps to keep children occupied: 'What will the thatching of the following stacks cost at 10 d. per square foot, the first was 36 feet by 27, the second 42 by 34, the third 38 by 24, and the fourth 47 by 39?' The Hertfordshire diarist John Carrington set his son similar problems that might have proved useful to old Master Lawrence: 'I desire to know how much timber there is in 24-foot long and 24-inches girt.' Beneath the sum Carrington observed that a six-hundred-year-old oak fell down in Oxford in June 1789, 'the girt of the oak was 21 feet 9 inches, height 71 feet 8 inches. Cubic contents 754 feet . . . luckily did no damage.' Perhaps a functional education at least.

This is a picture of sorts, of the men who went to fell that tree, of their education – or lack of – their cares and their material circumstances. It does not get us very much closer to understanding why they thought they had found a dragon's lair. Perhaps I am going about this back to front because the best way to get at the mental life of a nineteenth-century rural labourer is to take at face value the stories they told. The cultural historian Robert Darnton writes in his essay 'Peasants Tell Tales', that folk tales are one of the few points of entry into the mental world of peasants in the past, and the recurring motifs in early tales can shed light on the preoccupations of the people who told them – such as the tensions caused by the lack of food for all the family members and the preponderance of step-mothers with children of their own, in a world where it was fairly commonplace to lose a partner to illness or childbirth. While I have been asking what the life and education of an Ag Lab can tell us about the story, I might better have asked what the story can tell us about the life of an Ag Lab. They believed that dragons once lived in holes beneath yew trees. That may well be the most interesting thing we will ever know about them.

A postscript: I like to think that whatever happened that morning coloured the life of Thomas Skinner, that his encounter as a child with Piers Shonks and dragon's holes gifted him a curious mind and a life in search of other hollow places. Writing in 1926, a local historian in Anstey recalled in passing an old Gentleman Skinner who had found the entrance to the Blind Fiddler's tunnel and who 'took the greatest interest in antiquarian researches'.

9

To break a branch was deemed a sin,
A bad-luck job for neighbours,
For fire, sickness, or the like
Would mar their honest labours.

—from a ballad written after the illicit
felling of a tree in 1824

Master Lawrence and the others were walking into a story when they stepped out of their doors that still winter morning. Imagine the carpenter's yard as a tree's graveyard, boards and off-cuts and shavings of timber memorialising particular oaks or elms taken from woodland and hedgerows. Imagine gates and window frames that Lawrence remembered as branches, and entire cruck-frames that had once grown in Hormead Park Wood. 'The quality of a tree was remembered to the last fragment after the bulk of the log had been used,' wrote Walter Rose in *The Village Carpenter*. 'In any carpenter's yard there are piles of oddments – small pieces left over from many trees – but though they are all mixed up, it is usually remembered from which tree each piece was cut.'

Soon there would be loppings of a yew in Lawrence's yard.

At that hour, women would be fetching water in buckets hanging from yokes, carters were securing the traces to horses while young boys baited them. Old timers might already be warming themselves at the furnace in James Funston's Smithy. A man could speak freely there without being held to his word.

The track to the tree led south, following the boundary between Church Hill Field and Broadley Shot. Small children with chilblains hobble along in hard boots – off to pick flints or clean turnips. From the northern edge of Chalky Field it was little more than half a mile south and then west to Patricks Wood, and beyond the hornbeams lay Great and Little Pepsells where the labourers could set down their stoneware jars and their shovels and axes.

The spot was oddly remote. It is the landscape of M. R. James's ghost story 'A Neighbour's Landmark' that is one minute pictur-esque, the next, with the changing of the light, bleak, frightening and vulnerable to supernature. Imagine this spot on a grey winter's morning setting your axe to a village landmark and the only building in view is the tower of the church within whose walls an ancient legend sleeps. Marked by a small triangle where three fields meet, hemmed by three parish boundaries and two dark blocks of woodland, it was the kind of place where gallows once stood, or gibbets swung – places where suicides and strangers were buried. Yews are known to have been used as hanging trees. Such knowledge might well have worked upon the minds of those men that morning. W. B. Gerish is good on this, writing of an older time, of the medieval winter when 'The spirit world was abroad, riding in every gale, hiding in the early and late darkness of evening among the shadows of the farmhouse, of the rickyard, of the misty meadows, of the dark-some wood. Ghosts – we *talk* about ghosts, but our ancestors lived with them from All Hallows to Candlemas.'

R. M. Healey in his *Shell Guide* to Hertfordshire is generous about the countryside thereabouts, finding in it Samuel Palmer's elegiac landscape paintings, better Palmer's dark etchings from his final years after he had grown angry at the plight of the agricultural labourer.

In the right weather, the wrong weather, the view belongs in the old nurse's tale that troubled Jane Eyre's imagination, making her think of Thomas Bewick's engraving of a 'black horned thing seated aloof on a rock, surveying a distant crowd surrounding a gallows'. But so would many such views in England: the historian John Lowerson has written about the 'popular sense of an eternal cosmic battle between good and evil that is being fought out in an essentially rural English context'. Our yew site is a place as good as any for such battles, for stories, for putting ideas in men's heads about dragons and their slayers. Was it the place as much as the belief that a dragon once stalked those parts that would soon make them think they'd found a dragon's lair?

Farm labourers worked from 7 a.m. to 5 p.m. in the winter. Six shillings a week was a usual wage, but felling timber was paid by the load: one shilling for fifty cubic feet. You can do the working out. John Carrington's oak we met in the last chapter would have earned them fifteen shillings. Was it blood money enough? Were they superstitious about their task that day? No doubt there were those who thought that chopping down a yew brought bad luck. Plant lore is thick with injunctions against bringing down trees. The folklorist Jeremy Harte, writing about the Isle of Man, tells of the seemingly lonely places where 'locals know about the elder trees that should never be touched, not since the farmer hacked them back, and hanged himself in the barn that night'. But Harte is writing about fairies, and it is thorn trees and elders, not yews, that must be left alone. But a yew was also a sacred tree to many: 'A bed in hell is prepared for him / Who cut the tree about thine ears.' Did the men have sentiments similar to this final couplet from an old rhyme about the Yew Tree Well in Easter Ross, Scotland? A chill warning to those wielding an axe. The Yew of Ross in Ireland had to be prayed down by St Laserian because its wood was wanted, but no one dared fell it. Recall King Hywel Dda's tenth-century prohibition on felling yews associated with saints. Do similar injunctions survive far and wide in the collective memory? When the Victorian archaeologist Augustus Pitt-Rivers removed an old yew from a prehistoric burial mound in Dorset, the locals were not happy, even though Pitt-Rivers said the tree was dead: 'I afterwards learned that the people of the neighbourhood attached some interest to it, and it has since been replaced.'

John Aubrey relates the fate of the men who felled an oak in 1657 and in passing recalls the wife and son of an earl who died after he had an oak grove removed. These tales linger and still give pause for thought today to the sensitive and cautious: Harte writes, 'When we find that the N18 from Limerick to Ennis curves to go around a fairy thorn, we admire the knowledge of Eddie Lenihan, who campaigned to save the tree, as well as the prudence of the County Surveyor who knew of the risk involved in damaging it.'

Still, the Lawrences and the Skinners had their work to do, and so they savaged the roots of the great tree. Specifically the roots, I think. There is an engraving by Turner in his *Liber Studiorum* called 'Hedging and Ditching'. Two men are in a ditch in the ground fetching down a tree, not neatly chopping it down, but seeming to lever it out of the ground with pickaxes. A woman in a bonnet with a shawl over her shoulder walks by looking on. This is no rural idyll. The drawing has something in common with First World War art, with the pencil lines that suggest mud and stones, the thin leafless trees in the hedge, shredded of the fullness of trees. Grubbing up is an evocative expression. It is an unpleasant image, total and annihilating: trees torn violently from the soil. I think of Ted Hughes' Whale-Wort torn out by the roots and flung into the sea when he just wanted to sleep. It is the slow deliberate painstaking act of men with hand tools. Those in Turner's sketch might be doing hard labour; they look a bad lot, like pirates or smugglers – Turner was on the coast at East Sussex, so maybe they were.

Forget a neat V-shaped wedge incised with an axe prior to sawing. Dynamite and perhaps club hammers would make more sense than a copybook felling. An ancient yew with its hollows and split trunks and the irregular sprawl of its weary branches mocks the surgical approach. H. Rider Haggard, the author of the adventure stories *She* and *King Solomon's Mines*, gives the best and most plausible description of how the tree was felled in his *A Farmer's Year: Being His Commonplace Book for 1898*. He writes that there are two ways of felling a tree:

> one the careless and slovenly chopping off of the tree above the level of the ground, the other its scientific 'rooting'. In rooting at timber, the soil is first removed from about the foot of the bole with any suitable instrument till the great roots are discovered branching this way and that. Then the woodsmen begin upon these with their mattocks, which sink with a dull thud into the soft and sappy fibre.

This was known as grub-felling in East Anglia and was the common method for bringing down timber trees in that part of the country.

By Wigram's account, Lawrence and the other men had an uncommon amount of trouble with those roots. Perhaps their hearts were not in it, or something held back the full strength of their axe strokes. Did one of them stroke the scaly bark that yews can slough off to get rid of infections? Did it rattle under their fingers and the sap begin to run blood red? Fred Hageneder in his *Yew: A History* tells us that the yew is the only European tree that can bleed red sap. A feat that is scientifically unexplained, he says. The yew at Nevern in Wales is notorious for bleeding the blood of those buried in its churchyard. A bleeding tree might have given those men – any men – second thoughts. Or did the texture of its bark look like scales from a picture book dragon? In *Ulverton*, his extraordinary record of a fictional village across time, Adam Thorpe channels an old carpenter in an inn in 1803 regaling a visitor with his memories. He recalls the time the master carpenter chose an oak by smell, seasoned it for two years, then made a lid for the church font. 'Atween you an' I, though, I can spot a dragon in them patterns. I reckons as how there were a dragon in that tree. He'll avenge hisself one day.' Is this a brilliant bit of invention or does Thorpe know of a folk tradition among carpenters about dragons in trees?

They kept at it, but the tree would not yield. *Yet is thy root sincere, sound as the rock, / A quarry of stout spurs and knotted fangs, / Which crook'd into a thousand whimsies, clasp / The stubborn soil, and hold thee still erect.*

Eventually, they took a break. 'It was very hard work to get it down. The men had been at work all the morning, and went away to dinner,' wrote Wigram. In one of his later letters he put the story into the mouth of a local: 'They do say Sir, that the men could not get that yew Tree down. And at last they all went away to breakfast.'

It was an 'umbuggin job to remove such a tree. Why take so much effort to bring her down? Maybe someone wanted the timber. John Aubrey recalls the churchyard yew of his childhood in the 1630s, 'a fair and spreading ewe-tree . . . The clarke lop't it to make money of it to some bowyer or fletcher'. The lopping killed it.

Walter Rose gives us clues as to what would be going through a carpenter's mind as he stood in front of the tree, writing that when his father looked at trees he saw what could be made of them: 'In a stumpy butt, with large branches spreading off not far from the base, he would see four large gate posts, the spread of the branches to form the portion that would go into the ground.' Another would be large enough to split down the centre and quarter-up for coffin boards, or for rails or the slats of a field gate. He might have been calculating how much useful timber was in the Pelham yew. How much marquetry. How many writing slopes or clock cases were latent in the bole. More likely, Lawrence was counting how many poles could be sold to bodgers for the bows and hoops of the Windsor chairs made in vast quantities back then, with the very best given backs of yew.

'A post of yew will outlast a post of iron,' noted one naturalist in the 1830s. The Furneux Pelham Smock mill was modernised in those years, perhaps the year the tree came down, after James Seabrook the Younger bought the mill from his father and paid off the mortgage on it. Yew was excellent wood for cogs and pins, and its branches would yield fine barrel hoops for the fledgling brewing enterprise at Furneux Pelham Hall. The wood's waterproof qualities made it a favourite for buckets and palings. It had other uses besides, known to country folk: lengths of it were traditionally used for dowsing. It was also said that if you held a switch of yew in your hand while cursing your enemy they would not hear you.

No doubt some wanted the old tree down not because they valued its timber but simply because they did not want it in the landscape. They wanted it down, just as the doctor wanted rid of the elm in Hardy's *The Woodlanders*, because it oppressed Marty South's father as he lay on his deathbed. It is finally felled – by dead of night, but 'Little good it did poor old South, who was dead the next day from the shock of the tree's disappearance.'

The agricultural improvers detested the space taken up, and even the shadows cast, by hedgerow trees. Surprisingly to us, even those who loved the landscape may have wanted the old yew gone. Pollards, which often marked the boundaries of fields, were seen as ugly and had been under attack since the late eighteenth century – an old yew might be viewed with similar disdain by some. 'Not only were outgrown hedges tamed and excess trees removed. In many places hedges were grubbed out altogether . . . The grubbing of hedges was especially common in the high farming period after c.1830,' writes the historian of the East Anglian landscape Tom Williamson. Our tree was probably in the way of planting, or blocked a new drainage ditch. The Ancient Tree Forum publish a pamphlet for farmers on how to care for ancient and veteran trees. It contains a terrible map showing all the hedgerow trees that have disappeared from a single fifty-acre parcel in North Yorkshire since the middle of the nineteenth century, each standing tree a little green icon representing a surviving pollard or standard ash, beech, oak or sycamore. There are some fifty of them, but they are outnumbered nearly three to one by a mass of red 'X's in a circle representing a lost tree.

Little Pepsells was listed as pasture in 1837, and while it is unlikely that an old yew would ever drop enough leaves to poison stock, horses tied to yews have been known to die from grazing on them. Might the squire or his tenant farmer have taken a disliking to the tree for some such reason, or did they just need to invent winter work for men sent to them under the old Poor Laws? Remember that according to the Hammonds, 'degrading and repulsive work was invented for those whom the farmer would not or could not employ'.

What we do know is that this was not the only yew that disappeared from the landscape in the early nineteenth century.

In 1848 one archaeological journal lamented that yews were 'so reduced in number as to seem like the last of a once flourishing and noble race, mourning in their own decay over the magnificence of the past, and the desolation of the present'. In 1539, John Leland had counted thirty-nine yews at Strata Florida in Wales; they are the only ones he mentions in his famous itinerary around the British

Isles. Three hundred years later, only three of the famous yews were still standing. There is an engraving and article from *Gardener's Chronicle* in May 1874 with a description of the largest tree that is not unlike that of the Pelham yew in Wigram's letter: it 'was divided into two parts, leaving a passage through it, this was 22 ft in girth'. Beneath one of the three survivors was the traditional resting place of the fourteenth-century Welsh poet Dafydd ap Gwilym. It too disappeared after 1874, possibly during an archaeological dig of the Cistercian abbey at the end of the nineteenth century.

It is loathsome to think that our tree was felled indifferently, because it was in the way, or to give unemployed labourers something to do to earn their gallon loaf, but whatever their reason, it had to come down. On their return from breakfast, the sight that greeted them must have been something of a surprise. Was their approach a cautious one? Where they had wrestled with the tree half an hour before, there was now a large hole, a cavern even, and the tree had fallen into it. 'When they came back, that yew Tree had fallen down of itself; and when they looked, there was a girt hole right underneath it, underneath its roots, a girt cave like.' This in the words of the rustic voice Wigram used in his final account to W. B. Gerish. His 1888 letter to the *Hertfordshire Mercury* is less picturesque but more dramatic: 'On his return [he] found that the old tree had fallen, collapsing into a large cavity underneath its roots.'

Until I read about grub felling, I simply could not understand how a half-felled tree had fallen into a hole, but if most of the roots had been severed and there was a cavity under the yew, it would have been suspended by a few stubborn roots that eventually surrendered their charge to the hollow in the earth. After visiting several ancient yews, I could believe that one might collapse in on itself. The weight distribution is uneven as the heart rots away leaving heavy outer trunks and branches, twisted and over-balanced as the branches trail along the ground. The roots, severed and weakened as they would have been by the men's exertions, must have given way while they were at breakfast. At least that's the explanation needed to understand the 1888 version in which the tree falls into a large hole. The later version could be interpreted differently: the tree simply fell over and left a large cavity where the roots had been, but surely these countrymen were used to the holes left by trees that came down in this way, and would not need a supernatural explanation for the cavity.

'It's not unknown for voids to develop under very old trees,' wrote Wigram. It is certainly true that a cavern, or at least a hole, could have formed in the chalk under the shallow clay where the tree grew – it is not unusual for sink holes to form from erosion where the bedrock is limestone – and the weight of a tree no longer held steady by its roots could have brought in the ceiling of the cavity. It is not the only Pelham story of a cavity opening up in the chalk. Less than a mile to the east, on the other side of the Ash Valley, there is a tale recorded in the 1930s that the first church in the Pelhams was destroyed by Vikings or Pharisees (the local word for fairies) or, more prosaically, it collapsed into a hole that opened up beneath it.

She was down. 'It is done,' wrote Rider Haggard of another tree in another place.

A change has come over the landscape; the space that for generations has been filled with leafy branches is now white and empty air. I know of no more melancholy sight – indeed, to this day I detest seeing a tree felled; it always reminds me of the sudden and violent death of a man. I fancy it must be the age of timbers that inspires us with this respect and sympathy, which we do not feel for a sapling or a flower.

Ancient trees have personalities and attract stories; it is hard not to think that this was an event in the life of the village. A crowd must have gathered that morning, if not to watch the iniquitous act, then to see the cavity. We know the Skinner family kept loppings, which hints at the value of the highly prized wood. No doubt, other villagers kept pieces as well if they could — to make spoons and knife handles. Peter Kalm, an eighteenth-century Scandinavian traveller, left an account of a tree he saw chopped down in Hertfordshire, describing the surprising number of people on the scene, wanting the leaves and roots and twigs for fuel or to make baskets. I imagine a host of villagers turning up that day. Nothing of that prized wood would be wasted. John Aubrey's fair and spreading ewe-tree furnished him and the other schoolboys with *nutt-crackers* and *scoopes* to pull the flesh out of their apples. These would make fine souvenirs from a dragon's lair.

I have often wondered what was made of the yew. If anything has survived. I have started to keep an eye on the local antique auctions, hoping to find a Windsor chair from the right period. I know what I am looking for. The wood mustn't be too dark. The seat needs to be elm and shaped like the flagstones of a castle staircase, as if worn by years of use. And it has to be a stick back, no splat, with two hoops of yew, one for the back and one for the elbows, burnished to a rich honey, the tight grain bewitching and warm, taken from a tree with a dragon in its story. I'll know it when I see it.

10

Saint Augustine saith, that Dragons doe abide in deep Caves and hollow places of the earth, and the some-times when they perceive moistnes in the ayre, they come out of theyr holes, and beating the ayre with their wings, as it were with the strokes of Oares, they forsake the earth and flie aloft

—Edward Topsell, *The Historie of Serpents*, 1608

In the rocks of Jaffa, south of Tel Aviv, rest the last bones of the dragon that Perseus slew to save Andromeda. The skulls of similar monsters litter the Sivalik hills in Northern India, and on Turkey's Aegean coast the remains of fabulous creatures, which stalked the myths of Heracles, weather from the cliffs to astonish passing travellers.

Heracles' victory against the Monster of Troy is depicted most dramatically on an ancient Greek krater, or vase, now in the Museum of Fine Arts in Boston. Here is the beast peppered with arrows by the hero as he rescues the Trojan princess Hesione. It is a very peculiar monster: just a head, white and skeletal, but to the modern eye it is impossible to mistake what we are looking at – a fossilised skull of a prehistoric creature projecting from a rocky outcrop; it is a two-and-a-half thousand-year-old black-figure masterpiece of palaeontology.

The vase appears on the cover of Adrienne Mayor's *The First Fossil Hunters*, a compelling account of fossil finds in antiquity, which argues that dragons, griffins, cyclops and many other nightmares from the ancient world were inspired by the remains of dinosaurs and other prehistoric creatures. Mayor amasses accounts and archaeological evidence of encounters with giant bones in antiquity, alongside known fossil sites today, which dovetail neatly with the places where the legends of particular monsters first appeared.

In the first century CE, Apollonius of Tyana claimed to have seen dragon skulls in India where today we know the skulls of prehistoric giraffes, elephants and crocodiles are found in the famous Sivalik fossil beds. The Roman naturalist Aelian recorded the discovery of giant bones on the island of Chios following a forest fire and noted that the locals decided they must be the bones of a dragon: 'From these gigantic bones the villagers were able to observe how immense and awful the monster was when it was alive.' As for the dragons at Jaffa, biblical Joppa, a story from Ancient Rome tells how the consul Marcus Aemilius Scaurus held victory celebrations during which he paraded an immense skeleton found at Joppa, where tradition said the Greek hero Perseus rescued Andromeda from the dragon. One version of that myth even says that Perseus turned the monster to stone – petrified it, fossilised it perhaps?

W. B. Gerish entertained similar ideas about the origin of the Shonks' legend. Had those rustics in the Pelhams found some dinosaur fossils under the yew tree? He wrote to the Geological Survey enquiring about a dinosaur find and asked Herbert Andrews, the son of his friend and collaborator Robert Andrews, to walk across the road from his desk at the V&A to find out about the Cetiosaurus on display at the Natural History Museum. The younger Andrews kindly wrote back describing the dinosaur, which had been pulled from the Oxford Clay near Peterborough, but at the end of the letter cautioned, 'I don't think it is possible to see in him the Herts dragon.'

But Gerish wasn't to be put off; he had been collecting cuttings about fossil finds. One about an Ichthyosaurus found in Peterborough reveals what he was thinking: 'The preying habits of this hungry flesh-eater, with its wide mouth and long jaws so well armed with serviceable teeth, bring to mind the fabled dragons of the ancients and may well be possibly the origin of these myths.'

Was Shonks' dragon a Cetiosaurus, an Ichthyosaurus, or something else entirely, wondered Gerish. He wasn't alone in conflating dragons with dinosaurs. In one of his box files there is a tiny newspaper advertisement for a book with a humdinger of a title: *The Book of the Great Sea Dragons: Extinct Monsters of the Ancient Earth*. The author, Thomas Hawkins, was an unpopular and eccentric collector, amassing fossils in Devon at about the same time the dragon's lair in Great Pepsells was discovered. Hawkins believed his fossils were the remains of the giant creatures created by God in Genesis 1:21, the *Geodolim Tanonim*. Where most translators render this as the 'Great Whales', Hawkins argued for the far more exciting *Great Dragons*. In fact most of the dinosaur and ancient reptile fossils illustrated in his book are labelled as dragons (it was published the year before Richard Owen invented the word 'dinosaur'): 'Dragon from Lyme Regis. Discovered in 1835', 'Head of a Dragon from a village near Bristol', 'Dragon Plesiosaurus, from Street, Discovered in 1831'.

These scant remains of Gerish's fossil research were his attempt to build on an idea that had struck him as early as 1901 when he published his first Hertfordshire St George article in the journal *Folklore*: 'As to the dragon, fossil remains of extinct animals have often been found in the clay-pits of Hertfordshire, none of which, however, are of so recent a date as the medieval period. But the story may be very much older, dating possibly even from prehistoric times, and thus handed down from father to son it has become connected in the usual materialistic way with the monumental slab.'

This is oddly muddled. Gerish is not just thinking about the origins of dragon legends in general, but instead seems to have thought that a Cetiosaurus or other dinosaur was slain in prehistory by an impossibly early inhabitant of Brent Pelham and the story was passed down through the ages in the collective memory.

In the hierarchy of reasons Lawrence and the men may have had for presuming they had found a dragon's lair, number one would be because they found the remains of a real-life dragon. Number two would be something that they mistook for a dragon: large bones? We can be fairly certain that neither of these were in the hole. What other traces of an imagined dragon might have been revealed by the woodcutters' exertions? Earth scorched black by dragon fire, claw marks, treasure? How about a Roman mosaic of a dragon?

The idea of digging up something out of the ordinary would not have been alien to the men who knew that from time to time dull lumps of metal were pulled from the soil and could be turned into shillings and even pounds: a fabulous golden torque was found nearby a few years before, and some time in the 1830s labourers land-ditching unearthed a skeleton and a Bronze-Age founder's hoard. It is tempting to surmise that the woodcutters' attitudes to holes in the ground were conditioned by the fact that such treasure had been discovered in neighbouring fields. Treasure might even suggest the presence of guardian dragons, although the great folklorist and British dragon expert Jacqueline Simpson has pointed out that legends of dragons who guard treasure and those involving a dragon-slayer are not found together in England.

There was nothing in the hole, but in the same way that the Romans who found the fossils in Jappa assumed they had stumbled upon the remains of Perseus, those labourers' thoughts turned to Shonks because he was their text. There are two explanations for the part fossils played in the formation of monster stories in antiquity: either they started the stories, or the stories of monsters and heroes existed before the fossils were found, but those finds were explained in terms of the stories, and then in time the stories were modified by the finds. Perhaps the monsters took on the guise of the fossils: mammoths begat cyclops, Protoceratops – griffins, and Giraffokeryx launched a thousand dragons.

We know the story of Shonks and the dragon existed before the hole was found. There were no fossils, but superstition, the ancient yew, the dark winter's morning in a remote spot, and that great rent in the ground – together they were enough to suggest an extraordinary explanation.

It causes us moderns problems when the world of make-believe meets the everyday. We sometimes find it hard to imagine that people really thought these things: that dragons nested in a field. Weren't they just messing around? Ted Barclay stands in the vestry of Brent Pelham Church holding the remains of an old weather vane and declaring that it is one of Shonks' arrows. He is having a bit of fun. He does not really believe what he is saying – at least I hope not – but I am convinced those men did believe what they were saying. They believed it, because Shonks was the villagers' key text, the key to their cosmology. The historian Ruth Richardson has cautioned that to make sense of the past, 'we must come to terms with our own hostility to superstition'. It had been barely a century since an old woman in Brent Pelham was arrested on suspicion of witchcraft.

The writer Charles Nicholl has argued that Antonio Pigafetta, who chronicled Magellan's voyages, saw giants in Argentina because he expected to see giants. Why? Because he had read outlandish travellers' tales about them. In the same way Master Lawrence and the others would have expected to see a dragon's lair because they had grown up with the story of Shonks' and seen the dragon carved on his tomb.

We can hardly blame uneducated labourers for seizing upon the stories they knew best when scholars made similar mistakes, defaulting to Homer and the Bible to explain the world. When elephant bones were found with a flint hand-axe by the River Thames, some pointed to the Bible and said it dated from the Flood, whereas classicists thought the Romans brought the elephant to London in the first century CE and it had died in a battle with an axe-wielding Briton. (In fact, the axe is from a period when elephants roamed the Gray's Inn Road, some 350,000 years ago.) Ask a nineteenth-century labourer from the Pelhams who slew a dragon and they would answer Shonks and not St Michael or St George.

An incident in 1833 attests to how closely the Pelhams were associated with the Shonks legend. *The Country Press* for Saturday 20 April 1833 contained a case of local excitement from the Petty Sessions at Bishop's Stortford: 'for it seemed as if the whole Pelham population had come to town. This arose from a "set-too" amongst the fair amazons of that village, whose pugnacious propensities have been handed down ever since the memorable year of 1086, when Hun, who first tempted, was vanquished by O' Piers Shonks.'

Unfortunately no other record of this tantalising case has survived, but while it might be too large a claim to say that the Shonks legend was ubiquitous in that place, in those times, he was probably never that far from Pelham minds.

Or had something put them in mind of Shonks that morning?

Was something else going on that made those men eager to find evidence for the legend? Had someone questioned it and mocked the stories? In the 1840s, John Walker Ord interviewed a Mr Marr about the legend of Scaw the serpent-killer in Handale, North Yorkshire. Later Ord would write, 'Of course we could not gainsay these facts, especially as they were recited with a determination that rendered argument dangerous.' Challenging a legend had always been risky. In Bodmin in 1113 when a visiting French canon was foolish enough to scoff at the notion that King Arthur still lived he caused a riot. In Brittany at that time, it was said to be unsafe to assert in a public place that Arthur was dead: 'Hardly will you escape unscathed without being whelmed by the curses or crushed by the stones of your hearers,' reported Alain de Lille in the twelfth-century *Prophetia Anglicana*. If it wasn't dangerous to scoff, it was certainly foolish, and still is – who is to say that the 'set-too' among the Amazons of the Pelhams was not because someone was foolish enough to suggest that Shonks did not slay a dragon.

In *The Handbook of Folk-Lore*, Charlotte Burne cautions the folklore collector to conceal incredulity and amusement and to suppress their smiles when encountering local beliefs and customs. Was the Reverend Soames a little too mirthful about Shonks, and vocal about it too? On the other hand, he may have been sour-faced and prayed the yew down. As the author of the *History of the Reformation of the Church of England* he would have known that the palming ceremony on Palm Sunday was banned in 1569, yet it continued for centuries on hilltops and in remote corners. The yew was a popular substitute for palm leaves. When Soames preached against Catholic-leaning innovations, did he also try to dispossess his flock of their superstitions, counselling that the yew tree should come down and pouring cold water on local legends about dragons?

The discovery of the dragon hole meant the villages had something to throw back at their parson with all his book learnin'. How could anyone deny the truth of the stories now they had found the dragon's lair? *What do you say to that, Reverend?* If the discovery of the hole was a thumbing of the nose at authority, it may help us to understand the long-ago origins of the rest of the legends about Shonks. There are those who think that folk tales and legends were the folks' response to their struggles against the feudal classes, their struggles for a better life.

In the 1830s, the folks' traditions were under threat from even greater forces than the local vicar. Old ways of thinking about the world were changing. Charles Lyell's *Principles of Geology* was published in three volumes between 1830 and 1833, while a disciple of Lyell was gathering evidence on a voyage that would completely change the way we look at the world. Charles Darwin was scrambling through the impenetrable forests of Chiloé Island in the winter of 1834, catching foxes by striking them on the head with a rock hammer, and meeting native Christian converts who still 'pretended to old communication with the devil in certain caves' and so risked the fate of forebears who had answered to the Inquisition. In the eyes of men of science, the villagers in the Pelhams might have seemed equally suitable subjects for anthropological observation. Such rationalists would have soon explained away the hole in the chalk and derided the existence of dragons.

The way of life for those in the English countryside was changing more rapidly than at any time since the end of the Middle Ages; old beliefs and stories were disappearing as people turned their backs on the fields. The populations of cities like Manchester and Liverpool doubled in the first thirty years of the nineteenth century as labourers left the countryside in search of work. London saw its population increase by over 50 per cent to 1.6 million. This in a country of just fifteen million people. The first railway opened in September 1830 and was the prelude to the laying of 1,000 miles of iron and the synchronisation of clocks to the railway timetables before mid-century. Time itself was changing. The world was changing. Agricultural labourers were living in a countryside that had been pulled out from under their feet.

The agricultural revolution had changed everything. Customary rights of ordinary people were forgotten, enclosure meant they had nowhere to pasture their livestock, nowhere to collect wood or furze. The woods had been fenced for game by the new landlords from London, who were heedless of those customs that had been honoured time out of mind. Customs were replaced by laws.

It is for these new game laws that the social historians John and Barbara Hammond reserve their greatest ire in their classic *The Village Labourer*. The Laws of England that had shorn people of their rights and replaced their wages with charity, now threatened them with the gallows if they failed to resist the urge to vary their diet of roots by bagging a pheasant for the table. It is undeniable that, like William Cobbett, the Hammonds were purveyors of that particular style of the picturesque we might call the you-don't-know-you're-born school of history. Many historians would argue that things weren't as bad as they claimed, and that enclosure was an essential component of the agricultural revolution that ultimately brought better standards of living to all. Yet it is telling that the man who was the high priest of agricultural progress, the great champion of enclosure, Arthur Young, had second thoughts in later life: he thought the human cost had been too high.

The Swing Riots that began in Kent in the summer of 1830 were as much about resisting change to a way of life as about money. Captain Swing was the name signed to letters sent to farmers and landowners across southern England, threatening arson, machine breaking and murder. They went hand-in-hand with a series of uprisings starting in Kent in the autumn of 1830. Barns and hayricks were burned, the new threshing machines – which 'stole' winter work from labourers – were smashed, and unpopular overseers and parsons hauled from parishes in dung carts. The agricultural labourers were demanding higher wages, reduced rents and lower tithes (so the farmers could afford to pay the wages). But it was not just about poverty. One of the complaints of a mob at Walden in Buckinghamshire during the Swing Riots was that buns used to be thrown from the church steeple and beer given away in the churchyard on Bun Day. They wanted the customs continued, but the parson refused. Traditions and customs and rights were ignored. The Furneux Pelham overseers accounts once contained the item 'paid for ringing church bell for gleaners'. But gleaning – the right to pick up dropped corn during harvest – was being curtailed.

In 1834 there was a total overhaul of the Poor Laws, which would now be administered by Boards of Guardians in the big towns. Change was needed, but at the time it must have seemed like another of the links between a person, the place he lived, and the rights he had in that place, were being destroyed.

Belonging had mattered. Keith Snell looked at inscriptions on 16,000 gravestones in eighty-seven burial grounds to chart the use of the phrase 'of this parish' as in 'To the memory of Mr James Smith late of this parish who departed this life 5th March 1830 aged 63' and 'Ellen, beloved wife of Thomas Tinworth of this parish died June 2nd 1888 aged 64 yrs' – both in Brent Pelham churchyard. People had been proud of belonging, but by the 1870s examples became ever rarer.

Jacqueline Simpson has written that dragon legends 'foster the community's awareness of and pride in its own identity, its conviction that it is in some respect unusual, or even unique. That the lord of the manor should be descended from a dragon-slayer, that a dragon should once have roamed these very fields, or, best of all, that an ordinary lad from this very village should have outwitted and killed such a monster – these are claims to fame which any neighbouring community would be bound to envy.'

Those men did not only have a dragon legend to be proud of, they had a dragon-slayer in their village church and an ancient coffin lid to mark his resting place. Little wonder they thought first of dragons when they stared down into that great hollow in the earth.

Part II

Stone

11

Somewhere, perhaps, in the spaces between the pictures and the objects . . . lies a monument true to both us and the past.

—Mike Pitts in *Making History:*
Antiquaries in Britain 1707–2007

Little is known of Mr John Morice of Upper Gower Street, London, other than the fact that in the 1830s he contracted a severe case of *grangeritis*: a condition coined by Holbrook Jackson in his *Anatomy of Bibliomania* to describe a 'contagious and delirious mania endangering many books'.

Jackson was poking fun at the practice of grangerising or extra-illustrating books by re-binding them with pictures, often ruthlessly chopped out of other books. It was popularised by the followers of James Granger, a late eighteenth-century print collector and author. Although Granger did not paste his own vast collection of prints into published books, countless *grangerites* had theirs bound into his three-volume *Biographical History* (a catalogue of historical portraits from the reign of Egbert the Great to the Glorious Revolution). Granger's surname became a verb: the first edition of the *OED* defined *grangerise* as 'To illustrate (a book) by the addition of prints, engravings, etc., especially such as have been cut out of other books.' And some of the most notorious cases of grangeritis involved *grangerised* 'Grangers', including one that expanded the original three volumes into a shelf-full of thirty-six, each as fat as the binding would allow.

Other popular titles to inflate were county histories, and it is one of these that was the cause of Mr John Morice's affliction: Robert Clutterbuck's recently published *History and Antiquities of the County of Hertford*. In the 1830s, Morice developed such an affinity for the *History* that he expanded its three volumes to ten, adding over 2,500 illustrations. The result would become known as the Knowsley Clutterbuck (after Knowsley Hall, seat of the Stanleys, earls of Derby who owned it for many years) and has been called the most sumptuous extra-illustrated county history ever conceived.

The chances that anonymous Mr Morice had played a bit part in the long history of Piers Shonks' tomb were good because many of the illustrations were said to be original. When the Earl of Derby bought the volumes for 800 guineas in the late nineteenth century, the sales catalogue boasted of over 1,000 original landscapes, architectural views and portraits in neutral tints and watercolours, and 1,400 beautifully emblazoned coats of arms. A mere 550 additional engravings were acquired from other books. And this in a book that originally had only fifty-four pictures.

Among the best additions were those made in the 1830s by John Buckler and two of his sons, who appear to have landed their dream commission. The Bucklers were successful architects, but painting antiquities was their true vocation. Why draw new buildings when there were so many fine churches and manor houses to visit and preserve in ink? Reflecting on his career in 1849, John Buckler Snr wrote: 'To build, repair, or survey warehouses and sash-windowed dwellings, however profitable, was so much less to my taste than perspective drawing with such subjects before me as cathedrals, abbeys and ancient parish churches, that I never made any effort to increase the number of my employments as an architect.'

Following page 450 of volume ten are six extra folio leaves. Pasted neatly in is an engraving of Shonks' tomb, appropriated from some poor adulterated copy of the 1816 *Antiquarian Itinerary*. The picture is the *Itinerary*'s most important contribution to the history of the legend since the text was unoriginal. Drawn by the thirty-year-old Frederick Stockdale, an antiquary more often associated with the West Country, it is captioned 'Remains of the Tomb of O Piers Shonks, Brent Pelham Church, Herts'. The composition is a little cramped, but mostly accurate, and captures the relief of the carvings although Stockdale chose to frame them in a rectangle, ignoring the shape of the coffin lid, and so the essential tombness is lost.

On the page facing Stockdale's cannibalised drawing is something much more pleasing, real treasure: a unique sepia ink painting of Shonks' tomb slab seen from directly overhead. Unusually for the prints in the Knowsley Clutterbuck, the signature and date have not been trimmed off. In the bottom left-hand corner it reads *J. C. Buckler 1833*. This was John Chessell Buckler, the eldest son, notable for coming second to Charles Barry in the 1836 competition to design the new Houses of Parliament. He first came to Brent Pelham in 1831 and produced three sepia watercolours: one each of Brent Pelham Hall, Beeches and St Mary's Church – seen from the west or tower end. His father John Buckler visited the village in 1841 and painted a more complete view of the churchyard from the south-east, revealing that the nave was without a roof. John brought with him his youngest son George, who also painted three pictures in sepia: a view of the nave and font, another picture of Brent Pelham Hall seen from the churchyard, and lastly an interior view of the chancel screen with the two-faced royal arms mounted on them. The Bucklers liked to be thorough. The art historian Robert Wark has written that they were 'fond of documenting a building from several points of view and over a period of time, especially if new construction or changes of some kind were taking place'.

The date on the picture of the tomb, 1833, is different to the other pictures. J. C. must have returned to Brent Pelham that year expressly to document the tomb. Perhaps he feared the weather pouring into the roofless nave was taking its toll on the interior, or perhaps the light had simply not been good enough during his first visit.

Buckler's sketch picks out the four figures around a floriated cross, the large angel above it, and the dragon below. Of the eight known illustrations of the tomb, which predate the first known photograph in 1901, J. C. Buckler's best captures the work of the mason. He is prepared to sacrifice detail to impression. He is trying to show that this is stone, and stone of great antiquity: the smudged blank face of the angel, the wear on the other figures slowly and inexorably being smoothed back into the block of marble by the passing of time and its blows and caresses. For an architect, he is surprisingly undraughtsman-like here. It is a work of art and not just a record of the tomb at a moment in time. The art and craftsmanship of the mason inspired Buckler to create something much more than just a topographical record.

When Holbrook Jackson called *grangeritis* 'a contagious and delirious mania endangering many books', he was concerned for the hundreds of books cut up and ruined to create one vast work, such as James

Gibb's grangerised Bible, which ran to sixty vast folio volumes, 'each so thick that he could hardly lift it from the counter'. Jackson disapproved less, if at all, when books were not destroyed but instead collectors saved pictures from ephemeral publications such as newspapers and magazines or, better still, had new pictures specially made as John Morice did.

And yet Jackson, still tongue in cheek, called it a derangement for reasons other than the desecration of books for their prints. 'Those afflicted by the derangement,' Jackson writes, 'are the most flagrant of all book-defectives.' Why? Not just because they were handy with a pair of scissors, but also because they hunted for pictures 'of every person place and thing in any way mentioned in the text or vaguely connected with its subject matter'. The grangeriser Richard Bull epitomised this habit of wild deviation or going off at tangents: a footnote referring to Audley End in the Reverend Granger's *Biographical History of England* was an excuse to add fourteen large engravings of the palace to the volume. Although Alexander Sutherland was arguably the worst afflicted grangerite of them all, transforming the six volumes of Clarendon's *History of the Rebellion* into no less than sixty-one volumes in elephant folio – each nearly two feet high – with over 19,000 extra illustrations (including 743 portraits of Charles I alone).

Behind the hyperbole of Jackson's derision I sense a secret admiration for the grangeriser. Is their crime so very bad? After all, they give us unique pictures, and in some cases the only surviving record of buildings and views and monuments. On those days when I am overwhelmed by books, by my bookshelves, and the towers of books on the kitchen table and beside my bed demanding to be read, it has occurred to me that not just readers but writers ought to grangerise existing texts rather than fuel the anxiety of book lovers by making new ones. Paste in pictures, tip in reviews, scribble in the margins, insert maps and postcards, photos and poems and train tickets, draw pictures and diagrams, and eventually unpick the book and have it rebound. What else am I doing other than unpicking the story of Piers Shonks, collating what others have thought and said, chronicling my own journey, and inserting lots of new leaves? What better way to possess a much-loved text, to make it one's own, than to grangerise it? What did Jackson say? They hunted for pictures 'of every person place and thing in anyway mentioned in the text or vaguely connected with its subject matter'. Guilty as charged, and not just pictures. This book stands as testament to the technique; one that at times may be clumsy, but one by which hidden truths may be revealed. Something unique, and occasionally worth keeping, emerges simply from the juxtaposition of material. Putting all those Charles I portraits together in a particular order creates something that did not exist before; the deliberate or accidental meeting of one with another may reveal something or suggest something wonderful and previously unthought-of. Like my encounter with the Field of Cloth of Gold, here was a fingerpost pointing off the main highway to the trackways and holloways. Some would lead back to the main road, others would head across country to encounter – a pleasant surprise – other byways. Some would turn out to be dead ends, but they might be where the treasure is buried. All this hints at the process by which the legend itself came together and spread; a means to understanding how the folk legend grew by steady accumulation and accretion around the tomb – both deliberate and accidental – of images and rumours, half-remembered beliefs, the common store of folklore and tale, the theories of antiquaries and, only rarely, smatterings of historical truth.

The vogue for grangerising in the late eighteenth century was partly about the reinterpretation of the written word with the pictorial. The practice came into fashion just as the relationship between visual and verbal means of communication was changing. William Blake was mixing words and pictures to create something sublime, and the first illustrated Shakespeare appeared. This points us to the importance of the tomb as both image and text: its art to captivate and inspire us; its rich imagery, in which we can read its meaning, creatively and historically. It is likely that in the same way that a picture pasted into a book altered how the book was read, so with the passing of years the imagery of the tomb altered an oral tradition about somebody called Shonks. Perhaps. But only when I had exhausted that imagery – its original meaning and what it came to represent – would I have any idea of what that oral tradition might have been. *It will be what is left.*

The Knowsley Clutterbuck and the Buckler painting also pointed me to all those who had communed with the tomb to create images. Their drawings and paintings, with all their flaws – and the flaws contain their own important insights – helped explain the allure of the tomb and its capacity to conjure stories. The Bucklers and their fellow travellers (the prolific Mr Cole, the tragic Mr Oldfield, the meticulous Mr Anderson) are one of the organising principles of the second part of this book – the part that belongs to the tomb. They have wrestled with it in the shadows, tried to capture it, tried to decipher it. In many ways, the Shonks I tangle with here, is made of hatchings and brushstrokes on parchment: scribbles and shadows and smudges as much as percussions and chisel marks on stone.

12

. . . speaks to us from a forgotten world, drowned, mysterious, irrecoverable.

—May McKisack, *The Fourteenth Century*, 1959

At Barley in Hertfordshire, between the 13th and the 14th mile-stones, the Cambridge to London road forked south-east towards the small village of Burnt Pelham. The man enduring the sloughs and mires of these notoriously bad roads one morning in 1743 was the twenty-nine-year-old William Cole. He was destined to be one of the great antiquaries of his age, gouty and ink-stained and only comfortable among old stones or old parchment. A Hogarth painting from around the time of his pilgrimage to Shonks' tomb shows him standing in the background of a family portait examining old papers, perhaps less at home in the salon than in the muniment room. Would his scant worldliness stand the test of the man he was about to meet? Captain William Wright, the Lord of the Manor of Beeches, was known far and wide as 'a man of great parts and wickedness'.

'Great parts and wickedness.' The phrase is somehow picturesquely archaic without losing any of its force. *Wickedness* as a noun is stronger than the adjective and especially if applied to a grown man and one in a position of power. 'Great parts' is the quiddity of the character-isation. I understand it as great means, but also talents and roles in life. Returning to Cole's notes I find he considered the captain 'a man of great natural and acquired understanding [who] knows much more than he cares to put into practise'. I Google 'Great parts and wickedness' to see if it is a literary allusion, something Richardson or Fielding wrote of a lecherous squire, but draw a blank. It gave me a type and I hope that it is a fair reckoning, but it is a harsh epitaph for anyone.

I imagine Cole entering the village on a dun-coloured horse that morning (comfortable carriage rides and the eighteenth-century Enlightenment were a long time coming to the Pelhams). Only thirty miles from London now, and yet according to one observer, it was a place both isolated and secluded and thus prone to super-stitious fancies. Later, another would write uncharitably that, 'The three Pelhams are in a dark state. The people very ignorant.'

1743 was notable as the year that George II became the last English monarch to lead an army into battle, but it would not be surprising if some in Brent Pelham had not heard that George I had died sixteen years earlier, or that his son was now king and embroiled in the quarrel over who should rule Austria.

Captain Wright was infamously slothful. He drove the Reverend Charles Wheatly to devote the page in his ledger facing the captain's tithe payments to passages from scripture. He scribbled a proverb: 'I went by the field of the slothful and by the vineyard of the man devoid of understanding. And, lo, it was all grown over with thorns, and nettles had covered the face thereof, and the stone wall thereof was broken down.' (Proverbs 24:30–1). And ends with a psalm: 'A fruitful land maketh he barren: for the wickedness of them that dwell therein.' (Psalm 107:34). They are there as judgements and amulets against the captain's laziness and supposed malignity.

Wright was a notorious miser. When Cole arrived, he was horrified that he had to stable his horse in the dairy and to find only two rooms with glass in the windows. The captain was holed up in one of them with hogs and dogs and litter and lice and 'four strapping wenches who had nothing to do but obey their master and play at cards with him'. But Cole was willing to stomach the disreputable captain to satisfy his curiosity (and his taste for scandal). Wright was not only the current Lord of the Manor of Beeches, but also of the manors of Greys and Shonks, and, 'the famous old monument of Piers Shonks . . . was the only reason which drew me out of my own province of Cambridgeshire into a church of this county,' wrote Cole in a manuscript now in the British Library.

For all his bad parts, Captain Wright may have helped Cole. Perhaps one of his wenches accompanied him westward along the bridleway to the church and dangled a light while he pored over Shonks' tomb. It is a Hogarthian composition, the single-minded scholar peering earnestly into the niche of the ancient tomb, the buxom (is that what Cole meant by 'strapping'?) servant getting in his way, a suspicious sexton lurking in the background, and other stock village characters all arranged to lampoon Cole's curiosity and the decrepit parish church.

In his prime, Cole would have made a great study for Thomas Rowlandson, who liked to caricature antiquaries. One of his contemporaries wrote of him, 'With all his oddities he was a worthy and valuable man.' It is the oddities we are interested in, and Rowlandson would have captured them as he hunkered over a tomb, measuring the exact length of the nose on the effigy, as Virginia Woolf imagined Cole doing in a letter she wrote to him post mortem, after reading his diaries. He became wedded to historical research while at Clare College Cambridge in the 1730s and later at King's College, and, after being ordained the year after his visit to Burnt Pelham, he continued to put his research first. Woolf in her letter chastises Cole for not enjoying the eighteenth century. It was said he wanted to escape to the Middle Ages. She speculates that he was disappointed in love, which is why in later life he only loved his dun-coloured horse. He variously referred to his volumes as his wife, his children and his closest friends. By his death in 1789, he had compiled nearly a hundred large volumes of notes, transcripts and sketches, mainly on Cambridgeshire, and with remarkable industry; he told his friend Horace Walpole that 'You will be astonished at the rapidity of my pen when you observe that this folio of four hundred pages with above a hundred coats of arms and other silly ornaments, was completed in six weeks.'

He rarely showed his papers to anyone. They were bequeathed to the British Museum on the proviso that they would not be opened until twenty years after his death, but even this term of grace was said to have caused some alarm for fear of what he had written about those he disagreed with – particularly anyone who had dared to remove his beloved stained glass from windows. He had no time for modernisers. Cole predicted that posterity might not appreciate the work he had done for it and admitted that he had committed his most private thoughts and much 'scandalous rubbish' to his papers. They were indeed deplored, when they were finally opened, as licentious and even morally reprehensible for mixing gossip, scandal and his personal prejudices with his antiquarian observations. If the nineteenth century was prurient and unkind to Cole, the early twentieth century found his historical notes, his journals and vast collection of correspondence invaluable and fascinating (especially the tittle-tattle), all written in his beautiful, easily legible hand.

Cole took out his pen and ink that day in 1743 and made the earliest known sketch of the tomb. Like Buckler's painting, Cole's sketch was hidden away and forgotten; unlike Buckler's painting, it is not art. It is a scratching, an aide-memoire, and in both its virtues and flaws reminds me that it is no easy matter to identify the detailed carvings on the tomb, let alone their meaning. He did capture those features that make it such an intriguing and mysterious object: its position in the wall of the nave, the strange inscription above it, and the grey-black marble slab with its extraordinary medieval carvings around which stories had gathered for centuries.

In drawing it, Cole seems to be the first writer to have examined the carvings in detail, and he tells us that the middle figure holds a smaller figure in its lap. Earlier writers had called the former a man, but as Cole's sketch shows, it is an angel, a demi-angel, without legs, flying heavenwards, although the stumpy wings on Cole's angel look hardly capable of flight. He gives it a scallop-edged costume reminiscent of something you would dress a baby in for its christening. The face has the features of a stick man: a long stick for the nose, a small one for the mouth. Oddly, these give it a patrician feel, he is curly haired with sideburns on his chubby face, shaded to a flush, and more eighteenth century than thirteenth.

In his *Sepulchral Monuments* of 1786, Richard Gough would explain that the angel is 'conveying up a soul in a shroud, or sheet in the usual attitude' – the 'usual attitude' being hands together in prayer. The image of a small naked figure – in this case probably male – standing in a napkin held by one or two angels has since been called a 'stock symbol on monuments for the salvation of the soul'. The earliest known example can be seen on a beautiful slab in Ely Cathedral thought to commemorate Bishop Nigel who died in 1169.

Cole's drawing is a scratching, but it is lovely: it reveals more than it obscures, while being far from precise. We can see the coffin shape of the slab. At its head end, he has drawn the four animals that represent the Evangelists: an angel for St Matthew, a winged lion for St Mark, an eagle for St John and a winged bull for St Luke. Cole has drawn a lion because he already knew he would find a lion representing St Mark, but it bears only a faint resemblance to what the mason put there. Cole's lion faces us with the beard of an old sea captain, its forequarters raised semi-rampant upon a bow shape, its wings teardrops. Cole's lion is too naturalistic, but his eagle seems to have rigor mortis, its legs grasping for something in the moment of death when it should be clutching a scroll. It is lumpy, with a parrot's head, and looks incapable of flight. The bull or ox is dog-like, and St Matthew's angel is awkward and timorous, hugging himself against the draughty nave.

The cross below the angel and soul is more feather dusters than the foliaged arms of a cross fleury, and its central boss has four petals and not five – such details are important when they come from an age when everything could carry a meaning. None of Cole's sketches do justice to the hand of the mason, but he is not alone, the artists of Shonks' tomb have often led commentators astray because the tomb has eluded capture on paper. Looking at his renderings, it is easy to understand how later, less educated observers than him mistook the lion, ox and eagle for three dogs, which quickly became part of the story.

Standing by the tomb today in the quiet of the small church, the carvings are almost as evasive as they were when Cole wrestled with them; in some ways more so after another 250 years of wear. But we can see that the figures are more accomplished than Cole's impressions: the actual lion looks towards the south wall of the nave, to the observer's left and not straight at him. The mane is subtler, its wing is far more elegant and feathered, and the bow shape is a scroll under its right paw. Yet Cole conveys the great age of this slab and its strangeness that always unsettles me when I visit. St Matthew's angel holds an open book in its lap, but the most striking feature is its right wing, hanging over the edge of the stone as folds of drapery might hang over the edge of a bed – a subtle touch used by skilled masons at the time to indicate the recumbency of figures, but odd when applied to an angel's wing. Then there is the dragon, but we will return to the dragon in due course.

The carvings challenge us to unriddle them – black marble is hard to see in the recess – and they have been worn faceless and shiny with age, probably from the many hands that have tried to feel their shape, but perhaps also from the slippers of the priests who may have once walked on them (ignoring the ninth-century monition against such sacrilege: 'Let every sepulchre be esteemed sacred, and let it be adorned with the sign of the cross, and take care lest any tread upon it with their feet'). Cole, as he struggled in the half-light to see the figures concealed in the archway, could tell that the tomb was older than the church itself and he suggested that it had originally come from the chancel floor of an earlier church burned down in the reign of Henry I, in the fire that supposedly gave Burnt Pelham its name. Dragon fire, say some, muddling their stories.

The slab is an important piece of medieval sculpture. The masterpiece of a medieval mason. Nikolaus Pevsner, the architectural historian, has it as one of the two finest examples of stone effigy in Hertfordshire, calling it a 'very remarkable work'. And it would have attracted attention over the years for the quality and individuality of the workmanship on such an early tomb, regardless of any legends attached to it.

Shonks' tomb is an original work of art. It is something apart and liminal, sitting on the boundary between tombs with a simple cross and one or two crude symbols depicting the dead person's profession or calling – hammer and tongs for a blacksmith, say, or scissors and glove for a glover – and the grander effigial tombs with a life-sized knight in full armour.

By Cole's time, the slab had taken on a life of its own and the design on it had played no small part in conjuring the legend of Piers Shonks. It is easy to forget that this was set over the resting place of a man, not a legend. To commemorate his life? To send a message to the world of the living or the world of the dead? The design had a purpose in the thirteenth-century imagination, in the mind of the person who commissioned the tomb, in the ambitions of a stonemason.

The tomb is from a world where attitudes to death and the after-life were fantastically different to our own. And different to the world of Cole's day as well. There could hardly be a starker contrast between attitudes to death than those of the makers of Shonks' tomb and those of the Lord of Shonks' Manor some 500 years later. When Captain Wright died two years after Cole's visit, he was said by one contemporary to have enjoyed a 'long, wicked, atheistical life'. He left his brother the house, and instructions to serve but one pint of gin at the wake and to carry him to the churchyard in a carrion cart. Carrion: *dead putrefying flesh. Something vile or filthy. Rotten, loathsome.* Perhaps his refusal to fulfil the dying wish of someone so wicked precipitated the haunting that would one day lead to the demolition of the west wing of Beeches. Although a better candidate for any spectre may be one of Wright's mistresses whom he was rumoured to have murdered. On the captain's death, Cole appended more notes to his manuscript which change completely how we see things:

The late Mr Wright was one of the meanest objects I ever beheld, having no use of his limbs by his back broke by a fall from a horse . . . he sat without shoes, stockins or breeches, in a nasty greasy great coat and night cap and hat one would not have pick'd off a dunghill, and a shirt not chang'd I suppose since it was first bought.

It is inconceivable to our age that Cole mentions that Captain Wright was quadriplegic only as an afterthought. The beliefs and attitudes of all ages are perhaps irrecoverable, and we might despair of coming to grips with a thirteenth-century tomb when the eight-eenth century seems so alien, a collage of popular culture: Dick Turpin, Henry Fielding, Dr Johnson's *Dictionary*, Blackadder and the novels of Georgette Heyer. What people thought Shonks' tomb meant was key to the creation of the legend of Piers Shonks; what it originally meant was key to the real story of a real Shonks and why his remains were placed in such an unusual tomb.

13

Glory be to God for . . . All things counter, original, spare, strange
—Gerard Manley Hopkins, from 'Pied Beauty', 1877

In the closing years of the eighteenth century, a struggling artist by the name of Henry Oldfield made 1,500 unique drawings of Hertfordshire – of churches and tombs and coats of arms – and was then promptly forgotten for his pains. Within a few years of his death (a day that seems to have gone unnoticed and unrecorded) not even the drawings stood as a monument to his life and endeavours. If the story of Shonks' tomb is cast as a battle between memory and forgetting, no one better represents the changing fortunes of these old foes than the tragic Mr Oldfield and his terrible drawing of Shonks' tomb. A drawing so bad that I cannot help being fond of it, not least because its errors finally allowed me to make sense of the carvings on the tomb: to translate a message in stone sent from a world 800 years distant from our own.

It was the county historian John Cussans – he who claimed to have demolished Shonks' legend – who proved Oldfield's undoing, attributing his work to that of a schoolmaster called John Pridmore. The drawings became known as the Pridmore, or Dimsdale Collection, after Baron Dimsdale, who was supposed to have given Pridmore the work. To add insult to injury, Cussans condemned the drawings as ridiculous. He was scathing: 'Many boys, twelve years old, would do far better.' Cussans did, however, recognise that the pictures had some worth, writing that, 'Their value lies in the fact that no other drawings remain of many old mansions, churches, monuments &c which have been destroyed during the present century.'

Eventually and mercifully, a later historian, Herbert Andrews, whom we met replying to Gerish about a Cetiosaurus, rescued Oldfield from oblivion in the 1940s, when he paused to wonder how a schoolmaster found the time to wander around the county making so many sketches. Andrews solved the mystery when he came across a note in the margin of a sales catalogue in the British Library. The catalogue was for the collection of the antiquary John Meyrick, which was sold by auction on 21 April 1806. Lot 1794 of the *Biblioteca Meyrickana* consisted of 1,500 Hertfordshire drawings and an all-important pencil note revealed that they had been sold to Baron Dimsdale for £108. 3*s*. So the pictures had originally been owned by Meyrick and not created at the behest of the Baron. Following the paper trail, Andrews was able to establish that Meyrick himself had commissioned the art work from one Henry Oldfield, for the princely sum of 4*s*. apiece. Such antiquarian research can sometimes render a great kindness to the dead.

Cussans was not wrong about the quality of the work. The drawings are crude and inaccurate. 'He was not an Artist,' wrote Oldfield's cataloguer H. R. Wilton-Hall, but, like Cussans, tempered the criticism with the observation that 'thanks to him we can to-day see for ourselves the things that were as they were'. And that was the point of them. Topographical drawings were not expected to be artistic, they were meant as a record. Yet Wilton-Hall is generous. Oldfield's drawings are often not only crude but inaccurate as well.

Shonks' tomb is one of thirty-two drawings of altar tombs in the collection. It is catalogued as 'Drawing of altar Tomb – in brown' and is especially unsophisticated. If it had been a quick sketch in a notebook there would be less cause for complaint, as all the elements are just about there. The dragon is very odd, and among other imagined features, Oldfield has set a barb or arrowhead on the end of its tail. The strangest thing of all is that while most artists drew the slab in plan, Oldfield chose to draw it *in situ* under its arch, but obliquely, ignoring the rules of perspective and choosing more than one point of view; in some ways this is the drawing's chief virtue. The entire piece is made worse by the feeble effort to add colour: the flagstones are washed in a weak French navy blue, the walls are yellow and, while Wilton-Hall says it is brown, the tomb is in fact peachy; perhaps it has faded.

It is a poor topographical drawing, if topographical drawings are meant to be a photographic record. Oldfield wrestled with the tomb and was defeated by it. His efforts to depict the slab and its position in the wall are clumsy, and his figures are rough and inaccurate. Its strangeness is the drawing's redeeming feature. It emphasises the tomb's oddities. It is unsettling. More than any other of the nineteenth-century renderings, it captures the singularity of Shonks' memorial.

Monument of O Piers Shonkes in Brent Pelham Church Herts.

These early monuments with a cross on them, sometimes carved in relief, sometime incised, are known as cross-slabs – essentially a slab of stone with a cross on it. They might be a simple rectangular ledger stone for setting over a grave, flush with the pavement, or, like Shonks' stone, they might be shaped like a coffin lid with six sides. Your standard thirteenth-century monument was a stone coffin sunk into the ground, but with the lid still exposed and sitting proud of the floor as a grave marker. If the coffin was placed in the church, it might be left above ground and its sides decorated with simple carvings. It might even be placed in a niche.

Cross-slabs have been 'abused, neglected and forgotten' to take the title of a 2010 article on them by their champions Brian and Moira Gittos. The grander effigial monuments of the Middle Ages generally get all the attention, but with their origins in Christianised Rome, cross-slabs became the monument of choice for many in the twelfth to fourteenth centuries. Traces of pigment have been found on some slabs, and one of the reasons these seemingly humble stones continued to be popular with the wealthy is because many were originally brightly coloured. Count them with the loosest possible definition and several thousand have survived to some extent in the British Isles (albeit in fragments or with the carvings weathered away), but if we confine them to the high-status marble cross-slabs like Shonks' that came out of the Purbeck quarries in Dorset in the High Middle Ages, then there are a little over 800 examples.

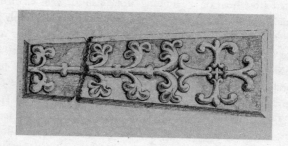

I have referred many times already to the thirteenth-century date, but how do we know? It is the cross heads that are used to date the slabs. Shonks' cross has four leafy terminals, each with five lobes. Its central boss is a rose with five petals, representing perhaps the Virgin Mary or the blood of Christ. Based on the style of foliage, the *Gentleman's Magazine* in 1852 first proposed a date for the tomb, a fairly precise 1200–1225. Pevsner gave only a vague thirteenth century, while the Historical Monuments Commission plumped for the latter part of it. The Gittoses favour a mid-century date, writing in response to the questions I bombarded them with to say, 'The leaves which make up the cross head are an elaborate form of "stiff leaf" which later in the century tended to be replaced by the naturalistic varieties.'

The crosses on the slabs come in a multitude of styles. The author of one early work on them wrote, 'The variety of designs in these stones is infinite; many too, admirable for the delicacy of execution, beauty and originality, both as regards the cross treatment and symbolic renderings.' It's been said that they followed no rule other than the wishes of the client, the architectural style of the period, the taste and skill of the craftsman, and the cost of the monument. One Victorian archaeologist wrote: 'Variety in their designs for monumental crosses appears indeed to have been regarded by the medieval artists as a no less important element than beauty and appropriateness.'

There are other slabs with crosses that are similar to Shonks': the floriated cross head on a Doulting Stone slab in Wells Cathedral is stylistically very similar although the four branches have only three lobes each. The most striking thing about the Wells cross is its resemblance to ironmongery, as if the stone cross is a copy of an actual processional or burial cross used in church services. These have a removable head and the stone mason has carved the bulge of the socket where the shaft would be inserted into it. At Furneux Pelham in 1297, we read there was an '*item i crux portatilis coram mortuis*' – a cross to be carried before the dead; at Brent Pelham simply '*i crux portatilis*'. It is tempting to imagine that the cross on the tomb resembled the one in the church that would be carried before a coffin during the funeral. The four ends of a bronze processional cross at the V&A, dated to the same period as Shonks' tomb, have the so-called stiff-leafed terminals very reminiscent of Shonks' cross. They look as if they themselves have been inspired by masonry – resembling the acanthus leaf capitals of classical architecture. We should not be surprised at the cross-fertilisation of styles and iconography between stonework and metalwork, not to mention manuscripts, wall paintings, stained glass and woodwork.

For the connoisseur of cross-slabs, the years 1250 to 1350 have been called the most interesting of the medieval period. 'A time of rapid growth, great energy, and exuberant vitality', observes one writer. It was a time when tomb-making was still largely the preserve of the same master masons who decorated churches, and Shonks' tomb seems to epitomise this. Its mason created something more original than most. Take the angel's wing falling over the edge of the slab's edge, intruding on the convex surface of the coffin lid's single hollow chamfer. Unique and highly unusual. The only slab that has anything like this is a Purbeck marble cross-slab for an abbess in Romsey Abbey, which has a leaf on the chamfer, but also a crudely carved arm eerily emerging from it to grip the shaft of the abbess's crozier or staff.

Writers have called it the *remarkable* tomb of Piers Shonks, or the *curious* tomb, the *peculiar, far-famed, celebrated, unusual, fine, interesting, most interesting, elaborate* and – on numerous occasions – *singular* tomb. 'A singular monument,' writes George Cooke in 1825. *Singular*: that is *unique, much beyond the average, extraordinary, eccentric or strange*. We should bear in mind that its singularity might not be because it was alone of its kind, but alone among its survivors. It has been estimated that only 10 per cent of cross-slabs have survived, perhaps even fewer. While stressing that you rarely see two cross-slabs that look the same, one Victorian expert called Shonks' tomb a 'curious' example that was not easily classified. The great Pevsner hardly ever mentions cross-slabs in his architectural guides to the English counties, even when they are the oldest object in the church, lament Brian and Moira Gittos, but he singles out Shonks' tomb for admiration, and the Gittoses themselves do not hold back, choosing it as one of two examples of a highly individual commission before concluding: 'Here is drama indeed and a unique composition.'

My favourite celebration of the tomb comes from the seventeenth-century writer John Weever. In his 1631 *Ancient Funeral Monuments* he copies an earlier account word for word, beginning his description with 'In the wall of this church lieth a most ancient monument', but in the unpublished draft of his book, Weever originally added something of his own, writing, 'In the wall of this Church lieth a wondrous strange ancient Monument.' The morning spent at the Society of Antiquaries reading through Weever's archive was more than worth those two adjectives from the poet.

Wondrous strange.

The wonder and the strangeness of it.

I stress this point, not only to elevate my chosen subject, but also because with few if any analogues, it is little wonder that Shonks' tomb puzzled antiquaries, as Richard Gough admitted. The critical examination of funeral monuments has been called one of the most important conceptual advances made by antiquaries during the eighteenth century, and Gough was the man chiefly responsible for this revolution. He was certainly the greatest examiner of tombs of that age; his magnum opus, the vast *Sepulchral Monuments*, still casts a shadow over commentators today. When Gough wrote that Shonks' tomb had long 'furnished matter for vulgar tradition, and puzzled former antiquaries', his stress is upon that word 'former'. Gough was eager to demonstrate that it was no puzzle to him; but in his haste to debunk vulgar tradition he dispensed with the singularity of the tomb and tried to group it with others, which bore no resemblance to it at all, and his taxonomy only adds to the puzzle.

The professed aim of *Sepulchral Monuments* was to use funerary monuments to understand the manner and custom of when they were made, which is one of the reasons why he is dismissive of the legends about the tomb, considering them not only vulgar but a later creation. Yet, if he had paid more attention to the tomb's stories, he might have come closer to understanding it. Ironically – although not necessarily surprisingly – the legends invented by locals to explain the tomb probably come closer to the real meaning of the carvings than the rationalisations of the expert Gough, but his reading has influenced almost everyone who has considered them since.

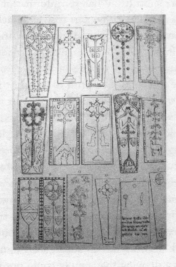

He wrote ponderously that the serpent is 'a two-footed dragon, pierced by the cross, whose point is in his mouth . . . the sculpture conveys the idea of the destruction of Satan by the cross of Christ, securing immortality to all who die in the faith of the gospel, as transmitted by the evangelists'. Few have questioned this simple interpretation. Some seventy years after Gough, when Charles Boutell published his *Christian Monuments in England and Wales* he wrote that the tomb at Brent Pelham 'denotes the triumph of the church by the cross being planted upon a dragon's head'.

In a round-about sort of way that brings us back to poor Henry Oldfield languishing in Hertford Gaol in May 1799, charged with not paying his debts. We know this because he wrote to Richard Gough asking for help and offering to make copies of his drawings. Gough went to great personal expense to fill his *Sepulchral Monuments* with as many drawings of monuments as possible, but they were not always of the best quality. One contemporary wrote about them rather snottily: 'Whatever information we may receive from his writings the delineating part is so extremely incorrect, and full of errors, that at a future period, when the originals no longer exist, it will be impossible to form any correct idea of what they really were.' Gough found a picture of Shonks' tomb from some-where. It was the first published print of it, but it is not attributed to anybody, and there is no date, although it must have been drawn before the book was published in 1786. It bears a striking resem-blance to Oldfield's drawing for John Meyrick. It is clumsy and shows the carvings in plan rather than the confused assemblage of the slab and pediment in its niche, but, most noticeably, the dragon has the same barbed tail that is missing from the tombstone itself. The main difference is the important thing: the drawing in *Sepulchral Monuments* clearly shows the separation between the cross and the carved tendrils coming out of the dragon's mouth, whereas the Oldfield–Meyrick drawing has an added shaft joining the cross to the tendrils. It is a drawing that simply could not have been made before Gough passed judgement on the tomb; it shows what simply is not there, and it illustrates Gough's words: 'a two-footed dragon,

128

pierced by the cross, whose point is in his mouth'. This is less hard to credit when we consider that topographical artists were known to write descriptions of monuments and then draw the pictures later from memory and their notes. If Oldfield used Gough's description to help him when he drew the tomb we can see how he got it wrong. Under the picture, Oldfield has written in red ink 'See Gough's *Sepulchral Monuments*'. Once again I am drawn to the significance of the encounter between text and image. As we will see when we look at the inspiration for the dragon in the next chapter, carvers did not just take their models from images of dragons; they appear to have used written descriptions as well. This constant metamorphosis from text to image to artefact and back to texts – both oral and written – is one of the keys to understanding the tomb and its legends.

If Oldfield had drawn his Meyrick picture from life, he would have seen that the carving entering – or perhaps emerging – from the dragon's mouth is not attached to the cross. It does not even look like part of the cross. This little detail matters. Boutell explained it away, writing that is was not an uncommon practice for the head to be separated from the stem, but he does not try to say why that is, although he does show examples. In his examples, the shaft is separate but still clearly a simple straight shaft, a stick, and nothing else. On Shonks' slab, the so-called shaft is two tendrils curling to the left and the right.

Gough's reading did not just lead Oldfield to draw an odd picture, it also led later writers up the wrong path. This is illustrated very nicely in the *Gentleman's Magazine* in 1852 when Gough's godson John Gough Nichols admits that the cross on Shonks' tomb is not 'united' with the 'flower' that pierces the dragon's mouth, but he decides that the whole must be a new variety of cross fleury, adding that this early English foliage is used to *engraft* the cross upon the dragon. There is an attempt to reinforce this point with a sketch of a tomb from a churchyard in Oakley, Bedfordshire. It is revealing that this was the best companion tomb he could find. It shows a cross fleury, with an obvious shaft, which merges with one of the limbs of a crude animal that looks nothing like a dragon and is probably a dog. It is irrelevant to any consideration of Shonks' tomb.

One writer in his commentary on Shonks' tomb says that it is not uncommon to find the cross on a cross-slab supported by animals. Lions and sheep and faithful hounds perhaps – but not dragons. Why would a cross be engrafted on a dragon on someone's tomb? In other words: why would a dragon be supporting a cross? It is not unusual to see a dragon being speared by a saint or archangel in religious imagery of the Middle Ages, or struck in the maw with a crozier by a bishop on a tomb, but in such cases the bishop is also standing on the dragon, the poor creature is being trampled underfoot because as the Book of Psalms commands, 'Thou shalt tread upon the lion and adder: the young lion and the dragon shalt thou trample under feet.' This is clearly not the case on Shonks' tomb. The antiquaries were very definitely puzzled – even if they did not know it.

To get at what was troubling me, why these readings were not *my* readings, I needed to look more closely at the dragon itself. I began to pursue it back through history, on a dragon hunt across the ancient world and through the literary and artistic landscape of medieval England.

14

What a dreary, monotonous, uneventful age we live in! We have sneered the ghosts and dragons away. We feed our children upon grammar and the multiplication table. Yet there are wonders still if we had but eyes to see them.

—Dr Augustus Jessopp, *Frivola*, 1896

What do we see today? What did they see 800 years ago? A creature emerging from the marble, its thick dark grey body arched into a horseshoe, like a devil's coachman roused for battle. Its long tail curls up, looping over itself as it tapers, terminating above the crest of its head in a curved point, like *gryphaea*, devil's toenails. It is a two-legged, two-winged dragon, or – heraldically – a wyvern. Its strangely stunted right leg projects forwards, while its left leg is tensed, stretched out behind and at full extension. It might be running westward – away from the chancel, the altar, the sanctuary. It has been petrified by the mason in the moment of attack. We are perhaps 800 years late and inured to the full visual effect, to its movement and menace. As Jorge Luis Borges once suggested, if we think of dragons as childish it is a modern prejudice because they appear too often in fairy tales. We have become blinded to their power because of our own 'crippling realism', in the words of the literary scholar Lesley Kordecki. They were not childish to the medieval mind.

The feet or hooves or claws have all but faded into the marble, but do the rear talons grip the stone, seeking purchase in that bottom corner of the slab, as the dragon braces itself against an assault? It bears the battle scars of the years: a chipped upper lip, the end of the tail flattened, the wing damaged, and the eye hard to decide upon, as if blinded. The long snout is wrinkled in a snarl; it is lupine, wolf-like, or is it lion-like, as the dragon's head in the Book of Revelation? Attached to the body of a fat snake, the head is quite vile, a deliberate perversion of nature, a thing perilous to body and soul. The more I look at it, the more malign it becomes, even now.

The medieval dragon is not what I expect dragons to look like today. It is not the dragon of Tolkien and his heirs. Its beard is most unexpected, a long three-stranded wavy goatee hanging down almost to the ground; as Edward Topsell tells us in his 1608 *Historie of Serpents,* which drew heavily on classical and medieval sources, some dragons are 'onely distinguished from the common sort of serpents by the combe growing uppon their heads, and the beard under their cheeks'.

The chisel marks where the head meets the body suggest a lizard or dinosaur's frill. Two long wavy ears protrude horizontally from the back of the head in a sign of aggression. The sculptor has closely observed the instinctive posturing of animals before a fight, and his dragon is not prepared to be just a symbol; it is far more natural-istic than the other carvings on Shonks' tomb, it is trying hard to come to life.

Whole wells of ink have been spilled trying to ferret out the origins of dragons, which were around in antiquity, and perhaps first appeared in the creation legends of ancient Mesopotamia. Explanations generally fall into five categories: they are memories of prehistoric creatures or based on their fossils; they were inspired by real and exotic animals such as pythons; their invention satisfied a psychological need; they were metaphorical, standing for battles of armies under a dragon banner, paganism, the taming of a river, or, in local stories, for an evil Lord of the Manor. Finally, of course, there are those who believed – still believe – that dragons really existed.

The creatures we think of as dragons in Greek and biblical legend were large and fierce, often multi-headed, and later they were suit-ably impressive opponents for saints and folk heroes. But early dragons were not always magnificent, and often appeared as support acts to other animals. From antiquity onwards, we meet the dragon running away from the sweet breath of the panther or strangling elephants with its tail. In his *Natural History*, the Roman historian Pliny's description of a dragon is of a large snake, a giant python or boa who drinks the blood of the elephant for the purpose of cooling his burning intestines, although he does not win the day, being crushed by the death throes of his opponent: when their blood commingled it made a wonderful red pigment – the true cinnabar – which must have been lusted after by the artists who later illustrated the medieval bestiaries.

In Alexandria, sometime in the third or fourth century, someone compiled the book known as the *Physiologus*, the prototype of the medieval book of beasts, or bestiary. Here were antelopes, bears and leopards alongside creatures missing from the zoos of medieval kings: the onocentaur, the phoenix, the echinemon, as well as relatives of the dragon on Shonks' tomb. For years, scholars have been mapping the relationships between the many bestiaries written in the Middle Ages, sorting them into families and tabulating the debts they owe to each other, as well as the odd occasion when a medieval scribe or poet got creative.

Bestiary texts evolved only slowly, borrowing from Pliny and Saint Isidore of Seville's great medieval encyclopedia, the *Etymologiae*, to flesh out the text of the *Physiologus*. The earliest manuscripts had only descriptions and no pictures. The *Etymologiae* describes the dragon as one of four serpents along with the anguis, the coluber and the basilisk. According to Isidore, the dragon is the greatest of all the serpents, with a crest, a small mouth, from which it sticks out its tongue, and a narrow throat through which it draws breath. It has no poison, and its strength is in its tail not in its teeth. It kills by entangling and suffocating its prey – the poor elephant again. They come from the fiery mountain tops of India and Ethiopia and live in caves, stirring up the air when they emerge. This seventh-century description is a dragon that the Shonks sculptor would have recognised and it changed little over the next 500 years. By the late thirteenth century when the tomb is being carved, some writers are giving dragons poisonous breath, but their tails are still their main weapon. Eventually someone untethers the beast from the earth and sends it aloft, but its wings are too puny, somehow it is 'lifted by the strength of venom into the air as if it were flying'.

We can imagine early artists turning these descriptions into pictures and carvings, carefully transcribing each quality into their art for other artists to copy in turn. Originally, dragons had walk-on parts under the descriptions of panthers and elephants, but nine hundred years ago, its star quality was finally recognised and it began to appear in its own right. We find a dragon pictured under an entry entitled 'Draco' in a bestiary known today as *Stowe 1067* (many manuscripts in our great libraries are named for the aristocrats who once owned them, or the country seats where they were once shelved – in this case Stowe House, home to the Duke of Buckingham and Chandos). It is a relatively poor manuscript produced probably in Canterbury some time in the 1120s. This dragon is not unlike Shonks', although here it is unfurled and sprouts a conical crest from the top of its head; its other features are common to dragons of the Middle Ages: two legs, two wings, a twisted or knotted tail, a goatee, ears sticking straight out of the back of its head, a frill and a forked tongue or flames exiting the mouth. The Stowe manuscript is unfinished: there are some twenty-eight drawings but over forty entries with spaces left for the pictures to be inserted later. The artist did not even get round to erasing his preparatory work, and especially interesting is the presence of a second dragon at right angles to the first. It is only a faint outline, a sketch or tracing in lead point, but this suggests that the finished dragon, like Shonks' dragon, was copied from a model that itself was copied from a model, and back through the centuries no doubt – to the last dragon drawn from life.

Draco

London, BL Stowe 1067, f. 5r draco

I searched the manuscripts for more models for Shonks' dragon and found many similar, with ears prostrate, two legs and small wings and the typical twisted or looped tail. A thirteenth-century manuscript in the Bodleian in Oxford has an uncoloured dragon in ink against a blood red background. It is hunting doves, which are sheltering in the Peridexion tree – a tree of life that repels the dragon. Here, the tree is split in two, and the dragon is crawling through the middle. In the same manuscript, a crude bottle green dragon recoils in fear from a panther. George Druce, the late Victorian botanist and bestiary expert, noted blue dragons with pink wings, pink ones with red and green wings, yet another brown and striped. One of my favourite pictures is from a bestiary now in the library at Douai in northern France – but said to be in the English style of illustration – it shows a distant relative of Shonks' dragon, sleek and red-headed, with blue and turquoise wings, lurking under a Peridexion tree. The branches are laden with birds, some looking ruefully at their enemy below, others hanging precariously from the branches like baubles: one has let go and is caught in the cross-eyed dragon's maw.

The consensus on what a dragon looked like in the Middle Ages is striking. The renderings of the bestiary illustrators perhaps made their way into pattern books or sketchbooks used by masons. There is only one such surviving medieval sketchbook of someone who may have been a mason, that of Villard de Honnecourt, now in the Bibliothèque Nationale in Paris. Between 1220 and 1250, Villard made some 250 drawings of architectural details, a menagerie of animals, kings and wrestlers. Here on the recto of folio 11 is a creature that is kin to Shonks' dragon. There is a short snout and a malign stare, wavy ears point backwards, and beneath the chin grows the goatee, its two legs perched on a frond of foliage, its small wings tucked back, its tail not looping but curling at the tip.

Without models, how would the masons have known what dragons looked like, unless of course they had seen one? If our mason believed that dragons plagued the land or had once done so – and I think he did, look again at the vitality of the carving – he would not have needed the evidence of his eyes. His, after all, was the world we find preserved in the late thirteenth-century map of the world kept at Hereford Cathedral, the finest Mappa Mundi of them all. As bestiaries did not distinguish between animals that we might separate into the real and the imagined, the Mappa Mundi

136

records the known world alongside relics from Greek myth: here is the Golden Fleece and the Minotaur's labyrinth. It is a map of time and space, of the imagination and belief as much as the physical world. Such a map was generous enough to contain the unicorn or monoceros, the Blemmyes with their faces in their chests, the scia-pods with one large foot to shield them from the sun's rays, the African troglodytes, who were very fast and could catch wild animals by jumping on them, the cynocephali – dog-headed men – and of course the dragons of India.

Dragons were very much part of English culture in the thirteenth century, but they were an endangered species set to go the way of the wolf and the wild boar; they were still abundant enough that bonfires were lit to keep them away on Old Midsummer Day. The twelfth-century liturgist John Beleth describes how bone-fires were made out of animal bones: 'For there are animals called dragons and these animals fly in the air, swim in water and walk on land, and sometimes when in the air they become aroused by lust, whence they often emitted semen into springs and rivers and because of that a deadly year ensued. So a remedy was found for this, that a fire should be made of bones and thus the smoke would drive these animals away.' Beleth was merely explaining why bone-fires, or bonfires, are lit on 24 June, the dragons were taken for granted.

The proto-scientist who went on to have an afterlife as a magician and alchemist, Friar Roger Bacon, complained that dragons were being stolen from thirteenth-century England and taken to Ethiopia, where their blood was in high demand. In fact, all the parts of a dragon were sought after. Pliny wrote that the fat of a dragon's heart, stored in the hide of a gazelle and tied to the arm with the sinews of a stag ensures success in litigation. Edward Topsell, learning from the ancients and bestiaries, noted that the 'fat of a dragon dried in the sun is good against creeping ulcers'. Its head 'keepeth one from looking a squint'. The 'Eyes being kept till they be stale and afterwards beate into an olyel with honey and made into an oyntment, keepe any one that useth it from the terrour of night visions and apparitions'. Magicians used the head and tail of dragons to make themselves invisible, while Saint Isidore thought that inside a dragon's brain was a precious gem called Draconite that had to be cut from a living dragon as it slept.

With every bone, sinew and inch of flesh useful for something, it is little wonder they vanished from England faster than the wolf, and little wonder that few remains have survived. Not so very long ago in County Durham, however, the antiquary Robert Surtees recalled being shown a piece of dragon's skin when he was a boy, 'like a piece of tough bull's hide'. This was said to be from the Lambton worm slain by Young Sir John Lambton on his return from the crusades.

It was in the second half of the thirteenth century that the dragon first entered the story of St George in Dominican Prior Jacobus de Voragine's medieval 'bestseller' *The Golden Legend* (it was removed again on the Pope's instruction 300 years later), although others have argued that Voragine invented nothing and must have taken the dragon from an existing legend. Dragons were suitable foils for saints because in Christian symbolism they had come to signify evil, the enemy, the devil.

To this dragon the devil is likened, who is a most enormous serpent. As it often rushes forth from its cavern into the air and the air glows around it, so does the devil, raising himself from the depths of hell, transform himself into an angel of light and delude stupid people with the false hope of glory and human joy.

These are the words of an anonymous bestiary text from 1235. Bestiaries from the *Physiologus* onwards were less encyclopedias of natural history than fables, with each animal there to teach us a moral, the Christian worldview of vice and virtue. To antiquity, animals and their behaviour contained lessons for how we should live our lives, and by the Middle Ages this had become codified into a complex set of stories and exemplars associated with animals both real and fantastic. Here is a key to the human mind.

The symbolism of the dragon in the stories, battling panthers and elephants, is straightforward. They are ciphers for evil forces in a world where all animals stood for something. The Anglo-Norman poet Philippe de Thaon, wrote, 'And know, that the dragon has the form of the serpent; it is crested and winged, it has two feet, and is toothed; by its tail it defends itself, and does harm to people. Tail, means end, as the theologians say; this is the meaning, that in the end truly the Devil will destroy those who shall end in evil.' It is a play on words and a logic that to us seems convoluted and forced, but de Thaon is in no doubt what a dragon represents in the High Middle Ages. It is Satan. Which leaves us with a puzzling question: why on earth would anyone put Satan on their tombstone?

To answer that we need to go back to the problem with the non-existent cross shaft that Gough described and Oldfield drew. What are those tendrils coming out of the dragon's mouth doing? Are they an elaborate and unique cross shaft, or something else? They look like a branch, gripped between our dragon's single fang and his three bared gnashers. This single branch divides into two three-lobed leaves. Nearly a quarter of a century after he penned the *Gentleman's Magazine* article, John Gough Nichols wrote again about Shonks' tomb in the journal *Notes & Queries*. Responding to a question from a correspondent about Shonks' tomb, he inched closer to a better interpretation of the grave slab, writing that there is architectural foliage emerging from the dragon's mouth. I cannot help thinking that the great publisher and antiquary has forgotten his godfather's judgement that the cross is piercing the dragon; he simply looked at a drawing of the tomb and recorded what he could see rather than what he was supposed to see. The cross is not mounted on the dragon, nor is it being thrust into the dragon's mouth. Something else is emerging from its mouth: foliage, the tree of life, a serpent's tongue, dragon's breath, flames?

Children's author and journalist Arthur Mee in the Hertfordshire volume of his *The King's England*, published in 1965, muddles many of the facts about the Shonks legend. He obviously has not done his research, and this is a blessing in disguise because he does not know what he is supposed to see; he says what he sees: 'Here is a dragon breathing fire.'

With the simple and rather obvious reading of flames, the tomb starts to make more sense. It is no anachronism to find a fire-breathing dragon in the 1200s. As early as the Anglo-Saxon epic poem *Beowulf* we encounter a dragon belching flame; it is the creature's chief characteristic in the popular imagination today, and it was familiar then. Several dragons in early bestiary manuscripts are portrayed breathing fire. An English bestiary dated to about 1300, now in Copenhagen, shows a green-headed dragon spurting flames as it flees from the sweet breath of a blue panther, and in a Harleian manuscript at the British Library a two-legged cousin of Shonks' dragon breathes fire at an elephant.

I look again at the drawing in Gough, on a page with over a dozen other slabs, none of which look anything like it. Its unique-ness stands out, and Gough's misinterpretation is emphasised by grouping it with these others. It belongs instead with the stone carving on the tympanum at Ault Hucknall in Derbyshire showing a cross separating a fire-breathing dragon and a warrior. The meaning is the same. There is a slab in St John's in Hagley, Worcestershire, which is not unlike Shonks'. It is cruder in style, but also has a separate cross fleury, and tendrils rising from the mouth of a small and cramped wyvern. The architectural foliage, the tendrils, look suspiciously like flames.

These dragons, like *my* dragon, are fire-breathers.

Some authors point to slabs with dragons that are biting the base of the cross, and say that is what is intended at Brent Pelham. It is a symbolism that recalls the wyrm imagery common on pagan graves where the serpent Nidhug from Norse myth gnaws on the roots of the world tree Yggdrasil. In 1963, the author Fred Burgess would offer an interesting twist on the same explanation: pointing first to a coffin lid in Tickhill, Yorkshire, which depicted the old pagan motif of dragons gnawing at the tree of life, he wrote, 'This emblematic representation of the eternal combat between Good and Evil also occurs on a fine Purbeck slab at Brent Pelham.' Not the triumph of Christianity, but a struggle, an ongoing battle. The only thing standing in between the dragon flames and the soul of the dead is the floriated cross, a shield, not a spear, not triumphant, but protective. As we shall see next, it is fire after all that was the defining characteristic of purgatory, the fire that cleansed souls.

15

Where is our humility? Is it reasonable for any modern to claim sufficient knowledge of the medieval era as to be able to 'pluck out the heart of its mystery'? We are all gropers in the darkness, and if all our little illuminations should coalesce so far as to cast an uncertain light on the subject of our study, that is the best we may reasonably hope for.

—Malcolm Jones, *The Secret Middle Ages*, 2002

Let us consider for a moment the main purpose of the decoration on a thirteenth-century tomb slab. The historian Nigel Saul is quite clear what it was for, it was 'commissioned to perform one function above all: to elicit intercessory prayer for the dead'. It is a concept alien to most today, but prior to the sixteenth-century Reformation, the dead were in dire need of prayers to hasten their passage through the nightmare of *purgatory*.

Purgatory was made official doctrine by Pope Innocent IV in a letter he wrote in 1254. It has been called the birth certificate of purgatory, but today historians argue that most of its tenets were in place centuries earlier – both among theologians and the folk. Prayers for the dead had been part of Christian life since the early church. In the fifth century CE, St Augustine had written that as God judges the dead, the prayers of the living could speed their journey to paradise. By the eleventh and twelfth centuries, this had grown into the belief that purgatory was an actual physical place (many thought the entrance was on an island in County Donegal) where the not-entirely-good and not-entirely-bad would go to be cleansed of their sins before admittance to paradise. Purgatory's greatest populariser was Dante Alighieri. His *Purgatorio* was the second book of his early fourteenth-century masterpiece *The Divine Comedy*, in between *Inferno* and *Paradiso* on the journey through the afterlife.

Purgatory was where the dead went to be purged or cleansed of sin, and the more prayers said for them by the living, the less time they spent there. No one wanted to spend long in purgatory. There, sinners were impaled on spikes or plunged into boiling cauldrons. 'Some were "fried in the fire as if they had been a fish in hot oil"; others were endlessly drowned and resuscitated and drowned again in pools skimmed with ice or eaten by monsters which excreted them whole so that they might be devoured afresh,' explains the historian Carl Watkins. 'Purgatory fire was to earthly fire as earthly fire was to its mere image in a painting; it burned fiercely but gave no light and never consumed its human fuel.' Souls in purgatory might be feasted on by adders and toads, nailed down in fields, or hanged by their lying tongues, depending on their crimes in life. Moneylenders were forced to drink molten gold, while thieves were boiled in it.

Mercifully, souls in purgatory were slowly making their way towards paradise, and it is little wonder that the dying were desperate to ensure a speedy passage by encouraging the living to pray for them. The wealthy established altars or even built chapels and bequeathed large portions of their estates to churches and religious houses in return for chantries where a priest would say mass for their souls for ever. In the early fourteenth century, Simon de Furneux – whose family gave their name to Furneux Pelham – sought permission from the king to give land to a nearby priory for two chaplains to pray for his soul and those of his wife and sons, at the priory and at an altar dedicated to St Katherine in

Furneux Pelham church. Simon was clearly worried about the amount of purging in store for him; in his will he left his London houses and rent to Sir William le Gros, but only in return for an annual payment of 6s. to purchase wine and candle wax for his chantry altars.

People were terrified of being forgotten, with no one to pray for them. Although All Souls Days on 2 November was a time when people prayed for all dead souls, your progress would be very slow if they were the only prayers you got. When Lucy, the first prioress of the nunnery at Castle Hedingham in Essex, died around 1230, a beautiful mortuary roll depicting her soul being lifted up to heaven was taken around the countryside to solicit prayers. Nearly 300 years later, purgatory was still going strong on the eve of the Reformation: in his will, Henry VII made provision for charities and a chantry chapel in Westminster Abbey, but also for 10,000 masses to begin immediately on his death: 1,500 in honour of the Trinity, 2,500 in honour of the Five Wounds of Our Lord Jesus Christ, 2,500 in honour of the Five Joys of Our Lady, 450 in honour of the Nine Orders of Angels, 150 in honour of the Patriarchs, 600 in honour of the Twelve Apostles, 2,300 in honour of All Saints. You could be forgiven for thinking that here was someone who was desperately in need of prayer to mitigate his earthly deeds.

The struggle for the soul between angels and demons at the moment of death had long been part of Christian belief. Funerary rites called on St Michael to fight off the demons and lead souls to their rest, and one eleventh-century prayer implored the archangel for protection: 'I ask and beg and pray you, St Michael archangel, who received the power of receiving souls that deign to take my soul when it will go out from my body and free it from the power of the enemy.'

Shonks' soul is held in a napkin by the angel, its little praying hands exhorting people to pray for it. Below, at the base of the tomb, a dragon breathes flames, and the only thing between the them and the soul is the cross. Shonks is guarded by the Archangel Michael and shielded by the elaborate cross with its central boss representing the Virgin Mary.

Above and to the side, the soul is encircled by the symbols of the Evangelists. It is rare to find them on a cross-slab of this early date, although they do appear on the bowl of a Tournai marble font at St Michael's, Southampton. They are more commonly found in manuscripts and on later brasses, and processional crosses.

The quartet of images famously surround Christ on the west front of Chartres Cathedral where, according to the cultural historian Christopher Frayling, they represent 'at a human level, the aspects of character which are most needed for salvation: intelligence, vision, sacrifice and courage'. Salvation is the key word. They were taken by the early Christian fathers from Ezekiel's of the animals in the Old Testament, and of St John's in the Book of Revelation; visions taken to represent the message of their gospels. St Jerome decided which animal went with which evangelist based on an ingenious – as in completely unconvincing – reading of the opening lines of the gospels, the Vulgate version of which often appeared on scrolls under their feet (or talons, hoofs or claws).

According to St Gregory, the symbols represented the four aspects of Christ, who was born a man, sacrificed like an ox, resurrected like a waking lion and ascended to heaven like an eagle. They are also among the most common images in first millennium illuminated gospel books, and it has been suggested that they were there to protect the scripture: 'apotropaic guardians of the sacred text'. Apotropaic: a difficult word that contains sorcery in its abracadabra count of syllables, something with the power to turn away evil.

In my reading, the Evangelists are on Shonks' tomb at his head and on each side not to boast of the triumph of Christianity through the gospel, but for the same reason as the cross: to protect the soul. 'Matthew, Mark, Luke and John, / Bless the bed that I lie on.' This well-known rhyme was the White Paternoster, and in rural areas in the Middle Ages and into modern times might be better known than the Lord's Prayer. It is a lorica, a protective verse. And the symbols on Shonks' tomb are this lorica visualised – a religious

incantation in stone designed to protect the soul and remind passers-by that Shonks is in peril, very much in need of their prayers to get him through purgatory and into heaven: pray for me, remember me, not for my deeds, but to save my soul.

As well as standing between Shonks and the flames of purgatory, if the cross represents a processional cross and is being carried in front of the soul on its way, it also recalls the journey of the soul through the trials of the afterlife. This journey is part of the rationalisation of the *viaticum*, a wafer given by the priest to the corpse in the offices of the dead; the word literally means to provide for a journey, to provide for the soul on its way. For anyone looking closely at Shonks' tomb, two medieval stories stand out because they combine journeys through the afterlife with the need for protection from fire. The first is that of St Fursey, told by Bede writing in the early eighth century. It is a vision in which three angels protect the saint from the demons and flames that lick at his feet – one clears the way and the other two protect his flanks. The second is perhaps more compelling still: according to the popular thirteenth-century *Early South English Legendary*, after his martyrdom St James the Greater was being taken for burial by his followers when they were waylaid by a fire drake belching flames at them. The followers hold up a cross between them and the flames and so destroy the dragon.

It is hard to escape the impression that whoever Shonks was, like Henry VII, he needed an awful lot of protection and an awful lot of prayers. That is no doubt a mistake, suggested by our distance from the thirteenth-century imagination, and he probably needed no more protection than anyone else, but nonetheless, it is a happy mistake for the storyteller, shared by those who would eventually fuel the legends about Shonks and the devil.

As Nigel Saul writes, a monument must arouse a reaction from passers-by or be of no value. What a reaction this singular tomb must have elicited in the thirteenth century and beyond. On one level it might represent the struggle of the soul, even the triumph of Christianity, but it also represents the triumph of art, because its beauty and rich symbolism continued to arouse a reaction long after people had forgotten how to read it and so began to rewrite the story it told: the story of a dragon-slayer in immortal peril.

The tomb challenges us, it speaks to us from across the ages, and look at how much it has to say if we take the trouble to translate it. The Reverend Cutts puts this so well in his 1849 manual of sepulchral slabs and crosses that I will quote him in full:

> By far the greater number of these ancient monuments have no inscription whatever, not even a name; nevertheless these stones are not dumb; they speak more justly and eloquently than long and laboured epitaphs. The cross upon them tells that a Christian lies in the grave beneath, its flowery form speaks of hope and triumph through the cross . . . the dragon at the base of another, pierced through by the shaft of the cross, tells how Christ bruised the serpent's head, and how we must overcome sin and Satan through the cross . . . and these sermons in stones are the more eloquent and impressive for being thus symbolically given; they speak to the imagination and the heart as well as to the reason.

Of course there are ideas here that work against my interpretation, but that is not a problem. The tomb is old enough, storied enough, mysterious enough and beautiful enough to contain many meanings. It may depict a soul protected from purgatory fire, the triumph of Christianity, the deathbed struggle between good and evil, and other things we are yet to see. The architectural historian A. Whitford Anderson gave us another option when he wrote dismissively that the carvings were 'evidently emblematical of the Resurrection'. But he was wrong to assume the meaning is evident.

In her exploration of the dragon in the Old English masterpiece *Beowulf*, Lesley Kordecki concluded that the medieval dragon acts as a symbol with several meanings. As we saw earlier, dragons as symbols appear in art and literature not just as signs, but as animals, yet they also symbolise things, such as power – in Christian art it is often the devil, in *Beowulf* it is a symbol of evil, chaos, pride, greed and other things too perhaps. Kordecki has written that the dragon 'projects rays of meanings, not just any meaning, which would result in no meaning at all, but a number of valid interpretations which enrich the poem . . . the treatment of the motif in Beowulf is ambivalent enough not only to allow different meanings but demands them as the most truthful way to represent Beowulf's complex situation'. We might say the same thing of the carvings on Shonks' tomb, not least about the ambiguity of that cross shaft, spear, vegetation, dragon's fire, which demanded that those who looked at it in the second half of the thirteenth century should put different meanings on it: those who commissioned it, those who carved it, and those priestly and lay observers who passed by it nearly 800 years ago, each understanding it in different ways. That ambiguity meant that it could be read by the most literate ecclesiast steeped in the writings of classical authors and the early church fathers, as well as by the uneducated illiterate peasant. It had something for everyone from the outset, and that also ensured its long-term success, because those qualities, that richness, meant that it transcended its original purpose and continued to fascinate and generate new readings over the centuries.

The author Bob Trubshaw, a wise voice on these matters, has written about marginal images, the so-called grotesques on corbels and springers in parish churches. He too counsels that we must guard against trying to give one definitive explanation to images from the past, that their meaning is 'slippery', and things might have different meanings to the client, to the priest and to the mason. The doctrine of purgatory was evolving still, what happened at the moment of death and following death was always open to question – we ought to expect the thirteenth century to leave us a multivalent conundrum, a riddle with more than one answer, something we need to look at from different points of view.

I got a chance to look at the tomb askance, one day in early spring as I was close to finishing this book. I returned to it with my friend, the photographer Dominick Tyler. As illustrators and painters found the tomb difficult to capture, photographers have been even less successful. There are postcards and pictures taken for local newspapers, which tend to show the tomb in its setting, but fail to capture the carvings in any detail. A. Whitford Anderson took a wonderful ghostly image of the surface of the tomb early in the last century, but it is much less helpful than the accurate and detailed scale drawing he made of the tomb at about the same time for the Victoria County History.

Dominick has come to St Mary's to attempt to capture the tomb for me and he spends three hours with different lenses, lighting it and trying to map it. We have spoken about it many times, and Dominick wants to stitch together an image of the tomb to show its entire surface in one view. As he works, the task puts him in mind of David Hockney's composite portraits, stitched together from photographic details. I had told him it would be difficult to photograph, that is how I lured him to the church, along with the promise of lunch in the Black Horse. He admits he had not realised how tricky it would be. Not only is the slab always in shadow, but, as he soon realises, 'There is no one angle from which you can see the whole tomb at once.'

The process is instructive and as he works I examine the tomb again, spotting things I had not noticed when I'd tried to describe it previously. St Matthew's angel's head is resting solicitously, tenderly against the folds of the napkin that holds the little soul. The soul is bearded and might well be wearing some sort of hat, perhaps a mitre? The ox's hooves are broken off, but they would have rested on top of the other side of the napkin, could the discolouring on the lion's mane be orange pigment? Three details have survived time and destruction more than others: the sharp paws of the lion, the balled claws of the eagle, and the stylised feathering on the angel's wing, which sits in lower relief than the rest of the carvings. I have to search glossaries to find the correct terms for this wing: *overlapping fish-scales* at the shoulder, *convex reeding* along its length to the tip – both showcasing the carver's extraordinary skill.

When I get the photographs back they reveal more than I could ever have seen with the naked eye, the macro lens, the lighting from the back and above give away so much (in the niche it is only ever lit from the south window – surely the mason never intended his work to be hidden in a niche). Most arresting are the chisel marks on the eye of the dragon, three crude incisions which we will soon look at more closely, and a red blob beneath the dragon which is probably a type of *scagliola*, a mixture of coloured plaster and paste used as a cheap inlay or to repair stonework in the eighteenth and nineteenth centuries, it is clumsy but better than other repairs with white and grey filler and patches that look like plain cement.

On the front left of the slab as you face it, between the scroll in the paws of St Mark's lion and the shoulder of the archangel's wing, is a small patch of marble that still holds a sheen, and Dominick chooses this to take a close-up of the surface of the stone. When I download it and open it on my laptop, the image is remarkable. I have been wrestling with an object from the Middle Ages, but for the first time I can see that Shonks' tomb is older than I had ever stopped to consider. It is made of millions of tiny fossils from the deeps of time.

16

Then might those genera of animals return, of which the memorials are preserved in the ancient rocks of our continents. The huge iguanodon might reappear in the woods, and the ichthyosaur in the sea, while the pterodactyl might flit again through umbrageous groves of tree-ferns.

—Charles Lyell, *Principles of Geology*, 1830

About thirty-six degrees north, in a lagoon, long ago, tiny river snails die in their multitudes and sink to the bottom of the brackish water – into shifting limestone-snail-shell-mud, stirred by the footfall of iguanodons. Continents drift, and a mason is carving angels and winged beasts on a stone coffin lid; his tempered point revealing the petrified whorls of endless little shells imprisoned in their matrix. Here they are, eight centuries later, abraded and polished flat, but shining and glorious on a tomb 140 million years old.

I make a pilgrimage to the Square and Compass in Worth Matravers, the Dorset pub most associated with stone carving and fossils, and there I find a perfect snail shell, three-dimensional, its whorls intact, projecting from a rough square of Purbeck marble. It is number seven in the glass cabinet in the little museum of fossils that the landlord Charlie Newman has collected from the beds of local limestone. It looks much like other snails dredged from ponds and puddles today, but the stone looks nothing like marble. Purbeck marble is not really marble, but a rough sedimentary rock, a limestone densely packed with the fossilised remains of *Viviparus cariniferus* an extinct river snail. It is found in the rock of the Isle of Purbeck in Dorset, and for about 200 years in the High Middle Ages was the most prized English stone. If Shonks' tomb is really of Purbeck marble, it is one of only eight such cross-slab coffin lids in Hertfordshire. There is other Purbeck marble: there are effigies and fonts, and the shrine of St Alban is fashioned from it, but a Purbeck marble cross-slab so far from home and from the coast is a rarity.

I have with me Dominick Tyler's photograph of the shiny corner of the tomb when I arrive in a gale on the southern Purbeck hills near Langton Matravers to meet Treleven Haysom at his quarry. Even though he is meant to have retired, Trev looks like he has just emerged from medieval diggings, or from a tumulus, an ancient lord of stone, bathed in the ghostly dust of the Isle. An eighth-generation quarryman, Trev is the greatest living authority on Purbeck marble, and I want his blessing. I want to know for certain that he thinks Shonks' tomb slab is genuinely a Purbeck slab. On ancient tombs that have lost their polish it is far from easy to tell.

He is slow to come to judgement. In fact, for some time, Trev seems to avoid looking at the close-up photograph I have put on the table, although he steals sidelong glances as we talk. I begin to think he is reluctant to break the bad news, since I have come all this way. He has visited much of the Purbeck marble in churches and cathedrals here and on the continent, and been instrumental in the restoration of many of them, but Trev has not heard of this strange tomb in Hertfordshire. When we spoke on the phone, he told me a long story about his efforts to examine a well-known Purbeck marble altar in an English abbey, which is definitely not Purbeck marble. He was priming me for disappointment.

At least Trev is very taken with the carvings on the tomb, particularly the dragon. The composition is like nothing he has ever seen on a coffin lid. Pointing at the close-up, he indicates a thin white line running for some inches from the shoulder of the angel's wing.

It is a calcite vein, he explains, a flaw in the stone that formed in the ground over millions of years and can be a weak point, depending on which direction it runs in the rock bed. In Purbeck they call it a 'list', in nearby Portland they have an even better term, 'snail-creep', and he points to a marble tile on the floor of the room we are sitting in; it too has a calcite streak, and as Trev explains how it formed I realise he is talking as if it is a given that my tomb came out of the same ground where these tiles were quarried.

'Wilkeswood,' he is saying, and then there's a long pause, 'or Dunshay.' Trev thinks that Shonks' tomb could have been quarried 800 years ago on Dunshay Manor.

Dunshay was well known as the sculptor Mary Spencer Watson's home from 1923 until her death in 2006. Although she worked very little in Purbeck marble, she is closely connected to the stone trade, having been inspired by the quarrying and restoration work she saw around her as a child. I like to think she would have liked Shonks' tomb, not only for its virtuosity, but also because of the symbols of the Four Evangelists, which fascinated her. Her own sculptures of the four creatures now guard the approach to Wells Cathedral. She is remembered locally for her sculpture of the *Purbeck Quarryman*, now in the churchyard at Langton Matravers. Dunshay is also the best known and best attested of the medieval quarries, because in the 1220s its owner Alice de Briwere gifted the Purbeck marble for Salisbury Cathedral – it is the only quarry that we can link with any degree of certainty to particular Purbeck marble carvings from the Middle Ages.

I walk to Dunshay the morning after meeting Trev, east into the sun, towards the sea. The Isle of Purbeck is not really an island, but is separated from the rest of Dorset by the River Frome at Wareham. Due south is Corfe Castle at the break in the chalk downs, where I begin my tramp, gazing up at the most dramatic castle ruins in England. The jagged walls of the broken keep and towers rise precipitously and defiantly from their extraordinary geological pedestal to haunt the skyline. It is the most ostentatious realisation of the potential of stone for miles around. A vast wyrm of chalk heads west, via Nine Barrow Down to Poole Bay and the chalk stacks at Handfast Point known as Old Harry Rocks. Beyond that it continues on the seabed, aligning on its natural continuation on the far horizon, where the Needles emerge from the sea at the Isle of Wight.

Walk south of the chalk into the valley, then up the dipslope of the south Purbeck downs and you are standing on the Purbeck limestone, tipped and folded confusingly by the same orogeny that raised the Alps thirty-five million years ago. By some counts, there are seventy strata within the Purbeck group, encompassing 160 million years or more of Earth's history. In their explorations of the stone they named feather and thornback and sky bed, the stonecutters of Purbeck travelled across deep time, to the boundary between the Jurassic and the Cretaceous. The marble in the upper beds makes up only a very small slice of the Purbeck stone. This most precious stratum of the group runs from west to east with complex inconsistency, and along that line of rock are the Isle's most famous medieval quarries: Dunshay, Quarr and Wilkeswood among them.

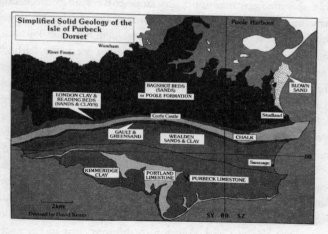

It is Dunshay I am most interested in now. The landscape approaching the Manor House and farm is roughed out by generations past, pitted with bowls where men have cleaved and wrenched the footings out, so the ceiling of the world has fallen in and the marble that once held up the land is many miles away holding up clerestories and vaultings, and memorialising men and women who died when Henry III was on the throne and the keep of Corfe Castle was rendered and painted white as the chalk. There is little for me to see other than the unnatural egg-carton grasslands. The earth hides its secret chambers. Tumbledown fields abandoned to woodland hint at workings, no less than barbed wire and electric fences that seem to be keeping you out of these hollow places, but if you were to hurdle them and explore, there is nothing to see over the false summits but more grass and dandelions, scattered on a surface like a force five at sea. Somewhere beneath my feet, down beneath those dandelions, beneath the turf and the mud and the shale, is a hollow space where Shonks' tomb was hacked from the earth.

In the nineteenth century, the stoneworkers of Purbeck dug shafts and tunnels to get at the freestone. The medieval quarries were small-scale and opencast – the ridden holes of Purbeck. Today, they excavate vast opencast quarries to get at the Purbeck stone, stone mind, not marble, which is only a small part of it. The marble is only mined rarely today, and it is not uncommon to read that it has been worked out and none is left. Workings were twice opened to repair London's Temple Church, first at Woodyhyde in 1842, and again near Swanage a century later following the Blitz.

Trev Haysom has specialised in conservation work. In 1993, he acquired the mineral rights to open ancient workings at Quarr Farm. I reach there ten or fifteen minutes after leaving Dunshay behind. There is a large, fading wooden signpost pointing to Swanage to the east and Kingston to the west. Just to the north is a fenced-off field half mown, half covered in long grass and tubed saplings. This is where Trev went in search of the marble. He did not know what the medieval stonecutters had left behind, but he knew that the marble bed slopes north, so he had a hunch where it might be. In the thirteenth century, there were no tracked excavators and no water pumps, so the water table and the sheer quantity of rock and clay that had to be moved meant there was always a point that the marble went too deep under the overburden for men with spades and mattocks. They gifted marble to the future. After finding ground disturbed long ago and backfilled, the quarrymen widened their hole north looking for virgin soil. Some twenty feet down, beneath brown shale and blue shale and rotten rag, they struck the topmost bed known as the blue marble. The 'best' blue it is called, and it is the same marble from which their forebears carved Shonks' tomb. Depending on where you are on the line, there might be two or three beds of blue (and if you are lucky there will be fossilised Iguanodon footprints too) and then beneath that there are beds of green marble, and beneath that beds of grey.

In the earth at Quarr, Trev found rocks with wedge pits to show that medieval masons had prepared to hammer in their gads to cleave a block of stone from its bed, but for some reason they had abandoned it. Nearby blocks of stone told an even more detailed story from the Middle Ages. There on the quarry floor, they had already been roughed into the unmistakable shape of coffins lids. One block had a crack in it that the stonecutters call a vent, and someone had probed it long ago with a punch. Other blocks showed the drokes made by the chisel as they cut away the waste. Why transport more than was necessary? This is how Shonks' tomb would have been cut from its bed, given its shape, and left thick enough to carve intricate figures in bas-relief.

I walk on through the wares, as these rough grasslands are known locally, from Quarr, through Wilkeswood, on ways lined with blue-bells. The wood is hollowed out, its centre pitted with great depressions that pull you towards them with a centripetal energy of ancient doings with chisel and hammer and the hope of glimpsing echoes of them among the tree roots and dark pools. Out of the old oaks, the farming landscape of the downs is laid out like compart-ments in a cabinet of wonders – is that why I find them so pleasing? Perhaps it is because the relationship between people and such a landscape has been refined over evolutionary periods of time, so that the pattern of fields in the valley and on the vast chalk barrow, which dozes like a sleeping animal with its muzzle in the sea – the image is Rena Gardiner's, the exquisite Dorset maker of books and not mine – the field pattern is really a map of the surface of the human cortex. Fields and wood and pathways, hedgerows and dry-stone walls are hard-wired to give contentment – a map of us at our best.

There were once many more quarries along the subterranean seam that starts in the English Channel at Worbarrow Tout in the west and extends east into Swanage and out to sea at Peveril Point. Here are two ridges of the Burr which underlies the marble (so called because freshly cut it looks like butter – *beurre*). The lines extend into the sea. Scramble down to the beach, and above you in the rock face, large slabs of marble are falling out of the cliff. They look nothing like marble, these grey brown slabs like baked mud. Who first realised what it might become? Did the Romans, who used it first, notice it here where land meets sea? Did they spy lumps of these strange cakes of ancient shells polished by the tides and waves and so called it *Marmor*?

The marble is only the top bed of the Purbeck stone. A short way further round the coast to the west is the rock ledge at Tilly Whim, where men braved the cruelty of wind and waves to extract the lower strata directly out of the cliff face and improbably lowered it to boats waiting on the water. What extraordinary labour was involved in removing this rock from the earth in the cliff faces and ridden holes and later in the mine shafts, even before the work of shaping hard and unpredictable rock into angels and dragons began. A thought occurs to me as I look out over the ledges at Anvil Point that must be a commonplace among scholars of burial practices; that we memorialise our dead with stuff torn from under the ground and brought into the sunlight, and we redress the balance by returning our bones to the dark earth, an ancient pact between people and stone. We read about the role of smiths in mythology but where are the mythical quarrymen toiling in the subterranean dark and heat to find the stuff from which we pave our streets and raise cities built of cathedrals and castles and tombstones?

> Old mammals, dinosaurs' tread, crocodiles
> congealed between the cliffstone's ammonites
> and marble's burnishable snail-whorls.
> Time, unmanned, in the rocks' mirror distorts

These lines, the language of aeons distilled to a rich quiddity, by the Dorset poet Paul Hyland, have been petrified too, carved into headstones. They are near the beginning of a beautiful stone time-line of facts and poetry that lead visitors from the Big Bang all the way to the arrival of mankind at the door of Durlston Castle. The castle, which is less a castle than a castellated Victorian house, was built by the 'King of Swanage', George Burt, a local boy made good trading stone in London. The timeline continues Burt's original project centred on a strange forty-tonne limestone globe he had made and hauled to a perch between the castle and the cliff edge at Durlston Head. It mostly boasts the extent of the British Empire in Burt's day, and is encircled by walls of stelae cut deep with Virgil, scripture and facts from a Victorian geography lesson, which time has worked into its own strange poetry of curiosity: *The carrier pigeon flies at the rate of forty miles per hour.*

The typographical art of these edifying rocks, meant to educate and amaze nineteenth-century tourists, as they gaze out to sea from the cliff tops, are the opposite of Shonks' tombstone and the religious imagery of the Middle Ages: in the past, images spoke to the illiterate, but today and for centuries the literate and illiterate have struggled to unriddle them. We need words to gloss the world and its ideas.

Further along the coastal path are well-chosen lines from Tennyson, who was poet laureate when the letters were cut:

An iron coast and angry waves / You seem to hear them rise and fall / And roar rock thwarted in their bellowing caves / Beneath the windy wall.

I had hoped while in Purbeck to fathom a connection between the carvings on the tomb and the environment, something in them that spoke of the meeting of the sea and rock and man. Here in those bellowing caves man had ventured to quarry stone at great risk, battling the iron coast and the angry waves. This was the Jurassic coast where the stone documents the history of millions of years of life on earth, not only tiny river snails, but Triceratops and Diplodocus and Ichthyosaur. Even prehistoric trees are captured in stone at Lulworth Cove. At the new fossil museum in Kimmeridge, built thanks to the efforts of the visionary collector Steve Etches, I watch a video of an ichthyosaur being painstakingly lifted from the shale, and for a moment those blows from the hammer on the chisel is a sculptor at work, revealing the dragon trapped in a block of marble, a creature from deep time. It is a process as painstaking as carving a tomb out of fossilised snail shells, and I am delighted to learn that Victorian museums employed actual sculptors to clean up the early fossil finds. Perhaps the early masons knew there were figures trapped in the rocks – dragons and flying oxen – waiting to be discovered and given new life.

The masons of Purbeck were known as marblers. They had their own guild or company from the sixteenth century, and possibly as early as the reign of Henry III. Probably the same men who hewed the stone from the bed of rock, roughed out its shape and removed the waste marble, would later carve the cross and figures surrounding it. Occasional mouldings have been unearthed at the farms near the old quarries, which would suggest that some carving took place near to the quarry face. Like carpenters picking out a tree for a particular job, they would choose the stone most suitable to their needs and, wanting to haul as little as possible, they would surely have roughed out the strange hexagon of Shonks' tombstone on the quarry floor, and knocked off as much waste as possible, before fetching the oxen to haul it elsewhere for more detailed work. Traditionally, it was thought that most carving was done on the bankers – the masons' low workbenches – on Corfe Castle's West Street, where thick heaps of scars, the fine chippings from working the stone, have been found. Historians have fretted over these details, but over the 200 years when the marble was at its most popular, it must have been carved at various places according to preference, season, weather and any number of humdrum factors. If they were working on one of the many churches being built in the thirteenth century or helping to build the gatehouse of Corfe Castle or the towers in the curtain wall, their workshop may have moved with them.

I have tried to see if anything on Shonks' tomb was accidental and dictated by the vagaries of the marble. It is now a traditional saying among Haysom's marblers that 'if you can't make a plum make a cherry, if you can't make a cherry, make a berry.' First they would regularise the thickness, wasting away the excess with small chisels. Then they would start at the high points, establishing a system to get the depth right across the tomb. Would they tackle the difficult drapery work on the angels first or last? The cross is in much lower relief than the rest of the carvings; could that have gone wrong initially?

Polishing the carvings and the background surface to make those snail shells shine like marble would have taken longer than all the rest of the masonry. They used stone on stone. At first they had to be fierce, taking a coarse grit, a natural sandstone rubbed with water, to remove the chisel marks, then a fine grit to work out the scratches. A hard day's work would go by quickly with little progress polishing just one of the lobes on the cross fleury. The stone would still be matt, or scratchy, so they worked an even finer stone over the whole surface until it looked like eggshell. Then with fingertips inured by years of this toil, it was time to use snake slip or perhaps cuttlestone. There are medieval accounts from Norwich Cathedral where goose fat is paid for alongside Purbeck marble – was it to lubricate the wheels of the wagons? Or for the final polishing and sealing of the marble? The polishing took longer than the carving, but the result was a remarkable sheen far superior, as any Purbeck marbler would tell you, to real marble. (The sight of white Italian marble in burial grounds 'is enough to put any man against the idea of dying' wrote the marbler Eric Benfield in his 1940s memoir.) At Haysom's quarry there is a small piece of marble carved with leaves, each finished to a different stage of polishing, the two small finished leaves took ten days to polish.

Trev Haysom is not sure that anyone in Purbeck had much to do with Shonks' tombstone – it is too exceptional, not like any of the other simple cross-slabs coming out of the quarries in those years on a medieval production line, but if it was not done on the Isle of Purbeck, it was done by a Purbeck marbler, not just by some local stone carver. It had to be someone used to working with the stone because it is such an unusual and unforgiving material. Strike it too hard with your punch and a bruise will travel down into its depths and spoil the marble.

There were marblers who were working in London on Westminster Abbey. They are given away in the thirteenth-century account books with names like Adam de Corfe. There were also imagers, a step up perhaps in skill from the men making mortars and capstones. Imagers made the Purbeck marble effigies from the time, stones with life-size knights and priests sleeping on their graves. I assumed that effigies were more advanced than cross-slabs, but that of Sir Henry d'Estoke in Wareham Church with his chainmail and drapery and a lion and griffin battling at his feet is one of the finest, but the detailing is not as intricate as on Shonks' slab.

I meet a sculptor friend James Copper for a pint, to ask him about stone, and he tells me that Purbeck marble was a stone with a threat. 'You want a stone that fights back, you want to have a conversation with it, and Purbeck is like that. You have to adapt to it, but you also have to become master of it as well, because sometimes you have to tell the stone what to do. It's a weird thing.'

Talking to James brings home the physicality of the craft. The sheer hard labour of the skill, which – not to glamorise toil – is part of the satisfaction masons must have got from their work. I can see those men standing there at the bankers in all weathers, strong men, perhaps stripped to the waist, shaping that stone with points and flats, taking off the surface, shards flying and drawing blood to the constant timpani of iron on stone. James has a super-stition that if he does not bleed when making a piece it is not any good. You have to take your knuckles off.

The labour in the act is borne out by the experience of modern masons at Salisbury Cathedral, who use traditional tools to restore sections of the Purbeck marble columns. A recent capstone on top of a colonette in the cloister took two months to make by hand, but with modern abrasives. When you have finished a piece of Purbeck marble you do not want to see it again for a long while, is the verdict of one mason. But for the marblers, the process was not monotonous insisted Eric Benfield in his memoir. Benfield baulked at the observation of a passing parson who was watching another stonecutter removing waste off a stone with a punch and a hammer. The parson remarked that it must be boring. The man had no idea of the years of skill and learning that were condensed into that act, wrote Benfield angrily and 'he does not know the interest in making something permanent: a stone that will go into a building and there outlast many generations.'

Whether a roughed-out coffin lid was sent north for further carving by marblers in London or elsewhere, a 370-kilo block of Purbeck marble had to make its way from the south coast of England to a Hertfordshire village some time in the middle of the thirteenth century. There was certainly an established trade in stone from the Isle of Purbeck. Between 1215 and 1235 an estimated 15,000 tonnes of marble was sent to Salisbury where it was used to raise 3,000 columns, some structural, but mostly decorative – the dark marble set off against the lighter freestone of the walls and great weight-bearing pillars. There is a story that when the well-known Purbeck quarryman–fisherman Billy Winspit was taken to Salisbury Cathedral in the last century and saw all the Purbeck marble columns, he exclaimed, 'Nobody's going to tell me there isn't a god.'

The marble was almost certainly shipped to Salisbury up the River Avon, and one of the reasons for the success of Purbeck stone was its proximity to water transport. There are old photographs of the stone workers in Swanage, hauling the stone by cart down slipways into the water at low tide to meet the boats. It is an extraordinary sight – how many blocks were lost to the water and gifted to the sea? In medieval times, it is thought that stone was shipped from the protected harbour at Ower Quay on the north of Purbeck, on the south side of Poole harbour. There today it is a silent mysterious place, accessible only by water or along rights of way across a large private estate. Lines of wooden stumps protrude from the water. The narrow strip of shingle between the fields and the harbour is green with seaweed, and strange oak trees grow horizontally from the bank as if yearning for the water before turning ninety degrees and reaching for the light. How many tens of thousands of tonnes of stone came along here in centuries past? Hauled on sleds across the heath and onto barges, the stone would float out past Furzey Island and the shallows of South Deep, out to the larger seagoing ships. 'The trade in marble coffins with their variously carved lids must have been enourmous,' wrote the local historian Dru Drury in the nineteenth century. 'So much so that one can visualise a steady daily procession of them wending their cumbrous way from Corfe across the heath to Ower Quay, the sweating teams dragging the groaning and creaking carts up and down the sandy track and across streams and skirting the many treacherous areas of bog before reaching their destination at the wooden jetty whence shipment was made to convenient distribution centres. Some weathered blocks are still to be seen here.'

Afloat in a cog and low in the water, clinker-built with a single stepped mast and a side rudder, they would ride the ebb tide an hour before slack water, keeping to South Deep Channel, misleadingly named, but deep enough, shooting for the vast chalk withies of Handfast Point and the English Channel. There a south-westerly and the flood tide would drive them east towards the Needles, steadily following the chalk bedrock, the water gathering at the hull, petrified into white marble filigree, intricate as a shrine. At Durlston Castle, there is a small display of stone and its fossils, not just animals and plants, but currents and ripples of water frozen in time in rock. The surface of the grey sea like the grey stone. The sailors, watching the clouds and the seabirds and the drift of seaweed, plumbing the depths with lead weights. It was a long and hazardous journey to Hertfordshire in 1250.

Maritime historians have looked for evidence of medieval ships in manuscripts, carvings and the seals of ancient ports. I have two red tiles at home bought a few years ago from the little museum at Dunwich on the Suffolk coast. The first shows the twelfth-century seal of the port: a symmetrical, clinker-built ship with high bow and stern, and single side rudder, foreshortened and projecting into the frame around the composition like the wing of St Matthew's angel on Shonks' cross-slab. There are castles fore and aft flying ensigns, a single central mast with a single square sail, which a smiling hooded figure appears to have just furled so they can catch the plentiful fish in the wavy sea beneath the hull. It is a picture of plenty, when Dunwich was a prosperous sea port by night and day, the sun and moon shining in the sky. It is before the great storm silted up the harbour and the bad times came, when they could no longer afford to build sea defences at the foot of the cliffs, and the church and monasteries were consumed by the insatiable sea. The second tile shows the new seal two hundred years later. Now the boat has no mast, no rigging, no castles, and no rudder. There is no sun in the sky, only the moon and stars – night has come to stay. The boat only has room for a doleful-looking king, said to be Edward III. Beneath it is a triangle of stylised waves. I have seen the image before. The seal design looks as if it deliberately apes the designs on grave slabs, as if the artist has drawn a sepulchral monument for the ailing town. The simple boat is the napkin, the king the soul. But most striking are the waves.

Beneath the central demi-angel holding the soul on Shonks' cross-slab is an odd triangular pattern between the angel and the cross. It is unusual and hard to read, and is maybe nothing more than a wavy pattern. The most obvious solution is that they are meant to be the fiery tongues of the Holy Spirit, or they represent clouds beneath an angel in heaven, but the Dunwich seal makes me think of the sea, of the waves beneath the forlorn boat. Perhaps this is the one tiny clue that the marbler who carved Shonks' slab came from the coast, where men wrestled with fish and stones in the waves along an angry coast, where if you needed angels guarding souls, you needed them out at sea, and when you said prayers for the dead they would often be for those lost to the tidal races and wrecked against those rocks that their land and livelihood were built from.

Basic as the ships were that we see on the Dunwich seal and elsewhere, we know that by the thirteenth century several English and French ports commanded vessels that could carry as many as 300 tuns of wine (that's nearly 77,000 gallons), but while the wine trade and the stone trade were well established, the journey was always hazardous along a coastline still littered today with wrecks driven onto the rocks. It was dangerous near the shore with the cliffs leeward, and the winds unpredictable. Coastal winds shoot out over the top of Old Harry Rocks for 100 yards then blow straight down, fierce enough to flatten a small boat. They would hardly enter the Solent from the hazardous west, instead staying well away from the coast and its sandbanks and strange currents, and travelling south-east around the Wight, towards St Catherine's Point where the first medieval lighthouse would be built some three-quarters of a century after Shonks' slab passed that way.

The coast itself would not be recognisable to a modern sailor; it has extended and retreated – the medieval shore at Camber is nearly 2 km inland today. Rivers changed their course – the Ouse between Newhaven and Eastbourne met the sea 3 km east of where it does today. Ports like Southampton and Portsmouth would have been there, but not in the same place. The Cinque Ports then were Hastings, Romney, Hythe, Dover and Sandwich, and this was before the dramatic changes of the later thirteenth century, when storms became stronger and more frequent – Hastings had not been put to the torch by the French, Old Winchelsea was yet to be breached, and the original Dover port at the estuary of the River Dour had not yet silted up. The Roman lighthouse at Dover and the castle at Rochester controlling the Medway are among the few seamarks that a modern sailor would recognise.

By the twelfth century, the marble itself had been shipped as far as Durham for use in the Galilee Chapel, but monuments went mostly to East Anglia and Lincolnshire. Shonks' tomb must have found a berth on a shipment to London, taking harbour at the Cinque Ports to await the tides needed for the journey around the Sussex coast and again into the Thames Estuary. In 1235 the king's representative at Purbeck sent a shipload of marble to London with a William Justise, who was paid £4. 3s. 4d. for the freight. 'God willing, I may send you one shipload before Whitsun and a third if I can find a ship to carry the said stone,' he wrote.

We get even closer to Brent Pelham with a mention in the 1229 Close Rolls of a ship loaded with marble heading for Waltham Abbey. Today, fragments of those marble shafts smashed at the Dissolution of the Monasteries, can still be seen in the walls of the church. To reach the abbey, the boat would have left the Thames south of Walthamstow and taken the River Lee north, although before that the stone must have been transferred from a coastal vessel to a smaller flat-bottomed shute. The Lee was navigable as far as Ware in the thirteenth century, where there was a regular wine and grain trade by river between the Hertfordshire market town and London. In the winter of 1258 Henry sent thirty-four tuns of wine to Westminster, from Cambridge to Ware by land, and from Ware by water to Westminster. That was the easier journey, downriver. Upriver was harder work, pushed by those on board with poles, or pulled from the river bank by men or horses or oxen.

At the port of Ware, the coffin lid would be less than fifteen miles from Brent Pelham. It is not inconceivable that the tiny River Ash, which rises just north of Brent Pelham as a winterbourne filled from the field drains and springs, would have been navigable for some distance upstream from its meeting with the Lee at Ware, maybe even as far as the Hadhams by raft or logboat. The cost of water travel was a mere sixth that of travel by land, so there was a high incentive to keep the ways open.

If the tomb had to go overland from Ware to the Pelhams, the route was well established. Our knowledge of the main medieval road network comes from combining royal itineraries, records of journeys made from universities and religious houses and, most importantly, the Gough Map (an anonymous fourteenth-century road map named for its finder, our old friend Richard Gough). In 1294, a consignment of 'treasure' was taken from Westminster to Norwich overland and, based on the Gough map, the route would have been London – Waltham Abbey – Ware – Barkway – Cambridge – Newmarket – Bury St Edmunds – Thetford – Norwich.

It took twenty-one carts, twenty mounted soldiers and eighteen foot soldiers nine days to make the journey. It is the section from Ware to Barkway we are most interested in, as that route would pass within less than three miles of Brent Pelham. There it would be met by local men with local carts and draught animals.

It is impossible to know for sure. The entire journey might have been overland, especially at a time of war, when the English Channel might be unsafe, but the cost of an overland journey of that distance would have far outweighed the cost of the freight. The mid thirteenth century was a time of relative quiet at sea, a truce with France just about held, so the sea and river journey is more plausible.

The journey only serves to emphasise how special a Purbeck marble tomb was in the thirteenth century: the rarity of the marble, the skill and labour to wrest it from the earth and fashion and polish this most capricious and intractable of stones; not least the cost and difficulty of transporting a heavy coffin lid to a landlocked Hertfordshire village from the manor of Dunshay on the Isle of Purbeck.

A coda: 'Near Studland, on a hillock, is a curious mass of sandstone called the Agglestone; the centre of superstition and legend,' wrote the Dorset artist and book maker Rena Gardiner. The route to this wonder is across a landscape that could still be stalked by dinosaurs.

The rock is astounding, balanced incongruously on a hill in the middle of a flat heath. Up close, it is otherworldly: wrought of Turner's sunsets at sea and ancient stardust, orange bleeding into blood red and luminous green.

Legend says the devil found it on the Isle of Wight and hurled it at Corfe Castle, shining annoyingly in the distance. Before it toppled over, it was called a logan stone, a holy stone, the Devil's Anvil. I cannot get it out of my mind. I have spent too much time thinking about rocks and how they have been forged by the earth, and how the earth is forged of them and how people have taken them from the ground to mark their dead. I am not godly, but later that day, exploring the chancel of St Nicholas Worth Matravers, I pick up the biro left there and request a prayer for the numinous and for the re-enchantment of the world, and then I head home.

Part III

Story

17

Between the facts of experience and the substance of a poem or novel, a creative intelligence has intervened, to transmute the historically real, which is transitory, into the imaginatively real, which, once brought into being, is preserved through the centuries.

—Richard Altick and John Fenstermaker,
1963

536. Three hundred years have passed since the mason carved the slab and Shonks was laid beneath it. *Let's talk of graves, of worms, and epitaphs.* For bones have been piled on top of bones in graves and tombs, and charnels and pits. Bones have been tumbled about and ploughed into fields at Crécy and Towton and Bosworth. In 1348, *a great vapour moved densely and hideously in the clouds, a great number of worms and vermin fell upon the earth so that many died of stench and hardly ten were left alive out of a thousand.* The vicar's pigs have rooted up the Pelham churchyard. Bones are hardly more secure in the walls and floors of the church, where the dead now favour alabaster over marble. Figures and brasses have replaced crosses. They too will pass. The last wolf and the last dragon have been slain in England, although not long ago a dragon was seen aloft over Calais, but you know that.

It rained blood in Rome, and flesh in Liguria.

They battle the parson over tithes, and they ring the bells for the dead, but they ring out of tune. They ring for Sir John Chamberlayne, who sends a red cow before his own coffin as a mortuary for the vicar in Brent Pelham. A century later, the last of the Chamberlaynes passes out of the story, but I have not told you their story yet. Masses are still being said for the souls of Simon de Furneux and his heirs and forebears. The lights are still lit before the altar, but not for much longer. Is Shonks in paradise yet?

Things have been black. Black Death, Black Prince, Black Monks, Black Friars, Black Books, Black Monday and Black Canons. Blackletter books are printed, and Bolingbroke's black arts are practised. Black Douglas falls and his bones are boiled, and a young king rides to Blackheath.

> . . . *let us sit upon the ground*
> *And tell sad stories of the death of kings:*
> *How some have been deposed; some slain in war,*
> *Some haunted by the ghosts they have deposed,*
> *Some poison'd by their wives: some sleeping kill'd*

We have told the bees of so many deaths that purgatory must be full, but no matter, purgatory itself will soon be assailed and will fall as Constantinople fell, as York then Lancaster, then York again fell. Even now, the sounds of the great battles of St Albans can still be heard when the wind is in the right direction. The bodies of two young boys remain entombed under a staircase in a tower. In 1483 *locusts swarm in Italy, afterward a darkening of the sun was seen and then came a great dying so that more than fifty thousand people died.*

Dante went to the afterlife for a final time, and the monks in Ravenna have hidden his bones. The Black Death kills the poet Dafydd ap Gwilym and he is buried by the yew trees in the Cistercian abbey at Strata Florida. Of another poet a scribe writes in the margin of a manuscript 'Of this Cokes tale maked Chaucer na moore'. *Of this Cook's tale made Chaucer no more.* The great poet is dead before the story is done. Death has triumphed. Popes and antipopes are gone to await their last judgement, hoping to behold the Beatific vision, but not before burning the Templars and burning those who deny purgatory. The three living kings have nothing on the three dead.

The seasons pass, and the coastlines change and change again, and ships litter the seabed of the Solent and of the Thames Estuary, and houses and churches sink too, but their bells keep ringing from the deep. In Pelham, the le Grey line fails after 300 years. What else can I tell you? How to convey the passing of time? The untold number of things that have happened while Shonks sleeps – things real and things imagined. I have a note to myself that tells me to be repetitive, to move you, the reader, towards the Reformation, from the birth of purgatory to its death, to give you a history of the crowded afterlife of the fourteenth and fifteenth centuries, to hint at all the battles, all the burnings and hauntings, all the deaths, all the prayers.

Three hundred years have passed, and Shonks has not been forgotten.

And now it is 1536, and the first saints are falling, pulled from their niches and smashed, their torsos sawn into building blocks, the Virgin Mary herself beheaded. Papal seals centuries old are torn from ancient vellum and cast into the sewers, while the tombs of bishops are ransacked for rings and croziers. Books – worst of all books – and wooden statues are used to fuel fires kindled to melt the lead from stained-glass windows and roofs. The Dissolution of the Monasteries (what a word: dis-solution) is just the beginning: in the coming decades, as the Reformation of religion in England gathers pace under Henry VIII's son Edward, anything considered Popish superstition, any image that is in danger of being idolised might be 'defaced, erazed, washt over, or obliterated'.

These last words are those of John Weever, who wrote of Tudor England that the 'Foulest and most inhumane action of those times, was the violation of Funerall Monuments. Marbles which covered the dead were digged up, and put to other uses.' Weever was the erstwhile poet who blessed Shonks' tomb with the epithet 'wondrous strange'. He travelled the country in the early decades of the 1600s gathering material for his great project *Ancient Funeral Monuments*. He wrote that he almost gave up the endeavour because there were not enough surviving monuments after the vandalism of the Tudor Reformations. 'Having found one or two ancient Funeral inscriptions or obliterated sepulchres, in this or that Parish church, I have ridden to ten Parish churches distant from that, and not found one.' The Elizabethan antiquary William Camden, renowned for his survey of Britain, put it even more strongly: 'I cannot without griefe remember, how barbarously, and unchristianly some not long since have offended, yea some *mingendo in patrios ceneres.*' By pissing on the ashes of ancestors. According to the historian, Phillip Lindley, a destruction rate of 90 per cent of medieval sculpture may be 'optimistic'.

We are fortunate to have Shonks' tomb.

Henry VIII may have begat the English Reformation, which stripped and laid waste the monasteries to fill the royal coffers, but he died a Catholic, believing in purgatory and ordering prayers and masses in his will, although not on the scale of his terrified father. It was his son, the boy King Edward VI, who saw the wholesale destruction of the inside of churches under the rule of his protector the Duke of Somerset. The 1547 First Injunction could have done for Shonks' tomb: 'They shall take away, utterly extinct and destroy all shrines, covering of shrines, all tables, candlesticks, trindles or rolls of wax, pictures, paintings, and all other monuments of feigned miracles, pilgrimages, idolatry and superstition: so that there remain no memory of the same in walls, glass windows, or elsewhere within their churches or houses.'

We do not know if the superstitions and stories about Shonks already clung to his sepulchre, but the iconography of the Four Evangelists would have been in trouble in the 1540s, and more so the 'usual aspect' of the soul, those little praying hands. That idea, those words that began so many epitaphs *Orate Pro Anima*, pray for the soul, had to be expunged as superstitious nonsense, particularly after 1549 when chantries for praying for the dead were dissolved and the whole notion of purgatory was officially abolished in England. Now, all of a sudden, the dead went straight to paradise, or to the other place. There was no longer any need to buy indulgences from the church that promised to shorten your suffering in purgatory – a practice which had become so money-grabbing and corrupt that it had fuelled the Protestant Reformation. The villain Bosola in John Webster's *Duchess of Malfi*, posing as a tomb maker, cracks a joke about the change in tombs: 'Princes' images on their tombs do not lie, as they were wont, seeming to pray up to heaven; but with their hands under their cheeks, as if they died of the tooth-ache. They are not carved with their eyes fix'd upon the stars, but as their minds were wholly bent upon the world.'

Someone must have taken chisel and bolster to Shonks' tomb to efface the offending details, and it looks like someone did, the faces of the angels have been crudely erased, and the hands held together in prayer are damaged, severed at the wrist. The whole surface of the tomb has been chipped and cracked, layers chiselled from the tendrils of flame, the dragon's snout hacked off. There is accidental damage and freeze–thaw damage, but it is not just the wreck of time, and it fits the pattern of how other tombs were attacked by the fervent, the thuggish, or the thieves of brass plates, who in the historian Richard Rex's phrase, were reformers who found a happy coincidence between their spiritual and their material interests. Some were simply doing as their betters instructed, others were relatives or parishioners removing the forbidden so as to protect monuments from complete destruction or removal.

Cross-slabs across the country were turned upside down in church pavements to hide their offending imagery. The antiquary Henry Keepe in his history of York wrote powerfully that many stone coffins and monuments were 'made the receptacles for rain water, mangers for horses, hog troughs to feed swine; and the lintel of many a noted senator or other deserving person [was] laid on the coping of some old wall'. And these were the lucky ones, at least they might be found again one day; many others were broken up for rubble. Little wonder that even in Purbeck most of the stones that have survived are broken fragments.

Some damaged images were deliberately left by the iconoclasts as a reminder that the old faith was dead, which may not always have had the intended effect. As historians of the period have pointed out, some of the damaged statues became even more powerful talismans with their scars. Shonks' tomb was lucky to escape with just a few, and it is these scars that are the first time that the tomb speaks to us since its making.

The tomb survived, and stories about Piers Shonks must have survived too, although the reformers were not partial to stories about knights and heroes. Such legends, passed down by word of mouth became associated with popishness after the Reformation. The Puritan William Fulke compared purgatory to 'the arguments of those vain fables that were wont to be printed in English of Bevis of Hampton, Guy of Warwick, and such like, where the arguments show how such a knight overcame such a Giant, how such a sorcerer wrought such a miracle, which are rolled as confidently as though they were true, and yet there is no man of mean wit so ignorant, but he knoweth them to be feigned fantasies'.

Plenty of people of great wit thought such stories were true, or saw the truths in them, and they passed the stories of Piers Shonks from father to daughter, mother to son. Then in 1596 John Norden arrived in Brent Pelham with his pen. He noticed a most ancient monument in the wall of the church.

Norden was a surveyor, who in the late 1590s embarked on an ambitious project to map and describe the counties of England. He called it *Speculum Britanniae*, literally the *Looking Glass of Britain*. After he had demonstrated the usefulness of his project by producing a volume on Middlesex, the Privy Council issued him with a warrant instructing people to assist him. It was also something he could show suspicious locals. England was still at war with Spain and, although the Armada had been defeated in 1588, there were other lesser-known invasion threats in the years that followed. The fear of outsiders was at a high pitch. In nearby Buntingford, government agents had shut down disreputable alehouses as places of possible sedition. Even without the suspicion of strangers, I imagine that locals may have been wary of outsiders turning up to survey maps and ask questions about the local area. Did Norden acquire the warrant because he had had difficulties elsewhere? A few years later, John Weever would be chased out of churches by suspicious church-wardens as he tried to record the inscriptions. Hertfordshire was the sixth county he surveyed. While we cannot say for certain that he visited Brent Pelham, his is the earliest known reference to the tomb, and Norden was unlikely to have copied it from elsewhere as he did with other entries for which the sources can be identified. It is also an uncharacteristically long entry. Typically, he gives only a map reference or a brief comment such as the one for nearby Hadham 'called Hadham *magna* where the Bishop of London has an auncient house.' Even more typically, he tries to guess at the meaning of the place name. His description of Stevenage merely tells us that that name derives from 'the steep standing of it on the edge of a hill'. In all, he wrote 192 entries, of which nearly 130 were no more than just a grid reference to his map, an alternative place name or an – entertainingly spurious – etymology. Another twenty-six have just a single line. The Brent Pelham entry is one of the remaining thirty-six more substantial descriptions, which were largely antiquarian.

What Norden was doing has been called chorography, or describing in detail the part of a whole, by which is meant describing parts of Britain through its rivers, and place names and archaeology. In practice, chorographers were more interested in the past than the present, and this was especially true of Norden. 'The only roads that interested him were Roman roads,' observes his biographer Frank Kitchen, and it serves to characterise his work and his leanings.

Norden had been working in the county just north of the Pelhams since the early 1590s as surveyor of Sir John Spencer's estates in Barley, and may well have known the tomb by 'common fame' and had ample opportunity to visit it along the same road that William Cole would use some 150 years later. He relied heavily on local knowledge, because when he was criticised for getting place names wrong in an earlier part of the *Speculum*, he responded by blaming the locals, who through their 'simplicitie or partialitie, may miscarry the most provident observer . . . and what I observe is from them, if the thing be hidden (as some time it is) from mine one view'.

Did one of these locals boast of Shonks' tomb? Or did Norden simply encounter it while using the church tower to survey the countryside? Christopher Saxton, Norden's main predecessor as a map-maker, was also given a warrant by the Privy Council that was more specific than Norden's, it read: 'see him conducted unto any towre, Castle, highe place or hill to view that countrey, and that he be accompanied with ii or iii honest men such as do best know the cuntry for the better accomplishment of that service.' It is likely that Norden operated in a similar fashion. Historians have argued about the method he used to make his maps: did he take sightings from high points to construct triangles on a baseline, then use simple geometry to measure distances, or did he physically traverse the landscape measuring from point to point? Whichever method he used he is likely to have followed the basic advice to all surveyors of the period: 'Go to a high place', but the evidence leans towards triangulation, which means he would definitely have climbed the steps and ladders of a lot of church towers. So it is surprising that he did not write about more funeral monuments – Shonks' is the only tomb described in the entire description of the county. If he spoke to anyone about it or about the legends of Shonks, they must not have been forthcoming or perhaps he chose not to report the tales they told. Instead, he simply gave a description.

In the walles of this church lyeth a moste auncient monument, a stone wherein is figured a man, and about him an Eagle, a Lyon, and a Bull hauing all winges, and a fourth the shape of an Angel, as if they should represent the foure Euangelistes: vnder the feete of the man is a crosse Flourie, and vndr the crosse a Serpent, he is thought to be sometime the Lord of an auncient decayed place, wel moated not farre from this place called SHONKES.

Before it was published as *Speculum Britanniae Pars: The description of Hartfordshire* in 1598, Norden presented a manuscript copy to his patron William Cecil, Lord Burghley, the queen's chief minister, it was in a limp vellum binding tied with green silk. The elderly Burghley hurriedly wrote 'Hartfordshire' on the front. There is only a tatty remnant of the green silk now hanging from that creased and blotted cover. The thin old leather has worn away at the corners. Creased and stiffened, it opens with reluctance to reveal the cockled pages. The first impression I got as MS.521 was removed from its archival case at Lambeth Palace Library was how small it is: only thirty-nine sheets thick and roughly the size of an A5 sheet of paper.

I rarely passed up an opportunity or excuse to look at an original document during my search for Piers Shonks, because you never know what you might find. Here the revelation was the map of Hertfordshire, on vellum across two pages, drawn and hand-painted by John Norden himself for Lord Burghley. Its margins are black with handling.

The symbols and lettering are very tiny and not easy to make out even with a magnifying glass. There is no key, but we know from his earlier survey some of the symbols he used for such things as market towns, castles, watermills, battle sites and beacons. There is no Shonks Moat, but Beeches is mapped for the very first time. There is Stoken Pelham, Pelham Furnix and Burnt Pelham written above a church, a smudge of light green below, and some strokes of the pen that might be symbols are to the immediate left of the church. I get excited; immediately over-interpreting them. One is a single large uncoloured tree. What great tree once stood in that country? A yew tree? Alongside the tree: a sort of scribble I can find nowhere else on the map unless it is the same as the hurried cartoon of lines by *Dane end*, which is meant to represent a battle. What battle ever took place near Burnt Pelham? I have inclined my head and zoomed into my photographs and tried to see a dragon in those pencil marks. Had the locals been regaling Norden with their stories after all?

18

In lapidary inscriptions a man is not upon oath

—Samuel Johnson, 1775

Things not written down 'slip away and wither as the sin of forgetfulness triumphs', the old Chronicle of Byland Abbey warned its monks. I like the idea that forgetfulness is a sin, that we have a moral obligation to remember our ancestors back through the generations: what was your great-grandfather's name and what did he do with his life? Most of us do not know, and most of us in turn will soon be forgotten. We should remember the old stories. *Tell ye your children of it, and let your children tell their children, and their children another generation.*

The sin of forgetfulness might well have triumphed over Shonks if it hadn't been for a jaundiced, foxed and seemingly liver-marked sheet of parchment, bound upside down at the back of Brent Pelham's eighteenth-century parish register. The sheet is now the rear free endpaper and the first of several pages of unrelated memoranda. It is battered at the long edges, and the bottom third is speckled like eggshell with ink from another page which no longer partners it, or perhaps because it was once honoured as a blotting pad. The top of the page is covered in writing, which begins: 'A Coppy of ye Inscription wch. was formerly over ye monument of Pierce Shonkes in ye North wall of ye Parish church of Brent Pelham, who departed this life Ano Dom: 1086.'

At the foot of the page, it is signed Tho: Tingge vicar.

Reverend Thomas Tingge's handwriting is a neat and legible italic with remnants of an older hand in the abbreviation 'y^e', (the 'y' is not a 'y' but the old character *thorn*, for the 'th' sound) and in the long *esses* and double *effs* (which are simply an old way of writing a capital 'F'.) His 'e's in the middle of words are backwards, and at the end are like rounded capital 'E's. I like his 'b's and especially his 'd's with their lovely big loops like the bights of ropes hitching them to other letters. As he reached the end of the verses, he loaded his nib again and the final lines stand out glossy black above his signature.

He gives us two inscriptions in Latin followed by English renderings:

> Cadmi ffama manet tantum tua ffama Georgi
> Posthuma, Tempus edax ossa, sepulchra vocat:
> Attamen hoc Tumulo, Shonkus qui perdidit anguem,
> Invito Satane, caute sepultus erat.

> Cadmus his ffame, St George his ffame alone remains
> Their Tombes & Ashes all are gone:
> But Shonks who valiantly ye serpent wounded,
> In spite of Satan, here he lyes entombed.

or thus:

> Tantum ffama manet Cadmi Sanctiqe Georgi
> Posthuma, Tempus edax ossa, sepulchra vocat;
> Hoc tamen in muro tutus, qui perdidit Anguem,
> Invito positus Demonae Shonkus erat.

> Nothing of Cadmus nor St George, those Names
> Of Great renown, survives them but their ffames:
> Time was soe sharp sett as to make noe bones

Of theirs, nor of their monumentall stones:
But Shonkes one serpent kills, tother defies,
And in this wall as in a fortress lyes.

It is undated, but we can guess that Tingge was writing at the end
of the 1600s, a century after John Norden first wrote about the tomb.
His note appears in the second volume of the parish register, which
was used for baptisms, marriages and burials from 1690 to 1773.
Tingge became vicar in 1693, but notes on the reverse of the inscription page and the one following, about tithes and parishioners and
the walnut tree in the churchyard, date from 1697. Henry Chauncy
reproduced the verses in his *The Historical Antiquities of Hertfordshire*,
published three years later. So we can guess at a rough date.

Are the verses an epitaph, a poem, or a riddle? Perhaps all three.
They allude to the dragon-slayers Cadmus and St George, and to
Shonks' own wounding or slaying of a serpent. They also introduce

189

the plot twist that Shonks defied another serpent, or even the devil. The second of the Latin verses is better, and that could be why there are two different versions – one simply refining and superseding the other. Perhaps Tingge was given the first inscription and decided to append his own, or the inscriptions had been preserved orally, and these were variants based on memory, or one or more authors drafted different versions of the lines. Too many 'or's. It could be the same person writing out the same thing four times, twice in English and twice in Latin, which would have been a normal school exercise for the time. Perhaps the most striking difference between them is the emphasis on the wall burial in the second epitaph: 'And in this wall as in a fortress lyes'. Could this be a clue that the tomb had been placed in the wall between the writing of the two verses, or that the position in the wall had become a more important element of the legend?

They were said to be 'formerly over the tomb', but hardly since its beginnings. Neither are likely to be thirteenth-century, although there is nothing in them that could not have been written in the Middle Ages. However, although most monuments had inscriptions, by 1300 they were short and formulaic. Elaborate classical Latin verses in hexameter, with biographical details and references to classical texts such as the Ancient Greek dragon-slayer Cadmus did not become fashionable until much later, and were associated with the period after the Reformation, when man's relationship with the afterlife and the purpose of tombstones had been turned upside down.

As we have seen, the main purpose of a medieval tomb was to ask for intercession for the dead – for people to pray for them in purgatory. Occasionally, they were also intended to be a memento mori, reminding passers-by that *as I am so you shall be*. And an inscription often began with the well-known *Orate Pro Anima* . . . Pray for the soul of . . .

A crucial change in the perceived purpose of funeral monuments occurred somewhere about the middle of the sixteenth century, says the historian Richard Rex in his study of epitaphs, 'a change which centred on the concept of remembering the dead'. Rex says that it can hardly be emphasised too strongly that in the Middle Ages the memory that the monument was meant to perpetuate was of a very different nature to that which appears under the Tudors. The art historian Erwin Panofsky stated it most succinctly: post-Reformation funerary monuments were about commemoration and no longer about preparation for the afterlife.

Before 1500, it was exceptionally rare to find a personal fact as simple as a date of birth, but now the dead were remembered as individuals, and inscriptions began to record their life and works. In the new world after the Reformation the dead were gone, they were no longer hanging around in purgatory, there was no point speaking directly to them or repeating the obit mass on the anniversary of their death. Secular memory, recording what you did in life – if you killed a dragon or defied the devil for instance – was now the key to a new kind of immortality. But the new epitaphs were not just filling the gap left by the old, Rex says that the same change can be seen on the Catholic continent. Renaissance humanism, with its emphasis on the individual, on virtue and glory and fame, also played its part. By 1480, English began to compete with Latin and within fifty years had triumphed. Only those who wanted to claim a certain educational or social standing still used classical Latin.

The Shonks verses were written at a time when a monument, in John Weever's words, was a 'thing erected, made, or written, for a memoriall of some remarkable action, fit to bee transferred to future posterities'. They were Elizabethan inventions, and if the carvings tell us what the tomb meant in 1250, the epitaphs are a clue to what the tomb meant in the late sixteenth century.

They are hardly great poetry, but in their favour, is their pithiness. The writer George Puttenham wrote *Of the poeme called Epitaph used for memoriall of the dead* in his 1589 *Arte of English Poesie*, praising those that were done with in a few verses that were 'pithie, quicke and sententious for the passer by to peruse, and iudge vpon without any long tariaunce'. By contrast he pours scorn on 'long and tedious discourses' that take 'halfe a dayes leasure to reade', and claims that he was once locked into a cathedral by the sexton because it took him so long to read someone's overblown epitaph.

The Shonks ones read like verses from the emblem books that were so popular in the Elizabethan period. These were rarely more than doggerel, and sought to give a moral to allegorical pictures of scenes from the Bible or classical authors such as Ovid and Pliny. The practice of writing verses to find the meaning in an object became widespread and an everyday gentlemanly accomplishment. A tomb seems an ideal topic for such word games. In her 1948 book on emblems, Rosemary Freeman wrote that it was natural for an Elizabethan man 'to scratch an emblematic poem on his friend's window pane, taking the brittleness of the glass for his "picture" and his theme'. Was it also natural to take an old tomb for a theme and set up an emblem above it? One writer of a popular emblem book from the period was the very learned Dr Andrew Willett, rector of Barley, seven miles north of Brent Pelham. His *Sacrorum Emblematum Centuria Una* comprised 100 emblems written to elucidate biblical passages. Like the inscription on Shonks' tomb they were written in English and Latin. Was the inscription just someone in the late 1500s looking at the grave slab set on its plinth in the wall and playing at emblem writing? Emblems are an interaction between word and image, something we see again and again in the Shonks' story, and yet they would normally describe the whole image, not just part of it. Where in the verses are the soul, the cross, the symbols of the Evangelists? The inscription over Shonks' tomb refers to only two visible elements: the carving of the dragon and the tomb's position in the church wall. Where does the second serpent spring from? The writer of the verses was not just describing the carvings: they must have known an old tradition about the tomb and its occupant, a story already told about someone called Shonks and handed down through the generations in the fields and by the firesides of Brent Pelham.

It was the county historian Nathaniel Salmon in 1728, who claimed that the Reverend Raphael Keene put these traditions into verse and set them over the tomb. 'The writing upon the Wall is modern,' wrote Salmon. 'Said to be done by a Vicar about a hundred Years ago, perhaps the long-lived *Keen*.' Salmon also surmised that Keene placed the tomb in the wall. Various authorities have insisted that the plinth and the setting are Tudor. And this would make sense when we consider the proclamation issued in the third year of Elizabeth's reign to repair any monument 'already spoiled in any Church, or Chapell, now standing'.

This was 1560, and Keene had already been vicar of Brent Pelham for twenty of the seventy-five years and six months he would famously spend in the incumbency. Keene administered to his flock through the reigns of six monarchs, a period that saw all the religious upheavals of the Reformation. He was popular enough after forty years as incumbent that one Jesper Wright had his son baptised Raphael on 12 June 1579. In all, during his years in office, six of his flock opted to name their child after the vicar, eight in total if we count Keene's third son and first grandson. It does not seem very many for such a long time, but Raphael was never a popular name in England and perhaps taking the name of one of the three archangels was especially dubious in the sixteenth century, when the saints and angels of the old religion were cast out of the churches.

Salmon was not sure about the authorship: 'The *English* might be of his Composition, but the *Latin* may have been put up long before, which I am the rather inclined to believe.' I like to think that Keene was the author, and as such, a man with a deep interest in the folk and their stories. A Hertfordshire Robert Kirk perhaps. Kirk was the Scottish Episcopalian minister who recorded the fairy-lore of his flock in the latter half of the seventeenth century, and 'threw his arms wide to enfold the beliefs of his parishioners, who collected the lore of the people, who was fascinated by their concept of faery . . . treated popular custom and opinion – and superstition – as worthy of intellectual interest and genuine respect.' It would be wonderful if Keene had all these attributes that the writer Marina Warner ascribes so warmly to Kirk and would help us understand how the legend of Shonks survived those years and prospered.

But Keene is an unlikely candidate for the Latin. It is difficult to conceive that a country priest of that period could have managed it, especially the second version. Ministers in the middle of the sixteenth century were notoriously ignorant. In 1551 only 168 of the 311 clergy in the diocese of Gloucester could recite something as basic as the Ten Commandments. Thirty-four of them did not know who wrote the Lord's Prayer, and ten could not even recite it. And in the diocese of Canterbury later in the century only 18 per cent of ministers were university educated. It appears that Keene was originally only the parish clerk and was not actually ordained until the 1560s. Since Brent Pelham was only worth £7 a year, it was not a benefice likely to attract an accomplished incumbent. There is little Latin in his parish register and scant sign of an imagination. His entries are terse and without comment, except on a single occasion when he refers to a woman uncharitably as a base child. They follow the same pattern throughout: 'Johan Larke, the daughter of Thomas Larke, was christened the xviiith day of March 1538'. His only Latin appears in the five marginal notes he made during his long incumbency: Henricus Rex, Edwardus Rex, Maria Regina, Elizabeth Regina and finally Jacobus Rex. Even the entry for his own wife's burial goes unglossed '1598 Anne Keene, the wife of Raphael Keene, clerk, was buried the xxth day of March'. But it is unfair to judge a man on so little evidence.

The Latin is more likely the work of someone who had a reasonable grounding in classical Latin verse and prosody, although it is fairly clumsy, and at best, grammar-school Latin. A better candidate for authorship would be Father Bennett, that is Thomas Bennett, the steward of the manor court who kept the manorial records in Latin for the Parker family, owners of the manor in the sixteenth century. If not Father Bennett, then someone else from the same household. William Parker, Baron Morley and Monteagle was something of a scholar and could well have been interested in the tomb and tales about Piers Shonks. Parker was also a prominent Catholic, a dangerous Catholic even. He sided with Essex in his rebellion against Queen Elizabeth and was said to favour Spanish military intervention to restore the old faith. (He is also the Monteagle who supposedly authored the Monteagle letter that alerted Parliament to the Gunpowder Plot and in so doing returned to royal favour.)

It is interesting to note that the inscription contains all those elements of popular Catholicism that survived the Reformation, according to the historian Ronald Hutton – death, salvation, miracles, prodigies, heroic action and moral behaviour. Was Shonks meant to step into the shoes of the saints as an example to people? Was his tomb intended to elicit prayer? Though purgatory no longer officially existed, it is the prayers for the dead that took the longest to abate.

It is hard to conceive of this as a deliberate Catholic inscription, but it might be taken as a thumb of the nose to the reformers and the iconoclasts of the previous generation, and in that sense it may be at least in part polemical, an attack on Protestant sacrilege of tombs. Shonks killed one serpent in life, but his second battle had been against those intent on destroying his tomb and his memory, our collective memories, our stories. And the mere survival of his tomb through the Dissolution and the Reformation was his second victory. Was the author boasting that he had defied the reformers? By the second demon or devil in the inscription are we meant to think of someone like Edward VI's Lord Protector Edward Seymour, or a local 'devil' who was keen to erase the superstitious memory of Shonks and see the sin of forgetfulness triumph?

The main message of both versions is a strange boast: that time has erased the bones and tombs of the likes of Cadmus and St George. They only have fame, whereas Shonks has fame and a monument to memorialise the fact that he killed a serpent as well as to protect his bones. The Greek heroes are scattered to the winds, but Shonks has found safe harbour. (In truth, St George's remains supposedly did survive. He was said to have a tomb at Lydda, in present-day Israel, where a church was built over it. Many of his relics were preserved, his head at Rome was lost and then found in 751 CE, and more relics were brought back from the Holy Land by Robert of Flanders at the beginning of the twelfth century.)

The medievalist James Binns has pointed out that the allusion to Cadmus may have a double meaning. As well as being a drag-on-slayer, Cadmus was renowned for giving the alphabet to the Greeks, as the inventor of writing. Could the poem be saying that while time consumes everything, writing endures and thus reputations are preserved? The only recognisable Latin tag is *Tempus edax [rerum]* – 'Time which consumes [things]' – which, like the legend of Cadmus, is from Ovid's *Metamorphoses*.

Epitaphs on this sort of theme were not uncommon in the period. The most famous are the two epitaphs on Sir Thomas Stanley's monument at Tong in Shropshire, which some think were written by William Shakespeare. One of them reads:

Not Monumentall Stone Preserves Our Fame,
Nor Sky Aspyring Piramids Our Name.
The Memory of Him for Whom This Stands
Shall Outlyve Marbl and Defacers' Hands.
When All To Tymes Consumption Shall be Geaven,
Standley For Whom This Stands Shall Stand In Heaven

The theme, as well as the six lines of rhyming couplets in iambic pentameter are uncannily reminiscent of the second English version of Shonks' second epitaph in English. There was a trend for epitaphs in Shakespeare's day that stressed the durability of the written word and the enduring reputation of the dead person in contrast to the vulnerability of their physical remains and their tomb. This is hardly surprising after what had happened to so many monuments during the sixteenth century. The Shonks inscription is certainly testament to the power of the written word and of storytelling. It energised and renewed the legends. As for the tomb and Shonks' bones, they were more vulnerable than the author realised, because they would soon have to defy even more devils.

In 1643, as England was rocked by civil war, a long battle was being fought not just on the moors, heaths and downs of England but in her churches. One salvo landed on Saffron Walden a few miles north of the Pelhams and is remembered in a bill sent to the churchwarden of St Mary's, Saffron Walden, for £2. 19*s*. It was William Dowsing's 'fee' for removing seven score and 18lb of brasses from the grave stones 'by an Ordenaunce of Parliament', among them a tablet commemorating the slaying of a cockatrice by a 'valorous Knight'. A pamphlet of 1669 records what happened: 'In these late times of Rebellion, it being taken for a Monument of Superstition was by the lawless souldiers broken in pieces, to show they were also of a venemous Nature as well as the *Cockatrice*.'

Such superstitious inscriptions were specifically targeted in the

Puritan war against idolatry and popishness. In their attack on the 'popish' innovations of Archbishop Laud, they set about completing the destruction of the earlier Reformation. We don't know if the zealous Dowsing or others of his ilk visited the Pelhams, but if a memorial to the slaying of a cockatrice – improbably half chicken and half dragon – was suspect, then words commemorating the slaying of a serpent must also have been at risk. If Dowsing or his soldiers didn't remove the inscription commemorating Shonks' valorous deeds, somebody did, because when Thomas Tingge recorded it in the 1690s, he did so because it was no longer on the tomb. It was *formerly* over the monument. The inscription had enjoyed about half a century to work its effect on posterity before Shonks was once again in the midst of a new struggle between memory and forgetting.

Between 1630, when Weever published his *Funeral Monuments*, and 1720, when Gough published his *Sepulchral Monuments*, some two-thirds of the monumental brasses in Hertfordshire, which had survived the Reformation, were lost to the Puritans' renewed attack on images and the vestiges of the old religion. They also had to contend with the wanton destruction of parliamentary troops, who were not averse to pillaging tombs and turning out the bones to hurl through stained-glass windows. Other attacks on images were more calculated and precise. Many brasses were removed or defaced by Dowsing, who was commissioned to implement the parliamentary ordinance of 1643 in East Anglia, requiring the removal of 'all crucifixes, crosses, and all images and pictures of any one or more persons of the Trinity or of the Virgin Mary and all other images and pictures of saints or superstitious inscriptions in or upon all and every church.' If that didn't cause enough destruction, on 8 May 1644, Lords and Commons approved 'An ordinance for the further demolishing of monuments of idolatry and superstition', including a list of things to be removed or defaced 'representations of angels, superstitious vestments, roodlofts, holy-water stoups and organs together with their cases and frames'. It explicitly speaks of 'images in stone, wood, glass and of images on church plate or other things used in worship of God'.

Monuments – as much as crucifixes and stained glass – were at risk from the desecrators and zealots acting in the name of the law. *Eikon Basilike* published ten days after the beheading of Charles I, and thought by many to have been written by the king himself, bemoaned 'the defacing of Monuments, and Inscriptions of the dead, which served but to put posterity in mind . . . are the effects of popular, specious, and deceitful Reformations'.

At Gazeley in Suffolk, the inscriptions on eleven slabs and on 'the back wall of a table tomb' were removed, and Dowsing noted in his journal that at Linton in January 1644 he gave orders to deface two gravestones. We know that he was active in the area around the Pelhams. It is impossible to say whether the damage done to Shonks' tomb was during the Reformation or during this later period of iconoclasm. Dowsing's work has been described as forensic rather than wanton. It would have been like his kind to cut off those little hands and remove the faces of the angel, leaving the rest intact. With its superstitious elements and its reference to St George, the inscription would not have sat well with this coldly destructive man, who believed he was doing God's work.

The Parliamentary ordinances specifically protected monuments that were not *commonly reputed or taken* for those of a saint. But images that were instructional of the old ways or a distraction to worship were destroyed. I can picture a struggle over Shonks. This was no ordinary tomb, but was it the tomb of a local saint? Was there a danger that the villagers would worship him? Was there popishness in its message? Was it okay to idolise local heroes? Was the inscription superstitious?

Thanks to the Reverend Tingge, the verses survived, and when Nathaniel Salmon published his county history in 1728, he wrote that the second verse was now over the tomb. William Cole drew it in situ in 1743. Later drawings show that it was changed again to make the English the main text, probably after the major restoration of the church in the 1860s. The inscription today appears to be the same as the one photographed at the turn of the twentieth century, stencilled onto a timber panel on the back of the wall in the arched recess.

O. PIERS. SHONKS

Who Died. Anno 1086
Nothing of Cadmus nor St George, those names ~
Of great Renown survives them but their fames; ~
Time was so sharp set, as to make no Bones
Of theirs, nor of their monumental Stones,
But Shonke one Serpent kills, tother defies,
And in this Wall as in a fortress lies.

Above, at an angle, in the left-hand corner are the first two lines of Latin:

Tantum Fama manet, Cadmi Sanctiq; Georgi
Posthuma, Tempus edax Ossa, Sepulchra vocat;

And in the right-hand corner the last two lines.

Hoc tamen in muro tutus, qui perdidit Anguem,
Invite, positus, Demonæ Shonkus erat.

There be of them, that have left a name behind them, that their praises might be reported . . . and their glory shall not be blotted out however hard the iconoclasts might try.

19

There was a young man of Brent Pelham,
When dragons were rife, who would fell 'em;
Since when there has been
Not the breath of one seen,
With such lasting success did he quell 'em.

—M. Tomkins, *Hertfordshire Countryside*, 1962

O ver the chancel screen in Brent Pelham church, there used to sit an unusual royal coat of arms from the reign of Charles I; unusual because it was carved on both sides so that the unicorn and lion had two heads, Janus-like, looking back and looking ahead, at the old religion and the new. 'They were quite unique,' wrote Reverend Woolmore Wigram. 'They stood on the screen and were to be looked at from the East & the West both; so they were constructed (like the Nineveh Bulls) with two faces each, and the Unicorn, necessarily, with two horns. And a very remarkable couple they formed.' The arms were erected in 1634, a date that commemorated the centenary of Henry VIII's Act of Supremacy, which began the Reformation in England. Coats of arms in churches often replaced the rood, or cross, and the accompanying statues of saints, which would have sat atop the screen dividing the chancel from the nave. They represent the line that divides the people either side of it from the visual and symbolic culture of Catholicism and the more austere culture of the Anglican Church.

Henry Bourne in his *Antiquities of the Common People* first published in 1725 explains vulgar superstitions as 'the invention of indolent Monks' who 'having nothing else to do, were the forgers of many silly and wicked opinions, to keep the world in awe and ignorance'. He may have been right, but how many folk beliefs came about because the symbols and rites of the old religion were forgotten (and there were no more monks to make sense of them)? It is not surprising that within a generation or two, men like Richard Gough, in their alienation from the exequies and terrors of a medieval death, which they dismissed as popish humbug, would misconstrue the imperative of a tomb like Shonks'. As for the uneducated, once they no longer grasped the old meanings of the carvings on Shonks' tomb, they took one look at the mysterious object and came to the obvious conclusion about its occupant – he must have killed the dragon pictured on it. After all, being slain was the generally accepted part played by dragons in the stories they had heard. In the *Golden Legend*, over a dozen saints have to overcome a dragon that is ravaging their neighbourhood.

If a monument must arouse a reaction from passers-by, what a reaction the tomb must have given at the time it was made. It is testament to the art of the mason that it has never lost its power to speak to people across the divide marked by that Janus-faced coat of arms – even once they no longer understood what it was saying. We can easily see why a dragon-slaying legend arose from the symbolic dragon carved on the tomb. There are often three stages in the life cycle of a folk legend: a mysterious object, the story that explains the mysterious object, and finally those who come along and try to explain the story.

The mysterious object might be a part of the landscape, like the Knucker Hole in Lyminster, Sussex, that probably inspired the story of a water-dwelling monster, or an object like the supposed thigh bone of the giant Jack O'Legs at Weston, or a tombstone such as the sixteenth-century one at Broad Hinton in Wiltshire where the damaged effigy of Sir Thomas Wroughton led to the legend that his hands withered and fell off after he threw a bible onto the fire – and if that were not punishment enough, all his children were apparently born without hands too. Many objects became mysterious as the medieval world and its codes faded away.

It is unlikely, but Shonks may have been slaying dragons in tales told long before the Reformation, and the story may have come about for reasons other than the mysterious object and its carvings. The mysterious object need not start the legend, but instead modify it and perpetuate it. In Shonks' case, the dragon-slaying story was at the very least given a helping hand by the inscription above the tomb. The inscription tells us that Shonks *perdidit anguem*, that is, he destroyed a serpent, and it associates him with St George, patron saint of England, most famous of dragon-slayers, and with Cadmus, the founder of Greek Thebes who killed a dragon and ingeniously sowed its teeth to raise an army.

Shonks has something else in common with St George: nobody associated either the saint or our hero with a dragon for many years. Writers had attested to George's martyrdom for centuries before the *Golden Legend* gave him a dragon to fight. Nobody paid much attention to that great killjoy Pope Clement VII's ruling that St George never did slay a dragon. The saint had been slaying them for too long by then, even in the villages around the Pelhams. Seven miles to the south in Bishop's Stortford, a canvas dragon on a wooden frame was operated by revellers during festivities and hired out to other villages. It must have come off particularly badly in the battles of 1482 when one William Northach was paid fourpence for 'mending the dragon'. It may even have been at large in the Pelhams, because we know it was leased to neighbouring parishes. In 1504, the churchwardens charged 4*d.* when it appeared 'in the Braughing playe'. The last we hear of it was in an inventory of church property some seventy years later, when it was said to have been sold, but 'w'owte the assent of the parisshoners ther'.

Though back into storyland giants have fled, / And the knights are no more and the dragons are dead.

The earliest account of a skirmish involving Piers Shonks has him slay a giant, with not a dragon or serpent in sight. When William Cole visited in 1743, he was told that Shonks killed, not a dragon, but an imp: 'the commonly known Tradition in the Parish which I have heard from many people there; that is that this Piers Shonk on a certain time accidentally met with a young Devil or Imp which he killed'. As time went by, the mysterious object with its dragon carving began to pull the story into shape. Edward Brayley in his *Beauties of England and Wales* published in 1808 says that the carvings on the tomb are the origins of a traditional tale in which the person buried there killed a serpent. Eventually, in 1827, in the weekly *Mirror of Literature*, we read about an actual dragon, and the story is fleshed out a little by the correspondent identified only as S. W. W.

In the time of Shonkes, a dragon infested these parts, annoying the inhabitants by destroying their cattle, &c. so that they were greatly troubled, and possessed no means of extirpating the enemy. In time, however, Shonkes stood forth, as the champion of the neighbourhood; and offered to kill the dragon or perish. He went armed with a bow and arrows, and accompanied by his two favourite dogs, sought the dragon and found him upon a hill (from thence called Shonkes' hill) about a quarter of a mile from the church. The dogs attacked the dragon and Shonkes contrived to wound him in a mortal part with an arrow, of which the dragon died. The dogs, however, were killed; and he himself wounded.

The folklorist Katharine Briggs offers an explanation for this fleshing out when she explains what happens when the distinction between folk legends and folk tales is forgotten: 'Folk Narrative is folk fiction, told for edification, delight or amusement, Folk Legend was once believed to be true . . . A difficulty arises when these tales are handed on by people who no longer believe them, for entertainment or as curiosities. Then they begin to be embellished with picturesque touches, new circumstances, and the legend becomes fiction.'

OLD TALES AND ⊗
BALLADRY ⊗ ⊗ ⊗

Dragon-slayings are perhaps particularly prone to this misadventure as in their original form they are so short on details – especially when it comes to the method of dispatch; Shonks is even shorter on details than most. In her dragon studies, Jacqueline Simpson has noted that when the hero is a knight 'it is surprising to observe how cursorily the actual combat . . . is often handled. We are given a general indication that there was a long, fierce struggle, in which the knight relied on the customary weapons of his class, but few details, if any, are supplied.' She notes wryly that the only exceptions

205

are where the accounts are relatively recent and the authors are known for their 'writing up'.

It is a shame that no folklore collectors were on hand in the thirteenth century or within living memory of the battle, to take down the details. The *Handbook of Folk-Lore* with its list of questions to ask about a hunt came several centuries too late: what days or times are thought auspicious for hunting? What are the preliminaries of a hunting expedition? What amulets, if any, are carried? How are the dogs treated, are they also charmed? And so on.

Frances Wilson, who was the daughter of a local blacksmith, wrote up the battle for the quarterly journal *The Reliquary* in the autumn of 1865.

> *Piers Shonks long pondered how to destroy the demon, and at last made the attempt. Having fasted and prayed, he started early in the morning, taking with him two powerful and savage dogs, and reached the garden at sunrise, where he found the demon just coiling himself in his tree. Shonk bent his bow, and praying meanwhile, discharged an arrow at the serpent, which immediately came down to attack his assailant. The two dogs at once fastened on the creature, and Shonk, after a hard contest, shot it through the heart.*

In 1902, Reverend Wigram must not have been aware of this account when he wrote of Shonks' encounter with the dragon in a letter, saying that 'the particulars of the fight were not recorded'. He need not have worried. They soon would be. Storytellers turned back to the tomb to embellish the tale.

The two dogs that had first accompanied Shonks in S. W. W.'s account in the *Mirror of Literature*, had, in a letter to the *Hertfordshire Mercury* sixty years later, become 'a faithful follower or henchman and three dogs of such surpassing swiftness that they were popularly known as winged'. We can understand why. The county historian Cussans wrote about the carvings on the tomb:

Simple and beautiful as these symbols are, they have given rise to the most absurd traditions. The most popular is, that Shonkes was a mighty hunter, and was always accompanied in his expeditions by one attendant and three favourite hounds, so swift of foot that they were said to be winged, and are so represented on the tomb. (The four Evangelists!)

The addition of the hounds in fox hunting country should be no surprise.

W. B. Gerish wrote three long articles about Shonks: the first two had little to say about the fight – but Gerish saved his best to last when he wrote in 1905 that Shonks and his hounds

sallied forth in search of the monster. The dogs soon gave tongue, and by their attacks and noise so distracted the attention of the dragon that it gave Piers an opportunity to thrust his spear into a vulnerable part and speedily dispatch it.

The erroneous interpretation of the carvings was now literally showing that Shonks killed the dragon by thrusting a spear into it, an image first conceived by Woolmore Wigram when he described the shaft of the cross as being like a spear, when it is not even like the shaft of a cross. It is the first mention of a spear in the history of the legend. The folk did not look at the tomb and see anything thrust into the dragon because there was nothing on the tomb, but Wigram and Gerish had read Gough's interpretation. In the *Mirror of Literature* in 1827, quoted above, we read that Shonks shot the dragon with an arrow – the first ever mention of any weapon.

By the late 1970s, the Hertfordshire historian Doris Jones-Baker had discovered that, 'Shonks at length found the dragon, and after a terrible struggle thrust his spear down the monster's throat, giving him a mortal wound.' And her Shonks was in 'full armour, with sword and spear'.

After that anything goes. In Kevin Crossley-Holland's *The Old Stories* Shonks rides into battle with his daughter Eleanor at his side and goes to with a dragon that 'blew out vile sulphurous smoke' before throwing out a jet stream of fire, which Shonks tries to avoid, trips and accidentally thrusts his spear down his enemy's throat. Such treatments brings Shonks into the tradition of comic or trick ways to kill a dragon. The best known examples are John Lambton's slaying of the Lambton Worm in County Durham with a suit of armour covered in razor blades so that when the creature wrapped itself around him it was cut into pieces and floated away in the river. Even more devious was Jim Puttock's strategy for killing the Knucker – a Sussex monster from a bottomless black pool – by feeding it a flour-and-water pie that slowed it down so much he could easily step in to deliver the fatal blow.

We are more than happy for Crossley-Holland to use poetic licence, he is not trying to get to the bottom of the story, but to delight and entertain and breathe new life into it. It is just another stage in the life cycle of a folk legend, and dragon-slaying was only the half of what was to come. While nobody originally bothered to write down the details of Shonks' battle with the dragon, what happened once the dragon was dispatched is another story altogether.

20

We carry within us the wonders we seek without us.

—Thomas Browne, *Religio Medici*, 1643

In Loving Memory.

These are the only words still legible on the tall headstone that marks the last resting place of Thomas Tinworth. He was Thomas Tinworth the bricklayer, and landlord of the Black Horse, whose grave is in Brent Pelham churchyard, a few feet from the north wall that harbours Shonks' tomb. Alongside, inches closer to the church, is a similar headstone marking the resting place of Thomas's wife Ellen, who died ten years before him in June 1888. Both have a deep roundel at the top; Thomas's holds a stone flower head, but the carving in Ellen's has broken away leaving an empty depression. Leaning against the backs are their little footstones: Thomas' with the date 1898 and the initials T. T. Ellen's is too mossy to read, but the inscription on her headstone has weathered much better: below her name is what the modern-day compilers of the *Hertfordshire Monumental Inscriptions* dismiss as a 'typical verse . . . refers to sudden death' – immured to sentimentality, they have not bothered to transcribe it.

Thankfully, W. B. Gerish was more inclusive and recorded it in his *Notes and Queries* column in the *Hertfordshire Mercury* back in 1915.

Sudden was the death of me
And great surprise to all,
When God did say I must away
Could I refuse his call?

Even closer to the church wall where Shonks lies is another memorial, tiny and crumbling. It belongs to the Tinworths' infant children, Rosetta and John. A small and simple broken cross, it is frogged like a brick and filled with moss and the much-worn remains of a flower that might once have been the same as that on their father's stone. Broken in two, it could easily be taken for two old bricks, and perhaps Thomas, the bricklayer, made it himself. John was born on 26 April 1852 and was buried nine days later. Ten years later, Rosetta was approaching her third birthday when she joined her brother in the ground.

Did the Tinworths stand heartbroken in that churchyard, looking south, and deliberately choose a spot near to Shonks' tomb? Of course, the tomb cannot be seen from outside of the church, but the wall of the nave of St Mary's is braced by two buttresses positioned either side of the north window. They flank the position of Shonks' tomb in the flint rubble wall. Some say they guard it, because on the left-hand buttress, at six feet and thirteen feet from the level of the graveyard, are two deeply incised and very curious crosses. Flouting expectations and symmetry, the right-hand buttress has just one cross, at four and a half feet from the ground.

In the early 1900s, the crosses generated a brief debate in the *Notes and Queries* column of the *Hertfordshire Mercury*. Were they consecration crosses, cut to mark three of the twelve spots where the bishop would have anointed the walls with oil? Twelve consecration crosses would normally be made inside the church and twelve outside to mark the separation from the ordinary, secular world beyond its walls, but permanent crosses are rare. They were usually just made with the chrism, the holy oil, and soon faded away. Occasionally, a chisel did fix them in place, or permanent crosses were prepared for the bishop to anoint, but exterior crosses are especially rare – although incised and indelible crosses might be thought necessary if you wanted to be certain that even the outer walls were holy ground belonging to God; if you wanted to be certain of sanctuary for someone buried in those walls, for instance.

Those at Brent Pelham are like Maltese crosses, cut an inch deep and as large as a handprint. Strictly speaking they are cross pattée. They do not really resemble the consecration crosses that survive in church walls elsewhere, which are normally enclosed in a circle. And why two crosses on one buttress and only one on the other? A trinity of crosses. W. B. Gerish ventured that they looked fresh and must have been cut during the church renovations in the 1860s, but at best they were recut or they replaced existing crosses, since there were definitely crosses there in 1808, said to have been lined with metal. That was the year Edward Brayley completed the seventh volume of the twenty-five volumes of *The Beauties of England and Wales* with the entry on Brent Pelham, which Brayley wrote himself: 'It would seem that O'Shonkes was a character much venerated,' he wrote. 'As the buttresses on the outside of the Church, which bound the place of his sepulture, are marked with *Crosses*.'

In April 1902, under the pseudonym Folk-lorist, one correspondent to the *Mercury* insisted that they were definitely not consecration crosses, but were cut expressly to mark Shonks' tomb. As well as the lorica of the Evangelists, perhaps the soul of Shonks needed extra protection from this trinity of cross pattée, not to mention the sanctuary of the wall of the church itself. They were probably wrong. They are most likely consecration crosses, although that does not mean that these spots were not chosen so that the crosses could stand sentinel to the tomb as well.

In 1884, the trustees of the British Museum bought over 1,500 engravings and drawings of Hertfordshire collected by the London merchant J. W. Jones, among them an anonymous watercolour entitled 'Brent Pelham Church, Hartfordshire, from the north'. It is a simple but attractive picture, more pale blue sky than light grey church. The nave has no roof, as in the Buckler sepias from the 1830s, and so the painting pre-dates the restoration of the 1860s.

The *raison d'être* of the picture is to show those small crosses, just two of them, one on the lower section of each buttress. The one on the right is the same as it is today, but the one on the left is larger and a slightly different shape. I know the artist paid particular care and attention to them because beneath the picture he or she has written, 'The Tomb of O Piers Shonkes is situated under the Window between the ✠ ✠ marked on Buttresses which appear to have been so marked to denote the peculiar sanctity of the intervening space'.

Examine those buttresses closely for clues today, and you will see that the original left buttress cross has been filled in with a mismatch of black flints that are uniform in colour compared to the other flints in the walls, but why that would be I don't know, unless the cross had worn to an unsightly shapeless indent in the stone. Whatever the case, I think the Tinworths put some store in the power of those crosses, even perhaps in the saintliness of Shonks. Thomas Tinworth might have carved the new crosses himself and blocked up the old one; they are rough and ready, certainly not the work of a skilled stonemason. One thing the correspondents in the *Hertfordshire Notes and Queries* did not ask themselves: did those three crosses represent Tinworth's two tiny children and his wife? They may well have done to Thomas Tinworth.

21

Such anecdotes, relating to such a man, even though they may be of doubtful authenticity, are not unworthy of preservation. The fabulous history of every country is part of its history, and ought not to be omitted by later and more enlightened historians; because it has been believed at one time, and while it was believed it influenced the imagination, and thereby, in some degree, the opinions and character of the people.

—Robert Southey

When was the last time a cook guilty of poisoning was boiled to death? Have you seen the *Lindworm* or dragon that is hanging in the town hall at Brun in Moravia? Is it a crocodile covered in pitch? Do you know of any other instances of dragons that were really crocodiles? Do you happen to know if John Bunyan was personally acquainted with Thomas Hobbes? And what is the derivation of 'cauking' as in, 'my servant never went cauking into the neighbours' houses'?

These were the pressing mysteries of the day on 28 December 1850, or they were if you subscribed to the journal *Notes and Queries*. Founded by William Thoms the previous year, *Notes and Queries* was the weekly house journal of antiquaries and folklorists – it was Thoms after all who had coined the term folklore – and has been described as a forerunner of internet forums where like-minded individuals could ask questions and get or give answers. Thoms expressed this elegantly on the masthead: 'a Medium of inter-communication for Literary Men, Artists, Antiquaries, Genealogists, etc.'

The last issue of 1850 was no. 61, and, as well as queries about *Lindworms* and boiling cooks to death, there were replies to questions from previous issues. One J. H. M. proposed a solution to the meaning of the word 'thwaites'. He thought it meant, 'a wood grubbed up and turned to arable'. (Like Great Pepsells in Furneux Pelham, he might have added.) J. H. M. was sticking his neck out, because it was *threads* – as we would call them today – on the meaning of words and pronunciations that generated the most replies and led to the most heated arguments. A query about how to pronounce the name of the Hertfordshire poet Cowper – he of the Yardley Oak – ran to a year's worth of spirited correspondence. Perhaps that is why most correspondents gave only their initials.

In each issue, the Queries and Replies were preceded by the Notes. Here people would write in with random observations on items they had stumbled upon or considered noteworthy. This was in the spirit of the journal's motto, taken out of the mouth of Dickens's Captain Cuttle in *Dombey and Son,* 'When found, make a note of'. Issue 61 opened with some ten pages of such notes, including one with the particularly intriguing heading of *The Pool of the Black Hound* (a folk tale about the laying of a restless spirit in Dean Prior, Devon). Then on page 513 was a note that might have caught your eye as you tackled your kippers that Saturday morning. It was headed rather vaguely *Similarity of Traditions.* Sent in by the thirty-eight-year-old solicitor, journalist and antiquary William Durrant Cooper, it began, 'Having recently met with some curious instances of the extent to which the same or similar traditions extend themselves, not only in our own country, but in Wales and France, I have "made a note" of them for your service.'

Among other similar traditions, Cooper had noticed that at Tremeirchion in Wales, was the tomb of a vicar who escaped a bargain with the devil by having his parishioners bury him 'neither within nor without the church, but in the wall itself'. There was a similar tradition at Rouen, where an archbishop had killed a man by hitting him on the head with a soup ladle. The archbishop had been buried in the wall of the cathedral, since he thought himself unworthy of a memorial in the church, but did not want to be buried outside of it. A burial in the church wall is supposed to be a burial in neutral ground, says Cooper. He then gets to the business we are interested in: 'A very similar tradition exists in Brent Pelham,' he adds, before quoting John Weever's cursory 1631 description of Shonks' tomb and giving a copy of the inscription over it, including the pertinent line: 'But Shonke one serpent kills, t'other defies / And in this wall as in a fortress lyes'. For many antiquaries and historians, it was the position of the tomb in the wall of the church under the central north window that most puzzled and attracted them. The first words written about Shonks begin, 'In the walles of this church lyeth a moste auncient monument'.

Wall burials captured the imagination and were something that would occupy the readers of *Notes and Queries* for many years to come. Although Durrant Cooper had sent a Note and not a Query, replies came all the same, albeit not with the immediacy we are used to today. The following year a correspondent styled mysteriously as *N* responded to Cooper's note. *N* said that tombs in the inside wall of churches are not especially unusual, but ones in the outside wall are rare. He gave several examples, and suggested that the reason people wanted to be there was so that passers-by would see them and offer intercessory prayers. Antiquarian interest in Shonks' position in the wall is curious, because his tomb was one of the more common wall burials, not one of the more unusual external immurements.

Richard Gough suggested that Shonks could have been a founder of the church – a lay founder perhaps, who paid for the nave, and so is commemorated there. This would be unusual for the time, as only after the mid fourteenth century are monuments thought to have spread out from the eastern ends of churches. Wealthy patrons usually wanted to be in the chancel near to the altar, or as near to it as possible – near to where the mass was said, near to the body of Christ. Founders are often associated not only with walls but also with the very foundations of churches. Recall D.E.'s query in the *Hertfordshire Mercury* in 1888: it didn't ask about a man buried in the wall but about a 'man buried under the foundation on the north side', to which *Ecclesiologist* replied, 'He may have been a builder of the church, or part of it, and it would be very natural that his tomb should be placed under its foundations, which is not an uncommon place for the sepulchre of the founder.'

It is not impossible that Shonks' bones are under the foundations of the wall, but that does not necessarily make him a founder of the church. One F. C. B. offered an alternative explanation in *Notes and Queries*. 'Did the custom arise from the more barbarous one of burying a living person in the foundation-wall for luck?' Certainly the great folklorist Laurence Gomme thought that skeletons buried in the walls of churches were evidence that bodies were put into the walls to protect the buildings from evil spirits. This is Shonks' legend turned upside down. The church wall is not a 'fortress' for Shonks, he is not in it for his own protection, he has been put there to protect the church.

Chambers *Book of Days*, first published in 1863, has an entry entitled *Sepulchral Vagaries* that talked about the 'peculiar kind of ancient burial . . . where the stone coffin, which contains the remains of the deceased, is placed within an external recess in the wall of a church, or under a low arch *passing completely through the wall, so that the coffin being in the middle of the wall, is seen equally within and without the church*. At Brent Pelham, Hertfordshire, there is a monument of this description in the north wall of the nave.'

Shonks' tomb does not pass completely through the wall today, and it is not possible to see the tomb from the outside, nor was it possible when the architectural historian A. W. Anderson photographed the consecration crosses on the left-hand buttress in 1912 leaving us an atmospheric shot of the exterior of the north wall. It is a ghostly image, shot through fog like a still from a Fritz Lang film, but there is no ghost and no tomb. It is tempting to believe that the *Book of Days* was right about the tomb passing through the wall and that the restorers altered this during the church restoration of the 1860s. The Victorian restorers were heavy-handed, as W. B. Gerish himself would lament about Brent Pelham: 'No church in Eastern Hertfordshire has suffered to so great an extent in this way from the "restorer".' Although he adds that, 'One can only express one's thankfulness that the same sacrilegious hands have spared the far-famed memorial to Piers Shonks.' There is no obvious structural evidence that the tomb once passed through the wall, and the matter is clinched by the anonymous early nineteenth-century watercolour of the consecration crosses that we met in the last chapter. It clearly shows the wall as it is today.

In fact, Shonks' tomb slab is only slightly more than halfway through the thickness of the wall, and must have been since it was bricked up – it is not as wide as the wall is thick – but if the position of Shonks' tomb has never been especially unusual, why did it draw so much attention? Is it the combination of an ordinary intra-mural burial, a far from ordinary tomb slab and, above all, a strange inscription that emphasises the fortress-like wall? Taken all together they fit very conveniently with the idea of a lorica formed by the symbols of the Evangelists, the floriated cross, and the consecration crosses on the buttresses outside.

The inscription also explains the reason for the wall burial. It was necessary because Shonks defied a serpent. Perhaps he was in the same situation as the ladle-wielding archbishop at Rouen – a good man who had sinned. In Shonks' case, if he had killed someone, we might assume that his victim was a metaphorical serpent and might have had what was coming, not an innocent struck down with a spoon. In 1888, in the *Hertfordshire Mercury's Notes and Queries*, one E. A. B. wrote that the devil 'declared he would wreak his vengeance' on Shonks for killing his dragon. The devil would 'have him when he died, no matter where buried, within or without the church, *excommunicated* or not for it is possible that at this time Shonkes may have been under a ban of the Church, and was meditating a return, by fighting against Satan.' My italics, because E. A. B. is speculating about the excommunication, reaching for a rational historical explanation. There was supposedly a similar case in Lichfield, which the mysterious *N* mentions in his 1851 reply to Durrant Cooper; he writes of a canopied tomb on the south side of the cathedral choir at Lichfield 'where we are told that the person interred died under censure of the church.' It has been suggested that when someone was buried in an outside wall it was because they died while still doing penance for their sins or while under excommunication and so were forbidden entrance to the church, and it is true that even bishops could not be buried in holy ground if they were in *anathema* at the time of their death. A wall burial could be a cunning solution to the dilemma and so save someone's soul from the devil. It was certainly better than risking the consequences of defying the church ban. Pope Gregory the Great wrote that church burial would make things much worse for those with heavy sins. He underlined the point quite terribly, recalling the example of two unworthies who were buried in a church: one's body simply vanished, and the other's was dragged from his grave by evil spirits.

In the *Essex Review* in 1896, one writer is uniquely damning of Shonks, declaring that he must have been a wicked man who would not be buried in consecrated ground. Not *could* not, but *would* not. If that is right, it puts Shonks on a par with another hero of English folklore, Hickonstern. In *Notes and Queries* in 1909, a correspondent with the buttoned-up name of Stapleton Martin wrote from Worcester asking for similar tales to that of Hickonstern, aka Hugo de Sturden, a hero of Gloucestershire legend, who 'died all but excommunicated, receiving the Communion only at the point of death, and that he was for his sins buried half within and half without that church.'

The circumstances around Hickonstern's death and interment in St Michael's Church, Winterbourne, were elaborated in 1803 by a Gloucestershire historian who wrote, 'A legend is preserved that this man had sold himself to the devil; and it was among the articles of the contract that he was to be carried to the church, after his death, neither with his feet or his head foremost, nor to be buried in the church or churchyard; to cheat the devil of his due, he directed that his body should be carried sideways to burial and that it should be buried in the wall of the church.' We are now firmly in Faustian small print.

A. R. Bayley wrote to *Notes and Queries* about a Dorset Faust. Anthony Ettrick was buried in 1703 in the Trinity Aisle of Wimborne Minster in Dorset. Ettrick was the 'magistrate who committed for trial the unhappy Monmouth when captured near Critchell after his defeat at Sedgemoor,' wrote Bayley, who must be the A. R. Bayley who wrote a history of the English Civil War in Dorset. 'Ettrick desired to be buried neither in the church nor out of it, neither above ground nor under; and to carry out his wish he got permission to cut a niche in the church wall, partly below the level of the ground outside, and firmly fixed in it the slate receptacle which is now to be seen. Into this, he ordered that his coffin should be put when he died.'

There are other versions of the Ettrick story. One claims that he had been involved in black magic in his youth and knowing that burial 'neither within the church nor without' was a formula to cheat the devil, he chose his strange sepulchre so as to escape a terrible fate. The formula is found in several folk legends earning it a tale-type from folklorists today: 'Devil is to get soul of man whether he is buried inside or outside of church, above or below ground. The man has himself buried in the wall of the church, partly in and partly out of the ground.'

Ettrick was not the only Dorset man to know how to beat the devil. John Minterne, an Elizabethan squire and conjuror, said to have stood nearly seven feet tall, was best remembered for jumping over the church steeple at Batcombe on horseback. At his death in 1592, he left instructions that he should be buried 'neither inside the church nor outside'. So he was buried in the wall. Although his tomb originally lay 'transversely across the wall', alterations mean that it has been cut in half, with one half inside the church and one half outside – with what effect on the fate of his soul we can only guess.

The idea probably has its origins in a classical legend about the Prince of Elis who was buried in a gateway because an oracle warned that he must not be buried *either within or without the city*. From ancient Greek myth to nineteenth-century Lincolnshire folklore: 'If a person sell his soul to the devil, to be delivered at a certain specified time,' wrote Edward Peacock in his 'Glossary of Lincolnshire Words', 'the vendor, if wary, may avoid payment by putting in the contract "be it in the house or outside the house", and then when the time arrives, sitting astride on a window-sill or standing in a doorway.'

At Aldworth in the Berkshire Downs there were once four effigies belonging to John Long, John Strong, John Ever Afraid and John Never Afraid. John Ever Afraid has now long since disappeared, but his tomb was set in the wall of the church. Colonel Richard Symons, a Royalist Officer during the Civil War, visited the church in 1644, writing of the tomb: 'The Common people call this John Ever-afraid & say farther that he gave his soul to the Devil if ever he was buried either in church or churchyard. So he was buried under the church wall under an arch.'

Shonks' position in the wall had been explained by the 'neither within nor without' ruse as early as the eighteenth century. William Cole wrote that Shonks killed an imp, 'to the no small mortification of the old one or great Devil who swore he would have him when he died let him be buried in Church or Churchyard: to elude which Oath Shonk order'd himself to be buried altogether in neither, but partly in one & partly in the other, that is in the wall of the church . . . This appears at first sight, to be a ridiculous sort of story:

however is very agreeable to the genius of the times it refers to, which dealt much in these kinds of cheating Nick.'

We may quibble with the strange logic of 'neither inside nor out', but we have to agree with Cole that it rings true as belonging to the world of medieval riddles and riddlers, of clever millers outwitting their betters with wordplay. In the early Middle Ages the devil was often shown as a fool. The ninth-century legend of St Dunstan has the saint seize Satan by the nose with a pair of red-hot tongs and make him dance. The story Cole told not only explains the position in the wall, but also explains the meaning of the inscription. It was retold and refined over the years. Herbert Andrews gave a good account in *Notes and Queries* in 1930. He was replying to a query from Olomouc in Czechoslovakia, where Otto Babler wanted to find examples of traditional English dragon-slayers. Andrews replied.

> *Instantly the death-struggles had ceased, the Evil One appeared, vowing vengeance on our hero for having destroyed his emissary, and threatening to have Shonks after his death, body and soul, whether buried in the church or out. Shonks modestly replied that his soul was his Maker's, and, as to his body, that should never be the Evil One's, for his burial would not be in the church or outside.*

Most of the analogous cases of other folk heroes and villains cheating the devil involve someone wriggling out of a Faustian pact. Shonks is unusual in that he has angered Satan rather than trying to cheat the devil out of a bargain – the Shonks version of the 'neither in nor out' tale type is a *suis generis* telling. There is one similar story, however, told at Tolleshunt Knights on the edge of the Essex Marshes, where it is said a knight angered the devil and so was buried neither within the church nor without to save his soul. Here is a hint of tales travelling via the village elites. In the Tudor period, the Lords Morley were Lords of the Manor in the Tolleshunts as well as in the Pelhams. Did the story travel with the household, with Father Bennet the manorial steward, who may have penned the inscription? I do not know which direction the tale travelled in, and which story came first.

The Tolleshunt tale is the closest to Shonks', but lacks a crucial element – the dragon. Shonks has the dubious honour of being the only dragon-slayer to be buried 'neither within nor without' a church, perhaps because dragons in English folklore are not normally associated with spiritual evil. But remember that Shonks' dragon probably had its origins in a carving symbolising Satan. The ever-shifting Shonks legend was morphing into something as unique as the tombstone over the hero's grave.

How this 'neither in nor out' works theologically is mysterious because the graveyard itself is consecrated ground, although that could make the wall of the church a liminal place between two consecrated zones and not necessarily a sanctuary but a place of great danger. In the 1920s, the folklorist Eleanor Hull wrote, 'To be neither within the house nor without the house or sacred place is ominous for there unseen and possibly evil influences have much power.' Is that the purpose of the crosses on the buttresses? To ensure the wall is holy ground, because we might say that they undo the riddle by making the tomb wholly inside the church? There come moments in the analysis of folklore and legend where try as we might, logic and facts will not close the circle and we are in danger of pedantry, of missing the point entirely. The tale is a neat solution to the conundrum set by the carvings, the inscription, and the position in the wall. It reconciles them all. It casts Shonks as the trickster, who gets one over on the devil. Others who manage that feat are the magicians of folklore, the dabblers in the black arts, who wield the formula as a spell, but Shonks is more Odyssean, the cunning warrior, and just in case that wasn't clear enough, someone decided to invite Robin Hood to the party.

22

Me: *You must have heard of Shonks*
Johnny: *Heard of it, but I can't believe it really, from Oxbury Wood he shot an arrow, didn't he? It's a long, long way there for an arrow to come from Oxbury Wood right across to the church isn't it?*

—Interview with John Brooks, who attended
Brent Pelham school in the 1930s

Even if we accept the low estimate of only 5,000 English long-bowmen at the Battle of Crécy in August 1346, with a modest firing rate of six arrows a minute, the sky would still have been vaulted with 30,000 arrows a minute (others estimate as many as 70,000). Little wonder that the French Chronicler Jean de Venette said that it was like 'rain coming from heaven and the skyies which were formerly bright, suddenly darkened'. They made a noise like a tempest, and the indiscriminate death toll must have been extraordinary. Edward III's English army, outnumbered at least three to one, left the field victorious.

If the battle of Waterloo was won on the playing fields of Eton, the famous English victories of the Hundred Years War were won on the village greens and archery butts of Plantagenet England. In Furneux Pelham behind the church and the house still known as Bowyers was the Shutting or Shooting Hill, where militia long-bowmen would build the skill and formidable strength to master a medieval warbow. Edward's grandfather, Edward I, realised the importance of longbowmen after they were used against the royal armies by Simon de Montfort's forces. Edward ordered that the best archers be picked and trained and paid well. The actor and longbow expert, Robert Hardy writes: 'It was Edward's genius to develop the longbow in tactical use and in individual power . . . "picked men" . . . under his guidance learned the techniques and disciplines, gained through long and arduous practice alone, of the great longbow drawn to the ear.' By the end of his reign English and Welsh longbowmen in the royal army were numbered in the thousands.

Many medieval households would have possessed a bow, many were obliged to. In Henry III's 1252 Assize of Arms all yeoman and townsmen were told to keep a bow and arrows. Later edicts ruled that bowmen had to practise regularly from a young age. We expect Shonks to have owned a bow and known how to handle it; in some versions of the story he even used it to slay the dragon. S. W. W., who tells us that 'Shonkes contrived to wound him in a mortal part with an arrow, of which the dragon died', then had the hero nock another to his bowstring one final time. After killing the dragon, Shonks set off home, but

the devil appeared to him, and told him that for his killing the dragon, wherever he was buried, whether in the church or out of the church, he would have him. Shonkes standing at a small distance from the church replied, 'I will shoot an arrow and wherever it falls, I will be buried'; he drew his bow towards the church, and the arrow entered one of the windows and descended into the bottom part of another opposite; so that when the coffin was placed there, it stood half in the church, and half out; thereby cheating the devil of the dreadful promise he had made of possessing him after his death.

S. W. W. claims the account was compiled from the different tales of the superstitious villagers. Or did S. W. W. use a little imagination and ideas taken from elsewhere? We might well guess that using a bow and arrow to explain the unusual position of the tomb might have been lifted straight from the legends of England's most famous folk hero. Robin Hood is a familiar interloper in other stories: 'minor occurrences and personalities of local interest were often conflated over the centuries with great figures, real or mythical, such as Robin Hood or Julius Caesar,' writes the historian D. R. Woolf. If so, then it was a relatively recent theft, since the notion that Robin fired his bow on his deathbed did not appear in the tales about the outlaw until late in their history.

The earliest stories of the outlaw's life relate his murder at the hands of a nun, whom he had asked to let his blood; she betrayed Robin and bled him to death. He died with no recourse to his bow and arrow. This fairly idiosyncratic ending had long legs and was still being told centuries later: Robin Hood's grave finally appears in an Elizabethan chronicle, but his resting place by the roadside is chosen by the treacherous prioress with still no bow and arrow to be seen.

Betrayal by bloodletting was still the main cause of Robin's death in a popular version of the legends, published in 1767 as *The English Archer; or Robert, Earl of Huntington, Vulgarly Call'd Robin Hood* at a price of 4*d*. But there for the first time we meet what the modern Robin Hood scholars Dobson and Taylor have called one of the most celebrated episodes in the entire Robin Hood saga, that is 'the dying outlaw's determination to shoot one last arrow to mark the site of his grave'. They suggest that this deathbed drama might have been invented following the discovery of one of the many supposed graves of Robin Hood. 'Exactly when this legend began, and whether it preceded or was invented to justify the discovery of a grave of Robin Hood within the Kirklees Estate, remain among the more insoluble of the Robin Hood mysteries.' There is a 1665 drawing of the simple cross-slab at Kirklees with the words 'Here lie robard hude' engraved crudely around the head end and thought to have been added to the slab long after it was made. The slab itself was destroyed when the railway was built in the nineteenth century, but not in the way we might expect: the navvies working on the tracks carried it away piece by piece because they believed it was a cure for toothache. And so folklore is the undoing of folklore.

The new version of the outlaw's death became a permanent part of the canon after it appeared in the broadside ballad *Robin Hood's Death and Burial* in Joseph Ritson's Robin Hood anthology in 1795. Having realised his undoing, Robin blows his bugle to summon Little John. His friend wants Robin to avenge himself on the prioress, but he refuses, instead saying:

> But give me my bent bow in my hand,
> And a broad arrow I'll let flee;
> And where this arrow is taken up,
> There shall my grave digg'd be.

Ritson's two-volume collection of Robin Hood ballads with scholarly notes and Thomas Bewick's engravings was a bestseller and went through many editions in the early years of the nineteenth century. It is not unreasonable to suppose that S. W. W. had read a copy and borrowed it for the story of Shonks.

A similar story was told about Bevis of Hamtoun, a hero of an early romance, who in one tradition is said to have hurled his famous sword Morglay – which is still in the castle armoury – from the ramparts of Arundel Castle in Sussex, and was buried where it landed. Again, this seems to be a very late addition to the story of a hero. Instead of a bow or sword, the giant Tom Hickathrift used a stone. He hurled or kicked it two or three miles from Tilney St Lawrence in Norfolk. In one account, it bounced off the church of Tilney All Saints and landed in the churchyard, marking the site of his grave, or in another, cracking the church wall where he was then buried. The variants are explained by the confusion over exactly which gravestone belongs to Tom: a lovely example of how these tales were formed to explain the mysterious or unusual object.

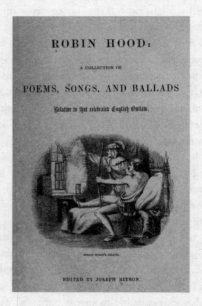

Neither of these stories appears to be older than either S. W. W.'s account of Shonks' death or the Robin Hood ballad; they borrowed the details from one or the other or some common ancestor. Closer to home there is a legend that dates from at least 1728 and may prove that the earliest account of an arrow fired to mark a grave may well belong not to Robin Hood but to another famous – but now largely forgotten – archer of English tradition: Strongbow. Nathaniel Salmon relates how Jack O'Legs, the giant from Weston, was hanged by the bakers of Baldock and 'made them at his Exit but one single Request, which they granted: That he might have his Bow put into his Hand, and where-ever his Arrow fell he should be buried, which happened to be in *Weston* Church Yard.' Was this version of Jack O'Legs's demise inspired by a memory of the lord of the manor who founded the church in the time of the Anarchy, Richard FitzGilbert de Clare, known as Strongbow for the military prowess that made him a rival to King Henry II? He was a mighty archer as his name implies and 'It is said his arms were so long, that he could touch his knees without stooping'. I learned this, to my surprise, from a little octavo volume from 1791 called *Anecdotes of Archery*, written by Henry George Oldfield, the tragically bad topographical artist who made a hash of Shonks' tomb.

Others have rationalised the Jack O'Legs story in other ways, saying that the arrow marked the spot where the future church would be built, which brings to mind again the legend of Barn Hall at Tolleshunt Knights where the devil was said to have hurled a beam declaring: 'Wheresoe'er this beam shall fall / There shall stand Barn Hall'. Instructively, as well as sharing the neither in nor out motif, Tolleshunt Knights has a version of the story known only from the 1970s in which the hero of the story was accompanied by three spayed bitches, which had a special power against the devil; they are suspiciously reminiscent of Shonks' winged hounds. S. W. W. was not only the first to write up Shonks' bow and arrow deathbed scene, but also the first to set down the report that Shonks was also accompanied by his hounds. Remember that Tolleshunt Knights shared the same lords of the manor as the Pelhams in the sixteenth century.

There is a sense that we are going around in circles with these stories as they borrow elements from each other, and it is impossible to disentangle these legends, or figure out which one should take priority over the others. These legends of bowmen, dragon-slayers and strange burials pollinate each other, fortify each other, and so carry the strain of other legends. In so doing, they increase their chances of survival. As Roberto Calasso has written, 'Stories never live alone: they are branches of a family that we have to trace back, and forward.'

That questions over land ownership should be settled by trials of strength, hurling stones or beams, or by shooting arrows and trusting in providence makes sense. This must have really happened; the bow was such a ubiquitous part of British life for centuries. To settle the fate of your body and perhaps your soul with the flight of an arrow is more surprising if these stories were genuinely old. The bow and arrow was certainly a weapon of chance and providence, and perhaps that was the point of the new explanation, no longer was Shonks a cunning man outwitting the devil, instead he was saved by luck and guided by divine intervention.

If the English longbow had a formidable fire rate it also had an impressive range, depending on the draw weight of the bow and the type of arrowhead, a professional archer could fire an arrow as much as 250–350 m. In another version of the Robin Hood legend, *Robin and Guy of Gisborne*, we read that during an archery contest they put pricks or long thin branches in the ground to shoot at, 'And sett them three score rood in twin'. That is 60 roods or 330 yards away. With that in mind, we cannot help asking whether Shonks could possibly have fired his arrow into the north wall of the church. There is confusion in the traditions about where he fired his arrow from and when. Johnny Brooks, who attended Brent Pelham school in the 1930s, was told that Shonks fired his arrow from Oxbury Wood, north of Beeches Wood, just under a mile from the church. Most writers have it that he died from his wounds in the encounter with the dragon and nocked his bow right there, others that he fired the arrow from his deathbed many years later. Both Pepsells field and Shonks' Moat are about a mile from the church in different directions. An improbable distance for the mightiest of archers. But S. W. W.'s very first account has the sense to place Shonks on his way home and near to the church. And we cannot quibble with that, although it is hard to see how an arrow could really have entered a south window of the chancel and hit the north wall of the nave.

This bothered Reverend Woolmore Wigram as well, and he set about to explain how it might have happened with a forensic analysis worthy of the Warren Commission. 'The chancel of the church was re-built about twenty-five years ago, and is now in a straight line with the nave,' began Wigram in 1888. He goes on to explain in detail how the original chancel was built, and that its south window used to look through the chancel arch, so that an arrow entering it could have struck the north wall of the nave.

You must not doubt that the arrow could have stuck in the flint wall. A medieval composite warbow made from the sapwood and heartwood of a yew tree might have a draw weight in excess of 50 kg. In the thirteenth century, Gwent archers would release arrows that could pierce the armour, saddle and horse of a mounted knight. They could literally pin enemies to their horses.

All of this is another way we are allowed to think about folk legends. We accept the existence of a dragon, and the appearance of a devil, but our belief crumbles if the arrow cannot be shown to have actually been shot through the window into the wall. Despite the fact that the tomb is older than the wall anyway, we demand internal logic. A magic arrow would have supplied that, but detracted from the world the folk legend occupies between fiction and fact. The arrow must fly out of the story and into the real world.

I will finish this chapter with the opening words of Robert Hardy's portrait of a medieval archer, it is based on his deep research, but is nonetheless an irresistibly romantic picture of the type. It won't be my last attempt to find a portrait of Shonks.

Broadly speaking he was drawn from the villages and fields, a man of small property, sometimes none, sometimes an outlaw or a poacher pardoned for service; a man of no great estimation in the world, but a man of country skills and strength, rough living and hard working, accustomed to things of wood and finding a pleasing familiarity in the wooden bow.

23

I know this story to be true because Sheldon told his daughter; Rosa.
Rosa told it to her daughter Estella.
Estella; in turn, told it to her son, William.
He then told me, his daughter; Patricia.
When my father finished this story he put out his hand and said,
'This is the hand, that has touched the hand, that has touched
the hand, that shook the hand of Abraham Lincoln.'

—Patricia Polacco, *Pink and Say*, 1994

'Many years ago, when the church was being restored, the gigantic bones of Shonke were discovered,' begins the earliest account of the tomb's opening. It was written some forty years after the event by one L. H. S., and published in *The Cliftonian*, the school magazine of Clifton College near Bristol. L. H. S. had spoken to a local farmer who told him:

A finger bone, which was twice the size allowed to mortal man,
was taken home by a farmer, who was then churchwarden. But
in the silent hours of the night, the spirit of Shonke so troubled
his conscience that on the next morning he restored the bone to
its rightful abode.

The 1888 letter to the *Hertfordshire Mercury*, which prompted Woolmore Wigram to write about the yew tree, also elicited a response from one W. H. N. of Watford: 'I remember some twenty years ago hearing a patriarchal old villager say that he either remembered or heard that on an excavation being made under the wall, near the monument, that bones supposed to be Shonks' were found.'

W. B. Gerish tracked down W. H. N. – William Henry Norris – to ask him if the bones had been put back where they came from, only to find that he was too late and that the old man had died. The bricklayer Thomas Tinworth, whose gravestone is today in sight of the crosses on the buttresses, remembered that his father explored the tomb in about 1835 during some repairs: 'He found that the recess went a long way down, and in digging into it he found some very large human bones.' This would suggest that Shonks' bones may well have been beneath the foundations.

The date the tomb was first opened is not certain. Tinworth said it was 1835, while the churchwardens' accounts show substantial bricklaying bills for 1832 and again in 1834. As we have already seen, J. C. Buckler drew the tomb in 1833, and drew it in a way that suggests he had a very clear view of the tomb slab – had it been removed from the niche?

Mary Ann Wisbey said it was opened in 1836. As a young girl, Mary Ann, a local farmer's daughter, sat with her feet on the tomb in the pew that belonged to Brent Pelham Bury. Sometime over the next seventy years, Mary Ann would reinvent herself as Marion, that name most resonant of English folk heroines. She was Marion Hudson, a retired housekeeper, when she was interviewed by a local newspaper reporter in 1903, who described her as 'an extremely interesting octogenarian'. He reported that about 1836 the tomb was opened by the churchwardens Mr Brand and Mr Morris, who each took a fingerbone from the tomb. 'One joint was as long as an ordinary man's finger,' and, she added in the low whisper of a wise-woman, 'the bones were double-jointed'. Morris 'never had any peace with his bone', and had to put it back in the tomb. In a letter

233

Mrs Hudson wrote to W. B. Gerish she recalled: 'Mr Morris put the bone he had in a glass in a corner cupboard but none in the house could rest so they put it back.' Brand also appears to have suffered, but not to the same extent. In a wonderfully quaint phrase, Mrs Hudson confided, 'He never knew the going of his bone.'

Are those bricklayers' bills paid to Thomas Tinworth senior explained by the opening of the tomb in 1832 when the bones were taken, and the re-opening in 1834 when they were replaced?

I have in my files a photocopy of page twenty-eight of a book called *Digging up Bones*. It is a diagram of the bones of the hand, and on its own is completely lacking in context. I suppose I kept it to better imagine Shonks' fingerbone. Which bone? The little digital phalanx or pisiform of the palm, or the larger metacarpal? They all look very tactile. Not reminders of our mortality, but lucky charms, netsuke, keepsakes to put in your pocket and make a wish on. Or something for the *Wunderkammer* (or Mr Morris's glass corner cupboard), like the 'Frenchman's Finger' bought from Franciscan friars in Toulouse by the seventeenth-century canon of Canterbury Cathedral John Bargrave for his own Cabinet of Curiosities (apparently they also offered to sell him a mummified baby.) If not the cabinet of curiosities, then the reliquary. Even better the reliquary. The index finger of St Thomas, Doubting Thomas, was kept alongside parts of the true cross and other marvels in the Basilica of Santa Croce in Gerusalemme in Rome – the very finger that had suspiciously prodded the resurrected Christ's wounds.

At the Second Council of Nicaea in 787 it was decreed that every altar had to have a relic of a saint or martyr. How on earth did a simple parish church in Hertfordshire acquire such a marvel? In 1297 there were four altars dedicated to St John, the Virgin Mary, St Katherine and St Nicholas, but they were reportedly unconsecrated and would not have had any saintly relics. They should have followed the example of Bishop Hugh of Lincoln, who was rather

Little Cokenag
Nr. Barkway,
Royston.
Oct. 2, 1903.

Dear Sir,

I am sorry I can't write what you want. I am very ill and can't use my hands properly. I will write as soon as I can. O Pier Shonks is not buried in Brent Pelham Church, but through the wall, half in half out. I knew well one of the Churchwardens that had the grave opened and each of them took out a bone from a finger just one joint and it was as long as a man's finger. Mr Morris put the bone he had, in a glass in a corner cupboard but no one in the house could rest so they put it back, Mr Brand the other churchwarden never knew the going of the bone he had it varnished. You see I can't write I fear you can't read it I'll try and write more fully soon, if any of your people were near I could tell them more than I could write. I have tried to write out the May song but can.

Oct. 26.

I have done the best I can in my weak state to write what you ask but am afraid you can't read it I went to Barkway to get information on the subject was caught in the rain and have had pleurisy, later on if I can finish I will do so.

Yours truly,

M. Hudson.

I can't connect my tale, but so the story goes. O Piers Shonk was in his garden the serpent went to him and said he would have him whether he was buried in the church or out of the church. Shonks said I'll shoot an arrow towards the church, where the arrow lodges I'll be buried the arrow went in a window and stuck in the opposite wall, please excuse all.

fond of another finger bone, supposedly that of Mary Magdalene. Unfortunately, it was still on the hand of the Magdalene at Fécamp in north-east France, so he went there and tried to bite it off, 'first with his incisors and finally with his molars'. (I cannot resist giving here John Bale's 1530 spoof and scatological list of relics, which included: a feather of St Michael's wing, one of Adam's toenails, one of Job's scabs, a fart of St Fandingo and a dram of the turd of St Barnabas. At least I think John Bale made this up – St Fandingo was surely a figment of his imagination – but it was not a million miles from the truth, as Calvin noted a few years later, both the Cathedrals of Augsburg and Trier claimed to have poor old St Bartholomew's penis.)

The theft of fingerbones is a chapter in its own right in the history of larceny. The most famous occurred at the opening of Edward I's tomb in Westminster Cathedral in May 1774. The occasion had been arranged by the same Richard Gough who wrote about Shonks' tomb in his *Sepulchral Monuments*. He was then director of the Society of Antiquaries and disgraced himself when he tried to pocket half a finger of Edward I. It had been pulled off while examining the dead king's signet ring. The Dean of Westminster made the shamefaced antiquary return the bone to the coffin. The story was put about by none other than that connoisseur of eighteenth-century gossip William Cole. No one seems to have minded a century later when someone stole a finger from the coffin of the Bible translator Miles Coverdale in 1840, it was put into a box made from his original coffin and is today kept in the Library of Trinity College, Cambridge.

John Morris regretted his grave robbery and put the bone back. Did he later connect it with his bad luck, or fear the avenging ghost of Shonks? In August 1837, Morris was farming the tithes and claims that farmers were deliberately leaving land uncultivated to deny him the tithe payment. 'He states the feeling of hostility against him for taking the tithes, to have got to such an extent as to have caused him great injury and that he is a very serious loser by the affair.' He should have left that finger well alone.

There is only one ghost story connected with Shonks, and it is a little dubious. It was told by Herbert Tompkins at the turn of the twentieth century in his *Highways and Byways in Hertfordshire*:

> One man, more fortunate than I, saw Shonkes under peculiar circumstances on a moonlit night. I do not know how many centuries have passed since the interview took place, and it is possible that the story has gained something in its telling; but I know that Jack O' Pelham had stolen his neighbour's faggot and had almost reached home with it on his back when it suddenly trebled its weight and Jack fell heavily to the ground. As he scrambled up he saw a man with very broad shoulders standing over him, and the man's aspect was so fierce that Jack swooned right away at the sight. That man was Piers Shonkes, who must have bribed Charon to ferry him back from the farther shades.

At Hathersage in Derbyshire, there is a story of a similar grave robbery. Dire misfortune was said to have befallen the men who raided the supposed thirteen-foot long grave of Little John, and their troubles only stopped when they replaced the bones. If Mr Morris or Mr Brand were troubled by Shonks' spirit, it would make a fine children's story, in which we do find out 'the going of his bone' – a gang of colourful village children and the ghost of Shonks are at the bottom of it. Imagining a children's story acts as a way of guarding us from the darker plots suggested. We are in M. R. James territory again, digging up whistles or crowns that should be left where they are, moving stones from the sides of wells, or peering into the hole in the fifteenth-century altar tomb in *An Episode of Cathedral History*, and wishing to God we hadn't.

But who does not want to peer into the tomb, the rabbit hole, the oubliette, the well, the tree, the hollow places of the earth?

Would you put your hand in and feel around inside? When archaeologists are searching for bones it makes a great news story: we are mesmerised by the unearthing of the famous dead: Richard III, recently found in a car park in Leicester. These bones can tell stories like never before thanks to the wonders of forensic anthropology.

Perhaps Ted Barclay and I could prise the lid off the tomb one night. But better not to. A while back I found a bone in a copse at the point where three parish boundaries met. I kept it outside superstitiously, until it transpired that it was an old cow bone. I preferred it when it was the bone of a suicide or a hanged man. A cow bone was not without interest to the local historian, since the field had been arable in living memory, but the old tithe records said it had once been pasture land where cows roamed. I didn't keep it, which was a failure of the imagination. As a boy growing up in Lichfield in Staffordshire there had been a wood where playground rumours said devil worshippers regularly congregated to sacrifice animals; back then, finding a cow bone would have been prima facie evidence of Walpurgis Night.

I might take a larger bone than a finger from Shonks' tomb. A giant's arm or thigh bone would weigh less heavily on the conscience than something as furtive as the tip of his finger. The thigh bone of the giant Jack O'Legs was once kept in the church chest at Weston in Hertfordshire, but was sold to John Tradescant in the seventeenth century and displayed in his Ark, or cabinet of wonders, at Lambeth, alongside such marvels as an ape's head turned into stone, a small piece of the true cross, a scourge with which the Emperor Charles V was said to have flogged himself, and countless other wonders natural and man-made. When that cornucopia went to Oxford, the 42 lb bone was one of the founding objects of the Ashmolean, and in *The Ashmolean Museum* by J. H. Parker, written in 1870, we read:

> *About the end of the last, and the early part of the present century . . . one of the curiosities shewn, which was especially attractive to the more ignorant of the visitors, was the Leg-bone of an Elephant, which was exhibited and labelled as the Thigh-bone of a Giant; and it was stated that this bone was bought of the Clerk of the Parish of Baldock . . . On the appointment of Mr John Shute Duncan as Keeper of the Museum, one of his first acts was to have the label erased from the bone, which is now in the Anatomical Department of the New Museum.*

The bone was listed in the 1836 catalogue at no. 109 as 'The femur or thigh bone of an Elephant', but what became of it has long been forgotten. Today we would display the bone because it was both the bone of an elephant and the bone of a giant. Destructive and supercilious rationalism was a third iconoclasm after that of the Reformation and the Puritans: the iconoclasm of the Enlightenment.

Tradescant himself showed more wisdom than the men who would later take charge of his collection. The Ashmolean Museum website tells us that, 'Tradescant made it clear that little priority was attached, by the collector himself, to one form of evidence over another, whether it be natural or artificial, real or imaginary. Within the encyclopedic context, all forms of data held equal weight when considered as parts of the whole of knowledge, and, as the Tradescant catalogue illustrated, the bounds of the encyclopedic enterprise could be extended to include objects both of myth and of reality.'

I am reminded of something M. R. James wrote in his essay on bestiaries for the Eton College Natural History Society in 1931 – wearing his scholar's hat not his ghost story writer's, though they were the same hat at different angles – he warns that it is useless to search for the one-legged nation shown on *Mappa Mundi*, and what a dull world it would be if there weren't such stories. It would certainly be a dull world if we proved with triumph that such a nation didn't exist. A world of forensic anthropology does not have all the answers. Writing in the seventeenth century, John Aubrey lamented that faeries had been scared away by such innovations as the printing press, we must be careful not to scoff away all memory of them as well.

24

Old Customs and old wives fables are grosse things, but yet ought
not to be buried in Oblivion; there may be some trueth and
usefulnesse be picked out of them, besides 'tis a pleasure to consider
the Errours that enveloped former ages: as also the present.

—John Aubrey, *Remaines of Gentilisme and Judaisme*, 1688

The disentombed are often mistaken for giants. The pioneering archaeologist and erstwhile soldier Reverend James Douglas used to tell a story about a skeleton found when opening a Saxon barrow near Chatham Docks in the 1770s. The three Irish soldiers, who were doing the digging, came running to report that they had found an enormous skeleton. He hurried to the spot but found the 'bones not exceeding the ordinary human stature'. Seizing a thigh bone, he measured it against one of the soldier's own, then, 'I belaboured the fellows with it for their natural promptness to magnify these casual discoveries into the marvellous.' Mr Douglas may have asked himself which is the worse crime: making the ordinary marvellous or the marvellous ordinary?

Writing at the end of the twelfth century, Gerald of Wales tells us that when the monks opened the tomb of King Arthur at Glastonbury, they found gigantic bones: the shin bone reportedly came up well above the knee of the tallest man there. In more recent times, when the stone coffin in the eastern crypt at Canterbury was opened in 1888, the bones inside were adjudged to have belonged to a man of at least six foot two inches, a fact which was taken by some as evidence that they could not be the bones of Thomas Becket because he was supposed to have been just under seven feet tall. The coffin was reopened in 1949 and 'Becket's bones' spent two years with Professor A. J. E. Cave at St Bartholomew's. When he finally submitted his report to the Cathedral, Cave concluded that the bones could not have belonged to the saint; he was also sure that they were not the bones of a man seven feet tall, nor even six foot two inches; the skeleton belonged to someone only five foot eight inches, an inch taller, incidentally, than the Anglo-Saxon skeleton exhumed from a gravel pit in the Pelhams, which Professor Cave had examined thirteen years earlier.

Writing about our supposedly lofty Anglo-Saxon forebears, the paleopathologist Don Brothwell, in *Digging up Bones*, hints at why we find giants in old graves: 'We sometimes find that the overall height of a skeleton within a grave (from the top of the head to the tips of the toes) appears to be well over 1.8 metres. However, it is often found on examining the long bones in the laboratory that the individual was in fact a number of centimetres shorter; the misconception has resulted from the fact that with decomposition of the soft tissues the bones had spread, giving a false impression of body size.' Brothwell adds that people wrongly assume that a large skull or jaw bone indicates an abnormally large individual. Or a large fingerbone perhaps? Just one of Shonks' joints was as long as an ordinary man's finger, confided Mrs Hudson, while the author of the 1872 article in *The Cliftonian* had heard a similar report, writing that Shonks' fingerbone was twice the size of an ordinary man's.

While the story of the dragon's lair began with the felling of the yew tree, the idea that Shonks was a giant did not begin with the discovery of the bones. The giant Shonks was already a well-established tradition and one that cannot be explained away by the tomb or its carvings; unless we count the simple fact that he *is* in a tomb in an English parish church and, as Richard Gough remarked, with his customary sneer: 'In almost every church a singular or unknown monument of any antiquity is given a giant.' Gough wrote this in 1786 and he knew well that some thought Shonks had been a giant. Nearly sixty years earlier, Nathaniel Salmon, the best of the county historians – because he took the most trouble over folk legends – left the earliest account of the giant Shonks, writing of a 'Relation given me by an old Farmer in the Parish, who valued himself for Being born in the Air that Shonk breathed. He saith, Shonk was a Giant that dwelt in this Parish, who fought with a Giant of Barkway, named Cadmus, and worsted him.'

Barkway is a Hertfordshire parish to the north of Brent Pelham; its giant had no other adventures and is known only through Salmon's account of Piers Shonks. As we have seen, Cadmus was an Ancient Greek dragon-slayer who found his way into the verse inscribed over Shonks' tomb, so we might assume that the name, if not the entire existence of this giant, was cribbed from the church wall. However, the Giant Shonks is not alone in the Hertfordshire and East Anglian countryside: a dozen or more miles to the west of Brent Pelham is Weston churchyard where two small gravestones fourteen feet apart are meant to mark the grave of the giant Jack O'Legs (who, as we have already heard, was hanged by the bakers of Baldock, bequeathing his thigh bone to a thankless posterity). Directly north of Brent Pelham is the church at Tilney All Saints near the west bank of the Great Ouse; there is the last resting place of Tom Hickathrift marked by an eight-foot long broken stone slab. Tom found fame when carrying ale from King's Lynn to Wisbech; he decided to take a shortcut across the wonderfully named Smeeth, a common haunted by a fierce local giant, who promptly attacked him with a giant club, but using the axle-tree of his cart as a weapon and its wheel as a sword, Tom killed his rival. There are those who think that Hickathrift descends in the folk memory from some giant god of the Iceni, or remembers ancient hill figures, standing stones and the old giants of Britain who were here under their leader Gogmagog when, according to Geoffrey of Monmouth, Brutus of Troy founded Britain. Some motifs in folk tales must be very old, as the stories are very old, but those who see the sun god and Bronze Age rites in every folk legend are usually missing the point, conflating the origins of giants with that of a particular giant.

Was Shonks remembered as a giant simply because giants are a commonplace of folk tales, flowing from the wellhead of legend haunting a prediluvian earth – there were giants in the earth in the days before the Great Deluge, says the Book of Genesis – the early Britain of Gogmagog and fairy tales? Are giants fated to infiltrate their fair share of the old stories?

Folklorists classify legends by thousands of tale types and motifs formulated over the last hundred years in a vast and never-ending taxonomy begun by the Finnish folklorist Antti Aarne in 1910. These tale types are further subdivided into motifs that appear repeatedly in stories around the world. The motif index has expanded greatly since then; giants can be found at F531, part of F, which is *Marvels in general*. F500–599 are remarkable persons, and F530 are exceptionally large or small men. F531 itself is subdivided into numerous, surprisingly specific categories. F531.1 is concerned with the appearance of giants, so at 531.1.3.3.1 we find *One-legged giants*. F531.1.5.1 is *Giantess throws her breasts over her shoulders*, and F531.1.1.1.1 is of course that stock character of folk tales, the *Giant with one eye in the neck which he covers with his lower lip*. Reading down the motifs whets the appetite for tales; especially when we find *Giant inflates self and floats through air*, and *Giant threads an elephant on a fish-hook*. Bob Trubshaw has joked that such classifying can turn into the worst kind of bug-collecting: 'Oh golly gosh, I think I've found the earliest-known Lithuanian example of motif Q493.1.'

Marina Warner, who has thought as deeply and sympathetically about our old tales as anyone, has cautioned against the downside of the universalising impulse 'which ipso facto looks for resemblances, not distinctiveness, erases historical and social conditions'. Grouping tales by motif can homogenise them and leads the taxonomisers to assume things about one legend because it has been classified with another, however superficial, or recently appended, that similarity might be when we dig deeper. Our attempts to reverse the entropy of language and folk tale can lead us astray. If we bear these cautions in mind, then the motif and tale-type indexes are useful and interesting. They are invaluable to anyone searching for stories and legends on a particular theme, and help us find tales that may have influenced each other. Besides, it is hard to claim that they erase distinctiveness when we comb through all the giant motifs and find F531.1.6.9. *Giant rooted to ground because his nails and hair have grown into the earth on account of his great age.*

The motif most relevant to Shonks the giant is simply, 'Giants wrestle with each other'. There is no 'Giant slays dragon'.

The wealth of sub categories does tell us that giants can mean many things. The giant who carries a church across a stream or bestrides a mountain, is very different to Piers Shonks. He is more likely to be *Giant carries man on his back*, than *Giant carries man in his pocket*.

F531.2 deals specifically with the size of giants, but tends to deal only with the gargantuan such as the *Giant lies underground with trees growing all over his body*. Some giants belong more to the everyday world than those we find moulding the landscape, striding across hilltops raising dolmens and hurling rocks. These test our credulity a little more than men who are merely taller than average – it is a fact we know from experience and from the *Guinness Book of Records* that exceptionally large people do come along from time to time.

W. H. Norris, who heard about the opening of the tomb from a 'patriarchal old villager', said that Shonks' bones belonged to a man nine or ten feet in height, and Thomas Tinworth, whose father saw the bones, said he was a man of great stature. The legend itself lacked such detail before reports of the tomb's opening reached the tale-tellers: the author of the *Cliftonian* article learned from a farmer that 'Shonke lived in the seventh century, and was a giant of huge proportions.'

In recent years, the Pelham website has been very specific: Shonks was apparently twenty-three feet high. It is a figure that originates with the geomancer and writer Nigel Pennick – the number twenty-three has some significance to geomancy – the art of finding meaning in patterns made by objects on the ground. The information came from an 'old lady' who 'was insistent that twenty-three was the correct number'. Pennick would later write that Shonks lived under an oak tree. Perhaps the well-informed old woman was insistent on that as well, but I pity the prodigious Shonks being crammed into a hole under a tree. Even Jack O'Legs only had to be folded in half once to fit him into his grave according to one account, and we have it on good authority that the skeleton in Shonks' tomb was only twice the size of an average person.

As early as the third century, the Greek writer Philostratus derided such reports: 'It is said that the heroes were ten cubits tall. This is a charming but misleading and unbelievable myth, if one looks at nature, in which today's individuals are the standard.' Even if we accept this dull sophistry, there is still the possibility that Shonks was unusually tall. The local historian Herbert Andrews wrote in 1930: 'But if Shonks was a man of ordinary stature he was, in biblical language, "a mighty man of valour", such as, in popular imagination would be pictured as taller than an ordinary man. His very name seems to bear this out, for Piers Shonks is none other than Peter Long Shanks or Peter of the Long Legs.'

On the evidence so far, it would be reasonable to conclude that Shonks was at the very least a lanky fellow in his day, but, fearful of an ugly literalism, I have neglected to consider the most telling clue of all. The average cross-slab is about six feet long, Shonks' cross-slab, his coffin lid, was an unusually small five foot six inches. I shall pass very quickly over that fact and recall instead that in the early 1860s when the church was restored, the tomb was opened once again. In an article that first appeared in *The Reliquary* in 1865, Frances Wilson, a local blacksmith's daughter wrote: 'The Sexton who showed us the church on my last visit, told us that a few years before, when the church was under repair, the tomb had been opened, when the bones were found heaped together, showing that it had been before disturbed.' This was six centuries after the tomb slab left the mason's hands, and we might expect them to have been disturbed a few times, especially since legend has it that the bones themselves might have been even older than the tomb. This most puzzling element of the stories holds out a promise of bringing us closer to the real Shonks, a man who, according to the inscription over his tomb, not only slew dragons but died some two hundred years before his tomb was carved; died in the year 1086, the year of the Domesday survey, under the Norman yoke, in the twenty-first year of the reign of William the Bastard.

Part IV

Name

25

*Mythical time had neither depth nor breadth. One might as well
wonder whether the adventures of Tom Thumb took place before
or after Cinderella's ball.*
—Paul Veyne, *Did the Greeks Believe in their Myths?*, 1983

In the twenty-first year after the Conquest of England by William
the Bastard, as the villagers of Peleham slaughtered their swine
and stacked underwood for their winter fires, their great champion
Shonks died in his bed with his eternal soul in the greatest peril.

1086 was a swinkful and sorrowful year with much untowardness
of weather. The chronicles say thunder and lightning killed many
men, so it is not surprising that the powerful found reason to go
south; a little to the west of Peleham, beyond the great yew tree,
Edgar the Aetheling, the last Anglo-Saxon claimant to the English
throne, left behind his Hertfordshire estates for Italy with a band
of two hundred knights. The Conqueror had sailed for Normandy
in August, but whereas Edgar would eventually return to his lands
and live out his final years on them in peace, King William would
never see England again. The following year he would succumb to
wounds, sustained when the pommel of his saddle drove into his
stomach during the sack of Mantes, in the Vexin.

Before William left England for the last time, he set in train a
great survey of the lands and landowners of the country that would
come to fill the pages of the Domesday Book. So it was that as the
hero Shonks neared his end, the King's commissioners visited the

gentle slopes of the Upper Ash Valley and came into the woods and the farmsteads of Peleham where the Hundred Court met by Edwin's Tree. They came to count the pigs and cows, and oxen, to inquire of the sheriff and reeves who owned each inch of plough-land, woodland and pasture. They must have known that thanks to Shonks they could pass through that country without fear now. Famine still ravaged the English countryside, and in the East men still watched uneasily for Viking longboats, but a much greater evil would come no more to those parts – for Shonks had slain the mighty dragon.

Peleham sat on the ancient road from Braughing to Great Chesterford, which passed beneath the boughs of ash and hornbeam covering the plateau east of the valley of the River Ash. The Vill was named after the Anglo-Saxon Peola who had lent his name to the Ham, or Homestead, some five hundred years earlier. It was out-of-the-way, yet not far from London and owned by Maurice, Bishop of that City. A Ralph, a Ranulph and other Norman lords held seven of the eight manors. The eighth, the smallest, was in the hands of Ealdred, a Saxon. But no Shonks is recorded in Domesday unless perhaps he is one of the two milites – or men-at-arms – who held a substantial three hides and one virgate of the Bishop's land.

Whether Shonks was a military man or not, no one records, but to battle a great serpent he must surely have been skilled in combat. Was he a Saxon thegn? Perhaps once a housecarl in the old king's elite bodyguard, hurling his throwing spear at the beast before finishing it off with a thrust from his hunting spear? Or was he a Norman knight, an adventurer who settled in Peleham after the Conquest, who charged the monster with his heavy lance? His name suggests a tall man, a long-shanks, and he must have been because he got close enough to the fire-breathing monster to hurl or thrust his weapon into the creature's flaming, wolf-like maw. And thus he delivered the simple ceorls or villeins of Peleham from a great terror and they could till the fields once again without fear.

As the years passed, people came to compare Shonks to the drag-on-slayers Cadmus and St George. Was he persistent and wise like Cadmus the founder of Greek Thebes and gallant and pious like the soldier George? When he died, the dragon was recorded in black marble so that posterity would not forget Shonks' great deeds. The carving shows a terrible serpent, a wyvern, with a beard and long ears and a long snaking coiling tail. Such animals were not unknown elsewhere in eleventh-century England: the Bayeux Tapestry shows a similar beast on the borders of Normandy when Earl Harold first met Duke William there in 1064. (Was Shonks among the retainers that day?). The death of the Peleham dragon was said to be a terrible loss to the greater dragon, to the Devil of medieval nightmares. And the villagers must have feared he would have his revenge; that he would have Shonks' soul whether he was buried in a church or not.

A priest lived on the land of the milites in 1086 and perhaps it was he who knew how to secure Shonks' safety in the afterlife. The great hero was buried neither within his church nor without, instead the marvellous slab of black marble was set deep into the very wall of the nave and Shonks lay in peace beneath that slab, and there he stayed – as in a fortress against Satan.

And eight hundred years passed.

On the back of a postcard I picked up on eBay, three holidaymakers, Mabel, Roger, and Richard write to their friend in Newcastle-on-Tyne to let him know that they are enjoying themselves 'immensely' down south. They are out on a short bicycle ride from 'the country "pub" in a lovely old village' where they are staying. I imagine they stopped at a church or two. Across an orange 1d. George VI stamp, is the fragment of a postmark: Brent Pelham, 20 August 1937. Another date adorns the flipside: A.D. 1086. The photographer has written it in white pen across the bottom edge of the postcard 'Shonks Tomb A.D. 1086 Brent Pelham 85341'. The black-and-white photograph is more grey and yellow, an early expressionist film, the flash intensely bright against the plaster above the tomb slab, which is little more than a sinister grey block under the arch. It looks as if it has been taken at dead of night in total darkness by a camera set up to capture an elusive creature on film. You half expect to see the startled red eyes of some scavenger caught in the blinding flash, or worse, but there is only a shapeless grey shadow seeping into the right-hand edge – just a flaw in the print, I expect. What it lacks in detail, in delineation, it makes up for in mood, and 1086, that most gothic date – AD 1086 – works hard to layer the photo with antiquity and profoundity as if the photographer has caught a moment in time long before 1937, as if the photo is itself an ancient relic.

It was John Weever in his *Ancient Funeral Monuments* who first left a date to puzzle posterity. Writing in the seventeenth century, lamenting the loss of memorials to the Reformation, while unwittingly preserving the memory of others that would soon be destroyed, Weever gives us little that is original about Shonks. In the published version, he quotes John Norden's brief note from the end of the previous century, but then he adds the line 'He flourished, Ann. à conquestu vicesime primo'; that is *In the twenty-first year from the Conquest*, or perhaps the twenty-first regnal year of William I, whose count of years began on 14 October (the date of his victory at the Battle of Hastings) and ran to 13 October in the following calendar year. William's twenty-first year was his last, and so ran until his death on 9 September 1087. A year in which, in that quaint but pleasing formula, Shonks *flourished*. A phrase that simply means *he was around*, and yet speaks to us of someone whose cups were flowing over, living life to the full and doing great deeds. Weever does not say that Shonks died in 1086–7. It was the Reverend Thomas Tingge who first wrote in the Parish Register above his record of the inscription *Pierce Shonkes, who died in 1086*. That Tingge records it as well, almost reassures us that Weever did not just invent it or make a mistake, muddling his tombs as he sometimes did. We assume the information came from the inscription over the tomb before it was taken down. However, the rough draft of Weever's work at the Society of Antiquaries does not include the date, although it does include a startling mistake, instead of Shonks, Weever writes St Honks, canonising the hero twice: in the text and in the margin. I can only think that came about from an inability to read his own handwriting, or someone else's transcript of John Norden's text, which he otherwise follows closely. Somehow, the mistake got cleared up between the draft and the published version, and the date was added, but from what source, we don't know.

Without the date, the hero and his deeds would exist outside of history. The places in the landscape associated with the name of Shonks do not transport us back to Norman England. The historical facts about the tomb slab, the carvings and their probable date, the niche, the wall, the church itself, none reach back to 1086. The date places the death of Shonks on a timeline along with undeniably historical deaths, which seem semi-mythical to us today: between the shootings of King Harold at Hastings and William Rufus in the New Forest.

Cadmus and St George have been given dates too. St George was martyred on 23 April 303 according to some accounts. Cadmus founded Thebes in 1493 BCE, at least according to my tatty copy of *Guy's Historical Table of General History*, which somehow finds dates for all sorts of mythical and semi-mythical events. In the fourth century CE, Eusebius of Caesarea calculated the age of the world, the day of Adam and Eve's fall and any number of dates from the Bible and antiquity (apparently Perseus decapitated Medusa in the year 650 of Abraham). We might be sceptical of his computations today, but he didn't just pluck them out of the air. I hope 1086 wasn't either.

The date furnishes the legend with an appropriate patina of antiquity, it is a cipher for 'a long time ago' and, as one writer on collective memory has pointed out, early dates can be part of a community's strategy to 'out origin' their rivals. How many villages can boast a local hero who witnessed the Conquest? For us, 1086 is the year of the Domesday Book and the Norman yoke, and the Conqueror is still on the throne, just. But if it was chosen to signify the distant past, why not the more famous 1066? Does its association with the Domesday Book suggest the Shonks legend had its origin in a land dispute? It is unlikely. And equally unlikely that it conjured up images of Saxons and Normans. The sense of the past, in the past, was not what it is today. We only have to look at historical paintings to see that our forebears thought that their forebears looked and dressed like them and favoured exactly the same clothing and architecture. As C. S. Lewis observed, Milton 'never doubted that "capon and white broth" would have been as familiar to Christ and the disciples as to himself'.

Certainly, for the uneducated farm labourer in the nineteenth century, 1086 is unlikely to have meant anything more than the passing of years and a past sufficiently long ago that dragons still stalked the land. The same goes for those who first put the date over the tomb. In Norden's and Weever's day, few, if any, knew that the Domesday survey took place in 1086. Turn to the great historical chronicles of the Tudor period, Raphael Holinshed and Polydore Vergil, and they both erroneously place the survey three years earlier. That doesn't mean that 1086 was without interest to them: 'About this season,' wrote Holinshed,

> the people in all places were pitifullie plaged with burning feuers, which brought manie to their end: a murren also came to their cattell, whereof a woonderfull number died. At the same time (which is more maruellous) tame foules, as hens, géese, & peacocks, forsaking their owners houses, fled to the woods and became wild. Great hurt was doone in manie places of the realme by fire, and speciallie in London, where vpon the 7. daie of Iulie a sudden flame began, which burnt Paules church, and a great part of the citie downe to the verie ground.

So a fine year for dragons and dragon fire. And that teasing reference to St Paul's, to which Pelham Arsa – Burnt Pelham mind you – would soon belong. All wonderful material for the imagination if not for the historian.

It may seem fruitless to spend any time pondering a date some two hundred years adrift of the day the mason took his chisel to the tomb. The traditional date of Shonks' death or flourishing can only be reconciled with the actual date of his tomb slab if we divorce the legend from the slab or decide that someone decided to venerate Shonks a long time after his death. Or was the thirteenth-century tomb slab appropriated in the sixteenth century to help preserve the old village story, which genuinely dated back to the Norman Conquest? Not for the first time, I resist itemising all the possibilities.

Herbert Andrews, writing in 1930, found an ingenious way to square the circle:

If, on the other hand, the legend records picturesquely a local event, instead of the devil let us put William the Conqueror, and for the dragon one of his Norman followers named Bech. The Saxon Shonks, beloved by his people for his prowess, is dispossessed of his lands by Bech, who treats him harshly and tyrannically: so Shonks slays the Norman and thereafter lives under the protection of the Church. Perhaps he had even been the builder of the Saxon edifice which preceded the present building and in his memory, enhanced by the passing of the years, the tomb was made for the reception of his bones when this church was built in the fourteenth century.

Here is Shonks as a new Hereward the Wake, fighting a guerrilla war against the Norman oppressors. By 1086, it is a little late for that, and perhaps not a good date to associate our hero with if the chronicler Henry of Huntingdon is to be believed. He wrote: 'In the twenty-first year of King William's reign there was hardly a nobleman of English descent left in England, but all were reduced to servitude and mourning, so that it was a disgrace to be called an Englishman.'

Ultimately, 1086 is part of the tradition that I may only be able to come at by writing Shonks into the eleventh century as I have tried to do at the top of this chapter, changing tack for a moment and, instead of peeling back centuries of imagination, attempting to come at him through a flight of fancy. As the folk have known all along, perhaps storytelling is the only meaningful way to get nearer to Shonks the man, if there ever was such a person.

Can we give Shonks a better date? There was the old farmer who in 1872 said that 'Shonke lived in the seventh century'. If that is not early enough, we could go back to W. B. Gerish: in 1921, the year that he died, Gerish wrote one final account of the Shonks legend, adding the surprise detail that the legend dated to before the coming of the Romans. More promising though is a rumour that half a century after Domesday our hero was flourishing in the Pelhams, his blood up, and quelling twelfth-century dragons while Christ and his saints slept.

26

How incurious are the majority of us, except on the subject which we deem the one all worthy of our attention. How many an antiquary, who has travelled miles to see a druidical monument has cried 'Pish' – at the legend with which his peasant guide would illustrate it, when reflection would have told him, that under the garb of fiction the truth of history is frequently concealed.

—William Thoms, *Lays and Legends of France*, 1834

In the spring of 1911, a young man called Cyril Fox cycled into Brent Pelham to explore Shonks' Moat. Most moats have no name or history, wrote Fox after his visit, but Shonks's, it appeared, had both: 'For as I wandered over the scarred and broken ground, I chanced on a labourer chewing on a contemplative straw; and being curious about a name so unusual as Shonks – a name with a harsh and uncompromising Saxon ring about it – I made inquiries, feigning complete ignorance.'

Fox listened carefully to the labourer's reply and wrote up his story for a newspaper. It was an unusual survival, an account of Shonks' fame that required no dragons, or giants or devils.

'My name is John Rolfe,' said he, 'an' I reckon I do know something about it, havin' been born in these parts, an' my father afore me. Now, this moat here is Shonks' Moat; here he had his house, an' here he lived an' died, spite of all who wanted to kill him.

For there's a mound at Anstey yonder that was once a gre't an'
strong castle, an' close by the church at Clavering is a moat wi'
white an' yellow lilies in it, an' on the ground inside that moat
was another gre't, strong castle. An' both of these were held by
lords, who took all the wealth of the land hereabout.' What did
they take? I asked. 'Why, they stole the cattle an' horses of the
farmers an' the squires, an' took corn from their barns; an' offen
the farmer himself was carried off; an' they made the poor folk
work for them. But this Shonks would have none of it, not he.'
John Rolfe nodded with great satisfaction, and proceeded to fill
his pipe.

Fox realised, with amazement, that he was listening to 'a tale of
the raids, plunderings, and oppressions of men who died seven
hundred years ago, a tale which had apparently been handed down
by word of mouth through the centuries.' Fox knew his history,
and placed the events described by Rolfe in the time of the Anarchy
of King Stephen and the Empress Matilda in the early twelfth
century – famously described by the Anglo-Saxon Chronicle as a
time so lawless that, 'The earth bare no corn: you might as well
have tilled the sea, for the land was all ruined by such deeds and
it was said openly that Christ and his saints slept'.

John Rolfe continued his tale, pointing to the neighbouring
villages of Anstey and Clavering – where castle mounds can still be
seen today – as the source of Shonks' troubles:

'This Shonks owned the land hereabout, an' one day a load of
corn which he had sent to market – to Stortford, maybe, ten
mile away – was stolen, waggon an' all, by the Lord of the Castle
of Anstey; he was most wrathful, an' said that all this wrong
doing an' harrying should stop, an' if the men of the three parishes
had any spunk, they could make it so. He was a main strong
man, an' the best shot with the bow in those parts; an' he got

men from the villages, Meesden an' Berden an' the three Pelhams, an' armed them; an' he digged this deep moat round his house, which was much deeper an' broader when he digged it than it is now. Well, he got his men, an' he set a watch on the ingoings and outgoings at Clavering an' likewise at Anstey; an' when the orders of the castles sent men to steal cattle an' fodder, as I told you, this Shonks knew about it from his watchmen; an' he took his men, with weapons an' bows an' arrows an' attacked them, they not expecting him, an' killed them. This he did again an' again, an' the cleverness of Shonks put heart into people, so that the lords hardly dared step outside their moats an' their walls. They was most wrathful with Shonks, an' came an' attacked him; but they cudn't get inside here, he fought so well.

'An' so the folk hereabout had peace, an' soon after the castles were pulled down. That were a main good job,' said John Rolfe meditatively.

'All the folk honoured Shonks,' the tale continued, 'as was right, seeing what he had done. As I said, he was a wunnerful shooter with the bow; an' one day when he was stanning inside his moat, looking west, as I'm looking now, an' seeing the spire of the church peeping over the hillbrow of Hartham Common, he shot with his bow, saying that where the arrow fell he would be buried; an the nearer the church the better, he says, shooting towards it. May be he did this out o' pride, so that when he died folk might know how far he could shoot. Anyways, the arrow, which he shot went clear of the hill an' stuck in the plaster of the church wall, an' this was thought good luck an' good shooting, too. So when Shonks died, as I have told you quiet an' peaceful in his bed, they buried him neither outside nor inside the church but betwixt an' between, for they put his coffin in a hole they made in the wall where his arrow had struck. An' the three Pelhams have never forgotten him, though his house be gone these many years.'

The complete absence of any supernatural or fanciful elements – other than the superhuman bow-shot – makes Rolfe's story completely different to any other account that has come down to us. Is it possible that Fox collected an unmediated oral tradition untainted by the feedback loop of written versions of the legend and the interference of well-meaning vicars and gentry? The story is an outlier.

Appearing in the *London Daily News* on 5 May 1911, the article bore the bracketed byline '(by Cyril Fox.)'. The name was familiar. Could the author be the eminent archaeologist Sir Cyril Fox? According to the biography written by his son Charles Scott-Fox, Cyril Fox was living in Stansted, Essex, some twelve miles from Brent Pelham from the middle of 1903. He was in his early twenties and working at the Bovine Tuberculosis Research station under the Cambridge bacteriologist Louis Cobbett. Both men were keen on history and archaeology, and Fox was able to revive 'boyhood memories of exploring earthworks with his father on the Isle of Wight, by cycling around the local area and recording local sites of archaeological interest'. Years later, the great archaeologist Sir Mortimer Wheeler conjured up a charming image of them exploring the countryside 'from the precarious altitude of a penny farthing'.

By 1911, when the article was written, both Cobbett and a twenty-eight-year-old Fox were based at the Milton Road laboratory in Cambridge, but they continued their excursions by bike into the surrounding countryside. 'Their common interests extended to all things historic,' wrote Charles Scott-Fox. 'From earthworks to cathedrals and farmhouses to ancient dykes and causeways.'

In the introduction to his breakthrough work, *The Archaeology of the Cambridge Region*, published in 1923, Cyril Fox recalls the cycle rides that took him as far afield as north-east Hertfordshire and the Pelhams. A prehistoric mound at Cole Green in Brent Pelham as well as Bronze-Age finds in Furneux Pelham find their way into the book. There is no mention of Shonks' moat, but he briefly discusses homestead moats over two pages in the Anglo-Saxon chapters, only to conclude that they probably do not belong to the Anglo-Saxon age: 'In view of this uncertainty, it is not proposed to include in this survey any of the homestead moats in our district.' I imagine him reluctantly putting aside the notes he made some years before on Shonks' Moat, recalling the day he met the bucolic John Rolfe.

Fox's long-standing interest in history and archaeology since boyhood and his later eminence in the field, give me some confidence that the account is an honest one. It is the first narrative to include an historical as opposed to a legendary Shonks. One we can believe in without too much suspension of disbelief. The fabulous elements are mostly tropes. The serpent of the inscription is a metaphor for the Lord of Anstey or Clavering. At the same time, I am not entirely sure what to make of it. Rolfe's description is a little too close to a dramatised retelling of the Anglo-Saxon Chronicle's version of the Anarchy, with a hammed-up yokel vocabulary to go with Rolfe's 'contemplative straw'. It is a little too literary, recalling the style of Kipling's *Puck of Pook's Hill*, published five years earlier, in which two children encounter characters from English history in the countryside near their home in Sussex. But that could just be in Fox's writing rather than in the raw narrative as he heard it. And we are not surprised that Fox told the story of Shonks' moat through the tale of John Rolfe when we read Mortimer Wheeler recalling Fox's deeply human approach to archaeology 'A potsherd, a mound, a barn, a button, what-have-you, were to him not mere *things*. The mind of a man or a woman had shaped them with a measure of skill and purpose to that extent they partook of humanity, were integral with humanity.' He was the best kind of archaeologist.

There is also the small matter of whether we believe that a folk legend can be passed by word of mouth for some twenty-five generations and retain – unbeknownst to the storytellers – a folk memory of identifiable historical events. It is certainly tempting to see this story as the one that was told before the carvings on the tomb got involved, but it is just as likely to be a practical man's rationalisation of the legend.

True or not, it bears studying, as an attempt to place the hero in an historical period more suited to the age of the moat and the tomb. It is also the longest oral account about Shonks I have come across. Fox's statement that he feigned ignorance of the legend so as to get a truthful account from Rolfe is convincing and consistent with the rules of folklore collecting. 'Treat other people's beliefs with respect,' counselled *The Handbook of Folk-Lore*, although it also added that you should not question locals for too long as they are likely to find it taxing to their brains, and warned that uneducated people would lie if frightened.

Rolfe does not sound frightened in Fox's account. The nearest John Rolfe I can find, during the years that Fox lived in the area, died at Bishop's Stortford in 1923 of senile decay aged eighty-one, and had been a farm stockman living in Takeley some fourteen miles from Brent Pelham at the time of the 1911 census, or it could have been his son, another John Rolfe, who was a farm labourer living with his father. Why either of them would be chewing a straw at Shonks' Moat when Fox visited is anyone's guess. Neither appears in the extensive lists of farm labourers employed at Beeches Farm in the early twentieth century, but the presence of one or the other is not incredible.

Glance at a map today and you can see that Brent Pelham with its homestead moats is flanked by Anstey and Clavering, with the remains of their castles. To the west is the 'Motte & Bailey' at Anstey, to the east the 'Castle (site of)' at Clavering over the county boundary. If you were inventing a story of the Middle Ages you could not ignore them, but equally in reality they must have played a significant role in life thereabouts. They are two of the earliest castles on the Hertfordshire–Essex border. Tom Williamson has noted that there are more castles in East than West Hertfordshire, where Domesday reveals that land ownership was complex and so

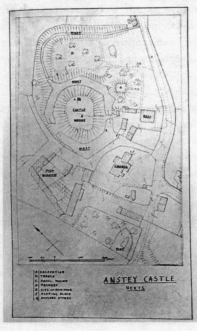

presented more opportunities for disagreements. He also adds that such castles were erected after the Conquest to protect sites from 'Baronial rustling' in times of unrest. But those garrisoned inside the castles were just as likely to do their own rustling in the local countryside, and worse.

The Lord of Anstey in the time of King Stephen was Geoffrey de Mandeville, a man said most to embody those terrible times when, as the Anglo-Saxon Chronicle reports, the king did not enforce justice and 'every rich man built his castles, and defended them against him, and they filled the land full of castles. They greatly oppressed the wretched people by making them work at these castles and when the castles were finished they filled them with devils and evil men. They took those whom they suspected to have any goods, by night and by day, seizing both men and women . . . I cannot and I may not tell of all the wounds, and all the tortures that they inflicted upon the wretched men of this land; and this state of things lasted the nineteen years that Stephen was king.'

Which all makes Mandeville, or one of his lackeys, a perfect candidate for Shonks' serpent. The medievalist J. H. Round, who coined the term 'the Anarchy', wrote that de Mandeville obtained Anstey Manor with its castle so as to strengthen his hold over the Lea and Stort valleys, and it is not far-fetched to imagine Mandeville's underlings, garrisoned at the castle, rampaging around the surrounding countryside stealing the *cattle an' horses of the farmers an' the squires, an' taking corn from their barns; an' offen carrying off the farmer himself.*

Revisionists have suggested that Mandeville was not all bad, but cannot completely exonerate him. The chronicle *Gesta Stephani* records that after Mandeville fell out with the king he sacked Cambridge and terrorised East Anglia. He 'raged everywhere with fire and sword; he devoted himself with insatiable greed to the plundering of flocks and herds'.

Over 1,000 adulterine or unlicensed castles were supposedly

destroyed by Henry II after the Anarchy. It is now thought that this number is greatly exaggerated, and the 'anarchy' of Stephen's reign was only in pockets throughout the country.

Clavering Castle survives as a moat and a series of complex earthworks, and it is something of a mystery. Some historians think it was that very rare thing – a pre-Conquest castle built by a Norman who came to England with Edward the Confessor in the 1040s. There were only five of them in the whole country. More recently, archaeologists have argued that it was more likely to have been built during the Anarchy and destroyed not long afterwards, or was not even a castle at all. If it was used during the Anarchy, we might hope that it offered resistance to Geoffrey de Mandeville's rebellion and any ravening of the local countryside, as it was held by Henry of Essex who was a royal constable of King Stephen's.

A little more is known about Anstey, and its history offers a longer time period when it may have played a part in the life of Shonks. Built shortly after the Conquest, it was still there in 1218 when Nicholas de Anstey was ordered to destroy the castle before mid-Lent so that no part of it should remain except what was built before the Barons' War against King John. Nicholas ignored his instructions and much of the castle was still standing seven years later when it was seized by the king on Nicholas's death. The last mention of it was in 1304. All of which gives us a reasonable time span to fit John Rolfe's account to a later historical event, closer to the age of the moat and the tomb.

The Anarchy was not the only time of unrest, and local lords and their retainers were still abusing their power long afterwards and long after Bad King John too. Weever's '1086', and Rolfe's Anarchy both seem vivid but unconvincing backdrops to the career of someone buried in that tomb. The historical Shonks was hiding elsewhere.

27

Monuments, names, words, proverbs, traditions, private records and evidences, fragments of stories, passages of books that concern not story, and the like, do save and recover somewhat from the deluge of time.

—Francis Bacon, *The Advancement of Learning*, 1605

Four years before he was decapitated by a London mob outside St Paul's Cathedral, Bishop Stapeldon had the rather less memorable distinction of being the first Treasurer to try to safeguard the records of the Exchequer before they were lost or ruined. The bishop was behind various writs in the 1320s that led to the famous 'Stapeldon's array': a mustering of the Treasury's papers in the White Tower where they were marshalled and arranged into twenty-four classes before returning to Westminster. Imagine many hundreds of wagons drawn east along the banks of the River Thames through Edward II's London, piled high with iron-bound chests, coffers, forcers, canvas bags, and leather pouches, tills, skippets and hanapers. Each was marked with a symbol as a clue to their contents: a letter, a monogram, sometimes a rebus or a sort of hieroglyph. Clasped hands for marriage papers. A Saracen's head for certain foreign records. 'Papers relating to rebellions would be marked, suggestively, with a gallows,' wrote the librarian Edward Edwards in the early nineteenth century.

Somewhere among all the tallies and rolls of animal hide was one particular rotulus that had started life in June 1288 in the great Westminster Hall where the notorious Chief Justice Thomas Weyland presided over the Common Pleas Bench (two years later he was forced to abjure the realm as an accessory to murder). The Common Bench was the court that heard civil cases between individuals, as opposed to those between subjects and the crown. After being handed in by the Chief Justice, the rotulus had probably spent a while in Hell, reputedly one of three medieval storage areas beneath the hall – the others being Paradise and Purgatory, of course – but once it was no longer a working document, it was carried across the street to the Chapter House in Westminster Abbey and bound with other rotuli between foruli, thick parchment covers. And it was to the Chapter House that it returned after its brief sojourn in the Tower of London, and there it sat mouldering until one day in the 1690s the Hertfordshire lawyer and antiquary Henry Chauncy happened to pull it from a heap.

It was a miracle it survived really, and a miracle that antiquaries like Chauncy were able to find anything at all among the public records. As a nation, the British were brilliant at creating records, but not so good at taking care of them, in spite of Stapeldon's valiant efforts centuries before. William Prynne was scathing in his condemnation of the state of things in the seventeenth century. Prynne, who was keeper of the records under the Stuart monarchs, complained in a letter to Sir Harbottle Grimston that he was being 'choked with the dust of neglected records (interred in their own rubbish for sundry years) in the White Tower; their rust eating out the tops of my gloves with their touch, and their dust rendering me, twice a day, as black as a chimney sweeper'. The records continued to be neglected in the following centuries, suffering from damp and rot and the attentions of rats and mice in the various repositories at Westminster: the Pell Office, the gatehouse of Westminster Palace, the Chapel of the Pyx, and the Chapter House of Westminster Abbey. These all sound like grand – if surprising

– repositories. At least they were better than the stores of the king's fishmonger, where, in 1687, someone discovered that all the records of the Court of Ward had been dumped. The fishmonger was suspected of embezzling many of the papers, although the embezzled ones probably had a greater chance of survival than those still in the storehouse, which were rained upon because the lead had been stolen from the roof.

To go through the innumerable eighteenth-century enquiries into the state of the public records with a highlighter is to emphasise confused heaps, dust, decay, damp, utmost disorder and filth. Papers *perished* or were *purloined, lost into private hands, suddenly discovered in corners, at risk of going up in flames,* or *in danger of utter perishing.* The last of these was a warning about the records in the Chapter House by the House of Lords Select Committee appointed to look into the matter in Chauncy's day. The Common Pleas rolls that we are interested in, were lying on the ground, for 'Want of Presses to put them in, the Dampness of the Ground having been very prejudicial to them', which is not surprising since the Chapter House itself 'was in ruinous condition and in danger of falling'.

The chaos puts me in awe of the heroic searches of the early antiquaries, like Henry Chauncy, rummaging through dirty parchment in the damp and the cold: there was no allowance for coal or kindling, so the working conditions for much of the year were freezing as antiquaries huddled over blackened and creaking scrolls and rotuli, copying them out before they became unreadable.

The 400-hundred-year-old roll that Chauncy alighted on referred to Simon de Furneux, Lord of the Pelhams in the thirteenth century. He made a brief summary of what he found, which is fortunate because for many years afterwards no other historians were able to locate the roll from Chauncy's description. He included it in his parish history of Brent Pelham, in passing, as one random piece of documentary evidence, writing that in the sixteenth year of Edward

I's reign, Simon de Furneux *distrained* a Gilbert Sank 'for his Homage and Service, and forty Shillings and six Pence Rent by the Year, Fealty and Suit of Court at Pelham Arsa from three Weeks to three Weeks'.

This dispute between de Furneux and Sank needs some deciphering, but first we must turn to another Hertfordshire county historian, Nathaniel Salmon, because it was Salmon who, a few years later, spotted the potential significance of Chauncy's reference. He asked if Sank might have been a variant of Shonks, and, therefore, if Piers might have been a relative of Gilbert's. The sixteenth year of Edward I's reign, that is 1288, is not too far out for the style of the cross-slab, although Salmon did not really know that at the time. He speculated even further, writing: 'Shonks is said to flourish Anno a Conquestu 21. Grant my Emendation of 221 and it suits well enough with the Distress to a Year'.

> *De Warrenis in cur. recept. in Scac. Rot. 45.* In the time of *Edw.* I. *Simon de Furneux* was Lord of the 𝕭𝖊𝖑𝖍𝖆𝖒𝖘, had a Grant of free Warren in them from King *H.* III. and upon a *Quo Warranto* brought against
> *Trin. 16 Ed.I. Rot. 24, cur. recept. in Scac* him, it was allow'd upon the View of the Grant: *An.* 16 of the same King, he distrained *Gilbert Sank* for his Homage and Service, and forty Shillings and six Pence Rent by the Year, Fealty and Suit of Court at 𝕻𝖊𝖑𝖍𝖆𝖒 𝕬𝖗𝖘𝖆 from three Weeks to three Weeks.

In other words Salmon, based on what Richard Gough would later call a 'train of amusing conjectures', suggested that Shonks really flourished not twenty-one years after the Conquest, but 221 years after it: that is 1287. The document he refers to as the *Distress* is dated in the Trinity Term of 1288, sometime between June and July, close enough for Salmon at such a distance. Peter or Piers, he continues, may have been a son of Gilbert, who got the distress against his father overturned and in so doing not only defeated a 'serpent' – who Salmon identifies as Simon de Furneux – but also rendered a service to the neighbourhood and so was venerated as a local hero.

Salmon's arguments are neat, albeit wildly speculative: a random legal document pulled from the dust by Chauncy is made into the only known record of the family Shonks in the thirteenth century – or at least the family Sank. The dates are made to fit with a spot of cabalistic conjuring, but Salmon also wants to have it explain the entire legend, substituting Simon de Furneux for the dragon, or the devil, or both, and a courtroom battle over a distraint rather than with a sword and spear in the farmlands of the Pelhams.

To understand this *distraint* requires a smattering of medieval law. In the Middle Ages a lord had the right to distrain or confiscate their vassal's chattels, that is their movable property, which usually meant their animals, so as to force them to perform a duty or pay a debt. This sounds a little like John Rolfe's account of local lords 'stealing cattle' or taking Shonks' load of corn on the way to market.

Distraint – making a distress – was often used to compel vassals or tenants to attend their lord's manorial court, usually every three weeks as is the case here. By the thirteenth century this *suit of court*, had become a great source of rancour, and has been called a humiliating reminder of a tenant's subordination to their lord. And lords tried it on, demanding suit when they had no right to it so as to assert their authority, or so they could impose fines or quit rents that were a handy source of income. As duties were customary and rarely written down, it was hard for a tenant to prove things one way or another. In the Provisions of Westminster of 1259, during the Barons' War against Henry III, it was decided that suit of court could be proven if it was in writing between a vassal and his lord or if the lord could show that the tenant had performed suit of court before a certain date, which, with seemingly picturesque randomness, was set as Henry III's first voyage to Brittany in 1230. When de Furneux distrained his tenant Gilbert Sank, he also demanded fealty, homage and service – in other words an oath from

Sank that he was de Furneux's man and acknowledgement that he owed feudal service in return for the land.

The document Chauncy had found was an *action of replevin* that Gilbert Sank had brought before the court – an action to recover his goods. This medieval Latin court record is now tired and stained, but safely in the National Archives. It tells a story about a village dispute over 700 years ago. Chauncy did not have all his facts straight and left out many of the details. In the original, we find Gilbert claiming that his goods were wrongly seized by Robert Bishop, Simon de Furneux's servant, who on the Friday after St Francis's day in the fifteenth year of Edward I's reign, that is 10 October 1287, seized two of Gilbert's bullocks and drove them to Simon's manor of Brent Pelham.

What followed were some legal un-niceties as both parties manoeuvred to have the court find in their favour. Gilbert argued that Simon had no right to make the distress. Simon countered by claiming that Gilbert held a messuage, that is a main house and outbuildings, and sixteen acres in Brent Pelham on Simon's manor, for which Gilbert was supposed to pay a rent of forty-six pence a year (not the shockingly large sum of 40s. 6d. that Henry Chauncy had misread) as well as homage, fealty and suit of court to his manor court in Brent Pelham. All these were in arrears, claimed Simon.

The outcome of the case is not recorded on the roll. And this would not be the last time that Gilbert and Simon squabbled in the courts. It was not an unusual case for the time. The terms of land ownership were vague, and there was often no written evidence of those terms, which besides could change at any time by verbal agreement. As late thirteenth-century legal actions go, it might not be out of the ordinary, but this dirty and stained block of text on membrane twenty-four of Thomas Weyland's Common Pleas roll for Trinity Term 1288 is the foundational document of any search for an historical Shonks. For all his wild speculation, and implausible as it may sound, Nathaniel Salmon might have really found a piece of the jigsaw: a record of a possible family Shonks, a relative of a folk hero, of someone who slew dragons and killed giants – assuming of course that Gilbert Sank and his bullocks had anything at all to do with Piers Shonks.

28

'As this world becomes increasingly ugly, callous and materialistic it needs to be reminded that the old fairy stories are rooted in truth, that imagination is of value, that happy endings do, in fact, occur, and that the blue spring mist that makes an ugly street look beautiful is just as real a thing as the street itself.'

—Elizabeth Goudge, at a meeting of the Romantic
Novelists' Association, 1966

Today the inscription above the hero's tomb commemorates not Piers Shonks, but 'O. PIERS. SHONKS'. That mysterious 'O' appeared some time between the Reverend Cole's visit in 1743 and the publication of Richard Gough's *Sepulchral Monuments* in 1786. Cole gave the name as 'Peirce Shonke' – with the 'e' before the 'i' – both in his drawing and in his text. This almost agrees with the Brent Pelham vicar Thomas Tingge's 'Pierce Shonkes', written in the parish register about 1695. Yet by the 1780s Gough tells us that: 'Over the lines is now written, O Piers Shonks.'

In a note to the *Hertfordshire Observer* in 1915, Frederick Gurney wrote from Bedfordshire: 'I wish some amateur antiquary would suggest a reason, however unreasonable, for Shonks absurd prefix of "O". It possesses a full stop, and is therefore not a poetical invocation, but an initial, surely. It has always puzzled me that it has puzzled nobody.'

It has puzzled me too. Surely not an initial. I like the suggestion, though immediately dismissed by Gurney, that it is merely the vocative 'O', as if the writer of the verses over the tomb were addressing the long dead hero with a melodramatically drawn out 'O'. 'O Piers Shonks, Nothing of Cadmus nor St George, those Names . . . '. An antiphony, chanted by the congregations of St Mary's for centuries to the attributes of their hero. O Piers, O Wisdom, O Courage . . . This is not too unreasonable; the full stop may have been added by mistake later as it does not appear in the earliest instances, but it is unlikely.

If not a vocative 'O', perhaps a genitive one, meaning 'son of'. This could be similar to the ancient and rustic-sounding formulation Tom O Dick O George O Bob – to identify a particular village Tom by appending a string of his forefathers to his name. It is a less familiar version of the *O'* in Irish surnames, or the *ap* in Welsh ones, David ap Rhys ap Owen. 'Sam o' Bill's o' Jacky Tordoff's' and 'Did ye see Long Tom o' Sally's on t'road?' are two of the examples culled by Joseph Wright for the *English Dialect Dictionary*. This would only really make sense if a name had been missed off, such as the Gilbert we met in the last chapter, who might be identified as Gilbert O Piers.

In his retelling of the legend, Kevin Crossley-Holland dubs him Sir Piers Shonks, with a nod to the common misapprehension that dragon-slaying was chiefly the purview of knights. Did 'O' simply act as a pseudo-title, something to distinguish the name, to mark it out from the ordinary?

The solution lies somewhere between 1598 and 1631. John Norden linked the tomb to the hero in 1598, but a careful reading reveals that he did not actually tell us the name of the occupant, he said he was lord of a *place* called Shonkes. When, thirty-three years later, John Weever noted the tomb in his *Ancient Funeral Monuments*, he wrote that the occupant of the tomb had been lord of a place called O Piers Shoonkes. The place and not the man was called O Piers Shoonkes: that is 'Of Piers Shonks'. The 'O' acting perhaps like the more familiar German 'von', or French 'de'. In the thirteenth century, land was always held 'of' somebody else. If you were the Bishop of London, you held it 'of' the king, at the next level of the pyramid, Simon de Furneux held land 'of' the bishop, Gilbert Sonke held land 'of' Simon, and a Thomas le Waleys held land 'of' Gilbert. Once enough tenants held land of you in a village, you might be said to have the beginnings of a manor. Did that 'O' indicate that the place Weever referred to was held 'of' Shonks manor? This is the most reasonable explanation; certainly more reasonable than any suggestion that the 'O.' with its full stop was an initial, in the way that some Americans favour using their first initial followed by their middle name: G. Gordon Liddy or F. Scott Fitzgerald come to mind.

The 'O' dispensed with, let's return to Shonks (or Shonke or Sonke and, possibly even Sank) which sounds tangibly Anglo-Saxon: a name you can hold in your hand like a farm implement or a weapon. Cyril Fox described it as 'a name with such a harsh and uncompromising Saxon ring about it'. It has about it what the poet Phil Roberts has called phonolexis, the association of sounds with certain connotations. That hard and spiky K and the monosyllable, its resemblance to 'shock': it is a word that vibrates, like someone striking an anvil. It is a good old Anglo-Saxon swear word. A curse. Something done with a dagger. In the dictionary, it appears as an obscure early modern word meaning 'to shatter', and a modern offensive word for a Jewish person, or Australian slang for someone engaged in illegal business activities comparable to 'shark'. 'Aussie expression Shonky = not legitimate, not on the level,' wrote a helpful tourist in the Brent Pelham Church Visitor's Book in 2010. Ultimately, it leads the ear to *shank* or *shanks and his pony* – to long legs and sharp implements.

The name goes with the age of the tomb. If Shonks means Longshanks, we only have to think of Edward I who was known by that name. In 1905, the prolific Victorian scholar Walter Skeat, who had recently written *The Place-Names of Hertfordshire*, passed judgement in a hastily scribbled letter to W. B. Gerish. 'It is quite certain that Schonkes or Shonks is a variant of Schankes,' he writes 'which occurs as a surname in the hundred-rolls and would now be spelt Shankes. It is, of course, a mere nickname, equivalent to long-shanks or long-legs.'

The great man is sceptical of the association with Sank suggested by Nathaniel Salmon (remember that Salmon, following Chauncy, missed off the final 'e' from the original document in which Gilbert Sanke appeared – such trifles are not pedantries to the hunter of etymologies), saying it would require the Norman scribe to make two errors: writing 'S' for 'Sch' and leaving off the 'S' at the end. What's more, whereas Shonks is of Anglo-Saxon origin, Sank on the other hand is a Provençal rather than a Norman name, and may even be the Spanish 'Sancho' in disguise, which itself is a problematic name – but has nothing to do with sainthood, warns Skeat.

So was Nathaniel Salmon barking up the wrong phonological tree when he associated the Gilbert Sank, who left a trace in 1288, with the legendary Piers Shonks? Three decades after Skeat passed judgement, the English Place-Name Society published its volume on Hertfordshire. As well as including some of the field names collected by the village schoolchildren, that we met in Chapter 5, its citations included the latest historical sightings of long-lost villagers who may have bequeathed their names to farms and ends and woods. One of these had been spotted among the Hertfordshire *Feet of Fines* for Easter 1289. Just under a year after Gilbert Sanke's disagreement with Simon de Furneux, he now appears as the tenant of land in Brent Pelham, still involved in a dispute with Simon. This final concord – 'final' hence 'fine' – is a beautifully preserved short document now bound into a red-cased volume at the National Archives, the top edge has the characteristic horizontal wave, where the bottom, or 'foot', of the parchment has been cut away from the copies above, halfway through the word 'chirograph', that is a document handwritten in duplicate or triplicate. The missing top section would have contained two or more copies of the text separated vertically by another wavy cut. The parts could be fitted together to prove their authenticity – like the silver sixpence in Kipps. The handwriting of the court chirographer is flawless, the name Gilbert fashioned from light and dark strokes of the quill and easily spotted even by an eye unused to a thirteenth-century hand. The Place-name Society's volume cited the foot of fine to explain the origin of 'SHONK'S MOAT', and they could be more sure than Skeat that the Gilbert in dispute with Simon was a member of the Shonks family, because in 1289 the scribe does not spell his surname S-a-n-k-e, he spells it S-h-o-n-k-e.

There is no doubt that Gilbert Sanke in 1288 and Gilbert Shonke in 1289 are one and the same. This agreement made between Gilbert Shonke and Simon de Furneux appears to be a settlement of the case started the previous year. It transpires that most of the land that Gilbert held of Simon was in turn held of Gilbert by his tenants: Thomas and Joan le Waleys. The clue that this is the same land under dispute is that Simon's demands are the same – forty-six pence rent, suit of court every three weeks and service. The service is now defined in the agreement as *scutage* – shield money – which was a cash payment in lieu of the military service that had originally underpinned the feudal system.

Each tenant was only responsible to the lord from whom they held the land, so in practice, Gilbert would have been obliged to warrant that Thomas and Joan were not responsible for any claim that Simon – a lord who was higher up the pyramid – made on them. In this case, however, it is likely that the two bullocks distrained were in fact the property of Thomas and Joan. Gilbert then had to intervene to protect his tenants. All of this suggests that Simon and Gilbert were at odds about the nature of the tenancy, and this agreement was where they finally came to terms. Untangling this and understanding the nature of land holdings in the thirteenth century is a specialist occupation. Many disputes were fictitious; feigned so as to record a transaction in the court records. This is hardly the stuff of legend. While Salmon has been vindicated and his link between Sank and Shonk shown to be uncannily astute, this run-of-the-mill land dispute does not seem sufficient to cast Simon as the dragon of the piece, and we are still missing our dragon-slayer Piers.

Having spent over twenty years from the 1860s preparing a definitive edition of Langland's fourteenth-century poem 'Piers Plowman', Walter Skeat might be even more authoritative about the hero's Christian name. Ted Barclay has joked that although Piers sounds Norman, surely Piers Plowman could not possibly have been Norman, as no Norman would have gone anywhere near a plough. Skeat knows otherwise, Piers is Petrus or Peter, and is indeed Norman. 'Piers Schonks' he writes, insisting on that spelling, 'is a compound of Norman and English such as would be possible after 1300, but not much earlier'. By 1325, the chronicler William of Nassington wrote that now some understood French and some Latin in different measures, but all understood English, educated and uneducated.

And so the name fits the date of the tomb slab, which is some relief when trying to comprehend a date irrevocably associated with a legend about a hero said to have flourished in 1086, centred on a tomb slab that is 200 years younger, in a church that wasn't built when the slab was carved, and a niche, pedestal, and inscription that probably come 300 years later. And no one knows when the bones in the wall actually date from. Were they originally associated with that tomb, and was the name?

The mind starts to play games with words: hoping for significance, looking for connections. For a time, I kept returning to the name Piers Gaveston, the most famous Piers of the period. Nathaniel Salmon invokes him, calling him 'the minion Gaveston', to remind his readers that Gaveston was sometimes styled Peter, as Shonks must have been.

Gaveston was brought to court by Edward I Longshanks – note the sobriquet. He was the favourite of Edward II, excommunicated by the church, murdered in Oxford in June 1312. His body wasn't buried until 1315 in the priory of Kings Langley in Hertfordshire, some forty miles west of Brent Pelham. What happened to his tomb at the Dissolution of the Monasteries? Is it relevant that Edward Newport, the man who bought Brent Pelham Manor in 1597 – the year before the first ever mention in print of the tomb – was also granted the Priory of Kings Langley, albeit in 1607? It is completely irrelevant, none of the dates fit, but I am now inured to wild speculation, and aren't such flights of fancy half of the fun of playing with folk legends? Even a useful way of thinking, far too neglected by timorous scholars?

I even started to doubt that Piers Shonks was a real name. Try the phonebook or Facebook: Shonks and its variants are thin on the ground. It sounds like a crossword clue. Perhaps that is why the 'O' was needed. Or a riddle, Piers or Pierce is too reminiscent of the idea that the cross is piercing the carving of the dragon, that his sword or spear or arrow is piercing the dragon of the tale. And Shonks, the supposed giant of a man with its echo of Shanks or Longshanks. If you were going to make up a medieval name for a medieval folk hero you could do a lot worse.

Except that Piers Shonks certainly did exist. I found him by chance one day in the Hairy Book.

29

To study something of great age until one grows familiar with it and almost to live in its time, is not merely to satisfy a curiosity or to establish aimless truths: it is rather to fulfil a function whose appetite has always rendered History a necessity. By the recovery of the Past, stuff and being are added to us; our lives which, lived in the present only, are a film or surface, take on body — are lifted into one.

—Hilaire Belloc, *The Old Road*,
1911

In a large blue clamshell box, on a table in a 1930s brick-faced block at the heart of London's Clerkenwell, sits an 800-year-old hairy book.

The Hairy Book.

It has had other names. In 1447, when Dean Thomas Lisieux catalogued the seventeen great record books of Old St Paul's Cathedral, thirteen of them were lettered *A* to *N* (there was no modern 'J', in case you were counting). The Hairy Book was *Book A* – or *Liber A* – not because it was the earliest, most beautiful, or most important, but simply because it was the largest at 15 by 10½ inches. It was already old then, and already nicknamed the Hairy Book, or rather *Liber Pilosus* to give it its proper Latin moniker.

Some 400 years later it was given the reference *WD1*. The East and West cupboards – or presses as they were called – in the gallery next to the cathedral library were identified by the letters W and E by the Victorian librarian William Sparrow Simpson. *WD1* was the first book on *Shelf D*, in *Press W*. It was still WD1 just before the Second World War, when Frank Stenton, the historian of Anglo-Saxon England wrote about, 'the famous Liber Pilosus; the great cartulary compiled for the chapter a few years before the middle of the thirteenth century'.

The 'chapter' Stenton referred to were the Dean and Canons of St Paul's Cathedral. There, in 1241, an unknown scribe began to copy many of the cathedral's charters to form a cartulary. His lettering was not beautiful, but administrative, 'a small rapid cursive hand', according to Marion Gibbs, who edited and transcribed the original contents of *Liber A*. Another hand partly rubricated the volume – adding capitals and marginalia in red. Above the first charter, the scribe wrote in Latin: 'In this book are contained copies of all the charters, chirographs and other diverse writings found in the treasury of the church of St Paul by London in the year 1241.'

It has survived for nearly 800 years, its importance magnified by the disappearance of twelve of the seventeen volumes known to Dean Lisieux. Over the centuries they had moved from the treasury to the vestry to the chapter house in Old St Paul's. During the Civil War, they were seized and lost, but were found again, largely by chance, by the antiquary William Dugdale and eventually returned to the cathedral. They survived more than one fire in the Tudor years, and in the Great Fire they were rescued by the clerk John Tillison and sent for safekeeping to Fulham and then back to Convocation House Yard while Wren was building the new St Paul's. Some were probably already lost by the time they were moved to the new chapter house. D vanished in the late seventeenth century. Only C's cover has been found. G, B and F went astray some time after 1699. The antiquary Matthew Hutton must be a suspect, as he was the last man known to have consulted them, copying out sections of them, including twelfth-century descriptions of the churches of Brent and Furneux Pelham. A fragment of *Liber B* turned up at Oxford's Bodleian Library many years later among the Richard Rawlinson collection. Bishop Rawlinson's motto was 'I collect and I preserve' and his biographer gives us some idea of the fate of so many lost books and manuscripts when she describes Rawlinson's efforts to save them: 'He did not confine himself to the traditional means of purchasing manuscripts through auctioneers and booksellers. He vastly increased his collections by seeking papers of historical interest that had been sold for scrap, scouring grocers' and chandlers' shops, and purchasing by weight important seventeenth-century archives. He also developed unrivalled skill in locating papers which had strayed and were thought to have been lost.' The annals of book collecting are at their most compelling when we read of pages snatched from the furnace at the last moment. The papers of the former Bishop of London Edmund Gibson were rescued from a London wine cellar by Sparrow Simpson as they were about to be sold as waste paper, and in 1949, an extraordinary 400 manuscript documents belonging to St Paul's were unearthed in a disused garage in Shenley, Hertfordshire. There is hope yet that the lost cartularies will one day be found – propping up a table leg in a farmhouse perhaps. Only I, K and L have survived the centuries alongside the Hairy Book. In 1829, these four books were still in the chapter house in the 'great wainscot press', but Archdeacon Hale removed them to the octagonal chamber above the dean's vestry. During the First World War, you would have found them hidden in the crypt, in the Second, they were secreted at the National Library of Wales and so dodged the bombs, which fell on the cathedral and destroyed many other precious records. The books came back to St Paul's after the war, but they struggled to look after them to modern standards. Finally, in 1980 the cathedral's archives found a new home at London's Guildhall Library. Like Shonks, the Hairy Book is a survivor.

Inside the clamshell box, the parchment folios are stitched into seventeenth-century heavy boards, with a battered white leather binding, that was once secured by two leather clasps which no longer close properly.

Lift it out respectfully and settle it on grey foam wedges to support the spine. Turn to the very end of the volume and find there, attached to the back board, the 137th sheet or folio.

Resist the urge to stroke it.

It is a sheet of parchment made from animal skin, but one side is unshaven, still hairy with bald patches, and piebald, but unmistakably the hide of a deer. The fifteenth-century index describes it as '*co-opertorium huius libri*' that is, 'the cover of this book'. And this hairy cover of deer skin would once have formed part of the limp binding for the original folios, 'limp' because there were no boards, a proto-paperback.

The cover was taken from a deer that was killed to make parchment for the scriptorium of St Paul's Cathedral while Piers Shonks was still in his prime and hunting in the Pelhams – we know this, because of what we will find in this book.

Inside it are a number of charters relating to Furneux and Brent Pelham, since the village churches had been annexed to the treasurer of St Paul's when that post was created in the mid twelfth century. Technically, both parishes were *peculiars* of St Paul's. The treasurer was the rector, who took an income from the great tithes and owned the rectory manors. In the 1230s, the treasurer was Alexander Swerford, a man whom the Hertfordshire chronicler-monk Matthew Paris would eulogise on his death as 'in elegance of form, in beauty of features, and a mind endowed with many forms of learning . . . has not left his like in England'. Some time between 1231 and 1242 he swapped a parcel of land with another Pelham landowner.

Halfway down folio *xx* in the Hairy Book is the only surviving version of this grant or gift, which recorded the deal. '*Sciant presentes et futuri . . .* ' it begins, with the customary formula of such documents, 'Know all people present and future.' and continues, 'I William son of Peter de Pelham Furneux have given, granted and by this my present charter have confirmed to God and the church of Saint Paul's in London and to Alexander, treasurer of the same church, two acres of my land with appurtenances in the same village, in exchange for two acres of land of the treasurers in Brendepelham.'

I had known about the charter for some years, long before I saw the Hairy Book in the flesh. It was catalogued and transcribed by Marion Gibbs just before the Second World War, and was of minor interest to me: a record of early land dealings in the Pelhams. But one day I happened to scan a copy of the Latin text all the way to the foot of the transcription, where I met the words *Hiis Testibus* – 'these witnesses'. What follows is a list of the men there when the deal was done. They would have viewed the land and witnessed the symbolic exchange of soil or turf. This was Livery of Seisin. There are nine named witnesses, and 'others' unnamed and uncounted; men like Walter Sarners, whose family originally gave their name to Brent Pelham a century earlier when it was called Pelham Sarners. Other witnesses were from outside the village, like Galfrido de Blaby and William de Alneto, who were probably there to represent the treasurer's interests. There are eight others in total: William son of Peter himself is the first name, followed by another local lord, Roger le Grey. Further down the list, between Warin the Carpenter and Henry de Wauncy, is a name that caught my eye: Petrus Sonke.

Petrus is the Latin for Peter, or Piers. It was just a name on the end of a sheet of parchment, but it was finally evidence that in the reign of Henry III of England, as the Mongols overran Russia, and Matthew Paris wrote his great Chronicle at St Albans, there was an historical Piers Shonks in the Pelhams. A man who, with the passing of time, would come to give his name to a little story that would be told for centuries.

Strange for a hero, a man of storybook deeds, that our primary evidence for his existence outside of legend is as a witness to another's dealings. Historians cannot agree exactly on what witness lists can tell us or what it meant to be a witness, other than the fact that they were there to attest to the validity of an agreement in the future should it ever be questioned. Does being a witness indicate power and influence, social status, rank, trustworthiness, or a family or feudal relationship with the parties to the deed, an interest in the terms, consent to the terms, or did they just happen to be nearby when a witness was needed? At times, no doubt all of the above. At the least, it must indicate that their word counted for something. Some historians have suggested that witnessing and having the right sort of witness was a status symbol, and the position of someone in the witness list was hierarchical: here Piers Sonke appears bang in the middle of the list of nine named witnesses. It is fair to conclude that he was a freeholder, perhaps one of the more important freeholders in the parish.

By the end of the next decade he was to become one of the most important men in the seventeen parishes of the Edwinstree Hundred.

30

I suppose you think you only have two eyes, but I always say there is a third which you can see with but which cannot be seen – that is, the Eye of Imagination. I don't mean that you should imagine things that are not true or that were never there, but you can imagine the people who used the tools and weapons you see in museums or find for yourself and how they used them, and then they are not just museum specimens any longer but part of life itself.

— Frederick W. Robins, *On The Track of the Past*, 1956

There were the king's justices, the commissioners, the sheriff, the coroners, the tithingmen, first finders of corpses, and the neighbours of the dead, four men from each town, and the reeves, burgesses, appellors, appellees, approvers, witnesses, sureties, attorneys, as well as the great and good of the county: the knights and barons, earls, bishops, abbots and all their household servants; not forgetting the officers of the court: the marshals, clerks, vergers, ushers, criers, sergeants and bailiffs. And among them all, it seems, was a dragon-slayer.

It was 27 April 1248, and this vast gathering of the county, as many as 5,000 people, came to Hertford for the opening of the first Hertfordshire eyre in eight years. On that Monday morning eight centuries ago, Thomas de Bocland, lord of the manor of Buckland north of the Pelhams and bailiff of both Odysey and Edwinstree Hundreds stood before the justices and nominated two substantial freeholders from each hundred to elect ten others to form a jury of twelve. The electors were one Roger de Cayly, who held land in Little Hadham, now remembered in the name Cayley Wood. The other would be remembered both in the landscape and in its stories – he was one Peter Shanke. With his fellow jurors, he stood and took his oath: 'This hear, O justices, that I will speak truth on the questions which you will put to me on the King's behalf, nor for any cause will I omit anything, but will act with all my might, so help me God and these holy things.'

And so across time – in a manner of speaking – we can at last hear Piers Shonks' voice; he no longer just bore witness.

An eyre of all pleas or a general eyre, as historians call them, were the itinerant royal courts, which visited the counties about every seven years. The name 'eyre' derives from the Latin word 'iter', meaning journey, because they were the travelling courts as opposed to the two main central courts, the Bench, or Common Bench, and the King's Bench, both of which sat at Westminster. Historians call them a *general* eyre because of the range of business the justices dealt with, and to distinguish them from the occasional special eyres set up for various reasons. The justices in eyre were there to judge the most serious criminal and civil cases, many of which had already been judged by lesser courts, to hold the powerful to account, to check and uphold the king's rights in the county, and to raise money for the crown by handing out fines for every conceivable infringement of thirteenth-century legal process.

The eyre that came to Hertford in the spring of 1248 had begun its circuit two years earlier in York. At Cambridge, the previous year, Henry of Bath, soon to be Lord Chief Justice of England, left his place on the Common Bench at Westminster to take over as chief justice of the eyre circuit. It would finally run its course the following year on The Strand in London after visiting thirty-two counties.

It was the sixth eyre to visit Hertfordshire since the first in 1198, and only the second for which the crown pleas have survived. Eyre records are scattered throughout the archives, but the most useful are the plea rolls, which belonged to the chief justice. A rare survival is the kalendar or list of jurors for each hundred. In fact, only Hertfordshire's survives for Henry of Bath's circuit, listing the jurors for the seven hundreds, one half-hundred, and the half-dozen or so boroughs, liberties and villages who presented to the justices separately. In the Edwinstree Hundred we have thirteen names, the bailiff and the twelve jurors, two of whom were the electors we are most interested in.

It is still just a name on a list, but if Piers Shonks' appearance in a witness list in the Hairy Book in the previous decade tells us that he was a leading man in his village, the kalendar confirms that he was one of the leading men of the Hundred, and certainly a freeholder, owning land outright that he could pass to his heirs. 'The great majority of the jurors were substantial freeholders,' adjudged the great legal historian Cecil Meekings. 'Men with sufficient standing and interest in affairs to be active in the business of their district.'

The jurors' main job was to respond to a series of articles or questions put to them by the court about events in their Hundred. They were asked to name those who had not pursued outlaws travelling through their lands, they were asked about treasure trove, the misdeeds of officials, and anyone who took bribes to ensure that corn and other goods would not be seized for munitioning castles. There were sixty-nine articles in all by the end of Henry III's reign, 150 by the end of the century. Some of them protected the rights of the king, many were intended to check corruption and abuses by officials, others to ensure that the crown was not cheated out of income, or that the powerful were not pretending to rights they did not have. After the articles were read, the jurors retired to prepare answers, most of which they would have compiled beforehand. Their responses were presented to the justices in a document called the *veredictum* – hardly any of which have survived. They did not have to answer all the articles, only relevant ones and the jurors could also put forward their own criminal indictments.

Immediately following the kalendar roll with its lists of names, are two long membranes detailing the crown cases presented by Shonks and his fellow jurors in the Edwinstree Hundred. For the most part, this insight into the world of Shonks is strange to us. There were alien things: outlawry and abjuration of the realm, sanctuary, banes which became deodands, trial by combat and trial by ordeal. Almost everyone was in mercy – that is fined – for something or other, the justices even fined themselves for being too lenient. Whole communities were fined for murdrum.

Murder at this time meant specifically a clandestine killing by an unknown killer or killers. The word 'murder' is not found in the court rolls, the clerks preferred phrases such as 'killed by evil-doers unknown' (although in Latin, of course). 'Unknown evil-doers came by night to the house of John le Novelhomme and killed him and Alditha his wife, Alice the wife of William Godgrom, Matilda her daughter, and Geoffrey son of Matilda.'

This is one of the numerous such killings in the crown pleas presented by Shonks and the other jurors. For some reason the jurors presented this massacre of a family as a death by misadventure and so were fined for 'false presentment'. Murder might be a word we do not encounter, but 'murdrum' is found everywhere, because murdrum was the fine imposed upon a district when it could not present a killer to the court to face justice; in other words, murdrum was the fine for what we call murder.

There was, however, a way in which communities – usually the Hundred or the manor where the murder took place – could avoid the fine. This is where presentment of Englishry comes in – literally proving that the victim was English and not Norman, because if you could do that, you did not have to pay the fine. The killing of an English person in secret by unknown evil-doers was of less concern to the crown. This is because the murdrum fine was introduced by William the Conqueror to discourage the killing of Normans in the years after 1066. It remained part of English law until 1340.

The Dialogue for the Exchequer written in about 1180 has a lawyer explain the concept to his pupil:

Murdrum, indeed, is properly called the secret death of somebody, whose slayer is not known. For 'murdrum' means the same as 'hidden' or 'occult'. Now in the primitive state of the kingdom after the Conquest those who were left of the Anglo-Saxon subjects secretly laid ambushes for the suspected and hated race of the Normans, and, here and there, when opportunity offered, killed them secretly in the woods and in remote places: as vengeance for whom when the kings and their ministers had for some years, with exquisite kinds of tortures, raged against the Anglo-Saxons; and they, nevertheless, had not, in consequence of these measures, altogether desisted, the following plan was hit upon, that the so called 'hundred', in which a Norman was found killed in this way when he who had caused his death was not to be found, and it did not appear from his flight who he was should be condemned to a large sum of tested silver.

At the eyre, the jurors presented a killing that led to a fine for the local community: '*Malefactores ignoti venerunt de nocte ad Domum Alicie que fuit uxor Alfrith Le Berebir . . .*' That is: 'Unknown evil-doers came by night to the house of Alice who was the wife of Alfrich Le Berebir and broke into the house and killed Alice and wounded Richard her son, leaving him for dead.' Someone called Reynald is tried for the killing but is released and because the community cannot present a murderer, the entire tithing – those adult householders responsible for the behaviour of the community – is arrested and eventually the neighbours agree to pay a fine of half a mark. This reads like strange justice to us.

Murdrum was applied in different ways throughout the country, and some areas were exempt. Likewise, different areas of the country proved Englishry in different ways, and the crown pleas on the court roll might include an 'Englishry clause' explaining how to go about it. In Meeking's Wiltshire eyre for 1249 'Englishry is presented in this County by three, namely by two on the father's side and one of the mother's side'. Of course if the deceased was also unknown, the men of the Hundred would hardly be able to produce two Anglo-Saxons from his father's family and another from his mother's. Nearly 200 years after the Conquest it was no doubt accepted that the murdrum fine was no longer about protecting Norman lives, but about making communities responsible for law and order and less likely to harbour a fugitive killer. In some areas of the country it may have been considered demeaning for a community to present Englishry when it was no longer relevant.

More alien still are deodands, inanimate objects responsible for someone's death. Their value had to be fairly assessed and then given to the crown, or to charity, usually the church. Lists of deodands in eyre records include: millwheels, cartwheels, pigs and even the timber of a house or a boat. Shonks presented a local case: John Pycok from Furneux Pelham was killed when he fell out of a cart onto a wooden fork; the horse and cart were declared deodands and valued at 7s. 6d. No one appears to have worried about the fork.

We are not surprised to find the alien so long ago, more surprising is that a quick study of eyre records equally challenges our ill-conceived notions of the Middle Ages – they were not as *medieval* as we expect them to be. Thieves rarely got their hands chopped off – lesser courts were often fined for being too severe, and people were often released for petty larceny if they could provide surety for their future good behaviour. It is also clear that close-knit communities were an important part of life in the thirteenth century, as was a sense of responsibility to your neighbours. The many were responsible for the actions of the few, and fines meted out were largely for lapses of collective responsibility. The groupings people shared: family, neighbours, tithings, parishes, hundreds, were very real.

The justices in 1248 heard how John Lambert broke Luke son of William's leg by striking his thigh with a stick. John was declared an outlaw but was captured fleeing and imprisoned at Barkway, but no plea was made in the county court, so the inhabitants of Barkway were fined.

We could be forgiven for thinking that the eyre was mostly about fining people to raise money for the crown. The first fine or amerce-ment was usually a sum paid up front by the jurors to cover the errors they were bound to make. Shonks and his fellow jurors paid a fine before judgement of forty shillings. Other fines would be made if they miscalculated the value of a deodand, if nobody had raised the hue and cry to pursue malefactors, and if the first-finder of a dead body was not brought to court along with four of the victim's neighbours. Laws around who had to attend coroners' inquests demanded an excessive number of people, and parishes and townships paid up rather than suffer the inconvenience.

The crimes on show that April 1248 were sometimes dramatic, sometimes tragic. One Margery sprang her husband Leonard, a

296

known thief identified by his clipped ear, from the prior's prison in Royston so that he could flee to the sanctuary of the Church of St Nicholas. Alexander the Mason was found dead in a field, probably killed by John de Stanton, who he had been arguing with earlier that day. Robert the Gardener of Stortford had already been hanged in a manorial court for theft; his brother was outlawed. Reynold the Carpenter was found drowned outside the castle gate. Unknown thieves came by night to the house of Robert de Seynts and burned his oven. Margery of Patemere, tried for many crimes, was hanged at Colchester before the Justices of Gaol Delivery. John Keyy and Henry de Erl were tried for theft of wheat and other goods and imprisoned at Royston Cross, but the jury found them not guilty, declaring instead that Ralph of Bendene had falsely accused them through hatred and spite, so Ralph was taken into custody.

Henry de Bocland, the sheriff's servant and no doubt a relative of the bailiff Thomas de Bocland, who had nominated Shonks as elector, had falsely imprisoned one Roger, who was accused of robbery. He had then taken one quarter and two bushels of wheat from Roger's wife without permission, so the tables were turned, Roger was released, and Henry was arrested.

John le Gunter was found hanged with his own belt in his chamber at Barkway, and even more tragically, Agnes daughter of Jordan, also of Barkway, fell into a vat full of warm mash and was soaked and died. Another name jumps out, John Schank – a relative of our hero? He was one of eight men accused by Adam le Porter of Anestye for assault and maiming, but Adam and his pledges got cold feet and did not come to court, so they were arrested as well, and everyone was found guilty.

There were a surprising (or not) number of churchmen in trouble. John, the parson of the church of Toppefeld, was accused of assault, robbery and breaking the king's peace. Clement, the parson of Aspedene, had killed Robert Cobbe, the reeve, with the help of the church clerk. Clement had fled and was outlawed. A Brother Robert assaulted Robert de Cockeye with an iron fork, leaving him with a scar two inches long. He also robbed him of four shillings and a silver buckle worth eight pence. Robert argued that the court had no jurisdiction over him, and he was committed to the ecclesiastical court.

Walter le Rus also pleaded benefit of clergy after he was accused of robbery and abduction of one Matilda. He was handed over to the Bishop of London. Walter didn't act alone. One of his accomplices was John Wymund, and one of the jurors had stood surety for the half a mark compensation he had to pay, perhaps he was a friend or kinsman with money. His name was Piers Shonks, or Peter Scanke, as the scribe spelled it on this occasion. Pen stroke by pen stroke made long ago on parchment, his existence and his world are slipping in and out of focus.

31

*Stories etch grooves deep enough for people to follow in the same
way that water follows certain paths down a mountainside. And
every time fresh actors tread the path of the story, the groove runs
deeper.*

—Terry Pratchett, *Witches Abroad*, 1991

The church of All Saints at Landbeach, on the edge of
the Cambridgeshire fens, has its own sepulchral mysteries. The
most unusual of them was discovered one day in the middle of
the eighteenth century when workmen decided to sacrifice a medieval stone carving to make way for a wooden seat. They prised from
a pillar a large square stone decorated with a carving of a rose. It
came away easily to reveal another stone, a one-inch thick oblong
the size of a pack of cards. Behind it was a cavity. One of the men
reached into the pillar and pulled out a curious sphere made from
two bowls of sycamore wood that had been cemented together.
Inside, they found a strange 'fibrous material' – probably spikenard,
an eastern plant used to make a thick perfumed oil – packed lovingly
around an object wrapped in linen. It was the blackened remains
of an embalmed human heart.

The story is only missing an old sexton, who chancing to wander
by implores the young men to put it back before too much harm
is done, and when they laugh at him goes away shaking his head
and muttering about something his grandsire, the sexton in his

time, told him about Sir C— who died a bad death in the time of one of the King Henrys, and about measures that had to be taken to stop him walking. And if not the heart of a restless spirt, then that of a saint, a holy relic concealed at the Reformation and venerated in secret. At the very least, there ought to be a legend about a crusading knight whose heart was brought home from the Holy Land at great peril by a noble Saracen and handed to his betrothed. It is a wonder no one has made one up, which may be instructive in itself: there is only a story where there is a story. Perhaps there was *nothing* for a tale to spring from. Was there no story to match to the heart because there was nothing especially unusual about the deposit? There have been a handful of similar findings in parish churches. One of the best known is preserved at the Pitt Rivers Museum in Oxford – a shrivelled heart in a lead heart-shaped casket that was also found in a niche in a pillar, this time in the crypt of Christ Church in Cork.

It was not unknown in the Middle Ages for the heart and even the bowels of a corpse to be buried somewhere other than the body, especially among the elite. The practice probably grew out of eviscerating the corpse of a high-ranking individual to stop it rotting when carried over a long distance to its place of burial – the job was done by monks or by butchers and cooks. Originally, the heart and bowels and other viscera would be buried where the corpse fell, and the body embalmed and carried home. From the twelfth century it was a particular English fashion to have the heart – the seat of the soul – and the body interred in different places, often as a symbolic or political act to stress the importance of the individual and his heirs to a particular place. It soon became a status symbol even when it was not actually necessary. And having your remains in more than one place could double the number of prayers said for your departed soul.

The practice was finally discouraged by a papal bull in 1299, but that did not put a stop to it. Thirty years later, Robert the Bruce's heart was removed from his body and taken to Spain by Sir James Douglas, who was said to have worn it in a casket around his neck. Some thought he was taking the heart to the Holy Land when he was slain in battle against Muslim forces. It eventually made it back to Scotland and was buried at Melrose Abbey (where it was uncovered during an archaeological dig in 1996). The hearts of King Edward I's mother Eleanor of Provence and his brother were buried with the London Franciscans. The heart of his first wife Eleanor of Castile and son Alphonso were buried with the London Dominicans. Other English kings had body parts scattered around at death. Richard I's body, heart, and bowels were all buried in different places. Henry I's bowels, tongue, eyes, heart, and brain were buried at Rouen, the rest of his body is elsewhere.

The posthumous travels of one seventeenth-century heart might have been invented by Walter Scott. James Graham, 1st Marquess of Montrose, a martyr to the Royalist cause in the English Civil War, was hanged in Edinburgh in May 1650. His body was dug up at night and his heart removed and embalmed. It was sent in a casket to his son in the Netherlands, and was eventually reunited with his bones at the Restoration when he was given a state funeral at Holyrood Abbey. So far so romantic, but his biographer David Stevenson adds, 'Yet myth would not accept that his heart had had so quiet a fate, and elaborate stories emerged of its being taken by sea to India, stolen by an Indian prince, brought back to Europe by land, and disappearing in revolutionary France.' Even in the eighteenth century itself, the custom was occasionally revived. Richard Rawlinson, whom we met saving manuscripts from rubbish heaps, was buried at Oxford, but not in one piece: his body was in St Giles' church, but his heart was in the chapel at St John's College.

At Landbeach, it is the discovery itself that is the story. What is it about finds in old churches that excite the imagination? The fleck of red pigment, spotted beneath the peeling whitewash that reveals a mural of St George slaying the Dragon, painted over during the Commonwealth, the hollow sound when you tap above the north door of the nave, which leads to the discovery of a bricked-up niche hiding an alabaster St Christopher carrying the Christ Child, forgotten timbers in the hayloft of the rectory stable that turn out to be tables of the Ten Commandments resting on fragments of the old rood screen; crumbling steps leading into a crypt full of lead-lined coffins, found when someone thinks to put a camera through the hole in the slabs when the pavement in the chapel is being repaired. The great age of churches, their proximity to so much death, the mysteries of an old religion – the rituals of which are only half-remembered and discredited as hocus pocus.

The heart in the pillar at Landbeach was a rare discovery, and both the Royal Society and the Society of Antiquaries exhibited it to its members before it was finally sent to the British Museum amid speculation as to whose chest it had once beaten in. The rector of Landbeach, Reverend Robert Masters, suggested that it had belonged to a former lord of the manor, 'one of the knightly family of Chamberlayne'. Masters was a fellow and historian of Corpus Christi College, Cambridge, which had owned the manor of Chamberlaynes in Landbeach since the fifteenth century. Its patriarch was Walter Chamberlayne. He had acquired the land in the 1240s, but unfortunately, it had been sold behind the back of its rightful owner, one John de Bere. When he found out and protested, he was murdered by two henchmen. Chamberlayne was suspected of procuring the murder and charged with harbouring the killers, but he was well connected – the Chamberlaynes were said to be the hereditary chamberlains of the Earls of Richmond. Claiming benefit of clergy, he secured a pardon from the king, following the intervention of the Bishop of Ely. The resourceful Walter would bequeath his name to two manors, the one in Landbeach, the other on the Hertfordshire–Essex border – in the mid-1200s Walter Chamberlayne of Landbeach was better known as Walter Chamberlayne of Brent Pelham, a close neighbour of Piers Shonks.

The Chamberlayne family papers were deposited in the archives of Corpus Christi College, where one day four centuries later, the antiquary William Cole spotted something of interest at the foot of an old deed; he added a note to the left-hand page of one of his papers on Brent Pelham beginning: 'I have seen a Deed in the archives of CCCC in which Peter fil: Willmi le Grey [Peter son of William le Grey] grants to Walt Camerarius for 2 marcs of silver an acre of land in Pelham arsa . . . witnessed by Peter Sonke.' Cole put a date of about 1240 on it based on another deed involving Walter Camerarius aka Walter the chamberlain or Walter Chamberlayne. He added: 'So by this one may guess at the time of Shonke's flourishing.'

Today, the deed Cole perused is still at Corpus Christi, in the library named after Elizabeth I's Archbishop of Canterbury, Matthew Parker. Enter the library from the New Court built in the 1820s and, as you approach the large portrait of Parker on the wall at the end, you will pass glass display cases with heavy green fabric covers. They are there to keep the light off some of the masterpieces owned by the college, including a copy of the Anglo-Saxon Chronicle dating from 890, one of the finest copies of Chaucer's *Troilus and Criseyde*, and most importantly of all, Parker Ms.286, St Augustine's sixth-century gospel – the oldest known codex in Britain and probably 'the oldest non-archaeological artefact of any kind to have survived in England'.

At the far end of the library, beneath Parker's sombre portrait, are simple archive cupboards, wood-framed mesh doors with heavy yellow curtains containing the clamshell boxes that hold the Chamberlayne Deeds. Cole's one is here, no. 21, a small rectangle of vellum, the narrow bottom edge of the grant folded up and slotted for the seal that once hung there, the writing is immaculate, running from edge to edge, hardly a millimetre of parchment wasted, the ink still a deep black from the incipit to the witness list at the end, and, in that list, the name Petrus Sonke – Petrus abbreviated to Pet with a small circle above the 't', here a scribal abbreviation for the missing letters 'rus'.

Envelope after envelope hold quitclaims, leases, grants and gifts from nearly 800 years ago. In the flesh they are nibbled and torn and dirtied by time and mice. The reverse of a quitclaim has been scribbled on by someone testing their newly cut pen, practising their 'b's and initial 'O's. Six times they have made a pen-trial 'Omnibus est notum quod multum diligo potum'. Everyone knows I like many a drink.

Again and again amidst the thirteenth-century legal Latin, the name Piers Shonks survives the ages. It is an embarrassment of riches. How could we have ever doubted his existence? In all he appears in thirty-eight deeds dated to some time after 1220 and before 1290. In thirty-seven deeds he appears as a witness, in one as a landowner and witness, and in one as someone who owes homage and service to his lord. Thirty-two of them are deeds bene-fiting Walter Chamberlayne. In the earliest document, he is witness to a grant to Walter of 2½d. rent of land in Brent Pelham. In the last he witnesses a quitclaim to Walter's son Henry, probably in the early 1280s. The majority of the documents have been dated between 1220 and 1270, the time of Shonks' flourishing.

We can be more precise because William Gravenel leased two brothers and their twelve acres of land for ten years to Richard Pincerna, and Peter Sonke witnessed the deal. It survives on a badly damaged membrane of vellum larger than all the others in the box and with a wavy or 'indented' top edge where it has been cut from another copy. It is folded in half, and unfolds reluctantly to reveal that the ink in the top half has faded to an almost unreadable watery orange. The top corner has been torn away, the rest is plotted with an archipelago of holes, but thankfully one crucial piece of information has survived: the date. It is the only thirteenth-century document witnessed by Piers Shonks that has a specific date: Michaelmas day 22 Henry III. In the twenty-second year of Henry III's reign at Michaelmas, Sunday 29 September 1238, the third quarter day of the year, when rents fell due. As the nights closed in and the beams swung with sides of bacon curing for the winter larders, Piers Shonks was in Brent Pelham in the company of other men from the Pelhams whose names we know, with Simon de Furneux, Adam son of Hugh, and others. When so little survives, something as meagre and simple, but precise as a date, is an epiphany, is fuel to the historical imagination, is an anchor in a sea of speculation.

We even know who wrote the name Peter Sonke on a sale by Warin Carpentar to Walter Chamberlain of two and a half acres, because the writer adds himself to the end of the witness list – Robert Pagan, 'who wrote this deed'. The deed is particularly notable for a lovely caramel-coloured wax seal of uncoloured beeswax and tree resin. It still hangs from it like an ancient toffee. The well-spaced lettering of 'S Warin Carpentar' around the edge – the 'S' for *sigillum*, meaning seal – attest to the high quality of the crafts-manship. In the middle, is a beautiful design of stylised tendrils and flowers.

These deeds of Walter Chamberlayne offer small glimpses into thirteenth-century village life, the names of the furlongs in the open fields, the freemen of the village and even some of the villeins, men who would normally have no memorial. They are full of references to the relics of feudalism: to homage and scutage and boon service. In another grant, in even neater handwriting if possible, Sonke's name appears twice, first as a landowner; 'two acres lie in the field called Aldwyk, viz. 1 acre and 1 rood between land of Henry de Wancy and land of Peter Sonke, and 3 roods between land of the said Peter and land of Robert son of Jordan.' This document is full of field names and landowners, another window onto Shonks' world: his neighbours Simon de Furneux, who we already know, Roger le Grey, Robert son of Jordan, Hamon le Grey, Alice de Wasseleshede and Roger Finecock. The landscape is here as well. The two-acre Bradecompe abutting on Tottesdiche, La Dune, which Henry le Wancy held as his wick, Cuttelcroft, Benleye, Longlondbroke, Prestlonde, Wycedesheye Wood, Taltebrege, Smalemad. You have to slow down and say them out loud several times to begin to unpack them – Long Land Brook, Wicked Ashy Wood. Many of the places in these deeds can still be traced today. On the field-map made by the schoolchildren in the 1930s, Aldwyck is Aldock, Redinke is probably Redland, Stotchingge is Stockings; not just on name evidence but on the description of the adjoining land. Selverlowe is Silver Leys, Wyggescroft is Wiggs Croat. Is Tottesdiche now Butcher's Dick, and Grimesmade now Grinders Mead? If we assume that many of the deals were concluded with livery of sesein – literally going to the field and exchanging a clod of soil – then when I stand in Cut Croat today next to Hall Wood I am in Cuttelcroft, an ancient close overlooked by ash and oak, the wheat crop ringed by hedgerows threaded with briar rose. Hammon le Grey held it in the thirteenth century, and his son William stood there with Piers Shonks and witnessed Walter Chamberlayne take possession of one acre between his father's land and Aldwyk and another acre between the Prior of Berden's land and land owned by Geoffrey de Sarners, and, like me, they heard the crickets fretting and the trill of birdsong.

Shonks appears in different guises. He is most commonly Peter Sonke, but also Peter Shonke, Peter de Pelham Sonke and even Peter Sconke. Henry de Wancy leases some twelve acres of land in eleven different parcels for four pence a year. The vellum with its top right-hand corner torn or nibbled away has been dated between 1220 and 1250 and here for the first time we find bookended between two other witnesses not Peter Sonke, but Peter Schonke.

Sonke and twelve other witnesses – the most of any deed, although the witness lists often end with the Latin phrase for 'and many others' – attested a grant to Walter Chamberlayne on vellum with a fine liquorice-coloured lozenge dangling from it. The seal has lettering around the edge and a shield in the centre that must have belonged to the creator Richard Pincerna. It is an armorial seal, perhaps it was a status symbol as is often the case with such seals, but Richard was probably entitled to it. That surname is telling and goes well with the Chamberlayne surname. The *pincerna* and the *camerarius* – the butler or cup-bearer and the chamberlain. These are not lowly household servants but important roles in a large feudal household somewhere. In other deeds, he is Sir Richard, and always appears second after Sir Simon de Furneux in the witness lists, who always appears first, apart from on one occasion when Richard's son Sir Robert appears ahead of Simon. It is Robert's first appearance, and it is tempting to see this as an avuncular gesture by Sir Simon allowing his young neighbour to sign first now he has come of age. They are witnessing the grant to Walter Chamberlayne of some arable land and also a meadow with the wonderful name Elfringemad – sadly not traceable today.

Piers appears in another mid-century list, once again written in Robert Pagan's immaculate left-sloping hand, not as a witness, but one of a group of 'sundry persons', Brent Pelham landowners whose homage and service is granted to Walter Chamberlayne for twenty marks by Geoffrey de Sarners. Here is the messy feudalism of thirteenth-century England in action. The sundry persons hold land from Geoffrey in exchange for homage – a ceremony where they would swear an oath of loyalty acknowledging Geoffrey's overlordship – and rent and service and the other incidental rights that go along with that. Geoffrey is not selling the land to Walter, but his overlordship of these men, his seigniorial rights, and inserting Walter in the feudal chain between the men and himself. Walter pays twenty marks, and promises homage to Geoffrey, and to pay scutage to Geoffrey's overlord. The rights Walter has bought will bring in a regular income and may bring in further income from time to time. It also includes an annual rent of 3s. and fourteen harvest boons receivable from William Ballard and his heirs and successors; that is fourteen days of work at harvest time. The most telling remnant of ordinary lives in medieval Brent Pelham though is the mention of Philip Hayl in the same deed. Unlike the 'sundry persons' who are all freemen, Hayl is an unfree villein and so he and his labour are granted to Walter as a person along with his goods, chattels and tenement. Villeins were by far the largest part of the population of England – here, in this deed, named and remembered. The villein paid for his land by working for the lord and with luck produced enough off that land to keep his family alive.

One of the greatest delights in going through the deeds, is to unravel the meaning of phrases that were the day-to-day legalese of feudal land-holding, but are romantic and whimsical to us – not too far from the round table. Homage, Service, Fealty, Scutage, Socage, Quit Claims, Boon Service. Some time in the middle of the century, Piers Shonks witnessed a sale to Walter not of land but of the feudal rights due from three men in nearby Clavering for an annual payment of a rose on St John the Baptist's day. It is on a poorly cut sheet of vellum, which looks as if it has been worm-eaten over the centuries. Its ink is browning. The men were Ralph ad Crucem (that is Ralph at the cross), Henry Prundhumme, and William son of Nicholas de

Clavering. Their overlord was William Bradehund, and the three men must have held land from William in return for feudal service, which might take various forms. It was this service that William was selling to Walter, making Walter their overlord. Why was the rent just a rose? The deal was really about the three shillings that Walter paid up front, but legally, because of the way feudalism had worked, there still had to be an annual payment of money or goods or service – in this case a nominal single rose. This happens today when the leasehold of a flat is sold for say 100 years, and a nominal ground rent or 'peppercorn rent' is charged because the legal device used to be the payment of a single peppercorn.

There are similar examples among these deeds. In one, Walter buys land and buildings in Brent Pelham for twenty-two marks and a pair of gloves each year, another deed for woodland has a rent of a pair of gloves worth 1½d. in value. In another deed Thomas son of Ralph acquires six doles of ten acres for of 1 lb of cumin at Christmas in lieu of service. That is worth significantly more than a nominal payment and may have been a way to inflation proof the rent (and raises all sorts of intriguing questions about the cost and availability of spices like pepper and ginger, and even frankincense, which appear in land deals in the thirteenth century.) In a slightly later grant Walter pays one rose every year to Alan the miller for fourteen acres. Ellis Peters took the idea as the basis for one of her Cadfael mysteries: *The Rose Rent*. Here the rent was for one white rose. A murdered monk and a vandalised rose bush are at the heart of the matter.

By the late 1270s Walter is dead. Where did he choose as his final resting place? Landbeach or Brent Pelham? All Saints church is at the centre of the village today, immediately south-west of the moated site where Chamberlayne's manor house once stood. It has little off-set lights in the octagonal spire, hooded windows like the openings in a dovecote – it looks as if something must be living up there. Wonderfully, crudely carved, fat-faced gargoyles on the south porch gawp at passers-by. Inside there are no remnants of the cavity where the heart was buried, but there is a surviving monument associated with the Chamberlayne family. It is a tall powdery-white and embarrassingly ornate arch over an empty recess.

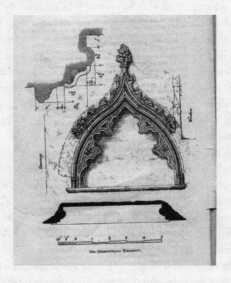

The Chamberlayne Monument.

It is nothing like the niche that houses Shonks' tomb, except it is also in the north wall of the nave, and is of almost exactly the same dimensions. It probably dates from the mid fourteenth century, at a time when the Chamberlaynes were still major landowners in both Brent Pelham and Landbeach. Did these niches reflect the tastes of the Chamberlayne family in two parishes nearly fifty miles apart? One final wild speculation: perhaps Walter Chamberlayne's body was laid to rest in Brent Pelham, but his heart was sealed in sycamore and consigned to a hollow in a pillar in the Cambridgeshire fens? The same heart that from time to time beat a little faster as Shonks related his latest adventure, pausing to stoop over a piece of parchment and sign his name.

32

. . . perhaps all writing, is motivated, deep down, by a fear of and fascination with mortality – by a desire to make the risky trip to the Underworld, and to bring something or someone back from the dead.

—Margaret Atwood, *Negotiating with the Dead*, 2003

The priest has given the last kiss of peace, the body has been washed, the dirige chanted. The bells are silent now, the tapers burnt down, the bier empty. *Eternal rest, grant them, Lord, and let perpetual light shine upon them.*

Piers Shonks is dead.

It is the early 1280s, Marco Polo is in Xanadu, Llewellyn the Last prepares for his final rebellion against Edward I, and in the Pelhams one Richard le King grants a house and land to Henry Sket. A Shonks witnesses the agreement, but it is not Peter any more, it is Gilbert. The same Gilbert we met when we first started following the name Shonks through the thirteenth-century archive. He was Piers Shonks' son. This is confirmed in the records of the 1287 Hertfordshire Eyre: Thomas le Waleys and his wife Joan who held land of Gilbert 'Shenke', brought an action against him, brandishing a charter to prove their case, a charter that had been agreed some years before with Gilbert's father. Gilbert's father was Peter Shenke, and he had died in 1281.

But just as the first Piers Shonks disappears from the witness lists to be replaced by Gilbert, a quarter of a century later Gilbert is succeeded by yet another Piers. He is there among the Corpus Christi deeds, first in 1306 as Peter Sconke, who owns land in Brent Pelham. He crops up several times in the deeds as Peter Schonke and later Peter Shonke. He was there on 13 June 1322 when a grant was signed and someone pressed their seal into the black wax, leaving a figure kneeling before the virgin and child on the front, and on the back a hollow made by their knuckle next to the whorl of an 800-year-old fingerprint.

On the Feast of the Exaltation of the Holy Cross in 1347, Peter Shonke witnessed a Chamberlayne deed for the last time. Teasingly, 1347 is the twenty-first year, not after the Conquest, as the inscription over the tomb has it, but the twenty-first year of Edward III's reign, it is also the year that the Earl of Arundel inherited the Manor of Berwick in Barkway, which he then granted to a Peter Shank for the term of his life.

This Barkway connection is not just another document with a name, mere proof that Shonks existed, or a sideways glance into his world, this is an ancient document that finally links the real-life Shonks to his legendary counterpart, not to the dragon legend, but to the earliest oral testimony we have, left to us by Nathaniel Salmon in 1728. It was a tale told 'by an old Farmer in the Parish, who valued himself for Being born in the Air that Shonk breathed. He saith, Shonk was a Giant that dwelt in this Parish, who fought with a Giant of Barkway, named Cadmus, and worsted him'; but that isn't all, Salmon then added, 'upon which Barkway hath paid a Quit-Rent to Pelham ever since.'

It is the one element of the legend I have yet to explain because this weird combination of battling giants and a quaint legal device, a quit rent, arises independently of the inscription or the carvings on the tomb. It is a lawyer's version of a fairy tale, where the loser doesn't forfeit his soul or his kingdom or a princess's hand in marriage, but instead has to write a cheque.

Unsurprisingly, a quit rent was originally a fee paid to be quit of something: a customary right or a feudal obligation. Just as land was usually held in exchange for money by the thirteenth and fourteenth centuries, rather than military service or agricultural labour, so other obligations had become monetised. A tenant could dodge his obligation to attend the manorial court by paying a fine or fee. And a community might agree to suspend its grazing or fishery rights for cash. If, for instance, Brent Pelham proved they had the right of pannage in woodland in Barkway, then they might agree to keep their pigs out of the wood in winter in exchange for a quit rent.

This could be all it took for a small village to garner bragging rights that begat a folk legend: a popular figure, a small landowner in Brent Pelham gains manorial rights in Barkway and proves his title to services and collects quit rents from villagers and perhaps from a local bigwig, who resents the upstart Shonks.

Ted Barclay has a more picturesque solution. For years, Ted has been telling anyone who asked all about the rent, but it was nothing so boring as a quit rent – it was a dragon rent. 'It is based on fact,' he insists. 'It was six shillings a year, I'm pretty certain, or that's what I was told by my grandfather.' Ted repeated the story recently on a local television feature about the church. 'Now people will say it was a ridiculous story,' he says into the camera, deadly serious, 'but there must be some truth in it because until 1900 Barkway paid us six shillings a year dragon rent for killing that dragon for them.'

Any documentary proof of dragon rent, giant rent, or any sort of quit rent has been lost – if it ever existed – but that doesn't mean there isn't some grain of truth in it. I wanted to marry these clues: the Barkway connection, the besting of a giant, the quit rent. In the 1970s, the Hertfordshire folklorist Doris Jones-Baker speculated about the giant Cadmus and where he must have lived. His home, she writes, 'was probably a stronghold similar to that of Shonks, a moated and fortified house so characteristic of the medieval Burys in the parishes that run along the Icknield Way and the chalk hills of north and east Hertfordshire. The most likely place was high up on Periwinkle Hill, opposite Rokey Wood and about half a mile from Barkway village, where there are still the remains of a small mount-and-bailey castle and the moat which surrounded it.'

Today, these remains have been almost ploughed out, and you have to take the fortification on trust. I assumed Jones-Baker simply chose Periwinkle Hill because of the trace of the moat, but the historian Tom Doig says that in the mid-1970s a very elderly villager in Barkway told a tale passed down to him by his grandfather. He said Shonks fought Cadmus on Periwinkle Hill over the ownership of a piece of land – he didn't know which land, but Barkway and Brent Pelham had always argued over it.

'And it's said that periwinkles grow where blood has been shed,' claims Tom. That gem sounds too good to be true and I can find no reference anywhere to back up Tom's plant lore, but it is far too good a tradition to ignore, even if it is an entirely new one. Blood was shed and so quit rent was paid. Doesn't the legend tell us as much? It was paid because Shonks worsted Cadmus.

There is one explanation that fits this strange amalgam of legend and land law. It involves a baston or staff nearly a yard long with a pointed head made of horn, a small wooden or leather shield or buckler, two champions, and the presumption in English law that *God will give victory to him that hath right.*

Duellum, judicial duel, trial by combat or battle, was a legitimate way of settling a land dispute in the English courts in the Middle Ages. Introduced at the Norman Conquest, it saw its heyday in the twelfth and thirteenth centuries. If Barkway were compelled to pay a quit rent to Brent Pelham after losing a fight, we might imagine the people of Brent Pelham, or perhaps one of the manors, claimed some common right over land and won, so that Barkway then paid Brent Pelham a quit rent in lieu of letting them exercise their right.

This could have been a local affair: some manorial courts claimed 'the right of judgement by fire, pit and battle', and charters have been found that granted manors the liberties of 'ordeal, battle and gallows'.

If the dispute was over land, then the land could not be 'a small thing such as an acre, toft or croft'. But fights could be over many things, such as fishery rights, the advowson of a church, or manorial customs and services. All of these could lead to a defence by battle. A plaintiff could even compel a court to defend its judgement by battle, and the court would then have to put up a champion.

While such cases would more commonly go to jury, defendants were entitled to deny a plaintiff's claim by their 'body or by another' – presumably because there was no other proof. Each party would then appoint a champion. Michael Russell, the most prolific historian of trial by battle, calculated that out of just under 600 disputes involving *talk* of battle in the early thirteenth century – that is an initial intention to settle things by combat – 123 led to actual fights. Thirty-eight of these were civil rather than criminal cases.

There are early examples in the Domesday Book. In Matlask, in Norfolk, 'the Earl of Richmond held land. A man of the king claims by offering ordeal of battle against the hundred, which witnesses it as belonging to the Earl. But a certain man of the Earl is willing to prove that the hundred witnesses the truth, either by ordeal or combat'. In other words, the Hundred Court had judged that the Earl of Richmond held the land, but the king's man said he would prove his claim to the land by battle against the Hundred Court. A man of the earl would act as the court's champion and defend its judgement. Perhaps here the plaintiff was prepared to do battle himself, although it was more common, and later obligatory, to appoint a champion. Originally the plaintiff's champion had to be a witness to the claim, or his father had to have borne witness to it and ordered his son to defend it – on the father's deathbed, it is sometimes said. This makes me wonder if it was prudent to ensure that there was a good loyal fighter among the witnesses to any land deals you made. Shonks was the most frequent witness to the Chamberlayne deeds in Brent Pelham.

Eventually, most people hired champions, and any pretence that they had witnessed a grant or deed was done away with. Occasionally, champions might still be loyal vassals, someone from the village with a reputation as a fighter: 'a mighty man of valour', for example, as Herbert Andrews called Shonks. Some hired themselves out as professional champions. There is even a cross-slab in St Mary Kilburn, North Yorkshire that must have been made to cover the bones of a champion. Either side of the cross shaft are the tools of the dead man's trade, a horn-tipped baston and a buckler. Robert of Clopton was a well-known champion, who fought for the Prior of Ware, a few miles south of the Pelhams. He was involved in at least another four cases over the next four years, but there is no record of him actually fighting. Often a famous champion was enough to intimidate the opposition into settling the case. Clopton was a champion in a notorious case where three other champions were also appointed, including the most infamous of them all, William Copeland, who fought one battle early in his career and never had to fight again, such was his fearsome reputation. Clients might sometimes, at great expense, buy up all the available muscle so their opponents would have to settle. A dispute over rights to fisheries between the Abbot of Meaux and the Abbot of York led to a battle in the 1250s. The Abbot of Meaux hired an extraordinary seven professional champions, but still lost. He must have wanted to win very badly, as hiring a champion was an expensive business. In 1292, the Chapter of Southwell, in Nottinghamshire, disputed the advowson of a local church with a rival landowner and hired the professional champion Meauton to fight for them, at a cost of £2 for just showing up. If it came to blows he would net a total of £46, an extraordinary sum, and on top of that he was paid a large retainer to be in attendance from the day of the wager until the day of the battle.

The wager came once the champions had been appointed. George Neilson described the ceremony in his 1891 *Trial by Combat*. Each champion 'bare legged, bare armed and kneeling, handed his glove with a penny in every finger to the judge. When the duel was awarded, the gloves were restored to their owners, and by command of the court exchanged. Thereafter the parties were ordered to take their champions to two separate churches, and "to offere there the five pennies which were in their gloves, in honour of the five wounds of God, that God might give the victory to him who was in the right".'

A time and place would be appointed for the battle, and then champions would have to swear not to use magic. In a dispute between the bishop and the Earl of Salisbury in 1355, the judges found on the bishop's champion 'many rolls of prayers and spells'. It now makes sense why you might need a dragon potion to give you success in legal battles: remember Pliny wrote that the fat of a dragon's heart, stored in the hide of a gazelle and tied to the arm with the sinews of a stag ensures success in litigation, but his recipe for invincibility might be more useful to the champion, all you needed for that was the skin of a lion and its marrow, the froth of a horse which has just won a race, the nails of a dog, and the tail and head of a dragon.

The baston and the small shield were the only weapons allowed, and if their bastons broke, the champions then fought on with 'their hands, fists, nails, teeth, feet and legs', as described in one late encounter. This sounds ferocious, but fights were rarely to the death; in fact, Michael Russell encountered evidence of only one fight that came to a tragic end, when the Abbot of St Edmundsbury's champion was killed in 1287, to the horror of both parties. Fights were often settled before they finished, and to end a fight a champion merely had to cry 'craven'. I say 'merely', but it was no small thing to utter that word: the early law treatise known as *Glanville* describes crying craven as the 'opprobrium of a lasting infamy, of that dreadful and ignominious word that so disgracefully resounds from the mouth of the conquered champion'.

We are not the only ones to find the whole concept alien: battle was not even popular 800 years ago, and contemporaries said it was unjust because the stronger party would win, not necessarily the party in the right, unless you expected a miraculous intervention by God or a saint. Russell says the medieval chroniclers complained about men with justice on their side who were beaten. And losing was costly. The plaintiff's champion, if vanquished, would be held a perjurer, fined, outlawed, and not allowed to fight as a champion again. On the other hand, victory could be fruitful. Not only in fees. Some clients are known to have granted land as a reward. In the late twelfth century, Stephen de Nerbon granted land in Coventry to William, son of Ralph of Filungel 'in consideration of a battle he fought for me'. In the thirteenth century, Roger of Reston gave John the swineherd three and a half acres 'for a certain battle that he fought for me and won'. Was Shonks given the manor of Berwick for fighting and winning and earning that quit rent? If so, there is a strange coincidence: the manor of Berwick was already associated with trial by combat. It was an outlying territory of the manor of Great Hormead to the south, and both were unique at Domesday – we might say they were the last surviving acres of Anglo-Saxon England. They were the lands of Edgar the Aetheling, the surviving heir to the English throne after the death of Harold II at Hastings. Edgar had granted both of his estates to a man called Godwine by 1086, and Godwine is thought to have been the Aetheling's champion who successfully fought a trial by battle for Edgar against Ordgar, an English knight who accused Edgar of plotting against William Rufus. Today, a field marked as Barwick Wood on old maps remembers the manor. It is an English field like so many others, baked golden with wheat in July, edged with ragwort and sorrel. On the northern boundary, the great elephant beeches of Earls Wood rise above hedgerows of hawthorn and buckthorn. A land of champions.

Legal historians say that by the late thirteenth century trial by combat was rare. But, if not trial by combat, then we have to accept the legend is a metaphor for some commonplace land dispute, and Shonks simply beat Cadmus in a court hearing. But that cannot be right because it is too dull, and we would be a sorry lot for making a tale out of it. That is not the raw material of legend.

No, Shonks was a mighty man of valour; he stood up at the moot by the ancient yew tree and offered to be their champion, with God on his side, he took up his baston and shield and worsted that bully Cadmus, proving an ancient right, and for that he was ever remembered. The name Shonks stayed attached to his moat and his wood and his manor, and people talked about his heroic deeds, of the day he was their champion, perhaps the time he stood up to the garrison of Anstey castle too, but that was the grandfather, and over time the two were remembered as one. Two or three hundred years hence people started linking the name Shonks to the tomb in the wall. It was already a special tomb, something remarkable, it might have been the earlier Shonks' originally, or it was an ecclesiastic's tomb, or one of the Chamberlaynes', but it was saved from an earlier church or from a priory and let into the wall. Nobody noticed it was an unusually small cross-slab when they started to exaggerate Shonks' stature, but they could hardly miss that snarling dragon and the other carvings, and so the legend grew.

There is a portrait of the champion Shonks on some fragments of thirteenth-century circular floor tile saved from the pavement of Chertsey Abbey in Surrey. Here is a fighter in black and white, wearing a loose knee-length smock and gartered hose on his legs. In his left hand he brandishes his horn-tipped baston, in his right hand – raised over his head as if ready to chop down with it – he holds a small rectangular shield. This is a champion in a trial by battle, down to the close-cropped bowl-shaped haircut prescribed by the rules of judicial combat, but this can't be Shonks – he is too sullen, his mouth turned down, his brow furrowed, his eyes fearful. Perhaps he knows that right is not on his side. He is a man about to receive a decisive blow, or one thinking hard about crying 'Craven!'

Shonks must be his opponent coloured mustard yellow. He wields the same weapons, but his baston is wound up ready to strike, his shield is blocking the other's shield, and his footing is on higher ground. His is the trustworthy face of a yeoman farmer, steadfast, and with the expression of complete equanimity allowed to the man blessed with physical courage and certain he is in the right. Shonks will be staring directly at his opponent, but taking no pleasure in getting the upper hand. At least that is how I imagine he looks, because even when the fragments of the tile have been reassembled, the fighter is still concealed. We can see half an ear and glimpse another short haircut, but his face is behind his shield. I can research, ponder and surmise all I like, but I will never get a complete, unobscured picture. It is an appropriate portrait of the giant, dragon-slayer and champion Piers Shonks.

Part V

Last Things

33

With myths, one should not be in a hurry. It is better to let them settle in the memory, to stop and dwell on every detail, to reflect on them without losing touch with their language of images. The lesson that we can learn from a myth lies in the literal narrative, not in what we add to it from the outside.

—Italo Calvino, *Six Memos for the Next Millennium*, 1988

Loitering in Brent Pelham church one day, measuring Shonks' tomb, I met a local man who asked me what I was up to. I told him I was writing a book about Shonks and he smiled and said his grandchildren love to come and see the tomb of the dragon-slayer. Then he asked me if I thought the story was true.

Bruno Bettelheim told a story about the psychologist Jean Piaget. A three-year-old girl asked him about an elephant's wings, to which Piaget responded that elephants don't fly. When the girl insisted, 'Yes, they do; I've seen them', he told her she must be teasing him. 'If Piaget had engaged in a conversation about where the elephant needed to fly to in such a hurry, or what dangers he was trying to escape from, then the issues which the young child was grappling with might have emerged,' wrote Bettelheim. 'Piaget would have shown his willingness to accept her method of exploring the problem. But Piaget wasn't trying to understand how this child's mind worked.'

Don't ask if dragons existed or not. There are better questions.

I have tried to be careful as I have probed and questioned and worried away at Shonks and his legends. I can hardly claim to have trodden lightly, because I was so curious about so much, but my intention was always to celebrate and enrich this little-known legend. I have tried not to break the butterfly on the wheel. C. S. Lewis tells us that that the fourteenth-century Scottish poet John Barbour set out the true reasons for studying history at the beginning of his most famous poem 'The Bruce'. 'Stories, even when untrue, give pleasure. But, if so, true stories well told ("said on gud maner"), ought to give a double pleasure; pleasure in the "carpying", the narrative as such, and pleasure in learning what really happened ("the thing rycht as it wes"). And thirdly, it is only fair to record the deeds of great men, for they deserve fame – "suld weill have prys".' Lewis gives a fourth reason that he found in the chronicler Froissart: as an 'ensample', that is by reading of valiant deeds, so 'the trewe and hardy may have ensample to encourage them'.

I want this book to do all those things. I especially want the double pleasure, but am worried that after pursuing the name Shonks through old parchments, I don't have much left, just the name, some picturesque legal terms, a supposition or two; no dragon, no giants, no superhuman feats of archery, no avenging devils, no cunning heroes, not even a dragon's lair.

This is not what I intended.

Instead, let us say that I have merely set the marvellous aside for a while, one marvel at a time, so as to take a good look at them in the round, and now it is time to put them all back in their rightful places. While there is certainly delight in trying to get at 'the thing rycht as it wes', the greater truths are in the tale that has grown over the centuries. Searching for a kernel of truth by trying to remove the legendary elements misses something, it gets rid of the best bits. The legend holds the deeper truths, about our hopes and fears, about how our imaginations work, what we value, and the effect that beauty has on us. It is the accretions to the event or object that originally inspired the tale that matter more. Ironically, as Paul Veyne has pointed out, without the legendary accretions the historical would not have survived anyway. Who would remember Piers Shonks if he had not become a dragon-slayer, a giant, a man who got one over on Old Nick? It is these fantastical elements that ensure the historical facts are remembered. They draw attention to the important things, the art, the storytelling, our capacity for wonder, the craftsmanship of a medieval mason, the countryside in which the story was soon rooted.

I am as interested in how we remember history as in what actually happened. How did the people of the Pelhams remember a village hero? As a dragon-slayer and someone who outwitted the devil by being buried in the church wall. The Marxist interpretation would be that the villagers told this story to flick their fingers at their feudal overlords; the doughty fellow through strength and cunning overcame overwhelming power and evil – no doubt this is what it took to gain a quit rent, or contest the ownership of land against a powerful lord.

What the villagers remembered down the centuries was that their champion killed a dragon that lived under a yew tree and angered the devil, but with the help of a bow and arrow he escaped his retribution by being buried in the walls of a church under a *wondrous strange* tombstone. Unlike most fairy tales, Shonks died happily ever after. I will even hazard a moral to all this: battle evil, even if at great peril. It is possible even when it seems impossible to avoid the traps of the devil. You will be celebrated for it down the ages.

Except you probably won't be. That is the point of Shonks: that he is remembered on behalf of all those others who have faced evil and prevailed but been forgotten. And that is his greatest triumph: Shonks has been remembered against all the odds. Why? The power of story and the power of art. Together they have withstood the iconoclasts, the pedants, and the dullards, with their hammers and their scratchy quills. When a tree or a tomb becomes a story, and a much-loved villager becomes a dragon-slayer, that is something very hard to destroy.

I was re-reading Cormac McCarthy's *Blood Meridian* as I

approached the end of this book, and there is a passage where the sinister Judge Holden sits in the desert copying primitive drawings into his notebook:

> *The rocks about in every sheltered place were covered with ancient paintings and the judge was soon among them copying out those certain ones into his book to take away with him. They were of men and animals and of the chase and there were curious birds and arcane maps and there were constructions of such singular vision as to justify every fear of man and the things that are in him. Of these etchings – some bright yet with colour – there were hundreds, and yet the judge went among them with assurance, tracing out the very ones which he required. When he had done and while there yet was light he returned to a certain stone ledge and sat a while and studied again the work there. Then he rose and with a piece of broken chert he scappled away one of the designs, leaving no trace of it only a raw place on the stone where it had been. Then he put up his book and returned to the camp.*

This is terrifying and sinister. I'm not even sure why this seems so apposite. It is partly the terror in forgetting, in being forgotten, in being eradicated. Evil triumphs. We will eventually forget our stories if we don't renew our capacity for wonder. Walter Benjamin has written that we are now much more interested in information than in wisdom, and information must be plausible, whereas wisdom from afar often employed the miraculous. I wanted this book to be the most complete monograph of an English folk legend ever written, a fascinating journey back through history, a detective story about the hunt for a folk hero, but as I researched and wrote and the years passed, I began to hope for something else as well – I began to hope that I was doing my bit for the re-enchantment of the universe.

This is not to be gullible or primitive, but it isn't an easy position to hold or defend. I am an atheist and a rationalist and I have problems with historical myth-making because in the wrong hands it can do great harm. You detect the most diehard folklorists grappling with the dilemma and justifying why they spend so much time with the make-believe.

If I ask you to believe in Shonks and his adventures, just ask yourself what harm did a belief in dragons ever do, and what do many of our beliefs do now? We congratulate ourselves on no longer believing such things, and we miss the point like all those people who threw away giants' bones or who wrote patronising lines about foolish beliefs. Kevin Crossley-Holland has written about the Cornish legend *How Joan Lost the Sight of one Eye*: 'To my mind, it's a metaphor,' he says. 'We can view this world around us in two different ways, it seems to say: with the eye that observes the physical, material, verifiable world, and with the eye of the imagination. Not only this: the story demonstrates how each of us needs both eyes, both ways of seeing, if we're to engage to the full with life here on middle earth.'

When my oldest son Max was a baby and learning to speak he held up a piece of buttered toast and said 'car', I said firmly, 'No, toast'. 'Car,' he replied, smiling. 'No, toast.' My wife Rebecca sighed and said, 'He's telling you his toast looks like a car,' and it did, the way he'd taken bites out of it had made the rough shape of a car. 'I thought you were supposed to be the imaginative one,' Rebecca said. I now think I wrote this book to prove that I can see when a piece of toast is also a car.

I certainly think of myself as the imaginative one, I am a writer, my wife is a doctor, she is supposed to be the rational, literal one, but I can be a know-it-all, I used to love debunking urban myths and local folklore. When I first started talking to locals about Shonks – people who had lived in the villages around Brent Pelham all their lives – to my shame I would rarely let them finish what they had to say, I would interrupt and set them right, after all I had been reading all about it. Then about the same time as the toast incident I read a report about an archaeological field trip in Sweden that changed the way I think about such things. In a wood, high on a horst in southern Sweden, there is an ancient monument, a hollow in the earth some 6 m in diameter and 90 cm deep that is thought to be an old trapping pit or wolf pit. When an international team of archaeologists visited it in the early 2000s they were sceptical that the bowl was anything special; it lacked many of the key characteristics of such pits, but the authors who wrote up the encounter were far less keen to set the locals right than I would have expected: 'So, what next?' they wrote.

> An archaeological excavation to examine the contents of the pit, digging our way down to discover (perhaps!) what it was? Even this might not lead us closer to the truth. And, finally, is that really what we want – always to find the truth? It may be that sense of place is greater if we give free play to people's imaginations. How likely is a simple little pit in the ground to engage the attention of both scholars and laymen, from the locality and from other countries, if we know everything about its function? Perhaps its function now, whatever it has been in the past, is to pose questions.

So don't ask if there was really a dragon. After all, 'it is heresy to say there wasn't a dragon', Ted Barclay reminds us emphatically, and he means it.

Let's ask a different question: would the world be a poorer place without dragons in it? And heroes like Shonks for that matter? It is a story from the landscape and the seasons and the weather and the mysteries of the last things and the gossip at the blacksmiths and the stories the old people half remembered. We have lots of hollow places and less and less to put in them. So if some misguided person asks you if Shonks really slew a dragon, remember those men who stood on the edge of the hole in Great Pepsells field, and envy them their ability to make sense of the world with dragons, and say, 'Of course he did', and mean it.

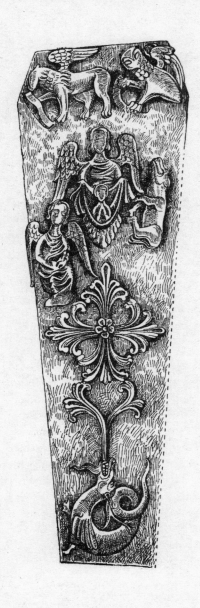

Acknowledgements

This book would have been impossible to write without the encouragement and kindness of many friends, and no end of complete strangers who responded to my requests for help and advice.

I started to take an interest in Shonks as long ago as 2007, and that year I spoke at one of the Folklore Society's legendary weekends about the yew tree and its felling. That talk formed the kernel of what would eventually become the first act or part of this book. Thanks to Jeremy Harte for accepting my offer of a talk and later for sending me copies of some of the geomantic writings about Shonks. Jacqueline Simpson was there that weekend in Sussex and suggested I write something, although I think she meant an article and not an entire book. Her work on dragons was an inspiration and some of the wisdom she shared with me that weekend has found its way into this book.

Another event from around the same time helped to motivate my initial research. At the annual meeting of the British Association of Local History, I listened to the Cambridge historian Evelyn Lord say that she was pleased with the amount of local history being written but regretted that much of it was too narrow, lacked ambition, didn't look beyond the village bounds to find a wider context, or consider how a local interest might bear on bigger themes. At least that's what I took from it. I doubt she had any intention to encourage the writing of a book like this, but it seemed like a challenge worth accepting.

Nick Connell at Hertfordshire Archives and Local Studies

encouraged and advised me from the outset. Not only did he help me to navigate my way around the papers of the Herts antiquaries he loves and knows so well, but every now and again I would receive an email from Nick with some new snippet he had spotted about Shonks. He was my go-to with Herts questions: 'Hello Nick, any idea who the photographer W.W.E. was?' Or 'Do you know anyone who's an expert on Barkway?' In the fallow years when much of this book lay in the proverbial bottom drawer, Nick never stopped nagging me to get it finished. His colleagues at HALS have aided me on many occasions too, helping me to read undecipherable handwriting, suggesting other lines of research, pointing me to the standard text on one obscure topic or another, or reminding me for the umpteenth time how to find a particular class of record.

My research took me further afield and I am grateful also to a number of institutions that have granted me access and/or assistance: the British Library, the National Archives, the Bodleian Library, Corpus Christi College Cambridge, the Mills Archive, the Society of Antiquaries, Lambeth Palace Library, Guildhall Library, London Metropolitan Library, Bishop's Stortford Library and Hertford Museum. More specific gratitude is in the notes.

No end of experts also feature in the notes. It constantly amazes me how generous busy people are with their expertise and time to someone who emails them out of the blue about Latin prosody, thirteenth-century travel, medieval iconography and so on. Special mention must go to Paul Brand. He won't know it, but his kindness and tact with someone wandering lost among the intricacies of medieval law spurred me on to finish this book. Hilary Wheeler at the Church Monuments Society responded to my enquiries and offered to put me in touch with Brian and Moira Gittos, who despite being busy with their own book on medieval effigies, helped me move beyond a merely impressionistic account of cross-slabs, patiently answering my questions and sending me extensive reading lists and suggestions, including an itinerary for my visit to the Isle of Purbeck. There, I am indebted to Trev and Mark Haysom who shared their unrivalled knowledge of Purbeck marble quarrying and ensured that I made the most of the week I spent in Dorset.

Closer to home, thanks are due to Ted and Lizzie Barclay, who welcomed me into Beeches several times to talk about Shonks and allowed me to tramp over their land on innumerable occasions. Thanks also to my friends and local historians Steve and Linda Bratt; they have always lent a willing ear to my musings and when I could only vaguely recall seeing or reading something that suddenly seemed vital for a particular chapter, Steve and Linda would usually know what I was after.

I must add, as is customary, but is particularly important in a book like this where I stray into so many areas of knowledge, that all the errors are mine.

My in-laws Rob and Wendy Mitten, my friends Ben Oliver, James and Suzy Roberts, Egbert and Penny Charlish-Jackson have always been there for me. Chris and Hannah Hines have supported me more than they know. Some years ago now, in a case of completely mistaken identity, David Burton accidentally resurrected my journalism career, continued to champion my writing and sent me on some cracking assignments. Thanks to all of you.

I am minded to extend my thanks much further back than the first time I wrote the name Piers Shonks in my notebook, because I was blessed with many amazing teachers at Christ Church Primary School and the Friary School, Lichfield. They gifted me a lifelong curiosity with almost everything and I am certain I would not have been a writer if it wasn't for John Burton, Jane Barker, N. T. M. and Jan Wilkowski (who will have no idea why, but it involves being set lines for messing around in art lessons).

To my wonder and delight, my extraordinary editor Arabella Pike shared my vision for this book, profoundly helped me shape it and re-ignited my self-belief. I want to embrace my agent David Godwin every time I see him as he embraced me and this project and made all the difference. To the ever patient Iain Hunt and Jo Thompson, and everyone else at DGA and William Collins who have helped make this book, thank you. I was told that Joe McLaren was a genius when he was asked to come up with a concept for the cover and that wasn't wrong; his eagerness to engage with my words was so heartening and has had amazing results.

My extraordinary friend, my dearest friend, the talented photographer and author Dominick Tyler has been there for me in so many ways over the years. No one is a better listener or wiser counsellor.

This book is dedicated to my mum and dad, who gave me far too happy a childhood for a writer. My children Max, Daisy and Caspar constantly challenge my pronouncements and shape and reshape my thinking. I have benefited from their wisdom and candour on countless occasions. My beautiful, kind, brilliant wife Rebecca is at once the most gentle and the most resilient person I have ever met. The time and space to write and read and think is but a tiny part of the debt I owe her, without her nothing would be possible. I love you. Thank you.

Chronology and select textual history

*c.*140 million years BCE	· Snail shells compact at the bottom of a Jurassic–Cretaceous sea. Purbeck marble is being formed.
After 61 CE	· The Romans build a road from Braughing to Great Chesterford. Where it passes through the countryside that will one day become the Pelhams, a yew tree grows alongside it.
1086	· Supposed date of Shonks' flourishing/death.
1100–35	· Reign of Henry I. There is said to have been a great fire in the part of the Pelhams that would become Pelham Arsa or Burnt Pelham.
1135–53	· The Anarchy of Stephen and Matilda.
13th century	· An anonymous stonemason or marbler – probably on the Isle of Purbeck – carves a remarkable cross-slab coffin lid for a client in Hertfordshire.
After 1220	· Peter Sonke witnesses a grant to Walter Camerarius of a rent of 2½*d.* on land in Pelham Arsa and quitclaim to him of 3 roods of land (CCCC09/24A/A1).
1220–40	· Grant to Thomas son of Ralph of arable land for a rent of 1 lb of cumin at Christmas in lieu of services (CCCC09/24A/A46A).
1220–50	· Peter Schonke witnesses a lease to Walter Camerarius of land in Pelham Arsa (CCCC09/24A/A23).
	· Peter Sonke witnesses a grant by Richard Pincerna to Walter Camerarius. Black seal with shield (CCCC09/24A/A26).

· Peter Sonke witnesses a grant of land including Elfringemade to Walter Camerarius by Richard son of the late Robert le Grey (CCCC09/24A/A30).

c.1220–70 · Peter Sonke witnesses a conveyance to Walter Camerarius of Pelham Arsa of the feudal rights due from Ralph ad Crucem Henry Prundhumme and William son of Nicholas de Clavering on annual payment of a rose on St John the Baptist's day (CCCC09/24A/F3).

· Peter Sonke is party to a grant to Walter Camerarius of the homages, rents and services of sundry persons, an annual rent of 3s. and 14 sets of autumn boon-service due from William Ballard and others; and Philip Hayl, his goods, chattels and tenement (CCCC09/24A/A40).

· Peter Sonke witnesses a sale to Walter Camerarius of two and a half acres of land for 3 marks and the remission of a yearly payment of 1d. Robert Pagan wrote this deed. Seal (CCCC09/24A/A14).

· Peter Sonke witnesses a quitclaim to Walter Camerarius for 12 marks of a tenement in Brent Pelham. The deed is written on a scrap of vellum previously used for a pen-trial of 'Omnibus est notum quod multum diligo potum' (CCCC09/24A/A17).

· Peter Sonke witnesses a grant to Walter Camerarius of an acre of woodland called 'Le Hoo' on annual payment of a pair of gloves worth 1½d. (CCCC09/24A/A37).

· Grant to Sir Walter Camerarius of a messuage and 14 acres of arable land, and a rood and half an acre of meadow. Annual rent: one rose (CCCC09/24A/A43).

1231–41 · Petrus Sonke witnesses a grant by William, son of Peter of Pelham-Furneux, to Alexander, Treasurer of St Pauls, from the Hairy Book, St Pauls *Liber A* cartulary CLC/313/B/012/MS25501 at London Metropolitan Archives.

no. 197 in Marion Gibbs, *Early Charters of the Cathedral Church of St Paul, London*, Camden Society, 3rd series, vol. 58 (1939), p. 156.

1238	· On Michaelmas Day 22 Henry III, Peter Sonke witnesses a conveyance by William Gravenel to Richard Pincerna of William Crisp and his brother Ralph with their property and 12 acres in Pelham Arsa for 10 years (CCCC09/24A/A6).
1240	· Peter Sonke witnesses a grant to Walter Camerarius by Peter son of William le Grey of an acre of land for 2 marcs of silver (CCCC09/24A/A21).
*c.*1245–60	· Peter Sonke is a landowner and witness in a grant to Walter Camerarius of 26½ acres of arable land with a messuage and all liberties within and without the town, four acres of meadow with a messuage and Wycedesheye Wood (CCCC09/24A/A3).
1248	· Peter Shanke/Scanke is a jury member in the General Eyre (TNA JUST 1/318, m.18). He also stands surety for John Wymund in the crown pleas (m.19).
1254	· 'The birth of purgatory' when it is officially recognised by Pope Innocent IV.
*c.*1280	· Peter Sonke witnesses a quitclaim to Henry Camerarius of 3 acres of land by William le Grey (CCCC09/24A/A49).
*c.*1281	· First Piers Shonks dies.
1280–1320	· Gilbert Sonke witnesses a grant to Henry Sket of a messuage with a house on it (CCCC09/24A/A54).
	· Gilbert Sanke witnesses a grant to Walter son of Henry le Chamberleyn of three acres of land (CCCC09/24A/A55).
1286	· Gilbert Shanke v Simon de Furneux action of replevin (TNA CP 40/63, m.34: image 4399d).
1287	· Agnes Shenke, wife of Gilbert Shenke, is plaintiff in an

assize of mort d'ancestor at Hertfordshire eyre. Agnes was the ward of the late Peter Shenke (TNA JUST 1/325, m.2).

· Gilbert Shenke and his wife Agnes are defendants in assize of novel disseisin at the Hertfordshire eyre (TNA JUST 1/325, m.3).

· Gilbert Shenke is defendant against an action of mesne at the Hertfordshire eyre (TNA JUST 1/325, m.9).

· Gilbert Swanke of Brent Pelham is non-suited in a writ of right at the Hertfordshire eyre (TNA JUST 1/325, m.11).

1288	· Gilbert Sanke brings an action of replevin against Simon de Furneux at the Common Bench. In Chief Justice Thomas Weyland's roll, 16 Edw I, Trinity term 1288 (TNA CP 40/73).
	This is the 'foundation' document in the search for a historical Shonks.
1289	· Gilbert Shonke and Simon de Furneux agree a final concord (TNA CP 25/1/86/43).
1306	· 15 December, Peter Sconke is a landowner in a grant to William, Chaplain of Streteford (CCCC09/24A/A50).
1322	· 13 June, Peter Shonke witnesses a grant to Richard le Chapman. Seal (CCCC09/24A/A58).
1347	· 14 September, Petro Shonke witnesses a quitclaim on the Feast of the Exaltation of the Holy Cross (CCCC09/24A/F9).
Before 1376	· Peter Shank is granted manor of Berwick in Barkway by Earl of Arundel, *Calendar of Patent Rolls Richard II 1396–9*, p. 578.
1534–6	· Split from Rome. Dissolution of the monasteries and destruction of images begins.
1539–1614	· Raphael Keene – alleged author of the inscription above Shonks' tomb – is vicar in Brent Pelham.

Before 1598	· John Norden visits Brent Pelham for his *Speculi Britaniae pars: A Description of Hartfordshire, Reprinted with the Addition of a Portrait of J. Norden and a Biography by W. B. Gerish* (Ware: G Price & Son, 1903; 1st pub. [London] 1598), p. 22. His presentation copy to Lord Burghley is MS 521 at Lambeth Palace Library.
1631	· John Weever, *Ancient Funerall Monuments within the United Monarchie of Great Britaine and Ireland, and the Ilands Adjacent, with the Dissolved Monasteries Therein Contained . . . Whereunto Is Prefixed a Discourse of Funerall Monuments, etc.* (London: Thomas Harper), p. 549. The draft at the Society of Antiquaries is 'A Breefe Discourse of Ancient Monuments . . .' Original drafts and collections for John Weever's *Ancient Funerall Monuments* (SAL/MS/127).
1642–51	· English Civil War.
1693–1725	· Thomas Tingge is vicar of Brent Pelham. In about 1695, he writes the inscriptions into 'Brent Pelham Register 2. Baptisms, Marriages, Burials. From 1690–1773' (HALS DP/77/1/2).
1695	· William Camden, *Camden's Britannia*, ed. and trans. Edmund Gibson, pp. 303–4.
1700	· Sir Henry Chauncy, *The Historical Antiquities of Hertfordshire*, vol. 1 (London), p. 284.
1723	· A tithe dispute: Rev. Thomas Tingge v George Hill [etc.] (TNA E134/9Geo1/Mich14).
c.1726	· Rev. Charles Wheatly is vicar, Vicar's Account Book (HALS DP/78/3/3), pp. 12–15.
1728	· Nathaniel Salmon, *The History of Hertfordshire; Describing the County, and Its Antient Monuments, Particularly the Roman. With the Character of Those That Have Been the Chief Possessors of the Land, [etc.]* (London), pp. 289–90.

1729–64	· Rev. Charles Wheatly's *Tithe Book* [for Brent and Furneux Pelham] *1729–1764* (HALS DP/78/3/2).
1743	· William Cole, 'Brent Pelham', *Extraneous Parochial Antiquities or an Account of Various Churches with Funeral Monuments, the Inscriptions in and About them in Divers Counties of England*, ff. 14v–27, Cole Manuscripts, vol. 5 (BL Add. MS 5806).
1757	· HACKETT, John, *Select and Remarkable Epitaphs on Illustrious and Other Persons in Several Parts of Europe. With Translations of Such as Are in Latin and Foreign Languages, and Compendious Accounts of the Deceased, etc.*, vol. 2, p. 228.
1769	· *A Plan of Beeches in the Parish of Bt. Pelham and in the County of Herts. Taken from an Actual Survey Made in the Year of Our Lord 1769 for the Use of Mr. [erased] and Mr. Parnel. Proprietor by their Most Obedient Humble Servant Hollingworth at Puckridge* (HALS D/ECn/P7).
1786	· Richard Gough, *Sepulchral Monuments in Great Britain Applied to Illustrate the History of Families, Manners, Habits, and Arts, at the Different Periods from the Norman Conquest to the Seventeenth Century. With Introductory Observations* (London: J. Nichols for the author), vol. I, p. Lxxxviii.
	· Anonymous drawing [poss. Henry Oldfield] in Richard Gough, *Sepulchral Monuments* – see above. Plate IV, no. 12. facing p. cix. The original illustration is in MS Gough Maps 225 at the Bodleian Library and is described in Bertram (2004) as '10a Burnt Pelham, Herts., coffin slab with elaborate cross, angel receiving soul, tetramorph and dragon, pencil drawing "to be engraved".' There is clearly no tetramorph. See Jerome Bertram, *Gough's Sepulchral Monuments: Being a Catalogue of Material Relating to Sepulchral Monuments*

in the Gough Manuscripts of the Bodleian Library (Oxford, 2004).

*c.*1800 · Henry George Oldfield, 'Monument of O Peirs [sic] Shonkes in Burnt Pelham church Herts' (HALS Oldfield Collection, vol. 5, DE/Of/5/234). In the Bodleian Library MS Gough Maps 224 is a better version and is catalogued in Bertram as '328 Burnt Pelham, Herts., late 13th century coffin-slab with cross and figures in relief in tomb recess, appropriated for Piers Shankes, 1686 [sic]; ink and wash drawing.' See Bertram (2004). When I saw this entry I got very excited, assuming this was a 1686 picture of the tomb, but 1686 is a mistranscription of 1086.

· Thomas Fisher, 'Brent Pelham Church, Hartfordshire, Monument in the North Wall of the Nave', Fisher (Miscellaneous) 18, Society of Antiquaries.

1808 · Edward Wedlake Brayley, *The Beauties of England and Wales: or, Original Delineations, Topographical, Historical, and Descriptive, of Each County*, vol. 7 (Hertfordshire, Huntingdonshire, Kent), (Vernor, Hood and Sharpe), pp. 189–90.

1810 · Hollingworth, *A Plan of Beeches Situated in the Parish of Brent Pelham and County of Hertford*, privately owned.

1816 · James Sargant Storer, *Antiquarian Itinerary: Comprising Specimens of Architecture, Monastic, Castellated, and Domestic, With Other Vestiges of Antiquity in Great Britain, Accompanied with Descriptions*, vol. 4 (London).

· John Grieg [engraver] after F. W. L. Stockdale [illustrator], 'Remains of the Tomb of O Piers Shonks. Brent Pelham Church, Herts', *Antiquarian Itinerary* – see above, p. 42.

*c.*1825 · 'A singular monument,' writes George Alexander Cooke,

A Topographical and Statistical Description of Hertford [etc], 2nd edn (London: Sherwood, Gilbert, and Piper), pp. 37–8.

1827 · Robert Clutterbuck, *The History and Antiquities of the County of Hertford: Compiled from the Best Printed Authorities and Original Records, Preserved in Public Repositories and Private Collections* . . . vol. 3, printed by and for Nichols, son, and Bentley, p. 452 (vols 1–3, 1815–27).

· S. W. W., 'Singular Monument at Brent Pelham', *The Mirror of Literature, Amusement and Instruction*, 17 February, no. 239, pp. 129–30.

After 1827 · Anon [Thomas Fisher?], Brent Pelham Church, Hartfordshire, from the north in *DRAWINGS and Water-colour Sketches, with Prints and Engravings, Illustrating the Topography of Co. Herts; Collected by J. W. Jones, to Accompany Clutterbuck's History of the County.* Five volumes. Paper; XVIth–XIXth cent., vol. iii, BL Add. MS 32350, f. 175. The catalogue reads ff. 174–176 Brent Pelham, Hertfordshire: Drawings: 18th, 19th cent. See the Trustees Minutes for 1884.

1831–39 · Rev. Henry Soames is vicar of Brent and Furneux Pelham.

1833 · J. C. Buckler, 'Monumental Stone in Brent Pelham Church', *Knowsley Clutterbuck*, p. 450F (HALS D/Z119/10/450E).

· 'Bishop Stortford Petty Sessions', *The County Press for Herts, Beds, Bucks, Huntingdon, Cambridge, Essex, and Middlesex*, 20 April, vol. III, no. 94, p. 3, c.3.

*c.*1834 · Yew tree on the border of Great and Little Pepsells is felled.

Before 1836 · Thomas Fisher, [Shonks' Tomb] At Brent Pelham, Hertfordshire published in the *Gentleman's Magazine* (1852) – see below. Fisher had died in 1836 and the

344

picture was sold at auction in March 1837: 'Lot 76 [finished drawings] of a Monument at Brent Pelham', *Catalogue of Interesting and Valuable Topographical and Antiquarian Works, by T. Fisher . . . Which Will Be Sold by Auction by Messrs Southgate and Son . . . March 15th, 1837* (BL 10368.e.3.(26.)).

1849 · Charles Boutell, *Christian Monuments in England and Wales, etc.* (London: George Bell), pp. 77, 104–5.

· Rev. Edward L. Cutts, *A Manual for the Study of the Sepulchral Slabs and Crosses of the Middle Ages* (London: John Parker), p. 31.

1850 · W. Durrant Cooper, 'Folk Lore: Similarity of Traditions', *Notes and Queries*, s1–II (28 December): pp. 513–14.

1852 · [John Gough Nicholls], 'Monument in Brent Pelham Church, Hertfordshire', *Gentleman's Magazine*, vol. XXXVII (New Series), pp. 444–6. With an illustration by Thomas Fisher – see above, 1836.

1863 · 'June 21st: Sepulchral Vagaries', *The Book of Days: A Miscellany of Antiquities in Connection with the Calendar*, ed. R. Chambers, vol. 1 (Edinburgh: W. & R. Chambers), pp. 804–8.

1864–76 · Woolmore Wigram is vicar of Brent and Furneux Pelham.

1862 · Kelly's 1862 Post Office Directory for Hertfordshire, p. 371.

1865 · F[rances] Wilson, 'The Legend of Piers Shonks', *The Reliquary, Quarterly Journal and Review; A Depository for Precious Relics Legendary, Biographical and Historical, Illustrative of the Habits Customs, and Pursuits of our Forefathers*, ed. Llewellyn Jewitt FSA, no. 22, vol. VI (October), pp. 98–9.

1866 · G. P., 'A Curious Epitaph', *Standard*, 24 January.

· J., 'A Curious Epitaph', *Notes and Queries*, s3–IX (17 March), p. 219.

345

J. H. L. [Joseph Hirst Lupton?], 'Curious Epitaph', *Notes and Queries*, s3–IX (12 May), p. 400. Responding to J.

1867 · J. G. N. [John Gough Nichols], 'Monument of O Piers Shonkes, At Brent Pelham, Co. Hertford', *Notes and Queries*, s3–XII (3 August), p. 97. Responding to J. and J. H. L.

1872 · John Edwin Cussans, *History of Hertfordshire, Containing an Account of the Descents of the Various Manors; Pedigrees of Families Connected with the County; Antiquities, Local Customs . . . Chiefly Compiled from Original MSS. in the Record Office and British Museum, etc.* [With plates, including a portrait.], 3 vols, vol. 1 (London: Chatto & Windus) [1870–1873], pp. 140–1.

· L. H. S., 'Epitaphs', *The Cliftonian: A Magazine Edited by Members of Clifton College*, vol. II (Bristol: Clifton College), pp. 45–7.

1876 · George Weight, 'The Tomb of O. Piers Shonks, in Brent Pelham Church, Herts', *Holiday Rambles in Essex and Herts*. Unpublished MS at London Metropolitan Archives (originally deposited at Guildhall Library). Plate 16 (CLC/270/MS00475).

· 'Shonk's Moat' on Ordnance Survey Map 1:2,500.

1880 · An Old Inhabitant, *A Guide to Hertfordshire with a History and Description of the Various Towns and Villages and Objects of Interest in the County* (Hertford: Simson & Co.), pp. 90–1.

1885 · 'Chronicles of English Counties: Hertfordshire', *All the Year Round*, 7 March, pp. 513–14.

1888 · D. E., 'Brent Pelham', *Hertfordshire Mercury*, 25 February, p. 4.

· Hertfordiensis/W. H. N. [William Henry Norris]/Ecclesiologist/'Brent Pelham', *Hertfordshire Mercury*, 10 March.

· E. A. B./W. Wigram/'Brent Pelham', *Hertfordshire Mercury*, 17 March.

· Hertfordiensis/'Brent Pelham', *Hertfordshire Mercury*, 24 March.

· J. E. Cussans, 'Query', *Hertfordshire Mercury*, 5 May.

· *Plan of Beeches Farm in the Parish of Brent Pelham, Herts* (HALS DE/Bc/P5).

1895 · *Handbook for Hertfordshire, Bedfordshire and Huntingdonshire* (London: John Murray), p. 8.

1896 · U. B. Chisenhale-Marsh, 'Folk-lore in Essex and Herts', *Essex Review*, vol. 5, pp. 142–62.

1897 · 'Shonk's Moat' on Ordnance Survey Map 1:2,500.

1898 · A. Whitford Anderson, 'Some Hertfordshire Churches', *Bygone Hertfordshire*, ed. William Andrews (London: William Andrews), pp. 152–75.

1901 · 'Query: Crosses on Buttresses at Brent Pelham Church', Hertfordshire Archaeological Notes and Queries, *Hertfordshire Mercury*, 5 October (EHAS). See 1902 for replies.

· W. B. Gerish, 'A Hertfordshire St. George', *Folklore*, vol. 12, no. 3 (September), pp. 303–7.

· [William Ellcock?], 'Tomb in Brent Pelham Church, Herts, 1901', published in 'A Hertfordshire St. George' in *Folklore*, plate X, facing p. 303 – see above.

· [W. Wigram], undated manuscript note from Watling House, St Albans (HALS DE/Gr/59).

1902 · Herbert W. Tompkins, *Highways and Byways of Hertfordshire* (London: Macmillan), pp. 306–9.

· W. Wigram, 'The Legend of O. Piers Shonks. Brent Pelham, Herts.', unpublished, undated, letter to W. B. Gerish, *c*.1902, HALS, Gerish Book Collection, Grangerised Cussans' History of Hertfordshire.

· W. B. Gerish, 'A Hertfordshire St. George', *Home*

Counties Magazine, vol. IV (London), pp. 289–94.

· Folk Lorist, 'Replies: Crosses on Buttresses at Brent Pelham Church', Hertfordshire Archaeological Notes and Queries, *Hertfordshire Mercury*, 7 April. Replying to EHAS.

· Q. W. V., 'Consecration Cross in Herts Churches', Hertfordshire Archaeological Notes and Queries, *Hertfordshire Mercury*, (date not found, see cutting in HALS DE/Gr/59). Replying to EHAS.

· R. T. Andrews, 'Moated Houses [etc.]', Hertfordshire Archaeological Notes and Queries, *Hertfordshire Mercury*, 6 September.

1903
· [R. T. Andrews?], Hertford Museum's Brent Pelham Bibliography, 3 MS sheets.

· Mrs [Marion] Hudson, unpublished typescript letter, 2 October (HALS DE/Gr/59).

· Mrs [Marion] Hudson, unpublished manuscript letter, 26 October (DE/Gr/59).

· H. T. Pollard, typescript relating Mrs Hudson's story [no date, *c*.1903] (HALS DE/Gr/59).

1904
· Herbert W. Tompkins, *Marsh-Country Rambles* (London: Chatto & Windus), pp. 214–16.

1905
· W. Wigram, unpublished letter to Gerish dated 12 June (HALS DE/Gr/59).

· W. W. Skeat, unpublished letter to Gerish dated 15 June (HALS DE/Gr/59).

· H. C. Andrews, unpublished letter to Gerish headed 'Cetiosaurus', n.d. (HALS DE/Gr/59).

· W. Wigram, unpublished letter to Gerish dated 6 July (HALS DE/Gr/59).

· W. B. Gerish, 'A Hertfordshire St. George; or the Story of O Piers Shonks and the Pelham Dragon', *East Herts Archaeological Society Transactions*, vol. III, part 1, pp. 61–70.

- 'Annual Report 1905', *East Herts Archaeological Society Transactions*, vol. III, part 1. pp. ii–iii.
- 'Proceedings of Archaeological Societies', *The Antiquary: A Magazine Devoted to the Study of the Past*, vol. 41, September, p. 357.

1909
- Stapleton Martin, 'Burial Half Within and Half Without a Church', *Notes and Queries*, s10–XI (6 February), p. 108.
- W. B. Gerish, John B. Wainewright, A. R. Bayley, 'Burial Half Within and Half Without a Church', *Notes and Queries*, s10–XI (20 March), pp. 230–1.
- A. Stapleton, R. B.-R., 'Burial Half Within and Half Without a Church', *Notes and Queries*, s10–XI (17 April), p. 318.

1910
- An inventory of the historical monuments in Hertfordshire/Royal Commission on Historical Monuments (England: HMSO), pp. 17, 19, 69–70.
- Postcard 'Shonks Tomb – Brent Pelham Church', *c.*1910 (HALS CV B.Pel/33).

1911
- W. B. Gerish, *The Folklore of Hertfordshire: A Brief List of Material Collected and Classified by [. . .]* (Bishop's Stortford).
- Sir Cyril Fox, 'Shonks – His Moat', *London Daily News*, 5 May. The copy among Gerish's papers is in HALS DE/Gr/59.

1912
- A. Whitford Anderson photographed the tomb and the crosses on the buttresses, *Hertfordshire Churches*, vol. 2 (HALS DE/X1042/7). See 1914 for his illustration.
- Allan Fea, *Old World Places* (London: Eveleigh Nash), pp. 41–2.

1914
- Helen Douglas-Irvine, 'Brent Pelham', *Victoria History of the County of Hertford*, vol. 4, ed. W. Page, pp. 92 and 98–9. With an illustration by A. Whitford Anderson.

· W. B. Gerish, 'Notes: Piers Shonks', Hertfordshire Archaeological Notes and Queries, *Hertfordshire Mercury*, 19 December.

· W. B. Gerish, 'Notes: The Churchyard at Brent Pelham [Pt1]', Hertfordshire Archaeological Notes and Queries, *Hertfordshire Mercury*, 21 November. See 1915 for Part 2. Both parts appear in *Epitaphs in Hertfordshire Churchyards: Vol. 1 A-R*, compiled by W. B. Gerish (HALS/H.9295).

1915 · W. B. Gerish, 'Hertfordshire Worthies', *East Herts Archaeological Society Transactions*, vol. VI, part 1, p. 54.

· W. B. Gerish, 'Notes: The Churchyard at Brent Pelham [Pt2]', Hertfordshire Archaeological Notes and Queries, *Hertfordshire Mercury*, 27 March.

· Frederick G. Gurney, 'Replies: Piers "Shonks" and Berwick in Standon', Hertfordshire Archaeological Notes and Queries, *Hertfordshire Mercury*, 17 April.

1921 · W. B. Gerish, *A Tour Through Hertfordshire: Setting Forth Its Legends, Traditions and Ghostly Tales* (Watford), pp. 7–8.

1930 · Herbert C. Andrews, 'Dragon-Killers in Tales and Legends', *Notes and Queries*, sCLIX (12 July), pp. 29–30 (in response to Otto F. Babler, 'Dragon-Killers in Tales and Legends', *Notes and Queries*, sCLVII, 3 May, p. 316).

1932 · D. C. Thompson, 'The Shonks Epitaph, Brent Pelham', *Notes and Queries*, sCLXII (2 January), p. 8.

· H. C. Andrews, Alice Earle, W. E. B., 'The Shonks Epitaph, Brent Pelham', *Notes and Queries*, sCLXII (16 January), p. 49.

· S., 'The Shonks Epitaph, Brent Pelham', *Notes and Queries*, sCLXII (20 February), p. 142.

1937 · *Shonk's Tomb*, postcard, postmarked 20 August.

1938   · J. E. B. Gover et al., *The Place-Names of Hertfordshire* (Cambridge: CUP), p. 185.

1946   · J. R. D., 'Hertfordshire Dragons', *Hertfordshire Countryside*, vol. 1, no. 2 (Autumn), p. 33.

         · F. S. Burnell, 'The Man in the Wall', *Folklore*, vol. 58, no. 3 (September), pp. 312–17.

1950   · Sir William Beach Thomas, *Hertfordshire*, *The County Books* (London: Robert Hale), p. 234.

1952   · Harold Adshead, 'Piers Shonks and the Dragon of Brent Pelham', *Hertfordshire Countryside*, vol. 7, no. 26 (Autumn), pp. 54 and 57.

1953   · Emilie Montgomery Gardner, letter to the rector of Brent Pelham, 5 December (HALS D/P77/29/1).

1962   · M. Tomkins, 'Limericks that Edward Lear Might Have Written', *Hertfordshire Countryside*, vol. 16, no. 67 (Winter), p. 281.

1963   · F. Burgess, *English Churchyard Memorials* (London: Lutterworth Press), pp. 105–6.

1965   · Arthur Mee, *Hertfordshire*, *The King's England*, rev. edn (London: Hodder & Stoughton), p. 42.

1966   · Betty Puttick, 'The Hertfordshire St. George and the Dragon', *Hertfordshire Countryside*, vol. 20, no. 83 (March) p. 311.

1968   · Will Bagley, 'Strange Tale of Long-Shonksy's Knucklebone', *Stevenage News*, 23 January.

         · Peter Jackson, 'From Brent Pelham: The Strange Tale of Piers Shonks – Giant Killer', *Hoddesdon and Broxbourne Mercury*, 20 December, p. 8.

         · T. P. E. [Ted] Barclay, *The Story of Brent Pelham* (n.d. late 1960s).

1974   · Doris Jones-Baker, *Old Hertfordshire Calendar* (London: Phillimore), p. 76.

1977   · Nikolaus Pevsner, *Hertfordshire*, 2nd edn, rev. by Bridget

Cherry, *Buildings of England* (Penguin; repr. 2000), pp. 22, 109–10.

· Doris Jones-Baker, *The Folklore of Hertfordshire* (London: Batsford).

· Nigel Pennick, 'Dragon Legends: No. 1 Piers Shonkes (Herts.)', *Journal of Geomancy*, vol. 2, no.1, pp. 4–5.

1978   · Jacqueline Simpson, 'Fifty British Dragon Tales: An Analysis', *Folklore*, vol. 89, no. 1, pp. 79–93.

1979   · Nigel Pennick, 'More on Piers', *The Ley Hunter*, no. 85.

1980   · Jacqueline Simpson, *British Dragons, Myth, Legend and Folklore* (London: Wordsworth, 2001; 1st edn London: Batsford, 1980), pp. 60, 65, 70, 74, 90, 93–5, 128.

1982   · R. M. Healey, *Hertfordshire: A Shell Guide* (London: Faber), p. 66.

1985   · Victoria Turner, 'Rich in Myths and Legends', *Herts & Essex Observer*, 11 April.

· Jennifer Westwood, *Albion: A Guide to Legendary Britain* (London: Granada), pp. 106–8.

1987   · Doris Jones-Baker, *Tales of Old Hertfordshire* (Newbury: Countryside Press), pp. 61–5.

1989   · Jennifer Westwood, *Gothick Hertfordshire* (Princes Risborough: Shire), p. 13.

· Frank Sheardown, *The Working Longdog* (Romney Marsh: Dickson Price), pp. 67–72.

1991   · Dr Stephen Doree, 'Nathaniel Salmon: Hertfordshire's Neglected Historian', *Hertfordshire in History: Papers Presented to Lionel Munby*, ed. Doris Jones-Baker (Hertford: Hertfordshire Local History Council), pp. 217–19.

· Arthur Mee, *Hertfordshire: London's County Neighbour* (King's England Press), pp. 54–5.

1992   · Victoria Maddren, *Who Was Jack O' Legs? An Investigation into the Legends and Customs of Baldock and the Surrounding Area* (Baldock, Egon), pp. 37–9.

1997	· Kevin Crossley-Holland, *The Old Stories: Folk Tales from East Anglia and the Fen Country* (London: Dolphin Paperbacks, 1999; 1st pub. 1997), pp. 50–6.
	· Nigel Pennick, *Dragons of the West* (Chieveley, Bucks: Capall Bann), pp. 61–5.
1998	· Clive Partridge, '100 Years of Archaeology: A Review', *A Century of Archaeology in East Herts*, ed. David Perman (Ware: Rockingham Press and EHAS), pp. 53–4.
	· John Timpson, *Timpson's Country Churches* (London: Weidenfeld and Nicolson), pp. 50–1.
1999	· Paul Dietrich, 'What's All This About Dragons?', *Herts & Essex Observer*, 23 December, p. 18.
	· Adam Fox, 'Remembering the Past in Early Modern England: Oral and Written Tradition', *Transactions of the Royal Historical Society*, 6th ser., vol. 9, pp. 233–56.
	· [PJL], 'List of Purbeck Marble Coffin-shaped Slabs Part XII', 'Additions & Corrections', *Church Monuments Society Newsletter*, vol. 15:2, winter 1999/2000, p. 48.
2001	· Alison Gates, 'Spooky Tales from Beyond the Grave', *The Crow*, 2 May.
	· Nicholas Connell, 'An Indefatigable Antiquarian: The Life and Work of William Gerish', *Hertfordshire's Past*, no. 51 (Autumn), pp. 23–31.
2002	· Robert Bevan-Jones, *The Ancient Yew: A History of Taxus Baccata* (Macclesfield: Windgather Press, 2004; 1st pub. 2002), pp. 126–7.
	· *Church Monuments Society Newsletter*, vol. 19:2, winter 2003, p. 16.
2004	· Antony Janes, 'The Slaying of the Brent Pelham Dragon', *Hertfordshire Life*, no. 49 (April), pp. 61–3.
	· Ted Barclay, 'The Story of Piers Shonks' (unpublished).
	· Lin Marsh, 'Piers Shonks the Dragon-Slayer', *Royals, Rogues and Rhymes*, commissioned by Hertfordshire

Music Service for the Hertfordshire Schools Gala 2004, Hertfordshire Schools' Symphony Orchestra, Massed Hertfordshire Schools' Choirs, Conducted by Patrick Bailey, at the Royal Albert Hall, 22 March (DVD/Black Swan Film and Video).

2005 · Jennifer Westwood and Jaqueline Simpson, *The Lore of the Land* (London: Penguin), pp. 335–8.

2007 · *Monumental Inscriptions of the Parish Churches of St Mary, Furneux Pelham, St Mary, Stocking Pelham, and St Mary, Brent Pelham*, ed. Janet and John Pearson, MI Series no. 87 (Hertfordshire Family History Society), pp. 53 and 66–7.

· 'Area 148: Anstey & Pelhams Plateau', *Landscape Character Assessment: Supplementary Planning Document* (Hertford: East Herts District Council), pp. 249–53.

2010 · Brian and Moira Gittos, 'Abused, Neglected and Forgotten: The Story of the Medieval Cross Slab', *Ecclesiology Today*, 43, pp. 29–44.

· Dave Bromage, 'The Devilishly Tall Tale of Piers, a True Legend', *Bishop's Stortford Observer*, 27 October, p. 15.

· Michael Smith, *Piers Shonks the Dragon Slayer* (sirgawainsworld.wordpress.com), 28 September.

2013 · Dave Bromage, 'Into the Dragon Slayer's Den to Pay Homage', *Bishop's Stortford Observer*, 9 May, p. 12.

2018 · David Whiteley, 'Now, a few weeks ago we were filming outside this church in a Hertfordshire village and a car pulls up and the chap inside said to me, "Have you seen the tomb of our dragon slayer inside the church?" – I said, "Dragon slayer? Beg your pardon!" This is the story.' *Inside Out East*, BBC TV broadcast, 26 February.

· Mia Jankowicz, 'Cold Christmas & Other Church Legends', *Hertfordshire Life* (December), pp. 35–7.

Notes

These notes are an assortment of citations, qualifications, clarifications, further acknowledgements, further reading, excuses, musings and one or two passages that I cut from the main text and sneaked back in here. They should be used alongside the chronology, where you will find all the books, articles, maps, deeds, public records and manuscripts that have played their part in transmitting the legend of Piers Shonks; in other words they directly refer to the hero and so are part of his story. Books not in the chronology are given in full when first mentioned (as are some that are when the occasion calls for it), and subsequently as a short-title reference. When I think the main text gives you enough information, there is unlikely to be a note unless I have more to say about it. So, for example, if the text refers to Kipling's *Puck of Pook's Hill*, I trust you can find that without any further help.

Abbreviations used

BL = British Library
CCCC = Corpus Christi College, Cambridge
DNB = *Oxford Dictionary of National Biography*
EHAST = East Herts Archaeological Society Transactions
EPNS = English Place-Name Society
HALS = Hertfordshire Archives and Local Studies
SOA = Society of Antiquaries
TNA = The National Archives
VCH = Victoria County History

A note on place names

There was originally one Pelham – Peleham in Domesday Book – then two, then three. Today they are, in order of size, Furneux, Brent and Stocking Pelham. This book is mostly about Brent Pelham (aka Burnt Pelham, Pelham Arsa and Pelham Sarners) where Shonks sleeps, and Furneux Pelham, where the dragon lived. The spelling and pronunciation of Furneux Pelham, is not without controversy. I favour the spelling Furneux and the pronunciation *furnix*. The alternative is the misguided Furneaux, pronounced *furnoh*. This, among other things, is a hyper-foreignism. I could say a lot more on the subject, but will forbear. I am glad that the two versions exist, because it is interesting.

Place names and field names are a movable feast, changing over time as we might expect, but also two or three variants might exist simulta-neously: on maps, in deeds and in popular usage, say. An example is Patricks Wood, St Patricks Wood and Partricks Wood; the first is used here. I have mostly been consistent with my choices, but might some-times opt to give the spelling that was used at the time I am writing about, especially if it sounds right to my ear. I think I have managed to avoid ambiguity. I use Johns a Pelham for the abandoned farm and St Johns Pelham for the abandoned medieval moated site although they are essentially the same place. Occasional further clarifications will feature below, if necessary.

Dummling set to work – this is taken from Edgar Taylor's first English translation of the Brothers Grimm tale 'The Golden Goose' in *German Popular Stories*, translated from the *Kinder- und Hausmärchen* collected by Jakob and Wilhelm Grimm, from oral tradition (London: Baldwyn, 1823). I am, of course, Dummling.

In the High Middle Ages – in case of any quibbling this is a formulation more romantic and pleasing to my ear than precise. By it I mean the *long* High Middle Ages, say from 1066 until the unhappy end of Richard II in 1400.

LITHETH AND LESTENETH AND HERKENETH ARIGHT – I cast around for a long time for the right opening to the book and especially to the prelude which is written in a different style to most of the other chapters. I wanted to signal this was the voice of a storyteller. Many traditional openings to folk tales act as a threshold for the listener to cross, from the real world to the world of story. I tried a few variants of 'Once upon a time', looking at the beginnings of old folk tales and medieval poems. I sounded out 'It befell in the days of . . .', which I stole from Malory's *Morte d'Arthur*, but that didn't work. For a while I settled on 'I had this from Bill Gerish, who had it from Nat Salmon, who must have had it from Jack Weever (and who Jack had it from is anyone's guess).' I can't remember where I got the idea for that from – I know I didn't invent the formula – but it was too hail-fellow-well-met.

In the end I stumbled upon the opening I use here, which sounds just right to my ear. It is strange enough, but simple and somehow familiar; writerly yet the product of an oral culture; hypnotic too in the right tones. It is tautological for emphasis but has been rendered with elegant variation as 'Hearken and listen and hold your tongue', but I prefer the simpler and repetitive, 'Listen and listen and listen well.' The story demanding our attention is 'The Tale of Gamelyn', a fourteenth-century folk tale which appears in several manuscripts of Chaucer's *Canterbury Tales*. It is found after the unfinished 'Cook's Tale', although scholars think Chaucer perhaps intended to use it as the basis for the 'Yeoman's Tale' when he got round to writing that.

I say I stumbled upon it, but I think I must have been deliberately flicking through the *Canterbury Tales* reading the opening few lines of each section until I hit upon the incipit of 'Gamelyn'. I didn't actually read the rest of the tale until much later when I discovered that it was more appropriate than I knew. The Victorian philologist W. W. Skeat, who we will meet again writing about the name Shonks, edited BL Harleian Manuscript 7334, which he says is the best and earliest version of 'Gamelyn'. His introductory notes explain how the tale is related to the Robin Hood ballads: Gamelyn was a forerunner to the more famous outlaw, whereas the Shonks legends were in turn influenced by Robin's exploits. The first two lines together make the opening an especially happy choice: 'Litheth and Lesteneth and Herkeneth aright, and ye shall hear a taleyng of a doughty knight.' A perfect fit for the dragon-slaying Shonks. See W. W. Skeat, *The Tale of Gamelyn* (Oxford: Clarendon, 1884).

She was – I intend this first unnumbered chapter as a *prelude*. Defined by the OED as 'a preliminary action, or condition, preceding and introducing one of more importance; an introduction, a preface; a precursor' and, especially, as 'a short, often extemporized, piece of music played before another in order to tune an instrument or allow an instrumentalist to warm up'. Notes on this opening section, written in a different style to much of the rest of *Hollow Places*, are wordier than for the rest of the book for reasons that I think are obvious.

the oldest living thing – people have attributed vast ages to old yews and in the prelude to the book I ponder whether the Pelham yew was growing in the Iron Age: did a scout from the Trinovantes tribe take his bearings from her? The Ancient Yew Group categorises ancient yews as those over 800 years old with no upper age limit, leaving open the possibility that there is a yew alive somewhere that has been around since the Bronze Age. The website ancient-yew.org is very informative. Also have a look at the leaflets at the ancienttreeforum.co.uk, especially 'Ancient Tree Guide No.4: What Are Ancient, Veteran and Other Trees of Special Interest?' Where the slow-growing yew is defined as ancient at 6 m or 19 feet in girth. A 36-foot yew is 'very ancient'. See Chapter 7.

wide plateau between the rivers Ash and Quin – this is the Hormead Wooded Plateau, a heavy clay interfluve between the Pelhams and the Hormeads to their west. It is so called in 'Area 146: Hormead Wooded Plateau', *Landscape Character Assessment: Supplementary Planning Document* (Hertford: East Herts District Council, 2007), pp. 226–30. I like the word *interfluve*.

time out of mind and beyond the memory of man. I encountered this particular phrasing of 'time immemorial' in a transcript of the court documents created when the Reverend William Bishop and his parishioner William Dalton fought a legal battle over tithes due in the Pelhams in the final years of Queen Elizabeth I's reign (see Chapter 3). Time immemorial was fixed by the Statute of Westminster in 1291 as the time before 6 July 1189, that is the date of the accession of King Richard I.

Editing the prelude one day it suddenly popped into my head as the wording I was after to mean a long time ago, in a suitably portentous way. The OED gives the excellent noun 'immemorialness' as having derived from the phrase. It is a delight to discover the poetry of legal documents, for more see the note on Widow Bowcock below.

that winter's morning – 'In November the felling of trees for the winter store of wood began,' writes Doris Jones-Baker (*Old Hertfordshire Calendar* (London: Phillimore, 1974), p. 230), and Walter Rose says that trees were felled for timber in the dead of winter when the sap was down (Walter Rose, *The Village Carpenter* (Cambridge: CUP, 1937)), but compare the writer H. Rider Haggard who describes springtime felling on his farm in his entry for 11 April in *A Farmer's Year: Being His Commonplace Book for 1898* (London: Longmans, Green & Co., 1899), pp. 137–44. Henry Bexley, the operations manager at Hatfield Forest, told me that it is best to pollard trees in the summer because the sap will seal the tree against infection. Trees pollarded when they are dormant are more likely to die.

'umbuggin *job* – a trawl of the dialect dictionaries turned this up: 'HUMBUGGIN, troublesome'. The example of the word in use is wonderful: 'A proper 'umbuggin job, as the grave-digger said when 'e come down onrespected (unexpectedly) on a skelington.' Mary Carbery and Edwin Grey, *Hertfordshire Heritage: Ourselves and Our Words* (London: John Green, 1948), p. 100. 'The yew is probably the hardest British tree to fell, or to remove entire,' writes Robert Bevan-Jones in *The Ancient*

Yew: A History of Taxus Baccata (Macclesfield: Windgather Press, 2002), p. 106. So I am right to call it an 'umbuggin job.

Pepsells – Sometimes Great and Little Pepsells have two '1's, whereas Pepsels and Pipsels have one. Just so you don't think I've been slapdash with the spelling of these most important fields.

For some twenty years – the calculation and location are mostly based on map and tithe record evidence. See notes to Chapter 8 below.

hail – in an early draft, I wrote 'rain' here but then I learned about the terrible hailstorm of 25 July 1738, which destroyed crops in the Pelhams and across Hertfordshire. Birds were said to have been killed, windows broken and branches knocked off trees by hailstones as big as hen's eggs. I expect they took their toll on our yew tree, although no doubt she had seen worse.

gather brushwood or flints – See Chapter 8 for what the historian Pamela Horn has to say about children's deadening occupations in the nineteenth century.

would have carved their names in her bark – see Chapter 8. You must allow me my 'would' on this occasion. While I have tried to be guided by the eminent Shakespearean James Schapiro, who in his *1599* tried to avoid 'awkwardly littering the pages that follow with one hedge after another – "perhaps", "maybe", "it's most likely", "probably", or the most desperate of them all, "surely"', we know considerably less about Shonks than we do about our greatest but still mysterious playwright, and so I have fallen back on rather a lot of hedges. There are 101 perhapses, 84 musts, 39 probablys, 7 maybes, 2 most likelys and, I'm afraid, 9 surelys in the book as I write this. I think they are unavoidable and hopefully not too awkward. My favourite strategy when in doubt is to ask a question: 'Did her shadow once fall on the Eagle of the Ninth?' But never without good cause. See the note on the Eagle below.

breakfasting on the bitter flesh – the aril is the flesh surrounding a yew tree's seed. The 'aril's juicy, sweet-tasting, somewhat slimy pulp is the only non-poisonous part of the tree,' writes Fred Hageneder in *Yew: A History* (Stroud: Sutton, 2007), adding that the 'bright red, nutritious aril' attracted birds that distributed the seed. They must also have attracted rural children who would supplement meagre diets with the berries and leaves of a variety of trees and hedgerow plants. Roy Vickery gives specific instances of children eating arils, the first from the late sixteenth century: 'When I was young and went to schoole, diverse of my schoole fellowes and likewise myself did eat our fils of the berries of this tree', and more recently in the 1940s: 'We knew that yew seeds were poisonous, but we would eat for its sweetness, the sticky red covering, which was known as red snot.' Roy Vickery, *Oxford Dictionary of Plant-Lore* (Oxford: OUP, 1995), p. 410.

strange things happen – says Nicola Whyte in her fascinating 'The Deviant Dead in the Norfolk Landscape', *Landscapes* (2003), I, pp. 24–39. She writes about parish boundaries and places where three parishes meet as liminal sites associated with gibbets and the burial of suicides.

Roman road – this is RR21b according to the classification system invented by that peerless enthusiast and documenter of Britain's Roman roads Ivan Margary. It is a local road running from the major Roman road hub near Braughing, south-west of the yew tree, to Great Chesterford to the north-east. Not far from the spot where the yew tree stood are the remains of the road's raised foundations – its agger – in Hormead Park Wood. Crop marks show its course passing just a few feet from the tree.

Eagle of the Ninth – this is no fatuous attempt to invoke the most famous of the Roman legions in Britain (famous because of the mystery surrounding its supposed sudden disappearance and because Rosemary Sutcliff wrote her wonderful adventure story about it and its lost Eagle standard). RR21b (see above) is thought to have been built after the Boudiccan Revolt of 61 CE, and linked Ermine and Stane Street at Braughing to the new fort at Great Chesterford, which according to archaeologist Warwick Rodwell was probably intended as the winter quarters for the new auxiliaries of the Ninth Legion, sent by the Emperor Nero as part of the campaign to encircle and punish the Iceni. See Warwick Rodwell, 'The Roman Fort at Great Chesterford, Essex' in *Britannia,* vol. 3 (1972) pp. 290–3.

Tandridge – an ancient yew tree in Surrey knitted together from wooden sinews. It is said that the original Anglo-Saxon church was built around the roots of the tree which was already old then. The tree is exceedingly old, but the story about the church is a pleasant fiction.

Crowhurst – another Surrey yew tree, but not just another yew tree. Twenty-eight feet in girth. Biblical. The mother tree. My favourite yew tree. One day someone will find a cave painting of it or a cuneiform tablet relating Gilgamesh's visit.

vermicular, flayed, mutating – I scribbled 'Beowulf' in my notes next to these three adjectives, but can't find them in any translation I own. I am guessing that the reference is to the 2007 movie, the CGI Grendel looked like a monster fashioned from old roots and reminded me of the ancient yews I had seen. I think I must have chosen these words to describe him.

Reverend Soames – Henry Soames was the vicar of Furneux and Brent Pelham from 1831 to 1839. He was a respected ecclesiastical historian. I have a sense that he was not very interested in his flock and was something of a bore, which may be a terribly unjust thing to say. See his entry in the *DNB*.

rumours of piglets – one in ten would belong to the vicar. See Chapter 3 on tithes.

Pipsels Mead, Nether Rackets . . . Lady Pightle – local field names. I will have a lot more to say about Pipsels Mead and field names in general as I go along, but for now you might like to know that John Field's *English Field-Names* (see note to Chapter 5 below) tells us that the 'Lady' probably indicates that it was a pightle dedicated to the Blessed Virgin for the maintenance of a chapel. Nether means lower down or further away. Rackets might be related to 'land where cloth was finished' on racks, but I doubt it as the field is too remote.

Fortingall – possibly the oldest tree in Britain. 'Possibly' is enough for me in this instance.

Peola – in 1904 Walter Skeat, the father of place-name studies (see note above on *LITHETH AND LESTENETH AND HERKENETH ARIGHT*), identified Peola's Homestead as the most likely meaning of Pelham based on a single occurrence of Peola as a personal name in an Anglo-Saxon charter. W. W. Skeat, *The Place-Names of Hertfordshire* (Hertford: Stephen Austin, 1904), p. 31. In 1598 the Elizabethan chorographer John Norden said that Pelham was named for all the Pels or springs in the Pelhams. There are a fair number of springs in the fields around Brent Pelham where the winterbourne Ash rises, but Norden's etymology was guesswork and fanciful. Skeat lamented that people who would never dream of trying to figure out Greek and Latin places names thought nothing of guessing at English place names without even the rudiments of Anglo-Saxon. There is no Old English word Pel: Norden had misread the Anglo-Saxon character for 'W' as a 'P'. The obscure word for a water spring was in fact the not so obscure word 'well' – nothing at all to do with Pelham. Place-name studies – and much else I write about in this book – are ringed with such pitfalls. No doubt, I've fallen into some of them.

longbows – see Chapter 22 for more on longbows and village archery butts. A young yew tree just 100 years old would yield about four staves of the sapwood and heartwood that made the best bows. Roger Ascham in his 1545 treatise on archery *Toxophilus* says that yew staves from the trunk were far superior to those from branches, implying that branches were sometimes lopped off and used, albeit for inferior bows. The best bow wood came from the continent, from Spanish or Venetian yew according to Oliver Rackham. The high demand for staves for longbows was a catastrophe for yew trees from which they have never recovered.

See Hageneder (2007) and Oliver Rackham, *The History of the Countryside* (London: Dent, 1987; 1st pub. 1986).

Generations pass while some trees stand – 'Gravestones tell truth scarce forty years. Generations pass while some trees stand *and old families last not three oaks.'* Wrote Sir Thomas Browne, adding a footnote on the gravestones: 'Old ones being taken up, and other bodies laid under them.' Sir Thomas Browne, *Urn-burial,* ed. W. A. Greenhill (London: Macmillan, 1896; first pub. 1658), p. 64.

Trinovantes – these were border lands early on: the boundary between the Catuvellauni and the Trinovantes Iron Age tribes. Worstead Lane, no doubt erroneously, has been called the latter's war path. See earlier note on Ash and Quin.

Widow Bowcock – 'not having the fear of God before his eyes but being moved and seduced by the instigation of the devil', the Lord of the Manor of Furneux Pelham John Newport stabbed poor Widow Bowcock to death in 1736. He had been trying to stab his maid but couldn't catch her and had previously been in gaol for running his manservant through with a rapier.

winged dogs . . . immense double-jointed finger bones that gave Mr Morris so much trouble – all in good time.

cursed be he . . . a landmark, which they of old time have set – a blending of two biblical quotations from the King James Bible: Deuteronomy 27:17 and Deuteronomy 19:14. The idea comes from M. R. James.

hard as yew wood – John Evelyn in *Sylva* says 'for the cogs of mills, posts to be set in moist grounds, and everlasting axel-trees, there is none to be compared with it; likewise for the bodies of lutes, theorbo's, bowles, wheels, and pins for pullies; yea, and for tankards to drink out of.' Evelyn didn't believe the yew was especially toxic and thought it fine for tankards. He was wrong. In the same section he tells the story of a yew that became sacred after the head of a virgin was hung up on it. He then – apropos of the word virgin – relates something from Pliny about the vestal virgins hanging their hair on a lotus tree in Rome, before adding 'But that is nothing to this.' He is my kind of writer. You have been warned.

Gone, the merry morris din – John Keats, 'Robin Hood' (1820).

'girt hole' – Reverend Woolmore Wigram hamming it up in a letter to W. B. Gerish. See 1905 in chronology.

HMS Beagle – what things to choose to typify an age, a moment, the passing of time? I research, make a list and then trust to my ear, my instincts and my theme. I selected Darwin here because he represents such a watershed in the history of human understanding. See Chapter 10 for more on what Darwin was up to in 1834.

Chapter 1

The Reader will rather excuse an unsuccessful Attempt – the full quote is 'Shonks will indeed afford us a little Amusement, if Conjecture may be admitted. Considering there is from Tradition some Ground to believe Shonk made a Figure in his Time; and considering it is not pro Aris & Focis, if our Story should be deemed fabulous, I will venture to say what seems to me probable. And the Reader will rather excuse an unsuccessful Attempt to clear up the Truth where so little Light is to be had, than giving Things up for nursery Tales to save the Pains of Inquiry.'

where the local fairies baked their loaves – this is the most interesting of these items ('There is more bliss in describing the nymphs than in describing medals,' declared Paracelsus. 'There is more bliss in describing the origin of the giants than in describing court etiquettes'). In the Pelhams there is a tradition that fairies used to bake bread in a dell in a field on the eastern slope of the Ash Valley. 'Whether a belief in fairies – locally known as "pharisees" – is widespread I cannot say,' wrote the local archdeacon in 1936. 'But the older people here still tell stories of what the "little people" did and said in the past, and I am seriously assured that there is, in the dell in Old Church Field, an oven in which they bake their bread.'

The dell is visible on old maps, represented by an amoeba of hatch marks and labelled 'Chalk Pit'. It must have been filled in some years ago as I can't find any trace of it now and who can say what has become of the poor fairies? The field immediately to the north of Old Church Field is called Silly Mead – Holy Meadow – and while walking there a few years ago I picked up an unusual piece of stone. At first, I had no idea what it was. Like the early antiquaries who couldn't distinguish between sharks' teeth and the stone age tools they called thunderstones and tongue-stones, I thought it was man-made owing to the regular and striking pattern of white dots punched into the dark surface, but turning it over in my hand I discovered that where it had been broken by the plough's mouldboard it resembled an ordinary piece of flint. Looking it up in a little book of Hertfordshire natural history, written for schoolchildren in the 1920s, I discovered the stone's pattern is in fact an imprint of the inside of a Micraster shell, which belonged to a type of extinct sea urchin that lived in the Cretaceous sea once covering our island. The hard flint grew inside the remains of the urchin which then eroded, leaving the magical stone. This was interesting, but more interesting still was how our ancestors solved the mystery of the stones: they called them fairy loaves. Now I had one of these loaves the fairies had baked and the archdeacon's tale about fairy ovens was solved.

I am with Walter Scott – I came across this in Dorson's *Folklorists* and used it before I learned the context (and ending) from Jennifer Westwood's *Albion*. It puts quite a different spin on its significance: In 1812 Sir Walter Scott visited Rokeby. His guide, J. B. S. Morritt, observed that he 'was but half satisfied with the most beautiful scenery when he could not connect it with some local legend, and when I was forced sometime to confess . . . "Story! God bless you! I have none to tell, sir" – he would laugh, and say, "Then let us make one – nothing so easy to make as a tradition."' See Richard M. Dorson, *The British Folklorists: A History*

(London: Routledge & Kegan Paul, 1968), p. 91, and Jennifer Westwood, *Albion: A Guide to Legendary Britain* (London: Granada, 1985), p. 371.

'Sir, it's one of the rummiest' – Herbert W. Tompkins wrote: 'Said a man to me once in Hadham, "Sir, it's one of the rummiest stories I ever heard, like, that 'ere story of Piercy Shonkey, and if I hadn't see the place in the wall with my own eyes I wouldn't believe nothing about it."' One of the rummiest quotes I've ever come across. See 1902 in chronology.

'You're writing a children's book?' – really best not to speak to people about a book you are writing, but when it takes such a long time and you are trying to justify what you are up to, sometimes you have to say something. This exchange was inspired by one I had with Duncan who fitted my living room carpet, which is now very moth-eaten and cat-scratched.

An early estate map – these are the trees in Shonks' Wood on Hollingworth's Plan of Beeches (1810), but on Hollingworth's earlier map of Beeches dated 1769, the shadows pool to the west – perhaps he surveyed it in the morning (HALS DE/Cn/P7). On the first 25-inch OS maps the sun appears to be directly overhead, but the second edition 25-inch maps of Hertfordshire published in 1898 clearly have the shadows to the east.

Oliver Rackham – on trees on OS maps, see Rackham (1987).

boundary sketch maps – on the Ordnance Survey and boundaries see David E. M. Andrews, 'Merely a Question of Boundaries', *Sheetlines*, 103 (August 2015), pp. 31–9, and David Fletcher, 'The Archive of the Invisible: The Ordnance Survey's Boundary Record Library', *Archives*, 25: 103 (2000), pp. 98–116.

'Hornbeam Stub' – boundary sketch map 1875 (TNA OS27/2451).

Piers O' Shonkes – I spell our hero's name Piers Shonks and it is given that way throughout unless I am directly quoting someone who spells it differently. The strange business of 'O' is dealt with at length in Chapter 28.

Italo Calvino – Italian Folktales, trans. George Martin (London: Penguin, 2000).

Charlotte Sophia Burne – The Handbook of Folk-Lore, new edn (London: Sidgwick & Jackson, 1914).

Joseph Strutt – quoted in Dorson (1968).

Chapter 2

a group of Edwardian gentlemen – for accounts of the East Herts Archaeological Society excursion to Shonks' Moat see 1905 in chronology.

stagnal – unlike the word stagnant, stagnal celebrates and delights in wetlands. Dominick Tyler champions it in *Uncommon Ground: A Word Lover's Guide to the British Landscape* (London: Guardian/Faber, 2015).

Kipling's 'Puck's Song' – first published in Puck of Pook's Hill (London: Macmillan, 1906) in the story 'Weland's Sword'.

anyone who has dug as much as a posthole – Rackham (1987).

moats were first and foremost a status symbol – I think Christopher Taylor proposed this idea. It is one of those things that when you first read it, you think, ah, how interesting, how clever. On reflection, I don't believe a word of it. No doubt, it will be on QI one day and irritate me. For more on moats: Christopher Taylor, *Village and Farmstead* (London: Philip, 1983); Tom Williamson, *England's Landscape: East Anglia* (London: Collins, 2006); and David Wilson, *Moated Sites* (Aylesbury: Shire, 1985).

trailbastons – Marc Morris, *A Great and Terrible King* (London: Windmill, 2008), pp. 346–8. It was F. W. Maitland who in 1893 wrote: 'There can be little doubt that it signified a "club-man", a vagabond with a big stick.' Cited in the *OED* entry for trailbaston, where they are defined as 'violent evil-doers'.

double white jonquil – see E. A. B. (1888) in chronology.

William Gerish – see Nicholas Connell, 'An Indefatigable Antiquarian: The Life and Work of William Gerish', *Hertfordshire's Past*, Issue 51 (Autumn 2001).

earliest large-scale Ordnance Survey – surveyed in 1863–86. Scale, 1:2,500 (Southampton: Ordnance Survey Office, 1878).

Monumental Inscriptions – *Inscriptions in Churches and Churchyards, Chapels and Burial Grounds in Hertfordshire, Collected by William Blyth Gerish* (British Library Add MS. 39271–39284 [1907–14]).

St Thomas Becket – John Butler, *The Quest for Becket's Bones* (London: Yale, 1995).

several replies – they appeared in the *Hertfordshire Mercury* on 10 March and 17 March 1888.

Chapter 3

Traditionally held in Brent Pelham – account book (HALS DP/78/3/3).

Tithes – on tithes, see Roger Kain and Hugh Prince, *Tithe Surveys for Historians* (Chichester: Phillimore, 2000); Herbert Lockwood, *Tithe and Other Records of Essex & Barking* (Chelmsford: Essex Record Office, 2006); W. E. Tate, *The Parish Chest*, 3rd edn (Chichester: Phillimore, 1983).

founding member of the Alpine Club – see *DNB* on Woolmore Wigram and *Alpine Journal*, vol. 1 (1863).

early local history manual – John Cox, *How to Write the History of a Parish* (London: Bemrose & Sons, 1879).

Alexander Pope – 'Memories of P. P. Clerk of this Parish' cited by Tate (1983).

shady deal done in 1160 – see Marion Gibbs, 'Early Charters of the Cathedral Church of St Paul, London', Camden Society, 3rd series, vol. 58 (1939), p. xxxv and no. 47, 192–3.

Wheatly set down – Wheatly's account book (HALS DP/78/3/2). This is the source for all local tithe payments in this chapter.

William Bishop v Richard Dalton – HALS DP/78/3/4. See also G. H. Cameron, *History of Furneux Pelham* (1935), unpublished (HALS DP/78/29/2).

Like Richard Hagger – the ancestors of Master Lawrence, the woodcutter, live on in the tithe accounts too. In 1728, William Lawrence of Stocking Pelham is paying a fixed rate of 5*s.* per annum for Pettycoat Mead – but in October 1731 pays part of his tithes with 18s worth of turnips from those he grows in Burnt Pelham Field. Another Lawrence pays 18*s.* in tithes in 1739, but Reverend Wheatly has written acerbically 'sed cavendu de futuro' – 'but beware of the future'. Lawrence continues to pay 18*s.* a year – 9*s.* at Lady Day and 9*s.* at Michaelmas – but in 1741, the vicar has been watching him keenly and makes a note that he had 48 sheep, 35 lambs and 6 cows that year. The following Lady Day his tithes have gone up to 20*s.* a year and he also has to pay a further 12*s.* 6*d.* tithe on the 'Aftermouth of the close'.

Chapter 4

The Variety of Wonders – Sir Henry Chauncy, *The Historical Antiquities of Hertfordshire*, vol. 2 (Bishop's Stortford: Mullinger, 1826; 1st pub. 1700), p. 321. Chauncy is writing about Sir John Mandeville who was born in St Albans.

W. G. Hoskins – *The Making of the English Landscape*, rev. edn with an introduction and commentary by Christopher Taylor (London: Hodder and Stoughton, 1992).

'On the Cannibals' – Michel de Montaigne, *The Complete Essays*, trans. M. A. Screech (Harmondsworth: Penguin, 1991).

Cussans – see 1872 in chronology. His curmudgeonly letter to the *Hertfordshire Mercury* begins with a moan about the traditions surrounding Henry Trigg in Stevenage. The landlords of the Old Castle Inn were selling copies of Trigg's will with the words changed to suggest he was still in the coffin: 'It is astounding how an absurd tradition survives. It matters not if an imposition has been exposed over and over again, credulous and weak-minded people will still fondly cling to romantic falsehoods.' Thanks to Nick Connell for drawing my attention to this.

Philip Pullman – *Folk Tales of Britain: Narratives*, vol. 1, collected and edited by Katherine M. Briggs with a preface by Philip Pullman (London: Folio Society, 2011).

Italo Calvino – *Italian Folktales*, trans. George Martin (London: Penguin, 2000).

still see it today – 'You can see it there still' is a chapter title in Simpson (1980).

Walter de la Mare – I first saw this quoted in Westwood (1985). The lines are taken from de la Mare's notes on poem 153 in *Come Hither: A Collection of Rhymes & Poems for the Young of All Ages*, new edn, vol. 1 (Harmondsworth: Kestrel, 1960).

mnemonic bridges – I came across this concept in Eviatar Zerubavel, *Time Maps: Collective Memory and the Social Shape of the Past* (Chicago: University of Chicago Press, 2003).

Coleridge – I see Alberto Manguel, *Packing My Library: An Elegy and Ten Digressions* (New Haven: Yale University Press, 2018).

Objects that locate legends – Adam Fox, in 'Remembering the Past in Early Modern England: Oral and Written Tradition', *Transactions of the Royal Historical Society*, 6th series, vol. 9 (1999), writes that the survival of physical evidence 'could be crucial in the preservation of local tradition' which was likely to die out 'if the landmarks or monuments which kept it in mind' were destroyed.

Chapter 5

parish magazine for March 1937 – Furneux Pelham Parish Magazine (Private Collection).

Burne said that – she added: 'And, to quote once more words read too long since to trace their source now, "if it be true that nothing human is without interest to man, then that which tells us of the thoughts and ways of our forefathers should be of the deepest and nearest interest to us, for it has had something to do with making us what we are"' (1914).

On field names – see

John Field, *English Field Names: A Dictionary* (Gloucester: Alan Sutton, 1989).

John Field, *A History of English Field-Names* (London: Longman, 1993).

Margaret Gelling, *Place-Names in the Landscape* (London: Dent, 1993).

C. H. Keene, *Field-Names of the London Borough of Ealing*, Field-Name Studies No. 1 (Nottingham: EPNS, 1976).

The Place-Names of Hertfordshire, ed. J. E. B. Gover et al. (Cambridge: CUP, 1938).

Rev. Prof. Skeat, *The Place-Names of Hertfordshire* (Hertford: EHAS, 1904).

A. H. Smith, *The Preparation of County Place-Names Surveys* (London: EPNS, 1954).

While editing this for the last time, I learned with delight that Paul Cavill has written *A New Dictionary of English Field-Names* for the English Place-Name Society. Some years ago, Dr Cavill encouraged my interest in field names and has always answered my enquiries with the kindness and tact that place-name experts must cultivate when dealing with enthusiastic amateurs.

Chapter 6

Beeches – this is the preferred spelling in the EPNS volume for Hertfordshire. Today the Barclays spell the name of their house 'Beaches'.

totally disarming habit – Zerubavel has something interesting to say about this: 'Being social presupposes the ability to experience things that happened to the groups to which we belong long before we even joined them as if they were part of our own personal past. Such an ability is manifested in the Polynesian use of the first-person pronoun when narrating one's ancestral history as well as in statements like "I smelted iron in Nubia" or "I built Timbuctoo" used to express a Barbadian poet's distinctly African memories.' Zerubavel (2003).

Comte de St Germain – I can't help but allude to the now obscure count as he has been a creature of my own imaginative life since childhood, put there by Francis Hitching's *World Atlas of Mysteries*. I recall reading somewhere that when someone was talking about Jesus, the eighteenth-century count was heard to mutter under his breath 'I told that Jew to be careful!'

stray Irish wolfhound – see 1989 in chronology.

six rooms were haunted – this surprising fact is reported by the VCH (1914) without offering a source.

Field of Cloth of Gold – Sydney Anglo, *The Hampton Court Painting of the Field of Cloth of Gold Considered as an Historical Document* (OUP, n.d. Repr. From *The Antiquaries Journal*, vol. XLVI, 1966).

In Our Time – 'The Field of the [sic] Cloth of Gold' on *In Our Time* (BBC Radio 4), 6 October 2005. Incidentally, 'cloth of gold' was a type of material and so the frequently encountered 'The Field of *the* Cloth of Gold' is incorrect. There wasn't just one big piece of cloth made of gold. We wouldn't write 'The Field of the Silk' but 'The Field of Silk'.

Chapter 7

Many thanks to Henry Bexley, operations manager at Hatfield Forest, and tree surgeon Ben Oates, both of whom very kindly talked to me about caring for ancient trees.

Melville – this quotation seemed so appropriate that I had to use it and replace the original epigraph to this chapter, which was 'Century after century they have continued to draw up from the earth their mighty nourishment; on their green umbrageous heads the rains and dews of a thousand years have fallen, and they now stand, at the present day, as monuments of wonder to the generations of men.' From 'On the Antiquity of Trees', in *The Mirror of Literature, Amusement, and Instruction*, 4 July 1840, vol. 36, no. 1013, p. 15.

yews in general: the two books I found most useful for this chapter were Fred Hageneder (2007) and Bevan-Jones (2002).

remarkable encyclopedic maps – Furneux Pelham Tithe Map 1840 at HALS DP/78/27/2 or DSA4/76/2, Furneux Pelham Tithe Award 1837 at HALS DP/78/27/1 or DSA4/76/1. The Tithe Commutation Act was in 1836. An amended map drawn up in 1861 renamed Pepsels as Pipsels and divided it in half, or rather into two parcels, one a fair bit larger, so there was a great field and a little field by Wigram's day, which explains the names he used. It is attached to the 1837 Award.

Of the 311 ancient Yews – I calculated the yew numbers from the database on the Ancient Yew Group website.

Oliver Rackham – *The Last Forest* (London: Dent, 1989).

geographical distribution of these curious trees – there are at least two more Hertfordshire yews worthy of mention. The nearest is in the churchyard at Little Hadham, but the most impressive survives only as an engraving: it was in the west of the county, in the grounds of St Mary's Church, Rickmansworth, and described in 1797 as having been struck by lightning and split into two. This is a 'lost' yew. The engraving shows two alien trunks growing away from each other amid the gravestones at precipitous angles. It is a creature from the pages of myth, with trunks like ill-formed giants, bewitched, corrupted, unsettling and hardened to wood and uncanniness by time and the dead tangled in their roots.

John Brand – see William Pulleyn, *Church-Yard Gleanings and Epigrammatic Scraps* [etc.] (London: Samuel Maunder, n.d., [1830?]). This is Pulleyn quoting Brand quoting Thomas Browne's *Urn-Burial.*

Hywel Dda – see Bevan Jones (2002).

Edwin's Tree – see VCH (1914), p. 3, which cites Assize Rolls 313 (6 & 7 Edward I), m.46.

At the turn of the nineteenth century – for the OS 1-inch maps see John Brian Harley, *The Old Series Ordnance Survey Maps of England and Wales, Scale 1 Inch to 1 Mile: A Reproduction of the 110 Sheets of the Survey in Early State*, in 10 volumes, vol. 1 (Lympne Castle, Kent: Harry Margary, 1981).

There are remarkable preliminary pencil drawings – 2 inches to the mile. Drawing 142 of 315 can be found on the British Library website at http://www.bl.uk/onlinegallery/onlineex/ordsurvdraw/

Mr Bryant – A. Bryant, *County of Hertford*, 1822 repr. by Hertfordshire Record Society, 2003.

Lord of the Manor's tenancy agreement – 'Lease for Seven Years', 1 January 1807 (HALS DZ/120/44444).

first President of the Board of Agriculture – see Susanna Wade Martins, *Farmers, Landlords and Landscapes: Rural Britain 1720–1870* (Macclesfield: Windgather, 2004).

The transformation of the ancient clay – see Tom Williamson, *The Transformation of Rural England: Farming and the Landscape, 1700–1870* (Exeter: University of Exeter, 2002).

Ashridge Park . . . Boarhunt yew – all these examples can be found in Bevan-Jones (2002).

Sir John Parnell – cited in the Landscape Character Assessment (2007): 'I know of no part of England more beautiful in its stile than Hertfordshire: thro'out the oak and Elm hedgerows Appear Rather the work of Nature than Plantation, generally Extending thirty or forty feet Broad, growing irregularly in these stripes, and giving the fields the air of being reclaimed from a general tract of woodland.' – Thomas Fuller, *The Worthies of England*, ed. J. Freeman (1952), p. 229.

one eulogist – J. G. 'Ancient Yew Tree Destroyed by the Hurricane in November 1836', *Saturday Magazine*, 4 February 1837.

Chapter 8

A select bibliography for this chapter would include:

Nigel Agar, *Behind the Plough: Agrarian Society in Nineteenth-Century Hertfordshire* (Hatfield: University of Hertfordshire Press, 2005). Nigel very kindly met me for lunch some years ago to chat about Hertfordshire ag labs.

George Fussell, *The English Rural Labourer: His House, Furniture, Clothing and Food* . . . (London: Batchworth, 1949).

Pamela Horn, *The Victorian Country Child* (Gloucester: Sutton, 1985).

Alun Howkins, 'The English Farm Labourer in the 19th C: Farm Family and Community', in B. Short, ed., *The English Rural Community* (1992), pp. 85–103.

J. S. Hurt, *Bringing Literacy to Rural England: The Hertfordshire Example* (London: Phillimore, 1972).

Valerie Porter, *Yesterday's Farm: Life on the Farm 1830–1960* (Cincinnati: David and Charles, 2006).

A Quaint Old Fashioned Place: East Hertfordshire in the 1830s. Writings of James Smith, edited with an introduction by David Perman (Hertford: Hertfordshire Publications, 1990).

Barry Reay, *Rural Englands: Labouring Lives in the Nineteenth Century* (Basingstoke: Palgrave Macmillan, 2004).

Eric Hobsbawm and George Rudé, *Captain Swing* (Harmondsworth: Penguin, 1973).

K. D. M. Snell, *Annals of the Labouring Poor: Social Change and Agrarian England, 1660–1900* (Cambridge: CUP, 1985).

Ian H. Waller, *My Ancestor Was an Agricultural Labourer* (London: Society of Genealogists, 2007).

Tom Williamson, *The Transformation of Rural England: Farming and the Landscape, 1700–1870* (Exeter: University of Exeter, 2002).

boundary trees 'were deeply scored . . .' – K. D. M. Snell, *Parish and Belonging: Community, Identity, and Welfare in England and Wales, 1700–1950* (Cambridge: CUP, 2006).

Robert Andrews went to Anstey – for details of Robert Andrews and W. B. Gerish at Cave Gate see HALS DE/Gr/6. In 1946 in *Hertfordshire Countryside*, in an article on Hertfordshire Dragons – the first mention of the yew tree since Gerish – one J. R. D. writes that a labourer called Skinner felled the tree. See 1946 in chronology.

1834 – Wigram does not say when Master Lawrence felled the tree. It was sometime in the first half of the nineteenth century, in the living memory of his informants James and his brother Thomas Lawrence. They were born within a few years of each other at the end of the eighteenth century and were related to the woodcutter. The cartographic evidence gives a *terminus post quem* of the early 1820s, while the detailed account in 1827 by S. W. W. says nothing about a tree or the dragon's lair, only that the battle was fought on Shonks Hill, where the hero lived, so I began to favour the 1830s as the most likely decade for the felling of the tree by a group of labourers that included at least one relative of the Lawrence brothers.

By the 1830s there are some 30 Lawrences I could send to chop down the yew. This out of a population of 64 families in 56 houses.

On one side of the family they were carpenters, on the other agricultural labourers. Canon Wigram's letters mention only a labourer, and later labourers, until June 1905 when he recalled that someone had credited a Master Lawrence with the felling. By 'Master' he might mean a master tradesman as opposed to a journeyman or simply be using a term of respect for an older man. Wigram's accounts are conflicting: he even suggests in one that it may have been James' and Thomas' grandfather who felled the tree, although he questions the identification. That would be the William Lawrence born in 1738. He died in 1821 at the age of 83 so if it was him, the tree fell at a much earlier date than the other evidence suggests – and far too early for Thomas Skinner. Someone had probably confused their Williams – James and Thomas' father was also a William and there were six William Lawrences alive in the Pelhams in 1831.

I returned again and again to the tithe records, the parish register and the trade directories, where Thomas and James appear year after year as postmasters and parish clerks. I set the facts alongside my interpretation of the maps, the nineteenth-century accounts of the legend, Wigram's letters and other clues which we will meet with in later chapters. For instance, not until 1865 is a tree mentioned in passing by Frances Wilson in her letter to *The Reliquary*. Remember that she was born in 1831 and grew up in the neighbourhood. As we shall see, the tomb was opened in the early 1830s and J. C. Buckler came to the village to paint it in 1833, which would surely have drawn the attention of the villagers and put them in mind of Shonks. 1834 was a good date to plump for.

Hammonds – J. L. Hammond and Barbara Hammond, *The Village Labourer* (Gloucester: Sutton, 1987; first pub. 1911).

17 per cent of agricultural labourers were out of work – Reay (2004).

wrote a prominent Essex land agent – Christopher Comyns Parker, *The Oxley Parker Papers* (Benham & Co., 1964).

loaf of bread – specifically a gallon loaf of second flour weighing 8lb 11oz; the actual amounts had been set by a group of worthies at the Pelican Inn in the village of Speenhamland on the morning of 6 May 1795.

Nathan Driver – *Report from the Select Committee on That Part of the Poor Laws Relating to the Employment or Relief of Able-bodied Persons from the Poor Rate etc.*, 1828.

considerably more families earned their living in England from trade – see 1831 census.

where were the ploughmen, the carters, the hedgers – Waller (2007).

'rural rides' – William Cobbett, *Rural Rides* (London: Penguin, 2001). Cobbett also bemoaned the labourers' hovels in Leicestershire 'made of mud and straw, and bits of glass or of old cast-off windows without frames or hinges frequently and merely stuck in the mud wall. Enter them and look at the bits of chairs or stools, the wretched boards tacked together to serve for a table, the floor of pebble broken or of the bare ground.'

James Fraser – quoted in Horn (1985).

Lord Carnarvon – see Hammond (1987).

'Hodge' – see Snell (1985) and Mark Freeman, 'The Agricultural Labourer and the "Hodge" Stereotype, *c.*1850–1914', *Agricultural History Review* 49, II, pp. 172–86.

according to one mid-century journalist – this is the horticulturist Sir Ronald Hatton, writing as Christopher Holdenby. As is the mysterious barrier of 'Ay, ay'; see *Folk of the Furrow* (London: Smith, Elder 1913).

Overseers accounts – HALS DP/78/5.

1816 report – *A Digest of Parochial Returns Made to the Select Committee Appointed to Inquire into the Education of the Poor: Session 1818* (London: House of Commons, 1819).

In January 1854, the Hertfordshire school inspector wrote – 'General Report, for the Year 1854, by Her Majesty's Inspector of School, the Rev. F. C. Cook […] in *Minutes of the Committee of Council on Education 1854–5: Elementary Schools* (London: Eyre & Spottiswoode, 1855).

A survey of over 500 labouring families in East Anglia in the 1830s – Reay (2004).

'One boy is a boy' – Horn (1985).

'getting up linen' – Hurt (1972).

At the first school inspection – Minutes of the Committee of Council on Education: With Appendices. 1845. (House of Commons Parliamentary Papers Online, 2005).

One school inspector a few years later – see Horn (1985).

The Hertfordshire diarist John Carrington – 'John Carrington, Senior, Memorandum Book. A Vellum-bound Volume, presumably John Carrington, Junior's School Arithmetic Book. Memoranda Haphazardly Entered, Mostly Undated [c1780–1789]' (HALS DE/X3/15).

This is a picture of sorts – I originally tried to elaborate on this, but it proved very difficult not to fall back on the Hodge stereotype and sound condescending. I didn't go as far as George Eliot who wrote in *Adam Bede* 'a peasant can no more help believing in a traditional superstition than a horse can help trembling when he sees a camel.' My touchstone was the story about the discovery of the Lewis Chessmen. A couple of years before Lawrence and his men were probing the roots of the yew, a local exploring a cave on the Isle of Lewis – according to one version of events – stumbled upon the Lewis Chessmen and was struck with terror that he had disturbed a nest of elves and gnomes. It starts to seem increasingly plausible that our labourers believed in dragons.

Robert Darnton – 'Peasants Tell Tales', *The Great Cat Massacre* (London: Penguin, 2001).

A local historian in Anstey – F. R. Williams, *Anstey: A Hertfordshire Parish* (Cambridge: Heffer, 1929), pp. 21–7.

Chapter 9

Some years ago when I first went looking for the spot where the tree once stood, I spent some time with the Hertfordshire archaeologist Isobel Thompson, looking at maps and the Historic Environment Records for that area. To my delight she even placed a small icon of the tree on the map. Isobel kindly handled several of my enquiries over the years including identifying the sinister cow bone – see Chapter 23.

To break a branch was deemed a sin – from a ballad written on the felling of the Mile Oak in 1824. The story is told in *Shropshire Folk-Lore*, ed. Charlotte Burne (London: Trubner, 1883). 'There are many old and famous oak-trees in Shropshire, but I do not find any records of traces of superstitions connected with them, except in the case of the Mile Oak which grew between Oswestry and Maesbury, and on which, according to a local 17th-century tradition, an arm of St. Oswald was hung after his death there in battle, 642 CE. In 1824 the then Lord Powis, to whom the tree belonged, wanted a slab of oak to form the top of a round table, and his Oswestry agent (who was engaged in disputing with a neighbour proprietor the right to the ownership of the famous tree) hastily cut down the Mile Oak for the purpose, without Lord Powis's knowledge, and then – found it would not supply a slab of the size required! In true Shropshire fashion a ballad bewailing the destruction of the fine old landmark was printed and circulated in the neighbourhood. In it occurs this noteworthy verse . . .'

Imagine the carpenter's yard – the opening of this chapter was inspired by Walter Rose (1937).

A man could speak freely – cited in George Ewart Evans, *The Pattern Under the Plough* (London: Faber, 1966).

used as hanging trees – Bevan-Jones (2002).

Gerish – see 1921 in chronology.

Jane Eyre – Charlotte Bronte's heroine is reading Bewick's 1797 *British Birds*. The sinister woodcut – one of Bewick's tale-pieces – appears at the end of 'Of the Grosbeak'.

Lowerson – John Lowerson, 'The Mystical Geography of the English' in B. Short, *The English Rural Community* (1992), pp. 152–74.

Labourers worked from 7 a.m. . . . fifty cubic feet – Arthur Young, *General View of the Agriculture of Hertfordshire* (London: Board of Agriculture, 1804).

Jeremy Harte – *Explore Fairy Traditions* (Loughborough: Heart of Albion, 2004)

A bed in hell – from a rhyme associated with the felling of a yew tree at Easter Ross in the early twentieth century – cited by Bevan-Jones (2002).

prayed down – ibid.

Pitt-Rivers – ibid.

John Aubrey relates – *Natural History and Antiquities of the County of Surrey* (London: E. Curll, 1719).

'Limerick' – Harte (2004).

Liber Studiorum – from about 1808. It is historically useful and also catches the right mood. The Tate has a watercolour and an earlier sketch of the scene from Turner's notebook when he was travelling from London to Portsmouth and back, and while looking it up for these notes I read Matthew Imms' 2008 description of the painting on the Tate website in which he quotes John Ruskin, the famous Victorian art critic, who also picked up on the sombre mood of Turner's rural scene: "'with its bleak sky and blighted trees – hacked, and bitten, and starved by the clay soil into something between trees and firewood; its meanly-faced, sickly labourers – pollard labourers, like the willow trunk they hew; and the slatternly peasant-woman, with worn cloak and battered bonnet – an English Dryad" . . .

'In an unpublished passage, he expanded on the condition of the trees themselves in anthropomorphic terms: "the expression of steady common-place-character in a bitter world. Some capacities of grace about the poor things once, had they been left to themselves or pruned wisely; some remnants of it even yet . . . for the most part hacked and blighted and cropped or withered away, hardly knowing whether they are still trees or only firewood. There is no tragedy allowed them neither, no pity to be had from anybody; they never can have had polite people to look at them. Advisable agricultural operations going on, bleak wind, angry clouds and vulgar people, penned, uncomfortable sheep – such life must they still bud and blossom for as best may be."'

common method – eighteenth-century agricultural writer William Marshall, cited in the *OED* under 'grub-fell'.

yew at Nevern in Wales – see Hageneder (2007).

Yet is thy root sincere – William Cowper, 'Yardley Oak' (1791).

John Aubrey – cited in Ruth Scurr, *John Aubrey: My Own Life* (London: Vintage, 2016), and taken from Aubrey's 'The Natural History of Wiltshire', *Gentleman's Magazine*, December 1847, p. 573.

Walter Rose – see Rose (1937).

How much marquetry . . . hoops of the Windsor chairs – I am indebted to my cabinetmaker friend Andy Chapman, who spent many hours talking to me about yew wood. It was Andy who insisted the tree would not have been wasted and was probably wanted for making Windsor chairs.

'*A post of yew will outlast*' – J. C. Loudon, *Arboretum et Fruticetum: Britannicum* (London, 1838).

Smock mill – see Cyril Moore, *Hertfordshire Windmills & Windmillers* (Sawbridgeworth: Windsup, 1999).

Williamson – see Williamson (2002).

Ancient Tree Forum – ancienttreeforum.co.uk

Hammonds – (1987; first pub. 1911).

one archaeological journal lamented – *Archaeologia Cambrensis: A Record of the Antiquities of Wales and its Marches and the Journal of the Cambrian Archaeological Association*, vol. III, 1848.

Leland – ibid.

cavity opening up in the chalk – it is perhaps telling that the Geological Survey map reveals the boulder clay over the chalk bedrock is at its thinnest near the site of the tree.

Pharisees – the Venerable Archdeacon Cameron (Late Vicar), *A Short Guide to Furneux Pelham Church and Parish*, Foreword by The Right Honourable Lord Cunliffe, 3rd edn (1969) [1st edn 1936].

Haggard – (1899).

A crowd must have gathered that morning – one Archer Houblon witnessed the felling of a large oak in Cambridgeshire in 1819 and wrote that upwards of 300 people attended to see it fall.

Peter Kalm – Doris Jones-Baker (1974).

I have often wondered what was made of the yew – at Beeches is a small pedestal table fashioned from the great Fairlop oak that once stood in Hainault Forest, its branches casting a shadow at midday that almost covered an acre. In the top drawer is pasted an entry from Robert Barclay's diary made the same year the Pelham yew was felled. He had passed the site of the lost oak and lamented the fall of a tree that had already been venerable when Domesday Book was compiled, recalling that he had bought the table and a snuff box from it when it blew over some years before. Surely local craftsmen would have made souvenirs from our yew tree too.

Chapter 10

Edward Topsell – The Historie of Serpents, or, the Second Booke of Living Creatures (London: W. Jaggard, 1608), p. 159.

For the opening of this chapter, I am indebted to Adrienne Mayor's fascinating study *The First Fossil Hunters: Paleontology in Greek and Roman Times* (Princeton: Princeton, 2001).

Thomas Hawkins – The Book of the Great Sea Dragons: Extinct Monsters of the Ancient Earth (London, 1840).

golden torque – the *Gentleman's Magazine*, September 1800, reported that a Hertfordshire labourer Izaac Bennett found a remarkable gold necklace, or torque, near Ware, not far from the Pelhams, while land ditching. He took it to his local watchmaker who, wanting to know the value of the gold, snapped off a piece and sent it to London to be assayed. Unfortunately, in the interim, 'perhaps from fear of having it claimed by the lord of the manor,' wrote Ronald Jessup in *Curiosities of British Archaeology*, 'the poor fellow sold his prize . . . for £20, scarce half its value in metal but a great sum to him none the less; and being instantly consigned to the crucible, every trace of this great curiosity had been lost.' (Fortunately, the watchmaker had made a drawing of it.) See Ronald Jessup, *Curiosities of British Archaeology* (London: Butterworths, 1961).

unearthed a skeleton and a Bronze-Age founder's hoard – in the 1840s, Lord Braybrooke at nearby Audley End had Bronze Age implements from the Pelhams in his museum room. The first entry in his museum book reads: 'No. 1. Bronze Axe End Celt. Found in a field at Furneux Pelham Hertfordshire called the 10 acre Hinden Field belonging to Mr Morris by a labourer land ditching – He found at the same time several others & sundry lumps of metal but of what nature he did not know.

He also found a small axe. There also was a skeleton & some black earth.'

R. C. Neville, *Catalogue and Account of the Celts* (*c*.1850) MS at Cambridge University Museum of Anthropology and Archaeology, GO2/2/10.

Simpson – (1980).

Ruth Richardson – Death, Dissection and the Destitute (London: Phoenix, 2001).

Charles Nicholl – 'Conversing with Giants', in *Traces Remain: Essays and Explorations* (London: Penguin, 2012).

Shonks and not St Michael or St George – in Thomas Hardy's *Woodlanders*, Mr Melbury explains to his workers why he gave his daughter an expensive education: as a boy, the parson's son and his friends came up to him and asked, 'Who dragged whom around the walls of what?' That was easy. It was 'Sam Barrett, who dragged his wife in a chair round the tower when she went to be churched,' answered young Melbury, but of course he should have said it was Achilles who dragged Hector around the walls of Troy. It is a lovely example of how people will turn to local tradition for answers, how they use their own texts to interpret the world in light of local tradition.

John Walker Ord – Jennifer Westwood and Jacqueline Simpson, *The Lore of the Land* (London: Penguin, 2005).

King Arthur – Christina Hole, *English Folk Heroes* (London: Batsford, 1948).

thumbing of the nose at authority – the folklorist Jack Zipes might say that this is the driving force behind many folk tales and legends.

'pretended to old communication with the devil in certain caves' – Charles Darwin, *Voyage of the Beagle*, 1839, Project Gutenberg text. Ebook, 2018.

Swing – Hobsbawm and Rudé (1973).

Snell – (2006).

Chapter 11

in the spaces between the pictures – Mike Pitts is writing about Stonehenge and the many images of it. In wrapping up his introduction to *Making History*, David Starkey singles out Pitts' contribution: 'the first antiquities, starting with that old romancer, Geoffrey of Monmouth himself, wondered at Stonehenge. We, with the benefit of almost two hundred years of scientific archaeology, understand it infinitely better than they. But when we see it in the half-light of a summer dawn, we are struck, not by the smug satisfaction of knowledge, but by a sense of ancient, atavistic wonder.' Starkey quite rightly calls this the 'proper antiquarian response'. It would also have a made great epigraph to one of my chapters. *Making History: Antiquaries in Britain 1707–2007* (London: Royal Academy, 2007).

Holbrook Jackson – *The Anatomy of Bibliomania* (London: Soncino Press, 1932).

On grangerising in general see: Robert R. Wark, 'The Gentle Pastime of Extra-Illustrating Books', *Huntington Library Quarterly*, 56.2 (1993): pp. 151–65. Also the *DNB* entry on James Granger and, naturally, John Carter's *ABC for Book Collectors*, 7th edn (London: Werner Shaw, 1994).

On topographical drawing in general see Ann Payne, *Views of the Past: Topographical Drawings in the British Library* (London: British Library, 1987).

On the Knowsley Clutterbuck see W. B. Gerish, 'A Notable County History', *East Herts Archaeological Society Transactions*, vol. I, part II (1900) (Hertford: EHAS, 1901), pp. 169–71. As well as the pictures in the Knowsley Clutterbuck, there are many more Bucklers in *Views of Hertfordshire: A Collection of Drawings by J. C. Buckler* (1793–1894), 4 vols (HALS D/Ebg). Several are also reproduced and framed at the west end of Brent Pelham church.

Reflecting on his career in 1849 – The Builder, vol. 10, 3 January 1852. Cited in a display on the Bucklers at the Old Forge Museum, Much Hadham.

reinterpretation of the written word with the pictorial – see Wark (1993).

Chapter 12

speaks to us from a forgotten world – the ellipsis is there in place of the poet William Langland. For May McKisack, it is Langland who speaks to us from a forgotten world. Shonks and his stories do too, but so do more recent contributors to this tale as this chapter proves. *The Fourteenth Century 1307–1399*, Oxford History of England, vol. 5 (Oxford: Clarendon, 1959), p. 527.

On William Cole see William Palmer, *William Cole of Milton* (Cambridge: Galloway & Porter, 1935) and the *DNB* entries on Cole – both Thompson Cooper (1887) and the current entry by John D. Pickles.

13th and 14th milestones – these are two of the famous Trinity Hall milestones – erected in the 1720s along the old London to Cambridge coach road by Dr Mowse, master of Trinity Hall, Cambridge. Today many of the stones are still standing along the B1368 and are the UK's oldest surviving set. This is the most obvious way for Cole to travel from Cambridge, south as far as Barley, bearing left just beyond Cumberton Bottom towards Brent Pelham. See Carol Haines, *Marking the Miles: A History of English Milestones* (Carol Haines, 2000).

notoriously bad roads – misreading Old English, the Elizabethan John Norden thought that Pelham derived from an Anglo-Saxon word for well and was so named because of the large number of springs in the area. Commenting drily on this in 1728 – a few years before Cole's journey – Nathaniel Salmon says there are no remarkable springs but adds, 'If he could have made out anything from the Sloughs, he might have found enow [enough] hereabouts, especially in Brent Pelham.' The *OED* defines a slough as 'a piece of soft, miry, or muddy ground; esp. a place or hole in a road or way filled with wet mud or mire and impassable by heavy vehicles, horses, etc.' See Salmon (1728). At the beginning of the nineteenth century Arthur Young noted in his diary that the roads around Pelham and Welwyn were the worst in Hertfordshire. Cited in the VCH (1914), vol. IV, p. 239.

Hogarth painting – this is now in the National Gallery of Ireland and entitled 'The Western Family', thought to have been painted by Hogarth in 1738. A few years later John Nichols described the painting in his *Biographical Anecdotes of William Hogarth*, identifying all the people in the frame, but including one person too many and naming three clergymen. There is only one obvious clergyman in the painting, and I originally assumed this was Cole, but the National Gallery of Ireland website suggests it is Archdeacon Plumptre. It could also be Mr Henry Taylor, a local curate. Cole must be the figure standing in the background behind the piano examining something he is holding up in his hand – some family papers perhaps. Nichols almost certainly got his information from Cole who perhaps was remembering who was at home with the Westerns that day, rather than who made it into the finished painting. Thomas Western was Cole's best friend at Cambridge.

'great parts and wickedness' – Cussans adds in a footnote 'The Revd. Tomas Tipping, of Ardeley, writes in the margin of a Chauncy's History, now in the possession of Hale Wortham of Royston, Esquire, "William Wright was succeeded by William, his natural son, fellow-commoner of Emanuel College, who led a long, wicked, atheisticall life, and dyed about April, 1745, ordering a part of Ginn, and nothing else, at his Funeral. A man of great parts and wickedness."' See 1872 in chronology.

dun-coloured horse – see Virginia Woolf below.

isolated . . . prone to superstitious fancies – reflecting on the tale of Shonks and the Serpent and other folktales and accounts of witchcraft, one anonymous nineteeth-century author wrote 'Such superstitious fancies are no doubt due to isolated and secluded conditions of existence; and not withstanding all the facilities of communication now enjoyed, and the fact of Hertfordshire being one of the home-counties, many parts of it are isolated and secluded still.' See 1885 in chronology.

'in a dark state' – this was the Reverend Upton in 1847 in his survey of non-conformism in Hertfordshire. Cited in *Religion in Hertfordshire 1847–1851*, ed. Judith Burg (Hertfordshire Record Publications, 1995). Thomas Fuller in his *Worthies of England* wrote: 'Some will wonder how this Shire, lying so near London, the staple of English civility, should be guilty of so much rusticalness', cited in Doris Jones-Baker (1977), p. 13.

the page in his ledger – see 1729 in chronology.

'with all his oddities' – Cole's friend Horace Walpole records the antiquary Michael Lort saying this. It is cited in the *DNB*.

Virginia Woolf – 'Two Antiquaries: Walpole and Cole' and 'The Reverend William Cole' in *Death of the Moth and Other Essays* (London: Hogarth Press, 1942).

his wife, his children and his closest friends – Cole wrote this in a letter to Horace Walpole. See *DNB*.

'scandalous rubbish' – this was Robert Masters' opinion. Cole and Masters were not on good terms. See Palmer (1935). We will meet Masters again in Chapter 31.

'stock symbol' . . . Bishop Nigel – the observation belongs to Brian Kemp who describes Bishop Nigel's slab in Ely as 'a large standing angel holding the diminutive soul of the deceased, a remarkably early use of what was to become a stock symbol on monuments for the salvation of the soul'. Brian Kemp, *English Church Monuments* (London: Batsford, 1980).

ninth-century monition – cited in Reverend Edward L. Cutts, see 1849 in chronology.

'long, wicked, atheistical life'. . . carrion cart – see Thomas Tipping above.

haunting – see Chapter 6 and note on haunting of Beeches.

Chapter 13

Hopkins – I was reminded of the Hopkins poem while reading Adam Thorpe's wonderful *On Silbury Hill* just at the right moment to appropriate the line for the opening of the chapter.

It was the county historian – Cussans' handwritten comments on the drawings are in his own copy of his history, HALS DE/Cu/11, p. 79.

Herbert Andrews – see H. C. Andrews, 'Henry George Oldfield and the Dimsdale Collection of Herts Drawings', in *East Herts Archaeological Society Transactions*, 11 (1942), pp. 212–24.

Wilton-Hall – see the catalogue to the Oldfield Collection online at archives.hertfordshire.gov.uk/collections/getrecord/GB46_CDEOf

On cross-slabs in general: Hilary Wheeler at the Church Monuments Society kindly put me in touch with Brian and Moira Gittos who were incredibly generous with their time, patiently answering my questions by email, sending me reading lists and drawing my attention to many of the other monuments I mention throughout the book. The Gittos visited Shonks' tomb in 2002, while researching the Church Monument Society's definitive *Survey of Purbeck Marble Coffin-Shaped Slabs*. A select bibliography would include:

Sally Badham, *Medieval Church and Churchyard Monuments* (Oxford: Shire, 2011).

S. Badham, B. & M. Gittos & P. Lankester, 'Survey of Purbeck Marble Coffin-Shaped Slabs', *Church Monuments Society Newsletter*, 10.1, 1994, pp. 4–11 (completed in 16 parts).

Rev. C. Boutell, *Christian Monuments in England and Wales* (London 1854).

Frederick Burgess, *English Churchyard Memorials: History and Representation* (London: Lutterworth, 1963).

L. A. S. Butler, 'Minor Medieval Monumental Sculpture in the East Midlands', *Archaeological Journal*, vol. 121 (1964), pp. 111–53.

F. Chancellor, *The Ancient Sepulchral Monuments of Essex* (Edmund Durrant & Co, 1890).

Frederick H. Crossley, *English Church Monuments A.D. 1150–1550: An Introduction to the Study of Tombs and Effigies of the Mediaeval Period* (London: Batsford, [1921]).

E. L. Cutts, *A Manual for the Study of the Sepulchral Slabs and Crosses of the Middle Ages* (London, 1849).

Brian and Moria Gittos, 'Abused, Neglected and Forgotten: The Story of the Medieval Cross Slab', *Ecclesiology Today*, 43 (2010), pp. 29–44.

Brian Kemp, *English Church Monuments* (London: Batsford, 1980).

P. Ryder, *Medieval Cross Slab Grave Covers in West Yorkshire* (Wakefield, 1991).

Nigel Saul, *English Church Monuments in the Middle Ages* (Oxford: OUP, 2009).

K. E. Styan, *A Short History of Sepulchral Cross-Slabs, with Reference to Other Emblems Found Thereon* (London, 1902).

Your standard thirteenth-century monument was – Crossley (1921).

Traces of pigment – Sally Badham, 'A New Feire Peynted Stone': Medieval English Incised Slabs?', *Church Monuments*, XIX (2004), pp. 20–52.

The author of one early work on them – Styan (1902).

One Victorian archaeologist – Boutell (1854).

At Furneux Pelham in 1297 – *Visitation of Churches Belonging to St Paul's Cathedral in 1297 and in 1458*, ed. W. Sparrow Simpson (London: Camden Society, 1895).

bronze processional cross at the V&A – see V&A website, Museum Number M.13-1952.

cross-fertilisation of styles – Dr Kirstin Kennedy at the V&A kindly responded to my enquiries about the relationship between cross-slabs and metalwork and suggested other items that showed evidence of this tendency in other media. The early fourteenth-century Swinburne Pyx, now in the V&A, has an image of the Virgin which looks very much like one in the thirteenth-century Peterborough Psalter, now at Corpus Christi College, Cambridge, while its Nativity scene is very similar to the Book of Hours produced a century later for the East Anglian gentlewoman Alice de Raydon. Neil Stratford at the V&A has concluded, 'The goldsmith must therefore have had access to the same copy books as the illuminators of these manuscripts.'

called the most interesting of the medieval period – Crossley (1921).

only 10 per cent – see Ryder (1991). It is estimated that 10 per cent have survived, but it may be as little as 2–3 per cent.

'curious' example – Cutts (1849).

'Here is drama indeed' – Gittos (2010).

one of the most important conceptual advances – Rosemary Sweet, *Antiquaries: The Discovery of the Past in Eighteenth-century Britain* (London: Hambledon and London, 2004).

languishing in Hertford Gaol – see *DNB*. It is the last time history hears from Oldfield, although a letter survives from Meyrick to Oldfield dated 1805, but as the author of the *DNB* entry says, there's no telling that he was still alive to receive it.

wrote about them rather snottily – this was the draughtsman Charles Stothard. Cited in Sweet (2004).

John Gough Nichols – the author of the *Gentleman's Magazine* article is anonymous, but in 1867 a correspondent signing themselves JGN wrote to *Notes and Queries* about the tomb and mentioned in passing that they had written the 1852 article in the *Gentleman's Magazine*. JGN is certainly John Gough Nichols, who was sole editor of the latter from 1850.

Oakley – incidentally, the Hertfordshire historian Reginald Hine tipped a newspaper cutting about the Oakley tomb into his copy of Gerish's *A Hertfordshire St George*. From 1941, the cutting says that the slab was being moved out of the churchyard and into the church for safe keeping. It describes the cross and – nota bene – the *dog* at its foot.

Chapter 14

What a dreary, monotonous, uneventful age – the first sentence of this quote is cited in *Lore of the Land* under the entry for the Bures Dragon. It is from August Jessopp's 'The Dying Out of the Marvellous' in *Frivola*, 1896; the essay first appeared in the *Illustrated London News*.

For dragons and bestiaries in general I found the brilliant *Medieval Bestiary* website invaluable and have leaned on it heavily: bestiary.ca

Lesley Kordecki's thesis *Traditions and Developments of the Medieval English Dragon* (Toronto: University of Toronto, 1980) is fascinating and comprehensive. It's a mystery why it hasn't been republished. Also useful was Ron Baxter's *Bestiaries and Their Users in the Middle Ages* (Stroud, Gloucestershire: Sutton Publishing, 1998).

Borges – see his *The Book of Imaginary Beings* (London: Vintage, 2002; first pub. 1967).

'crippling realism' – see Kordecki (1980).

five categories – Jacqueline Simpson gives a very useful account of the possible origins of dragons in general, as well as those of British dragon legends, in Simpson (1980).

Pliny – Pliny the Elder, *Natural History*, Book 8, 11 – cited on bestiary.ca

Physiologus and *Etymologiae* – see bestiary.ca and general works above.

'lifted by the strength of venom' – Hugo de Folieto in BL MS Sloane 278 trans. by George C. Druce, 'The Elephant in Medieval Legend and Art', *Journal of the Royal Archaeological Institute*, 76 (1919), pp. 1–73. All cited by bestiary.ca

We can imagine early artists turning these descriptions into pictures – much work was done in the nineteenth century on the relationship between the pictures in bestiaries and ecclesiastical sculpture and carvings. Were such carvings in churches intended to convey the moral lessons of the bestiaries? One of the more famous examples comes from the Norman doorway at Alne in Yorkshire, which depicts various scenes clearly taken from the bestiary stories such as the panther facing a winged dragon. 'The time when animal symbolism attained its highest development in the illuminated [manuscript] was during the 13th century, so that it is at this period we are most likely to find traces of it in the ornamental features of churches,' wrote J. Romilly Allen, father of bestiary studies. It is now a source of much debate whether Allen was right and how much of the bestiary narrative ordinary medieval churchgoers would actually understand in a carving.

Stowe 1067 – see bl.uk/catalogues/illuminatedmanuscripts/record.asp?MSID=7715 and, of course, bestiary.ca

thirteenth-century manuscript in the Bodleian – this is MS Douce 88.

George Druce – see above and also 'Animals in English Wood Carvings', Walpole Society, London (Annual Volume of the Walpole Society), 3 (1913–14), pp. 57–73.

in the library at Douai – this is MS 711 in the Bibliothèque Municipale de Douai.

Villard de Honnecourt – classes.bnf.fr/villard and Bob Trubshaw, *Mawming and Mooning: Towards an Understanding of Medieval Carvings and Their Carvers* (Marlborough: Heart of Albion, 2014), hoap.co.uk

John Beleth – spotted in Robert Bartlett, *The Natural and the Supernatural in the Middle Ages* (Cambridge: Cambridge, 2008). Professor Bartlett cites this as evidence that some medieval writers took the existence of dragons as a given.

Roger Bacon – 'It is certain that Ethiopian sages have come into Italy, Spain, France, England, and those Christian lands where there are good flying dragons; and by an occult art that they possess, excite the dragons from their caves. And they have saddles and bridles ready, and they ride the dragons and drive them at top speed through the air, in order to soften the rigidity and toughness of their flesh, just as boars, bears, and bulls are hunted with dogs and beaten with many blows before they are killed for eating. And when they have tamed the dragons in this way, they have an art of preparing their flesh . . . which they employ against the accidents of age and prolong life and inspire the intellect beyond all estimation. For no education which man can give will bestow such wisdom as does the eating of their flesh, as we have learned without deceit or doubt from men of proved trustworthiness.' Quoted in Lynn Thorndike, *A History of Magic and Experimental Science: During the First Thirteen Centuries of Our Era*, vol. 2 (London: Macmillan, 1923).

Robert Surtees – in his *The History and Antiquities of the County Palatine of Durham.* Cited in Westwood and Simpson (2005).

Arthur Mee – *Hertfordshire: London's Country Neighbour* (in his The King's England), rev. edn (London: Hodder and Stoughton, 1965), p. 42.

English bestiary . . . breathes fires at an elephant – the first is Kongelige Bibliotek, Gl. kgl. S. 3466 8°, f. 17v, and the second is BL Harley 3244 f. 39v which contains a second fire-breathing dragon, on f. 59r this dragon is a standout exception to the norm: it is large and red with four legs and two pairs of wings – it looks like an anachronism, as if someone's imagination has gone too far and they have adulterated the real dragon to create some fantasy of their own. There is no creature in nature with four functional legs and true wings, but it is closer to the dragon we would expect on our television screens today.

These dragons, like my *dragon, are fire-breathers* – a Romanesque sculpture from St Nicholas's Church, Ipswich, dated to the early twelfth century, shows St Michael on the left with a sword; a large Norman kite-shaped shield separates him from a dragon belching barbed flames, although some say it has a triple forked tongue – either way, this belongs with Shonks' dragon too.

biting the base of the cross – personal communication with Brian and Moira Gittos. The best example of such a dragon, from roughly the same period, is the one with a knotted tail biting the cross on the tomb associated – now controversially – with Princess Siwan the wife of Llewellyn the Great, Prince of Gwynedd, which is in Beaumaris church on Anglesey. Another slab at Bangor shows a small dragon holding the staff in its mouth. In both examples the dragon is in low relief and seen from above rather than in profile as on Shonks' tomb. The tomb of Archbishop Walter de Gray in York Minster has an impressive dragon with its head in profile, biting the end of his crozier; this is an effigial slab, but also from the mid-thirteenth century.

Chapter 15

Nigel Saul – (2009).

birth certificate of purgatory – this is Jacques Le Goff's famous phrase in his *The Birth of Purgatory*, trans. Arthur Goldhammer (Aldershot: Scolar, 1990; first pub. 1981).

in place centuries earlier – on this point and on the struggle of the soul at death, see Helen Foxhall Forbes, *Heaven and Earth in Anglo-Saxon England: Theology and Society in an Age of Faith* (London: Routledge, 2016).

some thought the entrance – this was St Patrick's Purgatory – there is a good account in Stephen Greenblatt, *Hamlet in Purgatory* (Princeton: Princeton, 2001).

not-entirely-good and not-entirely-bad – see Le Goff (1990).

sinners were impaled – my description of purgatory is heavily indebted to Carl Watkins in his *The Undiscovered Country: Journeys Among the Dead* (London: Vintage, 2013). He describes it so well, I wanted to paraphrase him as little as possible.

Simon de Furneux – see TNA C143/62/16. Simon's plans were entered on the Patent Roll for 28 July at Thirsk, in the North Riding of Yorkshire, where the ageing and ever-weakening Edward I spent a night while his son, the future Edward II, continued to pursue the broken forces of Robert the Bruce. Simon was not the only one whose thoughts were turning towards the last things. The king's itinerary had been painfully slow and for much of it he had been carried in a litter, but he persisted in trying to catch up with his armies. Earlier in the year, he had issued an ordinance about the Royal Forest, which included an extraordinary preamble to come from the mouth of a king: 'We are indeed inwardly tormented . . . tossed about by the waves of diverse thoughts, and are frequently troubled, passing sleepless nights, dwelling in our inmost soul.' Edward was a dying man himself when he considered Simon de Furneux's preparations for the afterlife.

The king granted Simon's request. The Patent Roll records a licence for Simon to grant to Thremall Priory '2 messuages, 167½ acres of land, 4 acres of meadow, 16 acres of pasture, 22 acres of wood, and 21*s*. 5½*d*. rent in Brent Pelham and Pelham Furneus for the maintenance of a chaplain to celebrate divine service daily for the souls of him and his ancestors in the church of St. Mary, Pelham Furneus, and a canon to do the like in the convent'. See Morris (2008) on Edward I. For Simon de Furneux see *Calendar of Patent Rolls, Edw I, 1301–7* (London: Eyre & Spottiswoode), p. 459, 34 Edw I, M.11 or TNA C66/127. It is not entirely incidental that the land Simon granted to the priory was the manor of Beeches and included Shonks' Moat.

Lucy, the first prioress – Mortuary Roll of Lucy, Foundress and First Prioress of the Benedictine Nunnery of Castle Hedingham, with Tituli (Responsive Prayers) 1–6, BL Egerton 2849.

in his will, Henry VII – from notes I took during the 'Death' episode of Helen Castor's BBC 4 documentary series *Medieval Lives: Birth, Marriage, Death.*

long been part of Christian belief – see Forbes (2016).

Funerary rights called on St Michael – Peter Marshall, *Invisible Worlds: Death, Religion and the Supernatural in England, 1500–1700* (London: SPCK, 2017) and Forbes (2016).

Christopher Frayling – *Strange Landscape: A Journey through the Middle Ages* (London: BBC, 1995).

'apotropaic guardians of the text' – see Jennifer O'Reilly, 'Patristic and Insular Traditions of the Evangelists' retrieved from xml.ucc.ie/chronicon/latinbib/oreilly.htm

White Paternoster – see Theo Brown, *The Fate of the Dead* (Cambridge: Brewer, 1979) and Iona and Peter Opie, *The Oxford Dictionary of Nursery Rhymes* (Oxford: Clarendon, 1951).

St Fursey – see Le Goff (1990).

Early South English Legendary – see Kordecki (1980).

Beowulf – Kordecki, ibid.

A. Whitford Anderson – see 1898 in chronology.

A. Whitford Anderson took a wonderful ghostly image – see 1912 in chronology.

Dominick wants to stitch together an image of the tomb – you can see the result at www.christopherhadley.co.uk/hollowplaces

scagliola – Mark Haysom (see Chapter 16) suggested this to me.

Chapter 16

Then might those genera of animals return – the quote appears on a stele at the end of the timeline at Durlston Castle. I read it metaphorically, not realising at the time that Lyell believed these prehistoric animals might literally return when the geological conditions were ripe again.

On Purbeck marble in general: the Gittos generously gave me some ideas for exploring the Isle of Purbeck as well as suggestions for reading about Purbeck marble. For background see the following texts which were invaluable in writing this chapter. A visit to Langton Matravers museum was also helpful. Treleven Haysom and his son Mark Haysom were exceptionally generous with their time and help.

S. Badham, 'An Interim Study of the Stones Used for the Slabs of English Monumental Brasses', *Transactions of the Monumental Brass Society*, vol. XIII (1985), pp. 475–83.

J. Blair, 'Purbeck Marble', in J. Blair & N. Ramsay (eds), *English Medieval Industries* (London, 1991), pp. 41–56.

J. Blair, 'Henry Lakenham, Marbler' in *Antiquaries Journal*, 60 (1980), pp. 66–74.

G. Dru Drury, 'The Use of Purbeck Marble in Mediaeval Times', *Proceedings of the Dorset Natural History & Archaeological Society*, vol. 70 (1948), pp. 74–98.

M. Edgar and A. Hinde, 'Stone Workers of Purbeck', *Purbeck Rural History*, 10:1, April 1999, pp. 75–90.

Paul Ensom and Malcolm Turnbull, *Geology of the Jurassic Coast: The Isle of Purbeck: Weymouth to Studland* (Wareham: Coastal, 2011).

G. W. Green, 'The Geology of Building Stones in Dorest, Hampshire, and Wiltshire, Together With Some Adjacent Parts of Somerset', in 'Building with Stone in Wessex over 4000 years', ed. Tim Tatton-Brown, *The Hatcher Review*, V, no. 45 (Spring 1998), pp. 5–17.

Treleven Haysom, 'Extracting Purbeck Marble', *The Hatcher Review*, op. cit., pp. 48–54.

John Hutchins, *The History and Antiquities of the County of Dorset* (Westminster: J. B. Nichols & Sons, 1861–73).

J. C. Mansel, 'The Marblers of Purbeck', *Papers Read Before the Purbeck Society* (1859–60), Wareham, pp. 191–214.

R. Leach, *An Investigation into the Use of Purbeck Marble in Medieval England*, (Crediton, 1978).

R. J. Saville, *The Stone Quarries of Langton Matravers*, 4th edn (Langton Matravers Local History and Preservation Society, 2017).

R. J. Saville, *A Langton Quarryman's Apprentice* (Langton Matravers Local History and Preservation Society, 2017).

Rex Sawyer, 'Jack Green – The Last of the Tisbury Masons', in *Hatcher Review*, op. cit. pp. 55–8.

James Sowerby, *The Mineral Conchology of Great Britain; or Coloured Figures and Descriptions of Those Remains of Testaceous Animals or Shells, Which Have Been Preserved at Various Times and Depths in the Earth*. Vol. 6 (London: Richard Taylor, 1829).

Tim Tatton-Brown, 'The Building Stone for Salisbury Cathedral', *Hatcher Review*, op. cit., pp. 39–47.

C. H. Vellacott, 'Quarrying', *Victoria County History of Dorset,* vol. II (London: VCH, 1908), pp. 331–44.

at his quarry – I met Treleven Haysom at W. J. Haysom & Son's Lander's Quarries on the Kingston Road, Langton Matravers. I use Haysom's in the text as shorthand.

Mary Spencer Watson – see Ilay Cooper, *Purbeck Arcadia: Dunshay and the Spencer Watsons* (Wimborne Minster: Dovecote, 2015).

open ancient workings at Quarr – see I. Cooper (2015) and Haysom (1998).

Rena Gardiner – Dorset: The Isle of Purbeck (Wimborne Minster: The Dovecote Press, 2016; first pub. 1969).

Peveril Point – there are several very enlightening displays on geology, coastal change and much else at the Swanage National Coastwatch Institute station at Peveril Point.

Dorset poet Paul Hyland – see his *Isle of Purbeck* (Wimborne Minster: Dovecote, 1998).

lines from Tennyson – his 'The Palace of Art', 1842.

delighted to learn – I briefly spoke with Steve Etches who told me this. Very special thanks to the lovely couple I met in the Greyhound Inn in Corfe Castle on the last night of my stay in Purbeck, who encouraged me to visit the Etches Collection before heading home.

Eric Benfield – *Purbeck Shop: A Stoneworker's Story of Stone* (Cambridge: CUP, 1940).

the labour in the act – on my drive home from Purbeck, I stopped off at Salisbury Cathedral and was lucky enough to bump into Carol, one of the stonemasons, who chatted to me about working with Purbeck marble.

370-kilo block – Corinne Whiting at Haysom's quarry estimated the weight of Shonks' slab for me with a simple formula – she multiplied the volume by 2.5, which gives a weight of 368 kilos.

15,000 tonnes of marble – see Stephen Hannath, *The Cathedral Rocks: The Earth Materials Used in the Construction of Salisbury Cathedral* (Stephen Hannath, 2010) and Gill Knappett, *Salisbury Cathedral Guidebook* (Stroud: Pitkin, 2015).

Billy Winspit – see Benfield (1940).

Afloat in a cog – I am extremely grateful to Bruce Murdoch of the Dorset Police Marine Section, who talked me through how you might sail from Ower Quay, out of the harbour and eastwards along the south coast. Sally Badham has counted and mapped surviving cross-slabs from Purbeck, showing at a glance that the majority were shipped to counties around the south and east coast, particularly to Norfolk – see Sally Badham,

'Evidence for the Minor Funerary Monument Industry 1100–1500', *Town and Country in the Middle Ages: Contrasts, Contacts and Interconnections, 1100–1500*, ed. K. Giles and C. Dyer, Soc for Med Archaeology Monograph 22 (Leeds: Maney, 2007), pp. 165–95, esp. pp. 179–81.

I consulted a number of very useful texts on medieval transport including:

G. J. L. Burnby and M. Parker, 'Navigation of the River Lee (1190–1790)', *Edmunton Hundred Historical Society*, 1978 Occ Paper (New Series), no. 36.

James Frederick Edwards, 'The Transport System of Medieval England and Wales: A Geographical Synthesis' (Thesis, University of Salford, 1987).

Mark Gardiner, 'Hythes, Small Ports, and Other Landing Places in Later Medieval England', in *Waterways and Canal-building in Medieval England*, ed. J. Blair (Oxford: OUP, 2007), pp. 85–109.

Evan Jones, 'River Navigation in Medieval England', *Journal of Historical Geography*, 26, 1 (2000), pp. 60–82.

John Langdon, 'The Efficiency of Inland Water Transport in Medieval England', *Waterways and Canal-building in Medieval England*, ed. J. Blair (Oxford: OUP, 2007), pp. 110–30.

John Langdon and Jordan Claridge, 'Transport in Medieval England', *History Compass*, vol. 9, issue 11 (2011).

James Field Willard, 'Inland Transportation in England During the Fourteenth Century', *Speculum*, vol. 1, no. 4 (Oct 1926), pp. 361–74.

maritime historians – see Edwards (1987).

The coast itself would not be recognisable – see *An Historical Atlas of Kent*, ed. Terrence Lawson and David Killingray (Chichester: Phillimore, 2010); Peter Murphy, *English Coast* (London: Continuum, 2009); *An Historical Atlas of Sussex*, ed. Kim Leslie and Brian Short; with maps by Susan Rowland (Chichester: Phillimore, 1999); and Christopher Daniell, *Atlas of Medieval Britain* (London: Routledge, 2010).

shipload of marble to London – see Blair (1991).

The entire journey might have been overland – Evan Jones at the University of Bristol kindly answered some questions I emailed him about medieval itineraries. He advised me to think about the precise political and economic conditions at the time as this could well determine whether the tomb went by sea or land. War with France, for instance, would make a sea journey too hazardous. Recent research suggests that many more valuable and bulky items travelled by land than has previously been thought.

Legend says the devil – see Hyland (1998).

Chapter 17

Between the facts of experience – Richard Altick and John Fenstermaker, *The Art of Literary Research*, 4th edn (New York: Norton, 1993), p. 144.

Let's talk of graves, of worms, and epitaphs – William Shakespeare, *Richard II*, Act 3, Scene 2.

In 1348, a great vapour – *The Book of Miracles* (Cologne: Taschen, 2013).

The vicar's pigs have rooted up the Pelham churchyard – this was alleged in a 1458 visitation of the churches – see VCH (1914).

It rained blood in Rome, and flesh in Liguria – *The Book of Miracles*.

Sir John Chamberlayne, who sends a red cow before his own coffin – see VCH (1914).

Black Death . . . Blackheath – chosen from entries under 'Black' in *Brewers Dictionary of Phrase & Fable*, 18th edn (Edinburgh: Chambers Harrap, 2009).

let us sit upon the ground – *Richard II*, op. cit.

We have told the bees of so many deaths – 'If there was a death in the family our custom was to take a bit of crepe out to the bee-skeps after sunset and pin it on them. Then you gently tapped the skeps and told the bees who it was who had died. If you didn't do this, they reckoned the bees wouldn't stay, they'd leave the hives – or else they'd pine away and die.' W. H. Thurlow quoted in Evans (1966).

sounds of the great battles of St Albans can still be heard – the first and second battles of St Albans in the Wars of the Roses were fought on 22 May 1455 and 17 February 1461, respectively. Doris Jones-Baker relates how they can still be heard on Holywell Hill (Jones-Baker, 1977).

The bodies of two young boys – I'm referring, of course, to the 'Princes in the Tower'. Some think that two skeletons discovered under a Tower staircase in the seventeenth century are the remains of the missing princes Edward V and Richard, Duke of York.

In 1483 locusts swarm in Italy – *The Book of Miracles.*

Dante went to the afterlife for a final time, and the monks in Ravenna have hidden his bones – see Butler (1995) for the fate of Dante's remains.

'Of this Cokes tale maked Chaucer na moore' – a scribal note at the foot of Chaucer's unfinished 'Cook's Tale' in the Hengwrt manuscript.

the Beatific vision – the sight of God, which many hoped for when they died.

The three living kings have nothing on the three dead – a common memento mori in medieval art, which depicts three living kings encountering their dead counterparts.

Papal seals centuries old – see *Art Under Attack: Histories of British Iconoclasm,* ed. Tabitha Barber and Stacy Boldrick (London: Tate, 2013).

William Camden – *Remains Concerning Britain* (1605).

Phillip Lindley – *Tomb Destruction and Scholarship: Medieval Monuments in Early Modern England* (Donington: Shaun Tyas, 2007).

The 1547 First Injunction – this was the royal injunction for 'The abolishing of idolatry and superstition'.

The villain Bosola – Act IV, Scene II. Cited in Marshall (2017).

Someone must have taken chisel and bolster – whether Shonks' tomb was damaged deliberately or by time we cannot say for sure; the angels' faces may have popped off with frost damage, but the removal of the little praying hands on the soul held in the napkin is very suggestive of deliberate damage by the iconoclasts of the sixteenth or seventeenth centuries. Close-up photographs of the dragon appear to show violent chisel marks.

Richard Rex's phrase – in 'Monumental Brasses and the Reformation', *Transactions of the Monumental Brass Society*, 14 (1990).

Henry Keepe – cited in Watkins (2013).

historians of the period have pointed out – see *Art Under Attack* (2013).

William Fulke – cited in Greenblatt (2001).

John Norden – Frank Kitchen's thesis on John Norden was invaluable – 'Cosmo-choro-poly-grapher: An Analytical Account of the Life and Work of John Norden, 1547?–1625' (University of Sussex, 1992).

Barley – see *John Norden's Survey of Barley, Hertfordshire, 1593–1603*, ed. J. C. Wilkerson (Cambridge: Cambridge Antiquarian Records Society, 1974).

Chapter 18

In lapidary inscriptions – James Boswell, *The Life of Samuel Johnson,* 2 vols (London: Printed by Henry Baldwin, for Charles Dilly, 1791), 1775 I. 514.

Chronicle of Byland – see Watkins (2013).

Tell ye your children of it, and let your children tell their children – the quote comes from the Book of Joel 1:3, but I found it used as an epigraph chosen by Stapleton Martin at the front of his *History of the Martin Family* (1908). We will meet Mr Martin in Chapter 21.

normal school exercise – correspondence with Dr James Binns who very kindly answered my questions about the inscription and made several useful suggestions.

Richard Rex – Dr Rex was also very generous with his time, answering my emails and making numerous suggestions. See his 'Monumental Brasses', op. cit.

Erwin Panofsky – *Tomb Sculpture: Four Lectures on Its Changing Aspects from Ancient Egypt to Bernini* (1964) cited in Paul Binski, *Medieval Death: Ritual and Representation* (London: British Museum Press, 1996).

Puttenham – in Chapter 28 of his famous work.

Rosemary Freeman – Rosemary Freeman, *English Emblem Books* (London: Chatto, 1948); on emblems see also Mike Bath, *Speaking Pictures: English Emblem Books and Renaissance Culture* (New York: Longman, 1994).

describe the whole image – Professor Mary Silcox at McMaster University kindly answered my queries on emblem books and suggested that a true emblem would have made use of all the imagery on the tomb.

Robert Kirk . . . Marina Warner – see Robert Kirk, *The Secret Commonwealth of Elves, Fauns, and Fairies*; introduction by Marina Warner (New York: New York Review, 2006).

notoriously ignorant – see David Hey, *The Grass Roots of English History: Local Societies in England before the Industrial Revolution* (London: Bloomsbury Academic, 2016).

£7 a year – benefices were valued in the Valor Ecclesiasticus of 1535. See VCH for Brent Pelham.

Ronald Hutton – see his 'English Reformation and the Evidence of Folklore', *Past and Present*, 148 (1995), pp. 89ff.

St George's remains – as described in Hole (1948).

Sir Thomas Stanley's monument – Simon Watney, 'Sky Aspiring Pyramids: Shakespeare and Shakespearian Epitaphs in Early Stuart England', *Journal of the Church Monuments Society*, XX (2005), pp. 103–16.

William Dowsing – see *The Journal of William Dowsing: Iconoclasm in East Anglia during the English Civil War,* ed. Trevor Cooper (Woodbridge: Boydell & Brewer, 2001).

A pamphlet of 1669 – *The Flying Serpent or Strange News out of Essex* retrieved from stmaryssaffronwalden.org/wp-content/uploads/2015/03/dixonhistorystm.pdf

forensic – see *Art Under Attack* (2013).

two-thirds of the monumental brasses – see T. Cooper (2001).

There be of them, that have left a name behind them – Ecclesiasticus 44:8–13. I happened upon this while trying to identify L. H. S. who wrote for the *Cliftonian* in 1872. It is an epigraph on the title page of *The Clifton College Annals and Register* for 1860–97.

Chapter 19

unusual royal coat of arms – these are now mounted above the entrance to the vestry in Furneux Pelham church, but were originally in Brent Pelham and shown in a George Buckler painting dated 1841 (HALS D/EBg/2/129). (George, brother of J. C. Buckler and the youngest son of John Buckler, is usually overlooked – the title of this collection at HALS is 'View of Hertfordshire: A Collection of Drawings by J. C. Buckler (1793–1894) In Four Volumes (1835–1840)'.) Wigram described them to Gerish in a letter of 6 July 1905. He concludes by writing, 'I preserved them for years at Furneaux [sic] Pelham Vicarage & left them there when I quitted it. I can tell you no more about them.'

three stages in the life cycle of a folk legend – I don't know if this is a well-known axiom among folklorists; Jacqueline Simpson suggested this to me in a conversation some years ago.

Knucker Hole in Lyminster – this and the several other local legends referred to in this chapter were found in Westwood and Simpson (2005), Westwood (1985) and Simpson (1980).

canvas dragon on a wooden frame – see Doris Jones-Baker (1974).

Katharine Briggs – see *A Dictionary of British Folk-tales in the English Language: Incorporating the F. J. Norton Collection* (London: Routledge & Kegan Paul, 1971).

Chapter 20

Hertfordshire Monumental Inscriptions – Monumental Inscriptions of the Parish Churches of St Mary, Furneux Pelham, St Mary, Stocking Pelham, and St Mary, Brent Pelham, ed. Janet and John Pearson, MI Series no. 87 (Hertfordshire Family History Society, 2007).

the crosses generated a brief debate in the Notes and Queries *column of the* Hertfordshire Mercury – see 1901 in chronology. For replies, including 'Folk-lorist', see 1902 in chronology.

In 1884, the trustees of the British Museum bought over 1,500 engravings and drawings of Hertfordshire – see After 1827 in chronology.

Chapter 21

Robert Southey – cited in Dorson (1968).

Patrick Leary's essay was very useful in writing this chapter: 'A Virtual Victorian Community', *Victorian Review*, vol. 25: 2 (Winter 2000), pp. 62–79. victorianresearch.org/nandq.html

All the articles and letters referred to in this chapter that discuss Shonks will be in the chronology, the others are:

N., 'Burying in Church Walls', *Notes and Queries*, s1–II (18 January 1851): pp. 37–8.

F. C. B., 'Mural Burial', *Notes and Queries*, s2–IX (2 June 1860): p. 425.

Francis P. Marchant, 'Dragon-Killers in Tales and Legends', *Notes and Queries*, sCLVII (1930): p. 358, and M. H. [Madeline Hope] Dodds, 'Dragon-Killers in Tales and Legends', *Notes and Queries*, sCLVII (1930): p. 388.

Victorian restorers – see 1914 in chronology.

anathema – I stumbled across a discussion of this in Barbara Tuchman, *A Distant Mirror: The Calamitous 14th Century* (London: Macmillan, 1979).

Pope Gregory the Great – Forbes (2016).

Essex Review – see 1896 in chronology. Laurence Gomme is cited here.

Gloucestershire historian – Thomas Rudge – cited in H. W. N. Ludwell, *A History of Winterbourne* (1972) on winterbourne.freeuk.com. I have a note to myself to use poor Ludwell, a local historian, as an example of the sort of pedantry I hate when reading about folk tales. Writing in 1972, he mocked the Hickonstern tale as untrue and – with the kind of astonishing insight I have repeatedly encountered with dismay on this quest after a folk legend – as an example of how historians get things wrong.

There are other versions of the Ettrick story – see F. S. Burnell (1947) in chronology.

tale-type – Ernest Baughman, *Type and Motif-Index of the Folktales of England and North America* (Indiana University Folklore Series No. 20), 1966. For more on tale types see Chapter 24.

Prince of Elis – the myth was preserved by the ancient Greek geographer Pausanias. He was writing of Aetolus Prince of the Greek city of Elis. Cited in Burnell (1947).

Edward Peacock – the full title is *A Glossary of Words Used in the Wapentakes of Manley, and Corringham, Lincolnshire* (London: 1889).

At Aldworth in the Berkshire Downs – see Westwood and Simpson (2005) and Westwood (1985).

St Dunstan – the point is made and the story told in Peter Stanford, *The Devil: A Biography* (London: Heinemann, 1996).

Tolleshunt Knights – see Westwood and Simpson (2005) and Westwood (1985).

spiritual evil – see Simpson (1980).

Eleanor Hull – *Folklore of the British Isles* (London: Methuen, 1928).

Chapter 22

John Brooks – spent all his working life at Rayment's Brewery in Furneux Pelham. He was always happy to share his memories of daily life in the Pelhams and committed many of them to lists and poems. He died on 16 October 2011, aged 86, and is buried with his wife Greta in Furneux Pelham churchyard.

Even if we accept the low estimate – Robert Hardy has written in detail about this, calling the mathematics 'beguiling and dangerous'. He talks about 3,000 archers firing 10 arrows a minute, that's 60,000 arrows every two minutes, but he doesn't suggest that they actually kept this up for an entire two minutes. He does suggest that a total of half a million arrows were let loose at Crécy. Hardy's *Longbow: A Social and Military History* (Sparkford: Haynes, 2012) was exceptionally useful when writing this chapter. My other key guidebook was the Folio Society edition of J. C. Holt's *Robin Hood* (London: Folio Society, 1989).

Robin Hood – as well as Holt, see above, I used R. B. Dobson and J. Taylor, *Rymes of Robyn Hood: An Introduction to the English Outlaw* (London: Heinemann, 1976).

Woolf – 'The "Common Voice": History, Folklore and Oral Tradition in Early Modern England', *Past and Present*, No. 120 (August 1988), pp. 26–52.

The slab itself was destroyed – this story is given in Ryder (1991).

Ritson – Joseph Ritson, *Robin Hood: A Collection of All the Ancient Poems, Songs, and Ballads, now Extant, Relative to that Celebrated English Outlaw: To Which Are prefixed Historical Anecdotes of His Life.* In Two Volumes. Illus. by John and Thomas Bewick (London: Printed for T. Egerton, Whitehall, and J. Johnson, Saint-Pauls-Churchyard, 1795).

Bevis of Hamtoun – or Hampton, who appears to have been appropriated by the storytellers of Sussex from his rightful home in Southampton. See Westwood and Simpson (2005).

giant Tom Hickathrift used a stone – see Westwood and Simpson (2005).

Salmon – see 1728 in chronology; also Jones-Baker (1977) and Victoria Maddren, *Who Was Jack O' Legs? Investigation into the Legends and Customs of Baldock and the Surrounding Area* (Baldock: Egon, 1992).

Calasso – in his *The Marriage of Cadmus and Harmony* cited in A. S. Byatt, *On Histories and Stories: Selected Essays* (London: Chatto & Windus, 2000).

how the original chancel was built – Wigram (1888). A. Whitford Anderson (1898) suggests that the chancel still wasn't straight after the restoration and gives an interesting though not uncommon explanation: 'Another feature of this church is that the chancel inclines from the nave several degrees to the north of east. This is said to be a common feature of Cornish churches, and is supposed to represent the inclination of our Saviour's head upon the cross.'

Chapter 23

Patricia Polacco – I saw this in Zerubavel (2003) and ordered a copy. I love those stories that begin with a very old man or woman saying 'Many years ago, when I was a child, my great-grandfather told me that when he was a boy, a very old soldier told him about the time he met . . .'

W. H. N. – [William Henry Norris] wrote to the *Hertfordshire Mercury*, 10 March 1888.

remembered that his father explored the tomb – see 1905 in chronology.

churchwardens' accounts – HALS DP/77 5/1. In 1832 the bricklaying bill was £5. 19s. 8d. This was the year after John Morris became churchwarden. Two years later the bill was £3. 14s. 4d. and a further 19 shillings for bricks and tiles. The sums jump out because there are scant other references to money spent on bricklaying and they are relatively substantial.

interviewed by a local newspaper reporter – see 1903 in chronology. Mrs Hudson also related her own unique version of the legend. It tells us a lot about the oral transmission of folk stories.

> *Shonks was in the garden and the Dragon came to him and said 'Let you be buried in the church or out of the church.'*
> *'Well,' he says, 'I'll fire my arrows where I stand and where my arrow falls there I'll be buried.'*
> *His arrow went through the window in the church and stuck in the wall opposite. The two greyhounds killed the Dragon.*

Digging Up Bones – see D. R. Brothwell, *Digging Up Bones: The Excavation, Treatment and Study of Human Skeletal Remains* (London, British Museum; Oxford: OUP, 1981).

'Frenchman's Finger' – *Making History* (2007).

Bishop Hugh of Lincoln – Christopher Frayling tells the story in Frayling (1995).

Bale's 1530 spoof – these appear in Bale's play *King Johan*. I cannot find where I read about Calvin's claim. Did I make it up? Did Calvin?

opening of Edward I's tomb – *Making History* (2007).

Morris was farming the tithes – see the Brent Pelham tithe file TNA IR18/3235.

Herbert Tompkins – see 1902 in chronology.

Little John – see Hole (1948).

sold to John Tradescant – see Westwood (1985).

John Aubrey – 'Before printing old wives' tales were ingenious, and since Printing came into fashion, til a little before the Civil-Warres, the ordinary Sort of People were not taught to read; nowadayes bookes are common, and most of the poor people understand letters; and the many good bookes, and a variety of Turnes of affaires; have putt all the old Fables out of doors and the divine art of Printing and Gunpowder have frightened away Robin Goodfellow and the Fayries.' *Remaines of Gentilisme & Judaisme* (1687–9), p. 68.

Chapter 24

James Douglas – see Jessup (1961).

Gerald of Wales – see Hole (1948) who gives the inscription from a leaden cross found in a tomb which stood between two stone pillars in the old burial ground at Glastonbury. It read: 'Hic jacet sepultus inclitus rex Arthurus cum Wenneveria uxore sua secunda in insula Avallonia'. The specificity of that 'second wife' is startling and convincing.

Digging up Bones – see Brothwell (1981).

Jack O'Legs – see notes to Chapter 22.

Geoffrey of Monmouth – see his twelfth-century *History of the Kings of Britain*.

tale types and motifs – see Stith Thompson, *Motif-index of Folk-literature: A Classification of Narrative Elements in Folktales, Ballads, Myths, Fables, Medieval Romances, Exempla, Fabliaux, Jest-books, and Local Legends*, revised and enlarged edn (Bloomington: Indiana University Press, 1955–8). For a good introduction to the Aarne-Thompson-Uther Tale Type Index – the ATU classification – read Cara Giaimo's article at Atlas Obscura: atlasobscura.com/articles/aarne-thompson-uther-tale-type-index-fables-fairy-tales

The ATU is online at mftd.org/index.php?action=atu

Marina Warner – Marina Warner, *Once Upon a Time: A Short History of Fairytale* (Oxford: OUP, 2014).

Nigel Pennick – Pennick, 'Dragon Legends: No. 1 Piers Shonkes (Herts.)', *Journal of Geomancy*, vol. 2, no. 1 (1977), pp. 4–5.

Philostratus – cited in Paul Veyne, *Did the Greeks Believe in Their Myths? An Essay on the Constitutive Imagination* (Chicago: University of Chicago, 1988).

tomb was opened once again – was this the last time the tomb was explored? The archaeologist Clive Partridge implied that it had been opened in the 1980s when he wrote in passing about Shonks' tomb before adding teasingly: 'I know this all to be <u>true</u> [his underlining] because in 1981 I was asked to carry out an archaeological and structural survey [of St Mary's Brent Peham], in advance of necessary restoration and drainage work and I can assure members that Piers still rests peacefully in his chosen place.' This seemed like a promising lead, but having looked carefully at the published report and the excavation notes archived at Hertford Museum, it looks as if the survey work came nowhere near the tomb. Clive Partridge, '100 Years of Archaeology: A Review', in *A Century of Archaeology in East Herts*, ed. David Perman (Ware: Rockingham Press and EHAS, 1998), pp. 53–4.

Chapter 25

Books I found useful when writing the opening section of this chapter include:

Domesday Book: A Complete Translation, Alecto Historical Editions, ed. Ann Williams and G. H. Martin (London: Penguin, 2003).

The Story of Domesday Book, ed. R. W. H. Erskine and Ann Williams (Chichester: Phillimore, 2003).

Lucien Musset, *The Bayeux Tapestry,* trans. Richard Rex (Woodbridge: Boydell Press, 2005).

Terrence Wise, *Saxon, Viking and Norman,* Men-at-Arms 85 (Botley: Osprey, 1979).

live out his final years on them in peace – 'Edgar Atheling, or Eadgar the Ætheling (fl 1066).' *DNB.* This is the archived version of the life. Edgar 'was taken prisoner at the battle of Tinchebrai on 28 Sept. 1106. The king freely released him, and he spent the remainder of his days in obscurity in the country, perhaps on his Hertfordshire property.'

a similar beast on the borders – this is, of course, poetic licence. The dragon stalks the bottom border of the tapestry directly beneath Guy, Count of Ponthieu, in the scene where Guy brings Harold to meet Duke William. Like many of the dragons in the tapestry's margins, it is out of the same mould as the one on the tomb. This one is also breathing fire.

rough draft of Weever's work – see note on Weever's manuscript under Chapter 13 above.

one writer on collective memory – Zerubavel (2003).

As C. S. Lewis observed – *The Discarded Image: An Introduction to Medieval and Renaissance Literature* (London: Cambridge University Press, 2012; first pub. 1964).

Eusebius – see Daniel Rosenberg and Anthony Grafton, *Cartographies of Time: A History of the Timeline* (New York: Princeton Architectural Press, 2010) and Veyne (1988).

old farmer – see 1872 in chronology.

before the coming of the Romans – see 1921 in chronology.

Chapter 26

Cyril Fox – the identification of Sir Cyril Fox and information about his movements are from: Cyril Fox, *Archaeology of the Cambridge Region* (Cambridge: University of Cambridge, 1922); Charles Scott-Fox, *Cyril Fox: Archaeologist Extraordinary* (Oxford: Oxbow, 2002); and E. M. Jope, 'Fox, Sir Cyril Fred (1882–1967)', *DNB*. I sent Charles Scott-Fox a copy of the article from Gerish's papers and he was convinced, writing back to say, 'This is certainly my father – typical of his very early writings.'

How incurious – William Thoms, *Lays and Legends of France* (London: George Cowie, 1834), p. vi fn. cited by Dorson (1968).

Tom Williamson, *The Origins of Hertfordshire* (Hatfield: University of Hertfordshire, 2010).

Anstey and Clavering – for more on these castles see first the monument records which can be retrieved from the National Record for the Historic Environment at pastscape.org.uk. Also: R. T. Andrews, 'Anstey Castle: Excavations on the Site of Anstey Castle', *EHAST*, vol. 2, pt 2 (1903); Jacqueline Cooper, 'Clavering Castle: A Mysterious Moated Monument', reprinted (with minor alterations and additions) from *Saffron Walden Historical Journal*, no. 9, Spring 2005. See saffronwaldenhistoricalsociety. files.wordpress.com/2014/01/clavering-castle.pdf; Derek Renn, *Norman Castles in Britain*, 2nd edn (London: John Baker, 1973); Derek Renn, *Medieval Castles in Hertfordshire* (Hertfordshire: Phillimore, 1971); VCH (1914) for Anstey.

Geoffrey de Mandeville – for the Anarchy, the now outdated but classic study is J. H. Round, *Geoffrey de Mandeville: A Study of the Anarchy* (London: Longmans & Co, 1892). For a very informative and more up-to-date version with information on the castles as well (my 'revision-ists') see Oliver H. Creighton et al., *The Anarchy: War and Status in 12th-century Landscapes of Conflict* (Liverpool: Liverpool University Press, 2016).

Chapter 27

Bishop Stapeldon – see M. C. Buck, 'Stapeldon, Walter (b. in or before 1265, d. 1326), Administrator and Bishop of Exeter', *DNB*.

one particular rotulus – see 1288 in chronology. I pieced together the history of the document this chapter is all about, along with the general conditions of state papers, from various sources. I began with TNA cata-logue *Discovery*, which includes a detailed description, arrangement and custodial history of record classes – in this instance for Common Pleas Rolls CP40.

Especially useful were:

Charles Cooper, *An Account of the Most Important Public Records of Great Britain, and the Publications of the Record Commissioners, Together with Other Miscellaneous Historical and Antiquarian Information* (London: Baldwin & Cradock, 1832).

Edward Edwards, *Libraries and Founders of Libraries* (London: Trübner and Co, 1865).

House of Lords Journal, 16 April 1719. See british-history.ac.uk/lords-jrnl/vol21/pp125-152#h3-0077

Thomas Weyland – see Paul Brand, 'Chief Justice and Felon: The Career of Thomas Weyland', *The Making of the Common Law* (London: Hambledon, 1992), pp. 113–33.

Chauncy – (1700) gave the mysterious marginal reference *Trin. 16 Ed I. Rot.24 cur. Recept. In Scac.* Basically a roll numbered 24 from the sixteenth year of the reign of Edward I that was kept in the Court of the Receipt of the Exchequer. Not very helpful as all sorts of classes of records were kept there. It wasn't until I read Paul Brand's *Kings, Barons and Justices: The Making and Enforcement of Legislation in Thirteenth-Century England*, Cambridge Studies in Medieval Life and Thought: Fourth Series (No. 56) (Cambridge: CUP, 2003) and understood that I was dealing with an action of replevin and what class of documents they could be found in, that I was finally able to unpick Chauncy – to my great delight. Professor Paul Brand has been exceptionally kind and helpful to me in the writing of the historical section of this book, patiently answering my – sometimes foolish – questions about the legal records of the the thirteenth century and providing me with leads I would otherwise have missed.

Chapter 28

Elizabeth Goudge – many thanks to Victoria Neumark for introducing me to Goudge's work, and this quote in particular, in *Slightly Foxed*, Issue 60 (December 2018).

Frederick Gurney – see 1915 in chronology. Gurney was a Bedfordshire antiquary who may have had some connection with the Barclay family of Brent Pelham. The Gurneys, like the Barclays, had been bankers and Quakers. It was Joseph Gurney Barclay who had bought much of Brent Pelham in the nineteenth century.

English Dialect Dictionary – ed. Joseph Wright (London: Henry Frowde, 1898).

retelling of the legend – see 1997 in chronology.

phonolexis – see Phil Roberts, *How Poetry Works*, 2nd edn (London: Penguin, 2000).

hastily scribbled letter – see 1905 in chronology.

wavy cut – for an example see the picture in Chapter 31.

specialist occupation – once again I am indebted to Paul Brand for helping me read and make sense of the final concord.

Ted Barclay has joked – see 2004 in chronology.

William of Nassington – see Melvyn Bragg, *The Adventure of English, 500 AD to 2000: The Biography of a Language* (London: Hodder and Stoughton, 2003).

Chapter 29

disappearance of twelve of the seventeen volumes – Geoffrey Yeo, 'Record-keeping at St Paul's Cathedral', *Journal of the Society of Archivists*, 8: 1 (1986), pp. 30–44.

his biographer – Mary Clapinson, 'Rawlinson, Richard (1690–1755)', *DNB*.

pages snatched from the furnace – see part XIX, 'The Misfortunes of Books' in Jackson (1932). Some stories are probably apocryphal.

Edmund Gibson – who incidentally added an entry for Shonks' tomb to *Camden's Britannia* when he edited it in the late seventeenth century.

400 manuscript documents – Yeo (1986).

Paris would eulogise – see David Crook, 'Swerford, Alexander of (b. before 1180, d. 1246), Administrator', *DNB*.

witness lists – see Susan M. Johns, *Noblewomen, Aristocracy and Power in the Twelfth-century Anglo-Norman Realm* (Manchester: Manchester University Press, 2003).

Chapter 30

On the general eyre, I have relied heavily on David Crook, both in his published work and his kind responses to my questions. See David Crook, *Records of the General Eyre*, PRO Handbooks No. 20 (London: HMSO, 1982). Also:

Collectanea, ed. N. J. Williams and T. F. T. Plucknett, Wiltshire

Archaeological and Natural History Society Records Branch, vol. XII (Devizes, 1956).

C. A. F. Meekings, *Studies in 13th Century Justice and Administration* (London: The Hambledon Press, 1981).

The 1235 Surrey Eyre, ed. C. A. F. Meekings with David Crook and Simon Neal, 3 vols (Guildford: Surrey Record Society, 1979–2002).

I must also thank the palaeographer Peter Foden for all his help, and in particular for transcribing and translating the crown pleas for me. See peterfoden.com

5,000 people – this is a crude guess. The medievalist Cecil Meekings estimated that for the Wiltshire Eyre in 1249, 4,000 to 5,000 people congregated at Wilton. This may be an overestimate for Hertfordshire, a much smaller county both by area and, in the thirteenth century, population.

Englishry – Meekings noticed that there were many cases where Englishry could be presented but wasn't. This was probably because it wasn't really worth the effort of hauling members of the victim's family to court. In practice, murdrum was not levied for every instance of murder, but was rather a charge based on the ability to pay, so once a district was liable for it in one case, there was probably little incentive to present Englishry for the others even when it was fairly straightforward to prove.

Chapter 31

Terry Pratchett – another gem spotted in the wonderful A. S. Byatt, *On Histories and Stories: Selected Essays* (London: Chatto & Windus, 2000).

Landbeach – on the church in Landbeach, Ray Gambell responded with kindness to my emails, sending me photos and extracts from his book. See: William Keatinge Clay, *A History of the Parish of Landbeach in the County of Cambridge,* Cambridge Antiquarian Society Octavo Publications No. 6 (Cambridge, Deighton, Bell [etc.], 1861); Ray Gambell, *All Saints'*

Landbeach: The Story of a Fen-edge Church (Cambridge: Milton Contact Ltd, 2009); Brian Walker, *Notes upon Discoveries Made During the Recent Restoration of Landbeach Church, Cambridge.* Antiquarian Communications, XIX, (1879), pp. 245–59.

embalmed human heart – on heart burials see: Katharina Rebay-Salisbury, Marie Louise Stig Sorensen and Jessica Hughes (eds), *Studies in Funerary Archaeology*, 5 (Oxford: Oxbow Books, 2010); T. F. Thiselton Dyer, *Church-Lore Gleanings* (London: Innes, 1891), pp. 130–4; Estella Weiss-Krejci, 'Heart Burial in Medieval and Early Post-medieval Central Europe', *Body Parts and Bodies Whole*, pp. 119–34.

his biographer – David Stevenson, 'Graham, James, First Marquess of Montrose (1612–1650), Royalist Army Officer,' *DNB*.

murdered by two henchmen – the claim is made in the VCH for Cambridge, 'Landbeach: Manors', *A History of the County of Cambridge and the Isle of Ely: Volume 9, Chesterton, Northstowe, and Papworth Hundreds*, ed. A. P. M. Wright and C. P. Lewis (London, 1989), pp. 141–4. British History Online: british-history.ac.uk/vch/cambs/vol9/. The primary sources have been published in the *Calendar of Close Rolls*, Henry III: Volume 10, 1256–1259, ed. A. E. Stamp (London, 1932). See 42 Henry III 1258, m.3, p.260, and 43 Henry III 1259, m.8, p.403. Also *Placitorum in domo capitulari Westmonasteriensi asservatorum abbreviatio: temporibus regum Ric. I, Johann, Hen. III, Edw. I, Edw. II* ([London], 1811), p. 148.

CCCC – I am very grateful to Dr Lucy Hughes, the archivist at Corpus Christi College, Cambridge, for her help and for showing me the Chamberlayne Deeds. For the connection between CCCC, Landbeach and the Chamberlayne family see Robert Masters, *History of the College of Corpus Christi . . . in the University of Cambridge; With Additional Matter, and a Continuation to the Present Time, by J. Lamb* (Cambridge, 1831).

All the deeds mentioned in the text can be found in the chronological table. Detailed descriptions are on the Cambridge University archives and manuscript catalogue Janus.

the oldest non-archaeological artefact – this is Christopher de Hamel in his wonderful *Meetings with Remarkable Manuscripts* (London: Allen Lane, 2016).

wax seal – seal experts Elizabeth New and Philippa Hoskin very kindly looked at images of the seals on the deeds at CCCC and described them to me.

moated site – if you have been reading carefully, you will remember I first introduced Ted Barclay up to his knees in floodwater here back in Chapter 6.

Chapter 32

local television feature – *Inside Out East*, with David Whiteley, BBC TV broadcast 26 February 2018.

Jones-Baker – (1977).

quit rent – the Hertfordshire historian Doris Jones-Baker seized on the grant of land to Peter Shanks, suggesting that Barkway may have had to pay him fines because he had 'View of Frankpledge' over Barkway. 'View of Frankpledge' was an old-fashioned way of saying that a manor had the right to hold a Court Leet and try crimes. However, Shanks was Lord of Berwick, which did not have view of Frankpledge. Berwick was in the hamlet of Nuthampstead in the parish of Barkway, but belonged to the manor of Great Hormead. This was a confused landscape which was still giving trouble to the mapmakers 600 years later when they had to draw detached bits of one parish in another and join them with arrows.

Tom Doig – personal communication during a pleasant hour or two in Tom's company in the Woodman Inn, Nuthampstead.

On trial by combat see:
   Georgina R. Galbraith, 'The Enfeoffment of a Champion', *Huntington Library Quarterly*, vol. 22, no. 2 (February 1959), pp. 143–7.

Peter T. Leeson, 'Trial by Battle', *Journal of Legal Analysis*, vol. 3, issue 1, 1 March 2011, pp. 341–75.

George Neilson, *Trial by Combat* (New York: Macmillan, 1891).

Michael John Russell, 'Trial by Battle', doctoral thesis (London: University of London, 1977).

Michael John Russell, 'Trial by Battle and the Writ of Right', *Journal of Legal History*, 1:2, pp. 111–34.

Michael John Russell, 'Accoutrements of Battle', *Law Quarterly Review*, 99 (1983), pp. 432–42.

Michael John Russell, 'Hired Champions', *American Journal of Legal History*, vol. 3 (1959), pp. 242–59.

Edgar the Aetheling – see N. Hooper, 'Edgar Ætheling (b. 1052?, d. in or after 1125), Prince', *DNB*. Also see the note on Edgar under Chapter 25.

Barwick Wood – is shown on 'A Plan of Several Farms Situate in the Parish of Barkway . . . 1728' (HALS D_ERy_P1).

trial by combat was rare – Michael Russell was unable to find any evidence of a battle that was actually fought after 1300, but he does appear limited in his sources, relying very heavily on the published editions of the Pipe Rolls, which still don't go beyond the reign of Henry III. Land disputes and other civil cases could be settled by duel in Court Leets, Hundred Courts and County Courts so wouldn't necessarily make it into the surviving sources. Russell pointed out that the great seventeenth-century legal scholar John Selden thought there were hardly any battles at all, but Selden based that judgement purely on the Year Books so had a very incomplete picture. It's likely that Russell did not have a complete picture either.

tile saved from the pavement of Chertsey Abbey – see Roger Loomis, *Illustrations of Medieval Romance on Tiles from Chertsey Abbey* (Illinois: University of Illinois, 1916) and Elizabeth Eames, *Catalogue of Medieval Lead-glazed Earthenware Tiles in the Department of Medieval and Later Antiquities* (London: British Museum, 1980). See britishmuseum.org/

research/collection_online/collection_object_details.aspx?objectId=13966
&partId=1&searchText=1885,1113.9081&page=1

Chapter 33

Italo Calvino – purloined from A. S. Byatt (2000) again.

Bettelheim told a story – Bruno Bettelheim, *The Uses of Enchantment: The Meaning and Importance of Fairy Tales* (London: Thames & Hudson, 1976).

C. S. Lewis – (1964).

Paul Veyne – (1988).

Marxist interpretation – see Jack Zipes, *Breaking the Magic Spell: Radical Theories of Folk & Fairy Tales*, revd edn (Lexington: University Press of Kentucky, 2002).

Cormac McCarthy – *Blood Meridian* (London: Picador, 1990).

Benjamin has written – Walter Benjamin, 'The Storyteller' in *Illuminations* (London: Vintage, 2015).

re-enchantment of the universe – Marina Warner writes that Gilles Deleuze and Felix Guattari called for the 're-enchantment of the universe' 'defying by implication the contempt for mythmaking, magic, and superstition that both Enlightenment thinkers and later interrogators of the Enlightenment . . . had expressed in scorching terms.' See Kirk (2006).

Kevin Crossley-Holland has written – in his preface to Katharine M. Briggs, *Folk Tales of Britain: Legends* (London: Folio Society, 2011).

archaeological field trip in Sweden – 'The Riddle of the Wolf Pit' in *Pathways to Europe's Landscape* (EPCL, 2003), historicengland.org.uk/images-books/publications/pathways-to-europes-landscape

List of illustrations

Pelham]. Detail from Ordnance Survey 1" Old Edition Map. Sheet 47, 18 April 1805; p. 78 'Black horned thing', Thomas Bewick's 'tale piece' to 'Of the Grosbeak' in *History of British Birds*, 1797; p. 80 'Felling axe' in R. A. Salaman, *Dictionary of Tools: Used in the Woodworking and Allied Trades, c.1700–1970* (London: Allen and Unwin, 1975); p. 81 'Grubbing axe' in R. A. Salaman, *Dictionary of Tools: Used in the Woodworking and Allied Trades, c.1700-1970* (London: Allen and Unwin, 1975); p. 89 Fossil from antiquity? Detail of Ancient Greek Column Krater (Mixing Bowl), Museum of Fine Arts Boston, Helen and Alice Colburn Fund, 63.420, photograph © 2019 Museum of Fine Arts, Boston; p. 105 John Grieg [engraver] after F. W. L. Stockdale [illustrator], 'Remains of the Tomb of O Piers Shonks. Brent Pelham Church, Herts', in James Sargant Storer, *Antiquarian Itinerary*, vol. 4 (London, 1816); pp. 106–7 J. C. Buckler, 'Monumental Stone in Brent Pelham Church', *Knowsley Clutterbuck*, p. 450F (HALS D/Z119/10/450E). Courtesy of Hertfordshire Archives and Local Studies; p. 112 George Buckler, 'South East View of Brent Pelham Church, Hertfordshire' (1841) in *Views of Hertfordshire: A Collection of Drawings* by J. C. Buckler (1793–1894), Vol II (HALS D/Ebg). Courtesy of Hertfordshire Archives and Local Studies; p. 115 Rev. William Cole, in John Nichols, *Literary Anecdotes of the Eighteenth Century*, Vol. 1 (London: 1812), facing p. 657; p. 116 William Cole's drawing of Shonks' tomb in *Extraneous Parochial Antiquities or an Account of Various Churches with Funeral Monuments, the Inscriptions in and About them in Divers Counties of England*, ff. 14v–27, Cole Manuscripts, vol. 5 (BL Add. MS 5806), courtesy Bridgeman Art Library; p. 122 Henry Oldfield, 'Late 13th century coffin-slab' in Bodleian Library, Ms. Gough Maps 224 / 328, courtesy the Bodleian Library, University of Oxford; p. 123 example of a 13th cross-slab (from Raunds, Northamptonshire), in Rev. Edward L. Cutts, *A Manual for the Study of the Sepulchral Slabs and Crosses of the Middle Ages* (London: John Parker, 1849) Plate L; p. 126 'Wondrous strange' in John Weever's 'A Breefe Discourse of Ancient Monuments . . .' Original drafts and collections for John Weever's *Ancient Funerall Monuments*. Society of Antiquaries (SAL/

MS/127) f. 186, copyright © Society of Antiquaries of London; p. 127 plate of cross-slabs including Shonks' slab in Richard Gough, *Sepulchral Monuments in Great Britain* (London: J. Nichols, 1786), plate IV, no. 12. facing p. cix; p. 132 drawing of the dragon on Shonks' tomb, detail from F. Burgess, *English Churchyard Memorials* (London: Lutterworth Press, 1963), pp. 105–6, courtesy Lutterworth Press; p. 135 drawing of a dragon from a bestiary, BL Stowe 1067. © Max Hadley; p. 145 drawing of symbols of the Evangelists, details from F. Burgess, *English Churchyard Memorials* (London: Lutterworth Press, 1963), pp. 105–6, courtesy Lutterworth Press; p. 146 drawing of the soul and archangel, detail from George Weight, 'The Tomb of O. Piers Shonks, in Brent Pelham Church, Herts', *Holiday Rambles in Essex and Herts*. Plate 16. London Metropolitan Archives (CLC/270/MS00475), courtesy LMA and City of London; p. 151 detail of viviparus fossils [Purbeck Marble] from J. de C. Sowerby, *The Mineral Conchology of Great Britain*, Vol. 6, (London: Richard Taylor, London) fig. 3, p. 12; p. 155 'Simplified Solid Geology of the Isle of Purbeck', postcard devised by David Kemp; p. 158 Trev Haysom. Author's photograph; p. 167 tile showing the post-1346 Seal of the Bailiffs of Dunwich. Author's Collection; p. 170 'Agglestone' detail from *Rena Gardiner, Dorset: The Isle of Purbeck* (Wimborne Minster: The Dovecote Press, 2016; 1st pub. 1969) p. 12, courtesy the Dovecote Press; p. 181 angel with damaged face, detail from Piers Shonks' tomb © Dominick Tyler; p. 186 Map of Hertfordshire from John Norden, *Speculi Britaniae pars. [etc]* Lambeth Palace Library Ms. 521, courtesy Lambeth Palace Library; pp. 189 and 190 Piers Shonks' tomb © Dominick Tyler; p. 205 Alec Buckels, 'Old Tales and Balladry' from Walter de la Mare, *Come Hither* (London: Constable, 1923), p. 413; p. 211 A. Whitford Anderson, 'North buttresses of nave, showing crosses', in *Hertfordshire Churches*, vol. 2 (HALS Acc. 3556). Courtesy of Hertfordshire Archives and Local Studies; p. 212 crosses on buttresses, detail from [Thomas Fisher?] 'Brent Pelham Church, Hartfordshire, from the north' in *DRAWINGS and Water-colour Sketches, with Prints and Engravings, Illustrating the Topography of Co. Herts; Collected by J. W. Jones, to Accompany Clutterbuck's History of the County*. Five volumes. Paper; XVIth–XIXth cent., vol. iii, BL Add. Ms. 32350, f. 175, courtesy Bridgeman Art Library; p. 228 'Robin Hood's Death' in Joseph Ritson, *Robin Hood: A Collection of Poems, Songs, and Ballads* (London: Ingram, Cooke & Co., 1853) Title page; p. 235 Mrs [Marion] Hudson, typescript copy of a letter to H.T. Pollard /W.B. Gerish, 2 October (HALS DE/Gr/59). Courtesy of Hertfordshire Archives and Local Studies; p. 238 Cow bone. Author's photo; p. 264 Cyril Fox (right) and Louis Cobbett at Blythwood Farm, Stansted, 1905 from Charles Scott-Fox, *Cyril Fox: Archaeologist Extraordinary* (Oxbow: Oxford, 2002). Fig. 8, p. 11; p. 267 map of Anstey Castle from R. T. Andrews, 'Anstey Castle: Excavations on the Site of Anstey Castle', *EHAST*, vol. 2, pt 2 (1903) facing p. 118; p. 273 detail from Sir Henry Chauncy, *The Historical Antiquities of Hertfordshire*, vol. 1 (London, 1826; 1st pub. 1700), p. 278; p. 288 Liber A, aka. The Hairy Book, London Metropolitan Archive. CLC/313/B/012/MS25501 f. xx © The Chapter of St Paul's Cathedral; p. 292 Peter Shanke, elector on kalendar of jury members in the 1248 Hertfordshire Eyre (TNA JUST 1/318, m.18), courtesy the National Archives; p. 307 'Grant to Walter Camerarius of an annual rent of 4s 2d payable by Anselm le Grey, William de Sarners, Richard le Grey and John Patrich.' Courtesy of Corpus Christi College Cambridge. CCCC09/24A/A 26; p. 310 'Chamberlayne monument' at Landbeach from Brian Walker, 'Notes upon Discoveries made during the recent restoration of Landbeach Church' in *Cambridge Antiquarian Communications*, XIX (1879), p. 250; p. 320 'A Judicial Combat' in Roger Loomis, *Illustrations of Medieval Romance on Tiles from Chertsey Abbey* (Illinois: University of Illinois, 1916), Fig. 38; p. 331 'Coffin-Slab in Purbeck Marble (Brent Pelham, Herts.)' in F. Burgess, *English Churchyard Memorials* (London: Lutterworth Press 1963), Fig. 26 p. 106, courtesy Lutterworth Press.

While every effort has been made to trace owners of copyright material reproduced herein, the publishers will be glad to rectify any omissions in future editions.

Index